Away for the
WEEKEND®

NEW ENGLAND

Away for the
WEEKEND®

NEW ENGLAND

52 Great Getaways in the
Six New England States
for Every Season of the Year

ELEANOR BERMAN

Fifth Revised Edition

Three Rivers Press
New York

Acknowledgments

My sincere thanks to the many state and local tourist offices who provided so much helpful information and guidance.

Copyright © 1985, 1988, 1992, 1995, 1998 by Eleanor Berman

Published by Three Rivers Press, a division of Crown Publishers, Inc.,
201 East 50th Street, New York, New York 10022.
Member of the Crown Publishing Group.

Random House, Inc. New York, Toronto, London, Sydney, Auckland
www.randomhouse.com

THREE RIVERS PRESS and colophon are trademarks of Crown Publishers, Inc.

Printed in the United States of America.

Maps by Susan Hunt Yule

Library of Congress Cataloging-in-Publication Data
Berman, Eleanor
     Away for the weekend, New England: 52 great getaways in Connecticut, Maine,
     Massachusetts, New Hampshire, Rhode Island, Vermont/Eleanor Berman.—5th ed.
     Includes index.
     1. New England—Guidebooks. I. Title.
F2.3.B47   1998
917.404'43—dc21   97-44622

ISBN 0-609-80169-4

10   9   8   7   6   5   4   3   2   1

Fifth Revised Edition

Contents

Introduction   vii
How to Use the Book   viii
State Tourist Offices and Regional Transportation Companies   xi
Bed-and-Breakfast Registry Services   xi
Hiking Information   xiii

SPRING

Sights for All Seasons in Woodstock   3
Getting Inspiration in Concord   8
Herbs and History in Connecticut   14
Rites of Spring on Nantucket   20
Admiring the Miracle in Providence   26
A Whale of a Time on Cape Ann   33
The Three Bs: A Maine Education   38
Antiquing in Old Connecticut   Woodbury 140 miles   45
Greeting Spring in Sandwich   51
City by the Sea: Portland, Maine   56
Crafts Spectacular in the Pioneer Valley   62
Savoring the Shore in Connecticut   68
Exploring Blooming Boston   75

SUMMER

Flying High in Quechee   87
A Summer Fling in Connecticut   Norwalk + Westport 160 miles   90
Scenery by the Sea in Ogunquit   96
On Top of the World at Mt. Washington   100
Looking for the Real York   106
Away from It All on Block Island   111
High Notes Near Mt. Monadnock   116
Visiting Martha's Vineyard   121
Moonlight and Mozart in Vermont   127
Scaling the Heights at Acadia   133
Supping with the Shakers in Hancock   140
Show-and-Tell at Lake Sunapee   148

Smooth Sailing in Boothbay Harbor   153
Discovering the Other Nantucket   159

FALL
Indian Summer in Kennebunkport   165
Inns and Arts of Vermont   s.w. 150 miles   169
Back to Nature on Cape Cod   177
Fair Weather at Fryeburg ,NH 180 miles   183
Leafing Through the Northeast Kingdom   188
Making a Pilgrimage to Plymouth   194
Fall Foliage in Franconia   199
Meandering the Mohawk Trail   205
Breezing Through the Past in Essex ,CT 133 miles   211
Mountains and Sea in Camden   215
A Bewitching Halloween in Salem   221
A Peak Experience at Killington   226
Bringing the Kids to Boston   232

WINTER
Merry Days at Mystic   241
Christmas Card Country in Hanover   245
Shopping by the Sea in Portsmouth   250
An Artful Weekend in Williamstown   253
Winter Carnival at Stowe   259
Stirring Things Up at Sturbridge   263
Happy Landings in Salisbury ,CT 150 miles   268
Wintering in the White Mountains   273
Back to Nature in Bethel   279
Beyond the Mansions in Newport   284
Boning Up on Cambridge   291
Sugaring Off in Grafton ,VT   299

MAPS
Massachusetts/Connecticut   306
Rhode Island   306
Vermont/New Hampshire   308
Maine   308

INDEX
General Index   311
Category Index   323

Introduction

New England has everything: craggy mountains and gentle rolling hills, placid lakes and the surging sea, quaint village greens and contemporary cities. Whether you want to ski or sail or lie on the beach, soak up culture or escape from civilization, spend a day in chic boutiques or in virgin woods, you'll find what you are seeking in this rich and remarkable six-state area—so rich, in fact, that it's almost a problem. In an area so packed with attractions, how can you decide where to start? Should it be the White Mountains of New Hampshire or the Green Mountains of Vermont, the beaches of Cape Cod or the rockbound shores of Maine, the "tall ships" at Mystic or the Maritime Museum at Bath?

Away for the Weekend invites you to sample them all, one at a time, as memorable weekend trips. In contrast to most guidebook writers, I have not separated the New England area by states or tried to list all the myriad attractions that each state has to offer. Instead, I have organized the getaways by seasons, and selected some of the very best places and special events to be found throughout the region at different times of the year.

There are a few things you should know from the start. The selections are admittedly personal, limited to locations and events I have visited and enjoyed, so not every single sightseeing attraction, lodging, or restaurant in each location is included. I've tried instead to pick only the best—places I've either been to myself or had recommended to me by local sources or frequent visitors. For this fifth edition, many fine, recently opened inns and dining places have been added.

Since New England country inns are one of the particular delights of the region, I've done my best to see and select special inns for each location covered, but keep in mind that this is a guide to destinations and events, not a guide to inns. The lodgings listed here are those convenient for each specific weekend, and in some cases that could mean only motels or hotels. Where there is a choice, I've given the inns, leaving the motel listings to local tourist guides or the Mobil and AAA publications.

In addition to inns, "bed-and-breakfast" establishments have become increasingly popular with travelers. There is sometimes confusion as to what constitutes "bed-and-breakfast." Small inns that serve only breakfast are listed here as inns. Lodgings that are rooms in private homes, with or without a private bath, are what is meant here by "B&B." These can be extremely pleasant places to stay, both because they are economical and because they offer the chance to meet residents and absorb some of the flavor of living in the area. Because it is impossible to mention every individual bed-and-breakfast lodging, I have included a list of areawide registry headquarters at the front of the book.

HOW TO USE THE BOOK

The format for the trips in *Away for the Weekend* assumes that you have a normal two-day weekend to spend, arriving on Friday night and leaving late on Sunday. Fortunately, with easy air travel to cities such as Portland, Maine, and Burlington, Vermont, trips that once were impractical for weekend driving can now be managed easily. Information regarding air transportation is included for each suggested trip, as is bus or train information for those who do not have cars or who might prefer not to drive in the unpredictable winter months in New England. There is also a symbol indicating destinations that can be visited conveniently at least in part without a car.

For each trip, there is a suggested itinerary for a two-day stay, with added suggestions to accommodate varying tastes and time schedules. When there is enough to do to warrant a longer stay, a symbol at the start will tell you so. When you do have more than a weekend to spend, you can use these itineraries as guides to planning a more extensive tour. If, for instance, you are touring the coast of Maine or the mountains of New Hampshire or Vermont, simply consult the maps and index for destinations that make for a convenient route.

Since the trips are arranged by season, you can read ahead about special events and make reservations before it is too late. Even when the season of a location described is not applicable to your schedule, the lists of sights and accommodations will apply whenever you go.

Because special activities change with the seasons, you may find some destinations listed more than once. In the case of Boston, there is a separate chapter for families who want activities best suited for children. A symbol identifying weekends most likely to appeal to families appears among the indicators at the start of each trip chapter. You are, of course, the best judge of which trips your own children are likely to enjoy.

In many cases, the trips suggested are deliberately out of peak season. The seashore, for example, can be twice as nice in spring or fall, when both crowds and rates are at a minimum.

The symbols that indicate these various categories are:

    = recommended for children

    = accessible at least in part via public transportation

    = recommended for long weekends

As for prices, these letters indicate the range for lodging in a double room and dining as follows:

I = under $80
M = $80 to $135
E = $135 to $199
EE = over $200

I = most entrées under $12
M = entrées averaging $12 to $20
E = most entrées $20 to $30
EE = over $30 (usually means prix fixe meals)

When prices bridge two categories, you will find two symbols. In seafood restaurants, a wide price range usually indicates the cost of lobster dinners, always the most expensive item on the menu. A wide price range for inns may mean that the less expensive rooms do not have private baths. Check with innkeepers to be sure.

When accommodations include meals in their rates, symbols will indicate this:

CP = continental plan (includes breakfast only)
MAP = modified American plan (breakfast and dinner)
AP = American plan (all three meals included)

For sightseeing attractions, the following dollar signs indicate adult admission fees. Children's fees are half the adult fee unless otherwise indicated.

$ = under $2.50
$$ = $2.51 to $5.00
$$$ = $5.01 to $7.50
$$$$ = $7.51 to $10
$$$$$ = Over $10

All of this information is as accurate as could be determined when the manuscript was turned in to the publisher. In the months that elapse between the writing and the publication of any book, places sometimes close unexpectedly, and rates can change even before they are put into print. For this reason, general price categories are used rather than specific rates. It is possible that even these general categories will change over time, with some of the places moving up into a more expensive range. Admissions fees to various attractions will undoubtedly go up as well, and hours sometimes change. So use this book as a guide—generally an accurate one—but *always* check for current prices when you plan your trip. Telephone numbers are included for this purpose.

If you discover that any information here has become seriously inaccurate or that a place has closed or gone downhill, I hope you will let me know in care of the publisher so that the entry can be corrected in the future. If you discover places I have missed or have suggestions for future editions, I hope you'll let me know that as well. Several places have been added or dropped from this edition as a result of suggestions from thoughtful readers.

The maps at the back of the book are simplified to make it easy to see where the suggested destinations are located. They are not reliable as road maps, so be sure to have a detailed map in hand before you set out. One way to get an excellent free map of each state in New England is to write to the travel or tourism office in the various states. These offices offer not only maps but excellent brochures on their states' attractions. Addresses are included at the end of this section, as are telephone numbers for the region's major transportation services.

In most cases, addresses for additional information also are given at the end of each itinerary. Do write well ahead of time, for the more you learn about your destination in advance, the more meaningful and enjoyable your visit will be.

One last warning: It almost goes without saying that when it comes to reservations in small country inns, you must plan well ahead or you will be disappointed. The same is true if you want to visit the shore at the height of the summer season or a ski resort during holiday periods. Most places offer refunds on deposits if you cancel with reasonable notice, so plan ahead—three or four months ahead is none too soon—and have your pick instead of having to settle for leftovers.

Writing this book has been a special pleasure. Having lived and traveled in New England for many years, I began with the impression that I already knew a great deal about the region and its most interesting attractions, but the more I traveled, the more I discovered that I had missed some special places, even in areas I had visited before. And the more territory I covered, the more I appreciated what a remarkable region this really is. I gained a new understanding of my heritage as an American by visiting the places where our nation was born, and new awareness of nature's extraordinary generosity in the beauty that is everywhere in this handful of fortunate states. With each update, I make new discoveries.

I hope *Away for the Weekend* will guide you to the same wonderful discoveries—as well as inspire you to find your own.

STATE TOURIST OFFICES AND REGIONAL TRANSPORTATION COMPANIES

Contact any of these state tourist offices for free maps and literature on attractions throughout their states, as well as for updated bed-and-breakfast registry listings:

Tourism Division
State of Connecticut Department
  of Economic Development
865 Brook Street
Rocky Hill, CT 06067
(860) 258-4355 or
(800) CT BOUND

Maine Publicity Bureau
PO Box 2300
Hallowell, ME 04347
(207) 623-0363

Massachusetts Office of
  Travel & Tourism
100 Cambridge Street
Boston, MA 02202
(617) 727-3201 or
(800) 447-6277

New Hampshire Office of
  Travel and Tourism
172 Pembroke Road
Box 1856
Concord, NH 03302
(603) 271-2343 or
(800) FUN-IN-NH

Rhode Island Department of Tourism
1 West Exchange Street
Providence, RI 02903
(401) 277-2601 or
(800) 556-2484

Vermont Department of Tourism
134 State Street
Montpelier, VT 05602
(802) 828-3236
(800) VER–MONT or
Vermont Chamber of Commerce
Box 37
Montpelier, VT 05601
(802) 223-3443

Reference numbers for major transportation companies serving New England:

Amtrak trains (800) USA-RAIL
Bonanza Buses (800) 556-3815
Peter Pan Buses (800) 237-8747
  or (800) 247-8560
Concord Trailways Buses
  (800) 639-3317
Vermont Transit Buses
  (802) 864-6811; in New England
  (800) 451-3292;
  in Vermont (800) 642-3133

BED-AND-BREAKFAST REGISTRY SERVICES

Covering Several New England States

New England Hospitality Network
(all New England states)
PO Box 3291
Newport, RI 02840
(401) 849-1298

Covered Bridge Bed and Breakfast
(Connecticut, Berkshires, Rhode Island
  shore)
69 Maple Avenue
PO Box 447A
Norfolk, CT 06058
(860) 542-5944

American Country Collection of Bed and
    Breakfasts
(western Massachusetts and Vermont)
1353 Union Street
Schenectady, NY 12308
(518) 370-4948

CONNECTICUT

Nutmeg Bed and Breakfast
PO Box 1117
West Hartford, CT 06107
(860) 236-6698 or
(800) 727-7592

Bed and Breakfast, Ltd.
PO Box 216
New Haven, CT 06513
(203) 469-3260

MAINE

Bed and Breakfast of Maine
377 Gray Road
Falmouth, ME 04105
(207) 797-5540

MASSACHUSETTS

Berkshire Bed and Breakfast Homes
(western Massachusetts)
PO Box 211
Williamsburg, MA 01096
(413) 268-7244

Bed and Breakfast Cape Cod
Box 341
West Hyannisport, MA 02672
(508) 775-2772 or
(800) 686-5252

Folkestone Bed and Breakfast
(Sturbridge, Worcester, and central
    Massachusetts)
PO Box 211
Williamsburg, MA 01096
(508) 480-0380 or
(800) 762-2752

Boston-Cambridge Area

ABC: Accommodations of Boston &
    Cambridge
335 Pearl Street
Cambridge, MA 02139
(617) 491-0274 or
(800) 253-5542

New England Bed and Breakfast, Inc.
PO Box 1426
Waltham, MA 02154
(617) 244-2112

Bed and Breakfast Cambridge and
    Greater Boston
PO Box 1344
Cambridge, MA 02238
(617) 720-1492 or
(800) 888-0178

Bed and Breakfast Associates Bay
    Colony, Ltd.
PO Box 57166
Babson Park Branch
Boston, MA 02157
(617) 720-0522 or
(800) 347-5088

Greater Boston Hospitality
PO Box 1142
Brookline, MA 02146
(617) 277-5430

Host Homes of Boston
PO Box 117
Waban Branch
Boston, MA 02168
(617) 244-1308 or
(800) 600-1308

Bed-and-Breakfast Agency of Boston
47 Commercial Wharf
Boston, MA 02110
(617) 720-3540 or
(800) CITY BNB

NEW HAMPSHIRE

New Hampshire Bed and Breakfast
33 Red Gate Lane
Meredith, NH 03253
(603) 279-8348

RHODE ISLAND

Bed and Breakfast of Rhode Island, Inc.
PO Box 3291
Newport, RI 02840
(401) 849-1298 or
(800) 828-0000

Anna's Victorian Connection
5 Fowler Avenue
Newport, RI 02840
(401) 849-2489 or
(800) 884-4288

Bed and Breakfast Newport, Ltd.
33 Russell Avenue
Newport, RI 02840
(401) 846-5408 or
(800) 800-8765

VERMONT

*Vermont Center Point Reservation
  Service*
PO Box 8513
Essex, VT 05451
(802) 872-2745 or
(800) 449-2745

HIKING INFORMATION

For Appalachian Trail, White Mountains, Monadnocks, and other hiking information throughout New England:

Appalachian Mountain Club
5 Joy Street
Boston, MA 02108
(617) 523-0636

For day hiking in Vermont:
Green Mountain Club
RR1, Box 650
Waterbury Center, VT 05677
(802) 244-7037
(Hiking Center open daily,
Memorial Day to Columbus Day,
on Route 100, Waterbury Center)

Merrell Hiking Center
Killington Resort
Killington, VT 05751
(802) 422-6708

**For hiking holidays and inn-to-inn
  tours:**
Country Inns Along the Trail
c/o Churchill House
RD 3, Box 3265
Brandon, VT 05733
(802) 247-3300

Hiking Holidays
Box 711
Bristol, VT 05443
(802) 453-4816 or
(800) 537-3850

Country Walkers
PO Box 180
Waterbury, VT 05676
(802) 244-1387 or
(800) 464-9255

Spring

Overleaf: *The rugged shoreline of Kennebunkport, Maine.*

Sights for All Seasons in Woodstock

Is Woodstock the most beautiful town in Vermont? It surely is in the running, and while nature is partially responsible, two notable American families are also part of the reason.

The late Mary Billings Rockefeller was the granddaughter of Frederick Billings, an early conservationist and Woodstock native, who went West long enough to make his fortune during the gold rush and have a town, Billings, Montana, named for him. He then returned home to establish a farm that became a model for dairy farmers and environmentalists throughout the state. Many of Vermont's green hills are the results of Billings's reforestation efforts. His granddaughter Mary married Laurance Rockefeller, a pioneer in conservation in his own right, who developed resorts that blended with and maximized the natural beauty of their environments.

Since the Rockefellers used the Billings family home in Woodstock as a summer home, it was almost inevitable that they would take an interest in the picturesque village, one that has been a favorite resort town since the original Woodstock Inn opened in 1893. Their efforts helped to build what is now one of the most exquisite towns in Vermont, preserved in a manner greatly abetted by the Rockefeller millions.

If Woodstock's village green seems somehow to be more perfect than that of other towns, it may be because they've buried the telephone and electric wires to prevent modern technology from marring the Colonial flavor. Most of the homes around the green were in place when General Lafayette passed through the village in 1825. Many were bought and meticulously restored by the Rockefellers, who leased them out to caring tenants.

The Rockefellers are also responsible for the "new" Woodstock Inn, built in 1969, as well as the Suicide Six Ski Resort and the Woodstock Country Club, which boasts a Cross-Country Touring Center, a Robert Trent Jones golf course, and a slew of tennis and paddle tennis courts. The Woodstock Sports Center provides year-round indoor facilities for tennis, racquetball, squash, and swimming. All this is available to inn guests—and for a fee, to anyone in Woodstock.

If that's not enough activity for you, hiking, biking, and riding trails also abound around Woodstock, helping visitors to make the most of the town and its natural amenities—meandering streams, covered bridges, and mountain views. Indeed, there's something for everyone in Woodstock, even if all you want to do is browse through a selection of fine shops.

Though this is truly a town for all seasons, Woodstock is a particularly lovely and welcoming destination in the soft green days of spring, that time of year between skiing season and summer when many areas offer little to do.

If you make your headquarters at the Woodstock Inn, on the green, you'll be choosing one of New England's classic resorts, traditional in style and surrounded by landscaped gardens. If there is any nip at all in the air, you'll likely be greeted with a welcoming fire in the huge fieldstone fireplace that dominates a whole wall of the lobby. The furnishings are country antique, the colors are subdued, and the spacious guest rooms are adorned with handsome traditional handwoven covers.

However, this is a resort hotel with over 140 rooms, not a cozy country inn. If something smaller is more your style, there are several lovely antiques-filled bed-and-breakfast inns in town, within walking distance of all the shops. There are some exceptional choices outside town as well.

Seeing Woodstock is easy, since everything is clustered within a couple of blocks of the green. More than three dozen historic houses, all still privately owned, can be seen on a walk along Central and Elm Streets, which intersect at the green. From Memorial Day on, you can visit one of the loveliest homes, the Dana House on Elm Street, an 1807 residence that was occupied by family descendants until 1944, when it became the home of the Woodstock Historical Society. It contains a fine collection of period furnishings (1800 to 1860), as well as many portraits, toys, costumes, and local memorabilia.

The rolling lawn behind the Dana House leads to the banks of the Ottauquechee River and a prime view of the Village Middle Bridge, which, when it was constructed in 1969 to replace the original, became the first covered bridge to be built in the state since 1895.

Two other covered bridges are located east and west of town on Route 4. The 1877 Lincoln Bridge, four miles to the west, is the only known remaining wooden example of the Pratt truss, a construction style that was favored later in hundreds of steel bridges across the nation.

Besides the wooden bridges across its river, Woodstock boasts five bronze Paul Revere bells. Four are in church steeples: the fifth is on display on the lawn of the Woodstock Inn. The 1808 Congregational Church on Elm Street houses the oldest.

Be forewarned that dozens of shops will tempt you to detour as you take a stroll through Woodstock. Original work by New England artists is found at Gallery on the Green, and Woodstock Folk Art Prints and Antiques has lots of whimsy and Americana. As you stroll, you'll spy more shops selling clothing, jewelry, gifts, and crafts. Almost everyone makes a stop at F. H. Gillingham & Sons, a general store that has been owned by the same family since 1886, to buy country housewares and Vermont specialty foods, including syrup and cheese.

This is also prime antiquing territory, with over a dozen shops in and around town and the handsome Antiques Collaborative at Waterman

Place, on Route 4 East near Quechee, a treasure trove of high-quality collectibles of every kind. For a change in sightseeing pace, visit the Vermont Institute of Natural Science. It offers nature trails on 77 acres and a Raptor Center, a unique living museum housing more than 40 birds of prey.

May 1 marks the annual opening of another Rockefeller project, Billings Farm and Museum. This is a working dairy farm that carries on the raising of prime Jersey cattle begun by Frederick Billings in 1871, plus a series of handsomely restored barns housing exhibits on Vermont family farm life in the 1890s. Outside are some of the best-looking bossys to be seen outside the pages of a storybook. To see sheep and cows grazing against the beautiful backdrop of rolling hills is to see classic rural Vermont at its best.

In the barns, you can greet the draft horses and pet the calves in the nursery. The restored and furnished 1890 Farm House includes a basement creamery where you can sample hand-churned butter and see how the house functioned as the hub of the farm operation a century ago. Beginning with traditional plowing early in May, there are special events on many weekends right through Christmas, when sleigh rides are available.

In future years, the Billings family home and surrounding woodlands across the road are to become the Marsh-Billings National Historical Park, paying tribute to both Woodstock's and the nation's conservation efforts and traditions.

Having seen the sights and shopped the stores, what else you choose to do in Woodstock depends a lot on the weather and your inclinations. If sports are your choice, the Indoor Center is always ready, the golf course is usually back to playing condition by May, and all-weather tennis courts should be available even earlier.

The Woodstock Inn can furnish you with maps of the most scenic recommended routes for bikers, hikers, or joggers; and horses are available for hire in South Woodstock, offering a pleasant way to see the scenery even during Vermont's notorious spring "mud season."

And there are many scenic side trips to be made by car. One will take you to Quechee to see the gorge and waterfall and visit the riverside shop of glassblower Simon Pearce in a magnificently restored mill. Another road leads to Windsor, a longtime political center of the state with its own parade of historic houses, including the Windsor House, which serves as a Vermont State Crafts Center displaying the work of some 200 state craftspeople. Simon Pearce has established a second glassblowing workshop here.

Still another route takes in the Crowley Cheese Factory and Weston, a thriving little shopping mecca that includes the Original Vermont Country Store and the Weston Playhouse, Vermont's oldest professional theater.

The most memorable side trip out of Woodstock, however, is available from late May, when the buildings are opened at Calvin Coolidge's birthplace, the Plymouth Notch Historic District, in the nearby tiny hamlet of Plymouth. Since Coolidge was not one of our more colorful presidents, this trip may not seem a tempting prospect, but it is actually a very special experience. Plymouth Notch has been called a "Yankee Brigadoon," a village virtually unchanged since 1923, when Coolidge was sworn in as president in the family homestead.

At the attractive small Visitors' Center, built of stone and with a Vermont slate roof, you will learn about Coolidge's life and about the modest frame house where he was raised—the home where his father, a notary public, administered the oath of office when Warren Harding's death cast Vice President Coolidge into the presidency. The house can be visited, providing a vivid reminder that ours is still a nation where a country boy can rise to greatness.

Within a distance of no more than two city blocks, you can also see the one-room schoolhouse built in 1890, the simple farm homes of Coolidge's family and friends, and the general store once operated by his father. Coolidge Hall, the vaulted room above the general store that was used by the village Grange for weekly dances, served as the 1924 summer White House office. It has been restored with an interpretive exhibit and original furnishings. Presidential gifts of state are displayed in the Visitors' Center in the Aldrich House, and a large collection of early farm implements is exhibited in a late-nineteenth-century barn.

Tastings are offered at the 1890 cheese factory that is still run by the Coolidge family, and you can buy a sample to take home. Six generations of the family, including the ex-president, are buried in the village cemetery.

To see the exquisite tiny church built by the townspeople of Plymouth in 1842 and still in use, to feel the continuity of life in this dot of a town, and to stand on the front porch of a humble home rich in mountain views is to understand some of the roots and reasons for our nation's strength.

You'll leave with a new appreciation of "Silent Cal" and empathize with his parting words when he left the White House: "We draw our presidents from the people. I came from them; I wish to be one of them again."

Area Code: 802

DRIVING DIRECTIONS Woodstock is on U.S. Route 4, reached from north or south via I-91 to I-89 North. It is 148 miles from Boston, 260 miles from New York, and 166 miles from Hartford.

PUBLIC TRANSPORTATION Nearest air service is at Lebanon, New Hampshire, 15 miles away. Amtrak trains serve White River Junction, 14 miles away, and Vermont Transit buses come into Woodstock.

ACCOMMODATIONS **The Woodstock Inn and Resort,** 14 the Green, Woodstock 05091, (800) 448-7900 or 457-1100, many money-saving package and sports plans are available E–EE • **Jackson House,** Route 4 West, Woodstock 05091, antique-filled 1890s home, ultraelegant E–EE, CP • **Charleston House,** 21 Pleasant Street, Woodstock 05091, 457-3843, 1835 Greek Revival town house within walking distance of shops and dining, tasteful furnishings M–E CP • **Ardmore House,** 23 Pleasant Street, Woodstock 05091, 457-3887 or (800) 497-9652, handsome 1850 clapboard Greek Revival home, convenient M–E, CP • **Canterbury House,** 43 Pleasant Street, Woodstock 05091, 457-3077, village Victorian M–E, CP • **Woodstocker,** 61 River Street, Woodstock 05091, 457-4432, 1830 comfortable village bed-and-breakfast inn, some larger rooms are ideal for families M–E, CP • **Winslow House,** 38 Route 4 West, Woodstock 05091, 457-1820, spacious rooms at bargain rates, I–M, CP. *Outside of town:* **Kedron Valley Inn,** Route 106, South Woodstock 05071, 457-1473, vintage quilts, fireplaces, country charm, set beside a brook and swimming pond in the horse country six miles from town; the nearby Kedron Valley Stables offers trail rides and carriage rides through the countryside M–E, CP or E–EE, MAP • **Apple Butter Inn,** Happy Valley Road (just off Route 4), Taftsville 05073, 457-4158, tastefully furnished, antique-filled 1840 inn with great charm, reasonable rates I–M, CP • **Maple Leaf Inn,** Barnard 05031, 234-5342 or (800) 51-MAPLE, Victorian in a quiet village, lots of fireplaces and whirlpools, on 16 acres, adults only M–E, CP • **Twin Farms,** Barnard 05031, 234-999 or (800) 894-6327, one of the most luxurious and tasteful hideaways to be found anywhere—and one of the most expensive; myriad sports and amenities, all food and liquor included in rates, which begin at $700.

DINING **The Woodstock Inn** (see above), traditional menu; E–EE, **Eagle Cafe,** I • **Kedron Valley Inn** (see above), "nouvelle New England," one of the area's best, E • **The Prince and the Pauper,** prix fixe, EE; bistro menu in lounge, 24 Elm Street, 457-1818, charming Colonial atmosphere, continental and nouvelle cuisine, I–M • **Barnard Inn,** Route 12, Barnard, 234-9961, Swiss chef, historic home, where Woodstockers go for special occasions, E–EE • **Wild Grass,** Gallery Place Building, Route 4, Woodstock, 457-1917, accomplished chef, eclectic and reasonable menu, I–M • **Bentley's,** 3 Elm Street, 457-3232, lively, casual, weekend entertainment and dancing, M • **Spooner's,** Sunset Farm, Route 4 East, 457-4022, informal fare in renovated barn, M • **Sweet Tomatoes Trattoria,** 23 Church Street, Lebanon, NH, (603) 448-1711, everyone's favorite Italian in the area, I • Also see Quechee, page 87, and Hanover, pages 245–249.

SIGHTSEEING **Dana House,** Woodstock Historical Society, 26 Elm Street, Woodstock, 457-1822. Hours: May to late October, Monday to Saturday, 10 A.M. to 5 P.M.; Sunday, 2 P.M. to 5 P.M.; open weekends in December. Free • **Billings Farm and Museum,** River Road, Woodstock, 457-2355. Hours: May through October, daily, 10 A.M. to 5 P.M.; also open weekends November and December, and from December 26 to early January. $$$ • **Vermont Institute of Natural Science and Raptor Center,** 457-2779. Hours: May to mid-October, daily, 10 A.M. to 4 P.M.; November to April, closed Sunday. $$ • **Walking Tours of Woodstock,** from Town Information Booth on the Green, 457-1042. Hours: June to October; Monday, Wednesday, and Saturday; 10:30 A.M. $ • **Plymouth Notch Historic District,** Route 100A, Plymouth, 672-3773. Hours: daily, Memorial Day to mid-October, 9:30 A.M. to 5:30 P.M. $$; under 14, free • **Kedron Valley Stables,** Route 106, PO Box 368, South Woodstock, 457-2734. Trail rides, carriage rides, inn-to-inn riding tours. Call for rates.

INFORMATION Woodstock Area Chamber of Commerce, 18 Central Street, Box 486, Woodstock, VT 05091, 457-3555.

Getting Inspiration in Concord

> By the rude bridge that arched the flood,
> Their flag to April's breeze unfurled,
> Here once the embattled farmers stood,
> And fired the shot heard round the world.
> —Ralph Waldo Emerson

It was on the nineteenth of April, 1775, that a brave band of farmers in Concord, Massachusetts, fired the fateful shots that started the American Revolution.

The spot and its significance—the bravery of the Minutemen who dared to fire against the mighty British crown—have been movingly marked and preserved to inspire us with patriotism even today.

It may be hard to associate the present placid, prosperous little suburban town of Concord with such bloody goings-on, but it's easy to see why the serenity of the town and the natural beauty of its countryside would have attracted a remarkable gathering of American literary giants to Concord nearly a century later. Emerson, who wrote *Nature* here, declared it a "fit" place for a poet, where a walk in the woods had "a breath of immortality in it." Hawthorne and Louisa May Alcott also lived and wrote here, as did Thoreau, whose Walden Pond is just outside of town.

With such an extraordinary blend of history to its credit, Concord is a fascinating place to visit. You actually need to take three separate tours to appreciate all this small town has to offer in the way of military and literary lore and early American architecture—and even then you haven't begun to enjoy the countryside.

Since its greatest fame rests on its pivotal role in the Revolution, it's well to start your tour of the town with a look at the Concord of 1775, a town of 1,600 people, mostly prosperous farmers, who were deeply involved in the movement to gain freedom from the oppression of Great Britain. As a place where Colonial supplies were being stored in anticipation of war, Concord became the target of a British confiscation mission. When General George Gage's troops left Boston for Concord on April 18, Paul Revere spread the alarm on his famous ride.

Drive up Monument Street, just beyond the center of town, and you'll come to the North Bridge, a reconstruction of the simple wooden bridge where the fateful encounter began. The spot is marked by the famous Minuteman statue, a young American farmer holding gun and plow, created by Daniel Chester French, who is also famed for his Lincoln Memorial statue in Washington. The bridge is now part of Minuteman National Historical Park, and the National Park Service has done its usual informative and tasteful job of bringing historical events to life. The site remains rural. You can cross the bridge and walk the path taken by the soldiers, following the action described on plaques along the way as you head gradually uphill to the Visitors' Center for a panoramic view of the entire scene. Weather permitting, there are guided tours as well.

Just before the bridge is the Bullet Hole House. A bullet hole may still be seen in the shed, where retreating British troops fired a shot at the owner. The home is now a private residence.

There are many other noteworthy remains of the events of that April 19 and of early Revolutionary War activities in Concord. You can see Colonel Barrett's farm, where a cache of arms, the target of the British army's mission to Concord, was hidden. At Monument Square you can climb to the top of the Old Burying Ground, where members of several Revolutionary War–era families rest, and see beyond it to the ridge that runs to Meriam's Corner, from which the patriots followed the retreat of the British on the road below.

Minuteman Park actually stretches all the way from Concord to Lexington along Route 2A, the road the British followed on their way from an early-morning skirmish on Lexington Green and again on their way back to Boston following the Concord battle, when further fighting took place all along the route. The Battle Road Visitors' Center on Route 2A just outside Lexington has its own exhibit room and a movie and orientation program. If you want to follow the entire sequence of events of April 19, 1775, you'll want to include not only the park but also the town of Lexington, another pleasant Colonial site with its own share of historic buildings.

But if you have just a weekend, you may prefer to stick to Concord, and by now you're probably ready for a lunch break at the Colonial Inn, a 1716 landmark right on the green in the center of town and another storage site for Colonial arms. As you munch your Colonial chicken pie or Boston scrod, you'll actually be starting your literary tour of Concord. Thoreau's family lived in the old part of the inn when it was still a private home; after the inn began taking in lodgers, it became known as Thoreau House.

You should also have noted another important literary spot, the home of Reverend William Emerson, Ralph Waldo's grandfather. The house, known as the Old Manse, was so close to the North Bridge that the reverend actually watched the Battle of Concord from an upstairs window. Descendants of the Emerson family lived here for 169 years, except for a period from 1842 to 1845, when Nathaniel Hawthorne and his bride, Sophia Peabody, rented the house. It was here that Hawthorne wrote *Mosses from an Old Manse.*

Hawthorne moved away to Salem but returned to Concord in 1852 to the home known as the Wayside, where he remained for the rest of his life. There's an orientation program and a half-hour tour there to tell you about him and the Wayside's other interesting residents.

The Alcott family also stayed at the Wayside while their home was being completed, but it was the Orchard House, where they lived for twenty years, that became the setting for *Little Women.* The tour here includes many of Louisa's mementos, including the costumes used by the Alcott girls when they gave their famous plays. Outside is the School of Philosophy, founded by Bronson Alcott and Ralph Waldo Emerson, the two leaders of the American Transcendentalist movement, a place where great thinkers of the day studied and spoke.

Emerson's own home, to which he moved in 1835 with his wife, Lydian, and remained until his death in 1882, is known simply as Emerson House. The guides will show you a collection of many of his books, personal effects, and furniture.

Thoreau, the only one of the resident writers who was a native son, loved the town and once wrote: "I have never got over my surprise that I should have been born into the most estimable place in all the world. . . ."

Thoreau's former home is now privately owned, and his wilderness outpost, Walden Pond, is part of a state recreational reserve, a busy place enjoyed by boaters, swimmers, and fishermen. Take a walk down the nature trail to the lovely pond and the stones that mark the site of his cabin, and you can understand why the spot inspired Mr. Thoreau.

Both Thoreau and Bronson Alcott spent time in the Old Jail in town when they refused to pay poll tax as a way to protest government-supported slavery. The incident was the inspiration for Thoreau's famous essay "On Civil Disobedience."

You'll learn still more about Concord's extraordinary group of writers at the lovely 1873 Concord Library, which houses their manuscripts as well as a statue of Emerson and busts of the others by Daniel Chester French.

The contents of Emerson's study and the furnishings of Thoreau's Walden House are on display at the Concord Museum, where a film and a six-gallery exhibition titled, "Why Concord?" explore the many facets of the town's unique history. Exhibit highlights include one of the lanterns that hung in Boston's Old North Church on the night of Paul Revere's ride and a diorama of the historic battle at the North Bridge. Some 15 period rooms show the evolution of the community from 1680 to 1880. The Thoreau Room has lots of memorabilia including his rough walking stick and spyglass and a tiny painted school desk from his Walden Pond cabin.

All of Concord's writers are buried on the Author's Ridge in Sleepy Hollow Cemetery, just above the town.

If all those sights are becoming overwhelming, take a shopping break downtown. These days, Concord is basically an upscale suburban town, but it has its share of interesting shops. You'll find a nice variety of galleries and gift shops, toys and teddy bears, as well as conservative clothing stores along Main and Walden Streets. There are two notable galleries with high-quality American crafts: Artful Image and the Lacoste Gallery. The Active Mind, on Walden, has an interesting selection of family-oriented games, puzzles, and software titles, many of which can be tried out in the store. Also, don't overlook the excellent gift shops at the Concord Museum, the Old Manse, and the Orchard House.

On Sunday, you might want to spend part of the morning on the architectural walking tour described in a brochure published by the Concord Chamber of Commerce. The brochure is available at the information booth on Heywood Street and at other locations around town. Guided tours are offered from May through October, leaving from the information booth at 11 A.M. on Saturday, at noon on Sunday, and on Monday holidays.

On your own, wander down Monument, Liberty, and Main Streets and along Lowell and Lexington Roads, along brick sidewalks bordering the green and on gravel paths just out of the town center, past lovely historic homes and white-spired Colonial churches dating from the early 1700s to the mid-1850s.

The 1750 home of Jonathan Ball now houses the Concord Art Association, which holds regular exhibits. Another only-in-Concord attraction is the Grapevine Cottage, former home of Ephraim Bull, who planted the wild grapes that eventually developed into the ubiquitous Concord grape. A plaque marks his accomplishment, and you can still see a grape arbor by the side of the house.

Finally, you can take your pick of places to get back to nature. There's the Walden Pond preserve, as well as the Great Meadows National Wildlife Refuge, whose Concord location is reached from Monsen Road, off Route 62. This is a great place for walking nature trails and spotting a great diversity of birds. Many waterfowl nest in the refuge's wetlands.

Or, if you'd rather glide along in a canoe, as Emerson and Thoreau once did, head for South Bridge Boat House in Concord on Route 62 and paddle your way along Concord's three rivers: the Concord, the Sudbury, and the Assabet.

If you have young children with you, take the ten-mile drive to the headquarters of the Massachusetts Audubon Society at Drumlin Farm in Lincoln. Drumlin is a 220-acre farm with lots of friendly barnyard animals as well as walking and hiking trails and a picnic area. Special programs for families, from sheep shearing to guided nature walks, are held on Saturday and Sunday at 11 A.M. and 2 P.M.

It's especially fun to make this trip around Patriot's Day, April 19, when both Concord and Lexington offer early-morning reenactments and other festivities to mark the date. The events, which change from year to year, are sometimes scheduled on a weekend rather than the actual day, so it's best to check with both chambers of commerce for the current year's schedule.

Concord is probably at its most beautiful in mid-May, when its fine Colonial homes are set off by the pinks, purples, and whites of flowering trees. But whenever you make the trip, you're almost sure to find the town a treasure trove of history, as well as a chance to emulate Thoreau and get back, at least a bit, to nature.

Area Code: 978

DRIVING DIRECTIONS   Concord is on Route 2, reached from I-495 or Route 128. Route 2A, the Battle Road, leads from Lexington to Concord. It is 17 miles from Boston, 248 miles from New York, and 138 miles from Hartford.

PUBLIC TRANSPORTATION   For many residents, Concord is a commuter outpost for Boston, so there is frequent train service from North Station. Phone 227-5070 for information. Many of the sights are within walking distance of the center of town.

ACCOMMODATIONS   Hawthorne Inn, 462 Lexington Road, Concord 01742, 369-5610, a lovely antiques-filled 1870 home on beautiful grounds that once belonged to Emerson, the Alcotts, and Hawthorne; just seven rooms, so reserve early, M–EE, CP • **Colonial Inn,** Monument Square, Concord 01742, 369-9200, prize location on the green, rooms in old inn or new motel wing, M–E • **North Bridge**

Inn, 21 Monument Street, Concord 01742, 371-0014, blend of inn ambience and hotel amenities, kitchenettes, in town center, M–E, CP • **Longfellow's Wayside Inn,** off Route 20, Sudbury 01776, 443-1776, a 1702 Colonial beautifully restored by the Ford Foundation and operated by a nonprofit trust—a charmer with just ten rooms, so reserve well ahead, M, CP • **Best Western at Historic Concord,** 740 Elm Street at Route 2, Concord 01742, 369-6100, good family choice, fitness room, outdoor pool, M, CP.

DINING   Aigo Bistro, 84 Thoreau Street, Concord, 371-1333, a touch of Provence, highly praised, M • **Walden Grille,** 24 Walden Street, Concord, 371-2233, varied menu, recommended locally, restored firehouse, M • **Colonial Inn** (see above), M–E, New England fare; lounge menu, I • **Papa-razzi,** 768 Elm Street, Concord, 371-0030, family-style Italian, pizza, I–M • **Willow Pond Kitchen,** 745 Lexington Road, Concord, 369-6529, roadhouse, nothing fancy, but good, homey food at good, homey prices, I • **Amigos del Norte,** 1200 Main Street, West Concord, 371-7000, Southwestern fare, M • **Longfellow's Wayside Inn** (see above), very popular, so reserve early, M–E • **Chez Claude,** Route 2A, Acton, 263-3325, longtime area favorite French restaurant, charming decor, M • **Lemon Grass,** 1710 Massachusetts Avenue, Lexington, 862-3530, popular Thai choice, I–M.

SIGHTSEEING   Minute Man National Historical Park, North Bridge Visitor Center, 174 Liberty Street, Concord, 369-6993. Hours: daily, 9 A.M. to 5:30 P.M. year-round. Free • **Battle Road Visitor Center,** off Route 2A, Lexington, 862-7753. Hours: mid-April to November, daily, 9 A.M. to 5:30 P.M. Free • **The Wayside,** 455 Lexington Road (Route 2A), 369-6975. Hours: April through October, Thursday to Tuesday, 10 A.M. to 5 P.M.; hours sometimes vary, so best to call. $$; 16 and under, free • **The Old Manse,** Monument Street at the Old North Bridge, 369-3909. Hours: mid-April through October, Monday to Saturday, 10 A.M. to 5 P.M., Sunday, from 1 P.M. $$ • **Orchard House,** 399 Lexington Road (Route 2A), 369-4118. Hours: April through October, Monday to Saturday, 10 A.M. to 4:30 P.M., Sunday from 1 P.M.; November to March, Monday to Friday, 11 A.M. to 3 P.M., Saturday, 10 A.M. to 4:30 P.M., Sunday 1 P.M. to 4:30 P.M. Closed January 1–15. $$ • **Emerson House,** 28 Cambridge Turnpike at Lexington Road (Route 2A), 369-2236. Hours: mid-April through October, Thursday to Saturday, 10 A.M. to 4:30 P.M., Sunday from 2 P.M. Adults, $3.50; ages 7 to 17, $$ • **Concord Museum,** 200 Lexington Road, 369-9609. Hours: Monday to Saturday, 9 A.M. to 5 P.M., Sunday from noon, shorter hours January to March. $$$ • **Concord Free Public Library,** 129 Main Street at Sudbury Road, 371-6240 Hours: Monday to Thursday, 9 A.M. to 9 P.M., Friday to 6 P.M., Saturday 9 A.M. to 5 P.M.; October to May only, Sunday, 2 P.M. to 5 P.M. Free • **Walden Pond State Reservation,** 915

Walden Street (Route 126 at Route 2), 369-3254. Hours: daily until dark. $ parking fee, charged April to October • **Drumlin Farm,** S. Great Road (Route 117, ½ mile east of Route 126), Lincoln, 259-9807. Hours: Tuesday to Sunday, 9 A.M. to 5 P.M. $$$ • **Great Meadows National Wildlife Refuge,** Weir Hill Road (north off Lincoln Road), Sudbury, 443-4661. Hours: grounds open daily, dawn to dusk. Visitor Center open daily, 8 A.M. to 4:30 P.M., except closed holidays and weekends in winter. Additional trails and observation towers in Concord, Monsen Road (off Route 62, 1 mile northeast of Concord center). Free.

INFORMATION Concord Chamber of Commerce, 2 Lexington Road, Concord, MA 01742, 369-3120.

Herbs and History in Connecticut

You'll find Sweet Cicely, an herb once used by the Elizabethans to polish furniture, and Tansy, which served the Victorians as an insect and moth repellent. For those in need of a little sympathy, there's balm lemon for your tea.

In fact, there's an herb for almost everything among the 300 varieties in 31 gardens at Caprilands, a one-of-a-kind 50-acre herb farm in Coventry, Connecticut. Visitors not only learn about herbs and their uses (culinary and otherwise), but are treated to a delicious five-course luncheon served in an eighteenth-century farmhouse and flavored with home-grown seasonings.

It's the perfect introduction to Coventry, a nontouristy town of wooded hills and bucolic back roads with history galore, a big lake for swimming, and unexpected discoveries, from antique dolls to fanciful puppets, nearby.

If you doubt that herbs such as sage can actually preserve a person's youth, you might have changed your mind if you could have met Adelma Grenier Simmons, the creator of the magical world of Caprilands.

Mrs. Simmons, who passed away in 1997 at the age of 94, was still signing autographs just a few months before her death. She first spied this land in 1929, a worn-out farm with 300 or so chickens running around in the run-down farmhouse. Farming was her weekend occupation then, and she first tried to establish the property as a goat farm, hence the name Caprilands, which translates to "Goat Lands."

When that didn't work, Simmons turned to herb farming and struck gold. One by one, the gardens were planted and lovingly tended until her initial vision was complete. Years of studying and growing herbs made her an authority, an author and lecturer known for her wit and whimsy. Her tradition is carried on in the talks given at Caprilands.

Visitors are free to stroll among the many gardens Simmons has created. They include a heart-shaped bride's garden, potpourri and old rose gardens, a silver garden (planted only with silvery plants), and a Shakespeare garden (filled with the herbs mentioned by the Bard). The newest addition, an identification garden, has markers giving names and uses for all kinds of herbs.

On the typical day here, at 11:30 A.M. a staff member gives an introduction to herbs, either on a walking tour or seated in a barn, its rafters festooned with sweet lavender and other drying plants. The herbal lore is both factual and fanciful and includes lots of fun herb trivia, like the fact that the leaves of the butterbread plant were once used as a primitive type of Saran Wrap. Afterward, guests are seated at tables crowded into the three main-floor rooms of the charming old farmhouse for a delicious lunch.

Shops in various buildings on the grounds also sell plants, seeds and garden items, gifts, fragrant herbs and seasonings, and herbal vinegars, mustards, and tea.

After lunch, depending on the weather, you may choose to spend the rest of the afternoon lazing on the beach in Patriot's Park, on the shores of Coventry's Lake Waumgumbaug. Or you can visit the authentically furnished 1776 red clapboard homestead that was the birthplace of Connecticut's officially designated "State Hero," Nathan Hale, the young patriot who said "I only regret that I have but one life to lose for my country."

Coventry is also antiquing country, with several multidealer shops along Main Street (Route 31) and a big Sunday flea market where you never know what you may find.

A stop not to be missed for anyone interested in antique dolls is Special Joys, at 41 North River Road, a bright pink towered Victorian that is a combination bed-and-breakfast, doll shop, and museum of owner Joy Kelleher's extraordinary collection of dolls, toys, and Stieff animals. Her treasures include early papier-mâché, bisque, and wax dolls; French fashion dolls; and unusual doll furniture.

Storrs, home of the University of Connecticut (UConn) campus, is about a ten-minute drive from Coventry via Route 44. On the way, you can detour onto Weaver Road (off Route 44 in Mansfield), for a unique little museum that is a delight. The Ballard Institute and Museum of Puppetry is named for the late Frank Ballard, who established the nation's first complete undergraduate and graduate degree programs in puppetry at UConn. The museum displays some of the over 1,000 large, fanciful marionettes and puppets that have been created for this renowned Puppet Arts Program.

Continue to Storrs to visit the main UConn campus and the William Benton Museum of Art, the official state museum. This campus was originally the site of an agricultural school, and the animal barns are well worth a visit—especially in spring, when there are lots of baby animals to admire. Be sure to stop at the UConn Dairy Bar to sample the rich mix they call "the granddaddy of homemade ice cream." Also check what's on at the Connecticut Repertory Theatre, on campus, where plays and musicals are presented from October through July.

Drive farther east on Route 44 to see more of the unspoiled northeast corner of the state, with woods for hiking, clear streams for fishing or canoeing, and village greens ringed by homes dating back to Colonial days. If you want to get out and walk in the countryside, there are 11 state parks and forests in the area and another half dozen preserves offering miles of hiking trails.

The area is divided into "hill towns" and "mill towns," the latter developed in the lower areas along the Quinebaug River. Most of the inns are in the rural villages on the hilltops.

There are many historic small bed-and-breakfast homes in these unspoiled villages, especially in Pomfret, a lovely town that is home to two prestigious prep schools. One of the most appealing of the inns is Cobbscroft, a comfortable 1800s home filled with art by the talented host and hostess. Artist Tom McCobb's art studio is on the grounds, and Janet McCobb runs a little shop there filled with wonderful handcrafts, including many of her own hand-painted pieces. The couple also offers weekend painting workshops.

Pomfret has two recommended eating places, the Harvest, for fine dining, and the informal Vanilla Bean Café, serving delicious home-made fare at reasonable prices. In warm weather, the Vanilla Bean grills outside.

This is a town where open space has been carefully preserved, making for beautiful drives and many opportunities to get out of the car and enjoy the countryside. Pomfret Farms, maintained by the Connecticut Audubon Society, has several miles of designated trails on 140 acres on Day Road (off Route 169) and offers guided walks and weekend workshops.

A delightful annual "Walking Weekend" in mid-October offers guided walks in Pomfret and all over the region; check with the Visitors District office for a full schedule.

Also in Pomfret are the Brayton Grist Mill and the Marcy Blacksmith Museum in Mashamoquet Brook State Park. The mill is an example of a one-man mill operation of the 1890s, still with its original equipment. The museum shows the craft of three generations of blacksmiths.

Antiquers will want to check out Pomfret Antique World, which includes some 90 dealers, and make the short detour to Putnam, an old mill town that has found new life as an antiquing center. More than a dozen shops can be found within two or three blocks of the village center. Stop at the Vine Bistro for a tasty lunch or a cappuccino in the outdoor courtyard. Mrs. Bridges Pantry, an antiques shop with a British bent, serves a proper afternoon tea with scones and clotted cream.

For one of the prettiest of the hill towns, turn north on Route 169 (you'll quickly see why it has been declared a National Scenic Highway) to Woodstock—not the famous one but a Connecticut country cousin—a village of stone walls and historic houses that date to 1686.

There is no Main Street as such here, just clusters of homes and occasional shops. About midway through the town, on the crest of a long ridge, is Woodstock Hill, where huge old trees shade handsome country houses spanning a couple of centuries in architecture. One that stands out is Roseland Cottage, a pink Gothic-style house built in 1864 for a wealthy gentleman named Bowen, a native who became a prominent New York newspaper publisher. When he returned to Woodstock to build his home, he installed the best of everything, right down to a private bowling alley. The house and its gardens and barns, now owned and operated by the Society for the Preservation of New England Antiquities, are open to visitors.

Woodstock is hardly a shopping mecca, but it does offer its own small group of shops—the Scranton Shops—near the intersection of Route 169 and Route 171. Fox Hunt Farms Gourmet and Cafe in this complex is an excellent stop for lunch. Windy Acres has dried and silk flowers as well as fresh blooms, and the Christmas Barn and Shop has 12 rooms of gifts, candles, tree decorations, and fabric. A mile off Route 169, on Woodstock Road in East Woodstock, is Brunarhan's, a furniture showroom where handcrafted pieces in pine and oak are available.

The gracious Inn at Woodstock Hill, set on 14 acres, is a recommended stop for lodging or dinner. Lord Thompson Manor, a stately 30-room beauty on 40 acres, is another excellent choice. It is located in nearby Thompson, a picturesque hamlet with stately trees and fine old homes, where the Vernon Stiles Inn has been serving meals to travelers since 1814.

Turn south on Route 169 for Brooklyn, another of those out-of-the-way spots off the tourist path. Friendship Valley, a charming inn in a historic home, has a hostess who delights in filling guests in on local history. Brooklyn's New England Center of Contemporary Arts is a rustic gallery with changing exhibits of work by living artists displayed in a four-story barn. The Golden Lamb Buttery is a unique dinner stop offering gourmet fare in a farm setting. Come early for a free hayride through the fields or to sit on the deck and watch the ponies, the donkey, and the horses graze.

If you want to plan an herb-flavored weekend, remember that reservations are a necessity at Caprilands, and the earlier the better. It isn't known whether luncheon dishes are laced with caraway, an herb said to bring those who eat it back to the place where they tasted it, but guests here do tend to return and to bring their friends—and the seats in the house fill up in a hurry.

Area Code: 860

DRIVING DIRECTIONS To go directly to Caprilands from Hartford, the best route is I-84 east (toward Boston) to exit 59, then I-384 east through Manchester and to its end, where I-384 becomes Route 44 leading into Coventry. Silver Street is off Route 44 on the right. From Boston, go west on the Mass Pike (I-90) until it merges with I-84. Take exit 67, Rockville-Coventry, off I-84 (Route 31 south), turn left on Route 44, and then take the second right onto Silver Street. Coventry is about 70 miles from Boston, 140 miles from New York, and 14 miles from the I-84 turnoff in Hartford.

ACCOMMODATIONS **Bird-In-Hand Bed and Breakfast,** 201 Main Street, Coventry 06238, 742-0032, charmingly furnished home, circa 1800, and a delightful guest cottage, I–M, CP • **Special Joys Bed & Breakfast,** 41 North River Road, Coventry 06238, 742-6359, two comfortable rooms above the shop, I, CP • **The Inn at Woodstock Hill,** 94 Plaine Hill Road and Route 169, Woodstock 06267, 928-0528, M–EE, CP • **Cobbscroft,** 349 Pomfret Street, Route 169, Pomfret, 928-5560, 1830s home filled with artistic charm, I–M, CP • **Karinn,** Route 169, Pomfret 06250, 928-5492, spacious, antiques, fireplaces, M, CP • **Clark Cottage at Wintergreen,** 354 Pomfret Street, Pomfret Center 06250, 928-5471, rambling Victorian on lovely grounds with views, I, CP • **Friendship Valley,** Route 169, Brooklyn, 06234, 779-9696, 1830s Colonial with authentic period ambience, M, CP.

DINING **Bidwell Tavern,** 1260 Main Street (Route 31), Coventry, 742-6978, historic spot, busy front bar, quieter back dining room, famed for 24 varieties of wings and 24 beers on tap, I–M • **Netto's at the Depot,** 57 Middle Turnpike (Route 44), Mansfield, 429-3663, American-Italian food in the old depot, I–M • **Cavey's,** 45 East Center Street, Manchester, 643-2751, known for elegant French dining, E–EE, **Cavey's Restaurant-Italian,** same address and phone, upstairs, M • **Altnaveigh Inn,** 95 Storrs Road (Route 195), Storrs, 1734 country farmhouse, Austrian cuisine, M • **The Golden Lamb Buttery,** Hillandale Farm, Bush Hill Road, Brooklyn, 774-4423, exceptional, open June to December, prix fixe, EE • **The Harvest,** 37 Putnam Street (Route 44), Pomfret, 928-0008, excellent continental menu, M–E • **Vanilla Bean Café,** 450 Deerfield Road, Pomfret, 928-

1562, a restored barn, very informal, I • **The Inn at Woodstock Hill** (see above), continental menu, M–E • **Vernon Stiles Inn,** Route 200, Thompson, 923-9571, charming nineteenth-century tavern, M • **The Vine Bistro,** 85 Main Street, Putnam, 928-1660, contemporary American cuisine, M.

SIGHTSEEING **Caprilands Herb Farm,** 534 Silver Street, Coventry, 742-7244. Visits to gardens and gift shops are free. Lecture and luncheon, May through December, $18 (check for any recent price change), reservations essential; high tea on Saturday and Sunday at 2 P.M. • **Nathan Hale Homestead,** South Street, Coventry, 742-6917. Hours: mid-May to mid-October, daily, 1 P.M. to 5 P.M. $$ • **Ballard Institute and Museum of Puppetry,** Willimantic Cottage, Weaver Road, UConn Depot campus (off Route 44), Mansfield, 486-4605. Hours: mid-April to mid-November, Thursday and Friday, 10 A.M. to 3 P.M., Saturday and Sunday, noon to 4 P.M. Free • **University of Connecticut,** Route 195, Storrs, 486-4866. Campus maps and information are available at the Information Booth on Route 195. Animal barns open daily, 10 A.M. to 4 P.M.; floriculture greenhouses, Monday to Friday, 9 A.M. to 4 P.M.; dairy bar, 3636 Horsebarn Road, Monday to Friday, 10 A.M. to 5 P.M., Saturday and Sunday, noon to 5 P.M. • **William Benton Museum of Art,** Route 195, University of Connecticut campus, Storrs, 486-4520. Hours: Tuesday to Friday, 10 A.M. to 4:30 P.M., Saturday and Sunday, 1 P.M. to 4:30 P.M. Free. • **Roseland Cottage,** Route 169 (on the Common), Woodstock, 928-4074. Hours: Memorial Day to Labor Day, Wednesday to Sunday, noon to 5 P.M.; Labor Day to mid-October, Friday to Sunday, noon to 5 P.M.; guided tours start on the hour to 4 P.M. $$ • **Brayton Grist Mill,** Mashamoquet Brook State Park, Route 44, Pomfret. Hours: late May to September, Saturday and Sunday, 2 P.M. to 5 P.M. Donation • **New England Center for Contemporary Art,** Route 169, Brooklyn, 774-8899. Open: May to November, Wednesday to Sunday, 1 P.M. to 5 P.M. Free • **William Benton Museum of Art,** UConn, 245 Glenbrook Road, Storrs, 486-4520. Hours: Tuesday to Friday, 10 A.M. to 4:30 P.M., Saturday and Sunday, 1 P.M. to 4:30 P.M. Free.

INFORMATION Northeast Connecticut Visitors District, PO Box 598, Putnam, CT 06260, 928-1228.

Rites of Spring on Nantucket

Spring comes late to Nantucket, bursting in at last near the end of April in a rush of blue skies, golden forsythia, and millions of bright yellow daffodils—an estimated three million at last count.

Weather-weary islanders celebrate the long-awaited end of winter gray with their own special spring rite, the Daffodil Festival, which fills the town with golden blooms and features a parade of antique cars and a tailgate picnic that have become island traditions. The weekend has grown to include the annual Basket Show by the Artists' Association, an annual inn tour, and a variety of entertainment that often includes morris dancers. Though it's a local party, everyone is welcome, and there are few more gala ways to usher in the season.

Preseason visitors to the island are rewarded with a glimpse of a Nantucket that is often obscured by the boatloads of summer tourists. In the mild and breezy sunshine of springtime, Nantucket's center is not a bustling resort at all, but a quiet and beautiful small town of 7,000 where everyone offers a friendly hello. Cobbled streets and sea captains' mansions become not a backdrop for the beach but the focal point of delightful walks into the past.

This is, after all, the historic island outpost, 30 miles out at sea, that was once the third largest city in Massachusetts, sending brave seamen to the far corners of the globe for the whale oil that lighted the lamps of the world. And weathered shingled cottages still mark the original farming settlement of the 1600s and the austere Quaker era of the early 1700s that preceded the prosperous whaling days.

Both simple cottages and stately homes remain, perfectly preserved by a turn of fate that seemed disastrous 141 years ago. A destructive business district fire in 1846, coupled with the discovery of kerosene and the resulting dwindling demand for whale oil that followed in the 1850s, sent Nantucket into an economic decline that lasted for years. Hard times meant that no one could afford to "modernize," so while the mainland was changing, Nantucket remained untouched, becoming America's largest living Colonial town.

Toward the end of the last century, visitors discovered that this beach-rimmed island was also a perfect vacation spot. New hotels went up, and islanders began to open their shingled houses to paying guests.

But world wars and the Depression slowed things, and the island's real renaissance did not come until the 1960s. It began with one man, Walter Beinecke, a wealthy summer resident who formed a corporation named Sherburne, after Nantucket's first settlement, to rescue and renovate the decaying wharves. Sherburne went on to acquire large portions of island real estate and to take over and renovate some of the better hotels.

Though Sherburne has sold its holdings, the development movement goes on—too much so to suit many who loved the island as it was. Strict ordinances have been passed to ensure that nothing spoils the island's remarkably preserved past. All new construction must conform to the simple shingled architecture of the original homes, so the church steeples and lighthouses remain the tallest structures on Nantucket.

A good place to learn about some of the people and events of Nantucket's rich past is the Thomas Macy Warehouse on Straight Wharf, where exhibits trace the island's development from whaling to summering. The warehouse is one of 13 sites, all open to the public with one moderately priced admission pass, maintained by the Nantucket Historical Association. These sites include the wonderful Whaling Museum; the Old Mill, which still grinds corn; the Old Gaol; the Quaker Meeting House; and the 1686 Jethro Coffin House, the oldest building on the island, re-restored after being struck by lightning in 1987.

But if the day is fine, there's no more pleasant way to explore than to take a walking tour of the town, starting on Main Street. It is interesting to note that the cobblestones that seem so picturesque today were put down originally for a very practical reason—to keep heavy whale oil drays from sinking into the mud.

The walking tour takes you past the Pacific Club, whose membership was limited to shipmasters who had whaled in the Pacific, and brings you to the corner of Main and Fair, where the R. H. Macy of retailing fame gave up his first storekeeping job with his father to go whaling, then became a forty-niner in search of gold, which he found when he eventually headed for New York to establish the store we know today.

Continuing on to upper Main, you pass the brick mansions of the ship-owning Coffin family, aboard whose vessel *Charles and Mary* Herman Melville once went to sea. The Coffins were responsible for planting the stately elms on Main Street as well as for bringing back and planting the pines, larches, and heather that have spread across the island landscape.

A few doors down on Walnut Lane is the Nathaniel Macy House, built in 1723 and now open to the public. Next comes one of the most fascinating sections of any street in New England: 12 magnificent whaling mansions built by various members of the Coffin and Starbuck families, testaments to Nantucket's wealth and taste. The three brick-columned Starbuck mansions that stand in a row have been the subjects of countless snapshots.

Wherever you walk, you'll run into more fascinating history and more historic homes that are now open to let you share it more intimately.

There's the house where Maria Mitchell, the most famous early female astronomer, was born. It's now the Science Center, open summers only, with exhibits portraying Mitchell's life. You'll also see various residences and monuments to the Folger family, including a memorial to Abiah Folger, wife of Josiah Franklin and mother of Benjamin Franklin. Facing Main on Pleasant Street, the Hadwen House, a Historical Association Property, has a beautiful 1850s-style garden in the rear that is maintained for the public by the Nantucket Garden Club.

Walk far enough in any direction and you're back to the ever-present sea that made Nantucket what it was in the past—as well as the popular spot it is today. Early in the year you can have the endless beaches to yourself, and although spring temperatures aren't normally warm enough for swimming, they are frequently perfect for beachcombing and tanning in blissful solitude.

Biking is another ideal spring pastime, taking you away from the cobblestones to wide-open vistas of cranberry bogs and low-lying moors of bayberry and scrub pine, the scenes that give Nantucket its faraway feel.

If you come for the Daffodil Festival, when you arrive you'll find Nantucket's cobbled Main Street festooned with yellow flowers in every store window and doorway; the bountiful and original arrangements compete for the coveted judges' blue ribbons for best window displays.

Prizes are awarded for Saturday morning's antique auto parade as well. The procession of classic cars from Model As to MGs parades past bystanders on Main Street; many of the drivers and passengers come in vintage costumes that match the ages of their cars.

The best part of the day comes when everyone follows the procession of contestants down the daffodil-lined road to the picturesque fishing village of Siasconset (known locally as 'Sconset) for a tailgate picnic party that just may be the most elegant event of its kind anywhere. Prizes are the lure once again, this time for the most artistic food display, and you'll see everything from a picnic for Raggedy Ann and Raggedy Andy to a caviar-and-champagne feast served to diners on velvet-seated gilt chairs brought along for the occasion. All the spreads are lavishly laden with daffodils, as are many of the diners. At one year's event, even a dog arrived wearing a yellow bonnet to mark the day.

The picnic ends before three o'clock, leaving time for a walk along 'Sconset's magnificent beach and through the twisting lanes of onetime fishermen's shanties that are now charming summer cottages—or, if you prefer, a look at the shops in Nantucket Village. There are a few T-shirt shops, but on the whole, very few geegaw souvenirs are to be found here. Most of the shops carry quality merchandise, much of it handmade, and browsing is a pleasure. Antiquers will find plenty of temptation—more than two dozen shops all around town.

One special place to watch for is Nantucket Looms, at the foot of Main Street, with its hand-loomed mohair scarves and other lovely woolens. The Spectrum, on Main, is a cooperative showing fine crafts, and Nantucket Folkworks, on Broad Street, features folk art by New

England artists. You'll find examples of the island's best-known craft, Nantucket Lighthouse baskets, in many stores around town. Each hand-painted ivory top is different, and since the price tags run into the hundreds, if you plan to indulge, you ought to have the fun of choosing from a full selection. The Golden Basket, on Main and at Straight Wharf; the Lightship Shop on East Chestnut Street; and Nantucket Basket Works, on Daves Street, are among the many places to look.

If you have time on Sunday, there are plenty of museums and historic houses to visit. The Peter Foulger Museum, with its mixed memorabilia of old Nantucket, and the famous Whaling Museum are both of special interest.

Sunday is also the start of the two-day annual Daffodil Show, sponsored by the Nantucket Garden Club in cooperation with the American Daffodil Society. You needn't be a flower worshiper to appreciate the unusual varieties and handsome arrangements.

The first show, in 1974, was the start of the island's daffodil mania. The Nantucket Garden Club set a goal of planting one million daffodil bulbs; eager islanders and naturalization have tripled the count, and the show lasts from March to May. Why daffodils and not tulips? Because while the island's deer population loves tulip bulbs, it seems that it doesn't care for daffodils.

The festival weekend, incidentally, has chalked up an admirable record of above-average weather, often sending happy visitors home with an early tan.

Off-season lodgings used to be sparse on Nantucket, but since the Daffodil Festival has begun to attract visitors, many hotels and inns open early. Many of the ship captains' homes and shingled cottages that abound here are now bed-and-breakfast inns, making for snug havens. Off-season prices are way down, good news on an island where it is hard to find moderate rates in midsummer.

Nantucket is distinguished among summer resorts for its large number of fine restaurants, and more of these are now open for the festivities as well.

There's a happy spirit of anticipation in the air in springtime Nantucket. Like the local homeowners, who can be seen putting fresh coats of paint on the shutters, shopkeepers and hotel and restaurant operators are busy sprucing up after the long winter. Hammers and paintbrushes are in evidence everywhere, and on Main Street, merchants are busily arranging new stock, awaiting the coming rush of summer customers.

There are some who love off-season Nantucket best in the fall, after the summer people have left, but though the island is handsome in its autumn hues, there's a feeling of renewal in the spring that is missing in the winding-down days at season's end. From its daffodil-strewn roadsides to downtown's winding lanes, Nantucket has just come alive, and it is a guaranteed spring tonic for early birds. If you can't make the Daffodil Festival, aim for the annual Harborfest, held the first weekend in June.

Area Code: 508

DRIVING DIRECTIONS   Nantucket Steamship Authority, PO Box 284, Woods Hole, MA 02543, 477-8600, runs boats to the island from Hyannis year-round for both cars and passengers. The trip takes approximately 2¼ hours. Hy-Line Cruises, Pier 1, Ocean Street Docks, Hyannis, MA 02601, 778-2600 or (800) 492-8082 (in MA only), has service for passengers from Hyannis by catamaran year-round, by ferry May through October. Both provide parking facilities if you want to leave your car. Island parking is not a problem in spring, but cars really are not necessary on Nantucket. Most of the activity centers within town, which is easily walkable. Bike rentals are plentiful, and you can rent a car or hire a taxi for a day's exploring. From June through September, shuttle buses connect major points. Hyannis is just over 80 miles from Boston, 271 miles from New York, and 187 miles from Hartford.

PUBLIC TRANSPORTATION   Several airlines service Nantucket from Boston, New York, Newark, New Bedford, Hyannis, and Martha's Vineyard; check the Nautucket Chamber of Commerce for a current list. Bonanza (800-556-3815) offers bus service to Hyannis from New York, Providence, and Boston. Plymouth & Brockton buses also run between Logan Airport, Boston, and Hyannis (746-0378).

ACCOMMODATIONS   Rates here are for summer; prices are considerably less out of season. Listings here have been open for the Daffodil Festival; check to be sure that your choices are still open off-season. All are zip code 02554. **Jared Coffin House,** 29 Broad Street, 228-2405, restored 1845 sea captain's mansion, elegant, E • **Harbor House,** South Beach Street, 228-1500, attractive resort complex with rooms in main house or cottages, pool, E–EE • **The White Elephant and the Breakers,** Easton Street, PO Box 359, (800) ISLANDS elegant resort hotels, EE • **Ships Inn,** 13 Fair Street, 228-0040, tiny cozy captain's home, E, CP. *Bed-and-breakfast inns:* **Brass Lantern Inn,** 11 North Water Street, (800) 377-6609, 1846 Greek Revival home with varied rooms, spacious quarters in modern annex, M–E, CP • **Carlisle House Inn,** 26 N. Water Street, 228-0720, tasteful, antiques-filled eighteenth-century home, M–E, CP • **Corner House,** 49 Centre Street, 228-1530, cozy 1790 home, screened porch and patio, M–E, CP • **Cliff Lodge,** 9 Cliff Road, 228-9480, 1771 sea captain's home, light and airy, harbor views from the roof walk, M–EE, CP • **Eighteen Gardner Street,** at that address, (800) 435-1450, fine 1836 whaling captain's residence, fireplaces, M–EE, CP • **Fair Gardens,** 27 Fair Street, 228-4258, cozy shingled guest house with lovely garden, M–E, CP • **Fair Winds,** 29 Cliff Road, 228-1998, water views from many guest rooms, E, CP • **Four Chimneys,** 38 Orange Street, 228-1912, stately 1835 captain's mansion, spacious and gracious, E–EE, CP • **Martin House Inn,** 61 Centre Street, 228-0678, attractive, good value, M–E, CP • **Roberts House,** 11 India Street, 228-9009, elegant 1880 home, fireplaces, large rooms, canopy beds, E–EE, CP; the same owners maintain the attractive **Meeting House Inn,** adjacent to the Roberts House, and the nearby **Manor House,** both with same rates • **Sherburne Inn,** 10 Gay Street, 228-4425, attractively decorated, stately nineteenth-century home, M–E, CP • **Cliffside Beach Club,** Jefferson Avenue, 228-0618, the only accommodations directly on the beach, but not open until late May; take note for summer visits, EE.

DINING   Opening dates vary from year to year; it's best to check. Most are small, so reserve ahead in season. **21 Federal Street,** 21 Federal Street, 228-2121, among the best in town, E–EE • **Straight Wharf Restaurant,** Straight Wharf, 228-4499, regional American, chic, E–EE • **DeMarco,** 9 India Street, 228-1836, excellent (and expensive) northern Italian, E–EE • **India House,** 37 India Street, 228-9043, choice of light or formal dining in a historic house, M–E • **The Boarding House,** 12 Federal Street, 228-9622, charming cellar café, E • **The Club Car,** 1 Main Street, 228-1101, dinner in a most elegant diner, E–EE • **Le Languedoc,** 24 Broad Street, 228-2552, excellent, sophisticated menu, E–EE • **The Woodbox,** 29 Fair Street, 228-0587, 1709 inn, beams, fireplace, E–EE • **Cioppino's,** 20 Broad Street, 228-4622, excellent seafood, M–E • **American Seasons,** 80 Centre Street, 228-7111, charming setting, folk art, choice of American regional dishes, E–EE • **Oran Mor,** 2 South Beach Street, 228-8655, newcomer with former Toppers chef, sophisticated international menu, M–EE • **American Bounty,** 60 Union Street, 228-3886, American fare served in a garden setting, M–E • **Obadiah's,** 2 India Street, 228-4430, seafood, cozy, reasonable, M • **Black-Eyed Susan's,** 10 India Street, phone unlisted, join the line for creative, economical ethnic dishes, M • **Arno's,** 41 Main Street, 228-7001, old standby, casual, uninspired but reasonable, M • **Moona Grille,** 122 Pleasant Street, 325-4301, American Seasons owners with a more down-to-earth menu, I–M • **Atlantic Café,** 15 South Water Street, 228-0570, casual, popular, I–M • **Cap'n Toby's Chowder House,** Straight Wharf, 228-0836, try the fried clams, I–M • **The Brotherhood,** 23 Broad Street, the local favorite for overstuffed sandwiches, inexpensive dinners, chowder, I. After dinner, you can dance to a rock band at the **Rose and Crown,** 23 South Main Street; hear quiet music at the **Atlantic Café** (see above); or listen to a pianist at **The Club Car's** bar (see above). Summer visitors also see pages 159–162; **Topper's** and **Chanticleer,** the island's two premier dining places, are not open for daffodil season.

SIGHTSEEING   **Daffodil Festival,** held annually the last weekend in April; Harborfest, the first weekend in June; contact the Nautucket

Chamber of Commerce office for current information • **Historic Nantucket Properties,** maintained by the Nantucket Historical Association, 2 Union Street, 228-1894. Hours: in season, daily, 10 A.M. to 5 P.M., off-season as posted. Visitors' passes— good for all of the following and more—are available at all locations. $$$$, or you can pay individual admissions. **Whaling Museum,** Broad Street at head of Steamboat Wharf, $$; **Thomas Macy Warehouse,** Straight Wharf, $$; **Fair Street Museum,** Fair Street, $$; **Peter Foulger Museum,** Broad Street, $$; **Jethro Coffin House** (oldest house), Sunset Hill off West Chester Street, $$; **Old Mill,** Mill Hill, Prospect Street, $; **Hadwen House,** 96 Main Street, $ • **Maria Mitchell Science Center,** 1 Vestal Street, 228-2896. Hours: mid-June through August 31, Tuesday to Saturday, 10 A.M. to 4 P.M. Combination ticket includes the small **Aquarium,** 28 Washington Street, 228-5387; and the **Museum of Natural Science,** 7 Milk Street, 228-0898; both with same hours, $$.

BIKE RENTALS **Cook's Cycle Shop,** 6 South Beach Street, 228-0800 • **Nantucket Bike Shops,** Steamboat Wharf and Straight Wharf, 228-1999 • **Young's Bicycle Shop,** Steamboat Wharf, 228-1151.

INFORMATION Nantucket Island Chamber of Commerce, 48 Main Street, Nantucket MA 02554, 228-1700.

Admiring the Miracle in Providence

You are cordially invited to visit Providence, Rhode Island, to see a miracle in progress. This isn't an exaggeration. For anyone who knew the city in the old days, the recent changes are nothing short of miraculous. An old industrial city in decline not so many years ago, Providence is in the midst of a remarkable turnaround. It began with the transformation of run-down historic residential neighborhoods, part of one of the nation's most lauded restoration campaigns. The work-in-progress is a rejuvenated downtown.

This is more than urban renewal; it is a complete remapping of the center of the city. For decades, the world's widest bridge, holding an unsightly network of railroad tracks and freight yards, obscured the Moshassuck and Woonasquatucket Rivers, two narrow waterways that snake through the city and converge to form the Providence River. The bridge has been ripped up and the rivers have been allowed to follow their scenic course through the town, edged by pedestrian walkways lined with park benches, trees, and flowering plants. You can now actually take a gondola ride or a kayak tour through downtown Providence and dine by the riverside. Local festivals are often celebrated with "Water Fire," a spectacular half-mile-long multimedia installation by local artist Barnaby Evans that literally sets the river on fire with twelve blazes mounted on granite piers in the river.

At the heart of the vibrant new city center is Waterplace Park, a four-acre gathering place framed by a one-acre pond and fountain, with an outdoor amphitheatre. It stands in the shadow of the historic domed State House Building, which still presides over Providence from its hilltop perch across the river.

Within walking distance of the park is the new railroad station that makes it easy to reach the city from Boston or New York. The old Beaux Arts station has been grandly restored into a new shopping and dining complex. A new convention center opened in 1993, attracting a posh Westin Hotel to the city. And instead of moving out, stores are coming in. Nordstrom's, Filene's, and Lord and Taylor will anchor Providence Place, a $300 million mall, office, and hotel project to be built not far from the State House lawn.

Along with the many physical changes, there has been a restaurant revival that has food critics singing the city's praises, all the more reason why Providence merits a weekend to discover how a city can transform itself.

An ideal time to visit is the second weekend in June, during the annual Festival of Historic Houses, sponsored by the Providence Preservation Society. For this one weekend only, visitors are able to go inside some of the exceptional private homes and gardens of the city's rejuvenated neighborhoods, with an emphasis on the College Hill Historic District, the area where the miracle began.

The district, which lies between the Brown University campus and downtown, was the earliest settlement in the state and the first center of the city. It is widely recognized as one of the most notable collections of early American homes in the country, one that is even more remarkable because these houses have been continually inhabited for more than 200 years.

Not long ago, College Hill was in trouble. Many of the older homes were in decay and were being torn down to make room for the expansion of Brown's campus. The group that formed to preserve College Hill faced a formidable task, but today its efforts are a model of what can be accomplished when a community cares about preserving its heritage.

On Benefit Street, the core of the restoration efforts, there are now more than 100 handsomely restored historic houses. The street has been dubbed "A Mile of History," and taking a stroll there is like stepping back to the eighteenth and early nineteenth centuries. The Nightingale-Brown House, built in 1792, is the neighborhood showplace, one of the largest eighteenth-century wooden structures in the country. Like many of the privately owned homes, it is sometimes open to the public on this special weekend to help raise funds for continuing preservation efforts, which have now spread to many other city neighborhoods.

The Festival of Historic Houses festivities usually begin on Friday night with a candlelight tour along Benefit Street or other streets in National Historic Districts. Changing areas are chosen for the House and Garden Tour, on Saturday afternoon, and tours for Sunday afternoon. Talks on various aspects of preservation fill out the schedule.

Typically, a dozen private residences open for the candlelight tour. Their carefully restored exteriors present fine examples of Federal, Greek Revival, and early Victorian detailing, while the interiors are both traditional and contemporary.

To add to the pleasures of the weekend, try to snag one of the rooms at the Old Court, a small inn perfectly located on Benefit Street. More accommodations on College Hill are available through Bed-and-Breakfast of Rhode Island (see page xiii). The restored Providence Biltmore Hotel, a landmark, usually offers special rates for house-touring visitors, as does the lavish new Westin.

The array of architecture on College Hill includes not only residences but house museums, churches, and grand mansions adapted for use as offices. Some of the mansions date back to the China trade era following the American Revolution, the time when many Providence traders made their millions. The area borders the historic Brown University campus, so visitors can also view the school's handsome quadrangles and stately buildings. In many ways, Brown's emergence as one of the most sought-after Ivy League colleges has paralleled the reblooming of its neighborhood.

Brown deserves a return visit for a closer look. Campus highlights include the 1770 University Hall, the John Hay and Rockefeller Libraries, and Wriston Quadrangle. The David Winton Bell Gallery, in the List Art Building, across from the main gate, presents changing art exhibits that are often worthwhile. Art exhibits are found also at the Providence Art Club, studios and galleries in two eighteenth-century houses off nearby Benefit Street.

The city's finest art collections, however, belong to the highly regarded Rhode Island School of Design (universally known as RISD, or "rizz-dee"), whose campus lies just below Brown. RISD's five-story museum on Benefit Street is first-rate, with everything from Oriental art to French Impressionists in its collection. The Pendleton House next door, was the nation's first example of an "American Wing" and is devoted to early American furniture and decorative arts.

Another RISD gallery is the Woods-Gerry, situated in a nineteenth-century Federal mansion, which displays the work of talented faculty, students, and alumni of the school. Many of them are world leaders in the designing arts. The gallery is on Prospect Street, which boasts other splendid mansions, most of them still private residences.

While you are in Providence, you may want to learn more about its founder, Roger Williams, one of the great champions of modern democracy, who planned the town as a model of religious tolerance. The Roger Williams National Memorial is in a park on North Main, the site of his original settlement. A slide show describes his life and the development of the site.

The First Baptist Meeting House, on North Main, with a Christopher Wren–inspired, 185-foot steeple, was founded by Williams and his followers in 1638—although the current building was actually constructed in 1775. Step in to see the massive Waterford crystal chandelier inside.

A statue of Williams stands at his burial place, on Prospect Terrace, a photographer's favorite spot for its panoramic view of the city and the countryside beyond. If you have children along, you'll also want to visit the Roger Williams Park, three miles south of the city, for its zoo and children's nature center. The Victorian park offers 430 acres of woods, waterways, and winding drives; a Japanese garden; and a classic carousel. The zoo's highlights include an African plains exhibit, a tropical rain forest pavilion, and a glass-sided habitat where polar bears swim.

One of the best features of a weekend in Providence is that the city is truly, as the brochures promise, a "walkable city," and most of the sights can be covered easily on foot. The main historic and cultural sights are marked with banners, and the Convention and Visitors Bureau offers a free "Banner Trail" map to point them out.

Noteworthy stops in town include the Rhode Island State House, modeled after the U.S. Capitol; the John Brown House, which John Quincy Adams called "the most magnificent and elegant private mansion that I have ever seen on this continent"; the gloriously restored 1878 City Hall; the 1707 home and garden of Governor Stephen Hopkins, a signer of the Declaration of Independence; the Museum of Rhode Island History, at Aldrich House, the former residence of U.S. Senator Nelson W. Aldrich; and the Providence Athenaeum, an 1838 Doric structure that was one of America's first libraries, as well as the place where Edgar Allan Poe courted Sarah Helen Whitman, a resident of Benefit Street.

Interesting boutiques and galleries are found on South Main Street, a block down the hill from Benefit Street. Many are housed in restored Colonial buildings. Wickenden Street has a cache of antiques shops— and cafés and coffeehouses like Café Zog and the Coffee Exchange in the 200 block that are favorite hangouts for RISD students.

Near downtown, at 65 Weybosset Street, look for the Providence Arcade, an 1828 covered shopping street that looks like an enormous Greek temple; it is said to have been the country's first indoor shopping mall. The downtown, which had been deserted by many stores, has been nicely taken over by Johnson and Wales University, which includes a noted culinary school. Where a vacant department store once stood is now the university's Gaebe Commons, with a college green and park benches.

Another part of Providence that should not be overlooked is the Federal Hill area, this city's thriving "Little Italy." Past the arch spanning Atwells Avenue, the streets feature Old World street lamps and fountains, plus a wealth of good eating, both traditional and contemporary.

But Italian is just the start of the excellent dining that has become one of the city's recent claims to fame. The couple who put Providence on the culinary map are George Germon and Johanne Killeen, husband and wife, who both graduated from RISD. Their creative Italian dishes at Al Forno have gained national praise. The list of other notable dining places continues to grow.

The old jewelry-manufacturing district around Chestnut Street is blossoming with favorite hangouts for young Providence such as the hip CAV (Coffee, Antiques, Victuals), where artwork and antiques are on display and for sale.

After dinner, you might want to see the latest offering by the highly regarded Trinity Rep theater company, one of the nation's leading regional repertory troupes.

Long an industrial town in the shadow of its worldlier neighbor, Boston, Providence has rescued the treasures of its rich past and come into its own as a livable and charming city. For those who knew the city only in the past, it is a transformation worth discovering.

Area Code: 401

DRIVING DIRECTIONS From north or south, take I-95; from west, take Route 44 or Route 6; from east, take I-195 to the center of Providence. It is 49 miles from Boston, 185 miles from New York, and 75 miles from Hartford.

PUBLIC TRANSPORTATION Amtrak trains, most major airlines, and Greyhound and Bonanza buses serve Providence. Bonanza provides frequent service to Boston's Logan Airport. You can manage the center of the city nicely without a car.

ACCOMMODATIONS Ask about weekend packages and special rates for the Festival of Historic Houses weekend. **The Old Court,** 144 Benefit Street, Providence 02903, 751-2002, 1863 home turned B & B in the historic district, M, CP • **Westin Hotel,** 1 West Exchange Street, Providence 02903, 598-8000, indoor pool and spa, M–E • **Providence Biltmore Hotel,** Kennedy Plaza, Providence 02903, 421-0700, M–E • **Marriott Providence,** Charles and Orem Streets, Providence 02904,

272-2400, M–E • **Days Hotel on the Harbor,** 220 India Street, Providence 02903, 272-5577, I–M • **Holiday Inn Downtown,** 21 Atwells Avenue, Providence 02903, 831-3900, M.

DINING   Al Forno, 577 South Main Street, 273-9760, the city's best known dining place, wood grill, Italian fare, M–E • **Café Nuovo,** 1 Citizens Plaza, 421-2525, prime location on the river, outdoor terrace, sophisticated menu, M–E • **Agora,** Westin Hotel (see above), 598-8011, elegant setting and fare, M–EE • **Capital Grille,** One Cookson Place, 521-5600, power dining for politicos in the restored train station, steaks are the specialty, E • **Federal Reserve,** 60 Dorrance Street, 621-5700, striking, soaring renovation of a period bank building, extensive menu, many New England specialties, M–E • **New Rivers,** 7 Steeple Street, 751-0350, eclectic contemporary menus, delightful café setting, M–E • **Rue de L'Espoir,** 99 Hope Street, 751-8890, French/California blend, interesting decor, informal, M • **Hemenway's Seafood Grill,** 1 Old Stone Square, 351-8570, the name says it, M–E • **Pot au Feu,** formal dining room for French fare, 44 Custom House Street, 273-8953, M–E; downstairs bistro, I–M • **Pizzico,** 762 Hope Street, 421-4114, Italian bistro, M • **Adesso,** 161 Cushing Street, 521-0770, California-style grill, innovative pastas, M–E • **The Gatehouse,** 4 Richmond Square, 521-5229, cosmopolitan cuisine, water views, outdoor terrace, live jazz on weekends, M–E • **Grappa,** 525 South Water Street, 454-1611, waterfront with a patio, flavorful food, prize selection of Italian grappas, M • **The Blue Grotto,** 210 Atwells Avenue, 272-9030, old-fashioned traditional Italian in Little Italy, M–E • **L'Epicureo,** 238 Atwells Avenue, 454-8430, elegant Little Italy dining, evolved from longtime local market, M–E • **Mediterraneo,** 134 Atwells Avenue, 331-7760, sophisticated European-style upscale Italian, M–E • **Christopher's on the Hill,** 25 Atwells Avenue, 274-4232, change-of-pace blend of French, Italian, Asian, and Mediterranean cuisines, M • **XO Café,** 125 N. Main Street, 273-9090, a newcomer with top reviews, M • **Down City Diner,** 151 Weybosset Street, 331-9217, trendy spot for good, reasonable food, I–M • **CAV,** 14 Imperial Place, 751-9164, sandwiches, salads, pastas for lunch and dinner; coffeehouse with live music after 9:30 P.M., with special desserts, I • **Geoff's Superlative Sandwiches,** 163 Benefit Street, 751-2248, *the* place for overstuffed sandwiches, I • **l'Elizabeth,** 285 South Main Street, 621-9113, Victorian decor, popular for afternoon teas and desserts and coffees at night, I.

SIGHTSEEING   Providence Festival of Historic Houses, early June. For current ticket prices and schedule, contact Providence Preservation Society, 21 Meeting Street, Providence 02903, 831-7440 • **Rhode Island School of Design Museum of Art,** 224 Benefit Street, 454-6500. Hours: September 1 to June 15, Tuesday to Saturday, 10:30 A.M. to 5 P.M. except Thursday, noon to 8 P.M., Sunday, 2 P.M. to

5 P.M.; rest of year, Wednesday to Saturday, noon to 5 P.M. $$; Saturday admission by donation • **Woods-Gerry Gallery,** 62 Prospect Street, 331-3511. Hours: during school year, daily except Tuesday, 11 A.M. to 4 P.M., Sunday from 2 P.M.; June and July, Monday to Friday, 11 A.M. to 4 P.M. Free • **Providence Art Club,** 11 Thomas Street at Benefit Street, 331-1114. Hours: September to June, Monday to Friday, 10 A.M. to 4 P.M., Saturday, noon to 3 P.M., Sunday, 3 P.M. to 5 P.M.; rest of year, Monday to Friday, 10 A.M. to 3 P.M. Free • **Brown University,** tours from Admissions Office, Corliss Bracket House, Prospect and Angell Streets, 863-2378. Phone for current hours • **David Winton Bell Gallery,** 64 College Street, in List Art Center, 863-2932. Hours: late August to early June, Monday to Friday, 11 A.M. to 4 P.M.; weekends from 1 P.M. Free • **John Brown House,** 52 Power Street at Benefit Street, 331-8575. Hours: March 1 to December 31, guided tours Tuesday to Saturday, 10 A.M. to 4:30 P.M., Sunday noon to 4:30 P.M. Adults, $$ • **Roger Williams National Memorial,** 282 North Main Street, 521-7266. Hours: daily, 9 A.M. to 4:30 P.M. Free • **First Baptist Church,** 75 North Main at Waterman, 454-3418. Hours: September to June, guided tours Sunday at 12:15 P.M. following the 11 A.M. service; July and August, at 10:45 A.M. following the 9:30 A.M. service. Church is open Monday to Friday, 9 A.M. to 3:30 P.M. Free • **Rhode Island State House,** Smith Street, 277-2357. Hours: Monday to Friday, 8:30 A.M. to 4:30 P.M., tours available from 9:30 A.M. to 3:30 P.M. Free • **Providence Athenaeum,** 251 Benefit Street, 421-6970. Hours: Monday to Friday, 8:30 A.M. to 5:30 P.M., Wednesday to 8:30 P.M., Saturday, 9:30 A.M. to 5:30 P.M.; closed Saturday in summer, open Sunday 1 P.M. to 5 P.M. during winter months. Free • **Governor Stephen Hopkins House,** 15 Hopkins Street at Benefit Street, 884-8337. Hours: April to December, Wednesday and Saturday, 1 P.M. to 4 P.M. Free • **Museum of Rhode Island History at Aldrich House,** 110 Benefit Street, 331-8575. Hours: Tuesday to Saturday, 11 A.M. to 4 P.M., Sunday, 1 P.M. to 4 P.M. $ • **Roger Williams Park,** Elmwood Avenue, 785-9450. Hours: park open daily, 7 A.M. to 9 P.M. Free • **Roger Williams Park Zoo,** daily, 9 A.M. to 5 P.M. in summer, shorter hours off-season—best to check. Adults, $$. *Walking tours:* 1½-hour walks with experts from the Providence Preservation Society, 831-8586, leave from John Brown House, 52 Power Street, July through September, Monday to Saturday at 10 A.M., Sunday at noon. $$$$.

INFORMATION Greater Providence Convention and Visitors Bureau, 1 West Exchange Street, Providence, RI 02903, 274-1636 or (800) 233-1636. Hours: Monday to Friday, 8:30 A.M. to 5 P.M.

A Whale of a Time on Cape Ann

Some places watch for the first robin or the first signs of green on the trees. On Cape Ann, the arrival of spring means just one thing: The whales are back.

"The other cape," as some call it, is the lesser-known northern Massachusetts strip, eight miles out to sea, that inspired onetime summer resident T. S. Eliot to write about "those who are in ships/whose business has to do with fish."

This is fishing country, all right, especially Gloucester, where some 150 million pounds of fish come in each year, the biggest catch of any port on the East Coast.

But fish aren't the whole story, by any means. Gloucester also boasts an art colony and an excellent theater company. And it shares its cape with Rockport, an artists' town, where a boulder-strewn seven-mile coastline, a harbor full of sailboats, and a picturesque cove packed with shops and galleries bring out both lovers of beauty and thousands of strolling summer shoppers.

In spring, it's the beauty that takes precedence—and it's also spring when Cape Ann takes on the title of "Whale-Watching Capital of the World." Sign on for a cruise and sign up at one of the lovely inns in the area, and you're ready for a rare weekend. If you're a chamber music buff, come in June and you'll be able to attend the annual Rockport Chamber Music Festival as well. The fine Gloucester Stage Company, which offers plays at its headquarters in an old warehouse, is also well worth a visit.

Just like clockwork every year, humpback, minke, finback, and right whales return here to the offshore feeding grounds of Jeffreys Ledge and Stellwagen Bank. They put on quite a show, especially the humpbacks. These showoffs breach the surface, flinging the entire lengths of their 50-foot, 40-ton bodies into the air, and then crash down with mammoth bellyflops, sending shock waves in all directions. They slap their flippers and bang their massive tails, and they blow clouds of bubbles into the air.

All this takes place within clear sight of the whale-watching boats. There are several ships to choose from, all about equal by most accounts. You may have more trouble deciding among the many nice places to stay in the area.

A personal favorite is the Eden Pines Inn, a simple clapboard Colonial perched smack on the water on a secluded road away from town, off Route 127A in the direction of Gloucester. This is an airy, summery hideaway with spectacular views from the oversize rooms. From the terrace, perched just above the rocky shore, you can almost reach out and touch the waves.

Another excellent choice nearby is Sea Crest Manor, an antiques-filled home once owned by a governor of Massachusetts. Set away from the town off Route 127A, with a view of the sea from its second-floor sundeck, it's the sort of gracious, civilized place where tea is served at 4 P.M. each day. Recent renovations have provided many rooms with picture windows facing the sea. Not far away, directly on the water, is the Captain's House, a small informal guest house with an unbeatable view.

On Route 127 North in the area known as Pigeon Cove are two appealing larger inns. The Yankee Clipper is a complex of three handsome Colonial houses, two of them on the curving lawn that runs right down to the water. The rooms vary, with the more traditional furnishings in the Bullfinch House, across the road. The owners of the Yankee Clipper also run the Ralph Waldo Emerson Inn, and both have pools for guests' use in warmer weather.

Old Farm Inn is an appealing 1799 farmhouse on five acres on Pigeon Cove, with warm country ambience, a caring host and hostess, and ready access to the beauty of Halibut Point State Park, just outside the door.

Those who prefer to be within walking distance of the shops will find some charming in-town bed-and-breakfast choices.

Rockport was never a major early trading port like some of its coastal neighbors; its broad harbor was unprotected from the elements until a breakwater was built at the turn of this century. The town was named for the granite beds in the surrounding hills, and cutting rock became its chief industry. The quarries attracted a large colony of Scandinavians, who served as stonecutters.

As the Scandinavians were arriving, so were the artists, attracted by the combination of Cape Ann's rugged coastline and its woodland beauty. The terrain and its luminous light have been magnets for painters and sculptors since the early eighteenth century, when Fitz Hugh Lane first began capturing the scene from a granite studio atop Duncan's Point in Gloucester. The Cape Ann Historical Museum has a comprehensive collection of his work. Winslow Homer also painted here.

As often happens when artists congregate in scenic spots, summer visitors followed. Gloucester maintained its fishing fleet, but with the completion of a major highway into town in the 1950s, tourism became Rockport's major industry. Even though the town is being developed rapidly and can be uncomfortably packed on a summer day, it retains much of its salty charm.

Most visitors head directly for Bearskin Neck, a spit of land extending out to sea and lined with fishing shacks now transformed into shops of every imaginable kind. You'll need no guide—just join the throngs and make the rounds of the stores and their scrimshaw, hand-blown glassware, pewter, leather, T-shirts, crafts, and clothing.

Take note of one of the shanties on an extension of Bearskin Neck; it's known as "Motif Number One" because it has been painted by so many area artists. The Rockport Art Association, housed in a restored tavern on Main Street, is the year-round center of the current art scene, which continues to flourish even though the subject matter has diminished since the shacks and ships' riggings gave way to shops and ice-cream stands. There are a number of interesting art galleries here, as well.

And there is more art to be seen in Gloucester, where the North Shore Art Association has its summer headquarters and a spacious gallery. You will pass them on the way to the Rocky Neck Art Colony, in East Gloucester, said to be the oldest art colony in the country; here you can watch artists at work as well as visit galleries and dine in picturesque restaurants. In town, pick up a self-guided walking tour of the harbor at the Cape Ann Chamber of Commerce. The tour will take you past St. Peter's Park, with views of fishing and lobster boats; the U.S. Coast Guard station; the *Gloucester Adventure,* a 121-foot fishing schooner open for touring; and the home of Fitz Hugh Lane, the well-known American painter whose works you can see at another stop on the tour, the Cape Ann Historical Association, which also offers art by the likes of Winslow Homer and many interesting artifacts of Gloucester and its cape. The City Hall has murals on the main floor and wonderful harbor views from the third; outside is the Fisherman's Memorial statue, a symbol of the industry that built the city. Come at the end of June for a real treat, the colorful blessing of the fleet at St. Peter's Park.

From Gloucester, it's a lovely ride to the Beauport Museum, way out on the water on Eastern Point Boulevard. This 26-room mansion, the home of Henry Davis Sleeper, a prominent antiques collector and interior designer of the 1920s, is a feast of decorative arts, with each room dedicated to a particular decor, from Oriental to Paul Revere.

Hammond Castle Museum is an unusual find in these simple seafaring environs. Mr. Hammond, it seems, was so taken with what he saw in Europe that he decided to build his own castle at home, complete with drawbridge, and filled it with Roman, medieval, and Renaissance pieces. The Great Hall here is worthy of a cathedral, with magnificent stained-glass windows at either end, a huge fifteenth-century fireplace, and an 8,600-pipe organ rising eight stories high.

You could easily fill two days viewing the whales, the shops, and the museums, but do leave some time to appreciate the rich natural beauty of the area. Take a walk south of town to the end of Atlantic Avenue and the Headlands, dramatic outcroppings of rock where you can look out to sea and back at the harbor and homes. Then drive to Pigeon Hill, at the end of Landmark Lane; this is a small park atop one of the highest elevations around, and affords you a soaring view.

Turn off Route 127 just before you get to the Old Farm Inn for Halibut Point, Cape Ann's farthest reach out to sea. Halibut Point is a 69-acre state park at the northern end of the peninsula with its own boulder-rimmed shoreline view, reached via a path through the woods.

The Eastern Point Sanctuary, in East Gloucester, is also prime hiker's territory, with many guided walks from the Coast Guard lighthouse. And then there are the beaches—two of them in town, more off Route 127A between Rockport and Gloucester. In between it all, you can feast on the freshest seafood to be found, everything from local cod and haddock to good old New England lobster. Make a note that Rockport is dry, so you'll have to bring your own wine for dinner.

With that exception, Cape Ann serves everything you need for a seaworthy weekend—with whales as an unbeatable main course.

Area Code: 978

DRIVING DIRECTIONS   Cape Ann is on Route 127, off Route 128, on the north shore of Massachusetts, 38 miles north of Boston, 246 miles from New York, and 136 miles from Hartford.

PUBLIC TRANSPORTATION   There is regular train service to Rockport and Gloucester from Boston's North Station, (617) 222-3200. It's possible to manage in the center of Rockport without a car.

ACCOMMODATIONS   *Bed-and-breakfast inns:* **Eden Pines Inn,** Eden Road, Rockport 01966, 546-2505, M–E, CP • **Seacrest Manor,** 131 Marmion Way, Rockport 01966, 546-2211, M–E, CP • **Old Farm Inn,** 291 Granite Street, Pigeon Cove, Rockport 01966, 546-3237 or (800) 233-6828, M, CP • **The Captain's House,** 109 Marmion Way, Rockport 01966, 546-3825, M, CP • **The Inn on Cove Hill,** 37 Mt. Pleasant Street, Rockport 01966, 546-2701 or (888) 546-2701, a 1791 Federal-style home just one block from the harbor, good value, I–M, CP • **Addison Choate Inn,** 49 Broadway, Rockport 01966, 546-7543, charming in-town home, Colonial furnishings, small pool, M, CP • **Sally Webster Inn,** 34 Mt. Pleasant Street, Rockport 01966, 546-9251, small, inviting decor, in-town location, M, CP • **Harborview Inn,** 71 Western Avenue, Gloucester 01930, 283-2277 or (800) 299-6696, small, well-decorated inn facing the water, walking distance to town shops and dining, M, CP; suites, E, CP. *Larger inns:* **Yankee Clipper Inn,** 96 Granite Street (Route 127), Pigeon Cove, Rockport 01966, 546-3407, E–EE, CP; EE, MAP • **Ralph Waldo Emerson Inn,** Phillips Avenue (Route 127), Pigeon Cove, Rockport 01966, 546-6321, M–E. *Motels with ocean views, pools:* **Ocean View Inn,** 171 Atlantic Road, Gloucester 01930, 283-6200, M–E • **Bass Rocks Ocean Inn,** Atlantic Avenue, Gloucester 01930, 283-7600, M–E, CP • **Cape Ann Motor Inn,** 33 Rockport Road, Gloucester 01930, 281-2900, I–M, CP.

DINING *Rockport:* **My Place by the Sea,** Bearskin Neck, Rockport, 546-9667, unbeatable location surrounded by water, outdoor deck plus attractive interior, eclectic menu, highly recommended locally, M • **The Veranda,** Yankee Clipper Inn (see above), formal ambience, sophisticated fare, fine views, M–E • **The Sea Garden,** 62 Marmion Way, Rockport, 546-3471, excellent reviews for this old-fashioned dining room, varied continental menu, seafood specialties, M • **The Greenery,** 15 Dock Square, Rockport, 546-9593, casual spot with harbor views, lots of green plants inside, seafood, regular menu plus lighter fare, I–M • **Peg Leg,** Beach Street, Rockport, 546-3038, informal, old favorite in town, I–M • **Brackett's Ocean View,** 27 Main Street, Rockport, 546-2797, the name says it, good family choice, I–M • **The Lobster Pool at Folly Cove,** 332 Granite Street (Route 127), Rockport, 546-7808, deck overlooking the bay, the place for chowder, lobster rolls, lobster in the rough, I–M. *Gloucester:* **White Rainbow,** 65 Main Street, Gloucester, 281-0017, 1830 landmark building, long known for excellent continental cuisine, M–E • **Thyme's on the Square,** 197 East Main Street, Gloucester, 282-4426, small café near the North Shore Art Association and Rocky Neck, excellent reviews, M • **McT's Lobster House,** 25 Rogers Street, Gloucester, 282-0950, everyone's favorite for basic fresh seafood and harbor views from the deck, I–M • **The Rudder,** 73 Rocky Neck Avenue, East Gloucester, 283-7967, seafood, picturesque waterfront views, I–M • **The Studio,** Rocky Neck Avenue, East Gloucester, 283-4123, another prime setting for seafood, big deck overlooking the harbor, M • For clams, drive to Essex, on Ipswich Bay, where some say the fried clam was invented and where **Woodman's,** Main Street, on the Causeway, 768-6451, is a local institution that fans say is worth the mob scene. Also excellent is **Tom Shea's,** 122 Main Street, 768-6931, right across the road.

SIGHTSEEING Whale watching off Cape Ann, usually half-day cruises, averages $23. Contact any of the following for current schedules and prices (all are zip code 01930): **Cape Ann Whale Watch,** Main Street, Rose's Wharf, Gloucester, 283-5110 or (800) 877-5110; **Capt. Bill & Sons Whale Watch Cruises,** 9 Traverse Street, Gloucester, 283-6995 or (800) 339-4253; **The Yankee Fleet,** 75 West Essex Avenue, Gloucester, 283-0313 or (800) 942-5464; **Seven Seas Whale Watch,** Seven Seas Wharf, Gloucester, 283-1776 or (800) 238-1776 • **Rockport Chamber Music Festival,** PO Box 312, Rockport 01966, 546-7391. Concerts by Manhattan String Quartet and others, Thursday through Sunday, mid-June through early July, at Hibbard Gallery of Rockport Art Association. Write or phone for current season dates and prices • **Cape Ann Historical Association Museum,** 27 Pleasant Street, Gloucester, 283-0455. Hours: year-round except February, Tuesday through Saturday, 10 A.M. to 5 P.M. $$ • **Rockport Art Association,** 12 Main Street, 546-6604. Hours: Monday to Saturday, 9:30 A.M.

to 5 P.M.; Sunday, 1 P.M. to 5 P.M. Free • **Gloucester Stage Company,** 267 East Main Street, Gloucester, 281-4099. Hours: mid-May through October and December; phone for current schedule and ticket prices • **North Shore Arts Association,** 197 East Main Street, Gloucester, 283-1857. Hours: early June to September, Monday to Saturday, 10 A.M. to 5:30 P.M., Sunday, 1 P.M. to 5:30 P.M. Free • **Beauport,** 75 Eastern Point Boulevard, Gloucester, 283-0800. Hours: mid-May to mid-September, Monday to Friday, 10 A.M. to 4 P.M.; mid-September to mid-October, also Saturday and Sunday, 1 P.M. to 4 P.M. $$$ • **Hammond Castle Museum,** 80 Hesperus Avenue, Gloucester, 283-7673. Hours: June through August, daily, 10 A.M. to 6 P.M.; May, September, October, Wednesday to Sunday, 10 A.M. to 4 P.M.; rest of year, Saturday and Sunday, 10 A.M. to 4 P.M. $$$ • **Halibut Point State Park,** Gott Avenue (off Route 127), 546-2997. Hours: guided tours on Saturday morning, 9:30 A.M., mid-May to late October.

INFORMATION Cape Ann Chamber of Commerce, 33 Commercial Street, Gloucester, MA 01930, 283-1601 or (800) 321-0133; Rockport Chamber of Commerce, Route 127, Box 67, Rockport, MA 01966, 546-6575.

The Three Bs: A Maine Education

The time is 3:00 A.M. on a chilly spring night, a good time to be snuggled in bed under a New England patchwork quilt. So why are all those cars still out in a parking lot in Freeport, Maine?

They belong to sportsmen, savvy shoppers, insomniacs, tourists, and the just plain curious from every part of the country, part of some 3½ million people who stop day and night, year-round, at one of America's shopping phenomenons, the L. L. Bean retail store, a one-of-a-kind emporium that is open for business 24 hours a day, seven days a week.

Mr. Bean's enterprise has developed into a major tourist attraction and a Maine institution, one that has transformed Freeport into a shopping mecca. Two nearby neighbors—Bowdoin College, in Brunswick, and the Maine Maritime Museum, in Bath—are also long-standing institutions, each reflecting another facet of the state. Put the three Bs together and you'll have a weekend that is a pleasure-filled Maine education.

Leon Leonwood Bean never dreamed what lay ahead in 1912 when his intense dislike for cold, wet feet led him to create a new kind of hunting shoe with leather uppers on rubber overshoe bottoms. Armed with a mailing list of Maine hunting license holders, he advertised that with his new product their feet would be "properly dressed for hunting bear or moose." He guaranteed "perfect satisfaction in every way," a promise that proved expensive when 90 of the first 100 pairs sold were returned with their bottoms separated from the boots.

But Bean was true to his word. He gave refunds, borrowed more money, perfected his product, and started mailing out more catalogs; this time, things went well. Under Bean's grandson, Leon Gorman, the company now does over a billion dollars in annual sales.

Today their mammoth flagship store, decorated with granite paths, pine beams, and a 7,000-gallon indoor pond stocked with trout, has been described as "a cross between Bloomingdale's and a forest glen." You'll find everything for the outdoors, from canoes to clothing, and recently the store has added an Outdoor Discovery program with courses to teach you how to make the most of all that equipment.

The new L. L. Kids store, adjacent to the main store, opened in 1997 and was built to resemble a traditional Maine sporting camp, and with interactive features like an electronic climbing wall and a simulated mountain bike "test ride," complete with jolting handlebars and sound effects. There's also a two-story waterfall and a trout pond with windows so visitors can observe nature at gill level.

Across the road is a factory store stocked with irregulars and markdowns at bargain prices. *Bargains,* in fact, has become the watchword in Freeport, as some 150 discount stores have opened to take advantage of the crowds drawn to Bean—everyone from Laura Ashley to the Yankee Candle Company. Mixed among the outlets along Main Street are some unique stops like Abacus, with fine American crafts; Maine's Edgecombe Potters; and Buttons & Things, offering thousands of kinds of buttons.

All of this makes for mammoth traffic jams along Main Street (Route 1), almost obscuring the fact that Freeport is a fine old New England town with a history dating back to 1683. It was here, at the Jameson Tavern, that the treaty was signed separating Maine from Massachusetts in 1820, and there are several notable homes to be seen, including the 1830 Harrington House, now home of the Historical Society and a house museum and shop. Ask here about visits to the society's Pettengill Farm, a nineteenth-century saltwater farm with exhibits of early coastal farm life

The Gore House is perhaps the most historic quarters of any of the McDonald's restaurants anywhere.

If you get tired of the crowds, you can leave them behind for Wolfe's Neck Woods State Park, a beautiful stretch of land along the shore, or head for the Mast Landing Sanctuary, another lovely spot for a walk, maintained by the Maine Audubon Society. If the weather is conducive, there is a public beach at the town's Winslow Memorial Park, where you will also find a launching site on the Harraseeket River, a favorite for canoeing.

Starting in mid-May, head for the picturesque harbor at South Freeport and enjoy delicious lobster and the best lobster roll I've tasted in Maine at the Harraseeket Lunch and Lobster Company. Several cruises are available from the harbor, including seal and osprey watches.

Freeport's handsome Harraseeket Inn puts you within walking distance of L. L. Bean, and more bed-and-breakfast inns are opening all the time, making Freeport increasingly a destination in its own right. However, you can also choose to make your headquarters in the more peaceful atmospheres of nearby Brunswick or Bath.

Brunswick is a town filled with fine homes and history. Much of it centers around Bowdoin College, Maine's proudest educational institution, whose heritage goes back to 1794 and whose alumni list includes the likes of Henry Wadsworth Longfellow, Nathaniel Hawthorne, Admirals Peary and MacMillan, and President Franklin Pierce. Free campus tours are offered, but you can easily stroll the handsome 40-building campus and see the main sights on your own. Bowdoin's museums merit some time.

The Walker Art Building collections span the centuries and the globe, but most notable are the American paintings—such as Gilbert Stuart's portrait of Thomas Jefferson, and other portraits by Copley and Eakins. There are many Gilbert Stuarts, including a portrait of James Bowdoin III, son of the Massachusetts governor for whom the school was named. Bowdoin commissioned a number of works and then bequeathed his collection to the college in 1811, giving it one of the earliest college art collections in America.

The second campus museum, the Peary-MacMillan Arctic Museum, honors the exploits of two adventurous explorer alumni, who were the first to reach the North Pole. If you've ever wondered what it took to make this historic trip, here is the place to find out. The museum features nearly life-size, painted cutout figures of Peary and MacMillan in Eskimo dress, and interesting artifacts from the expedition, including the odometer, telescope, and navigational instruments they used. Stuffed polar bears and walruses give some notion of the animals they found on their journey, and another section of exhibits details the life of the inhabitants of the Arctic in the first half of this century, with examples of their clothes, tools, carvings, and paintings.

Both the college and the area between Federal and Maine Streets are historic districts, and a walking tour will reward you with a look at some of the finest of the area's remaining homes. Among the beauties are 63 Federal Street, once the home of Harriet Beecher Stowe, and 25 Federal Street, the residence of Longfellow and his wife when he taught at Bowdoin in 1829. Lincoln Street is lined with Greek Revival homes, unchanged since they were built in the 1840s. One exception is the house at No. 3, a 1772 structure that was moved here and altered. It is considered the oldest home in the village.

Park Row homes date from 1798 to the mid-1800s, with the Italianate brick double house at 159-161 Park Row deserving special note. Guided tours from the Pejepscot Historical Society Museum, No. 159, take you through the building next door, the Skolfield-Whittier House, furnished just as beautifully as it was in 1863. Also of interest is 6-8 College Street, a onetime station on the underground railroad that shielded slaves en route to Canada. Number 26 College Street was the boyhood home of Pulitzer Prize–winning poet Robert Peter Tristram Coffin.

Finally, Civil War buffs should note the 226 Maine Street home of General Joshua L. Chamberlain, who was also a governor of Maine and a president of Bowdoin College. It is now a museum with many original furnishings and memorabilia tracing Chamberlain's life, including Civil War relics.

If you return in summer, the Bowdoin campus is the setting for the Maine State Music Theater, presenting Broadway musicals. And a Summer Music Festival of chamber concerts takes place at the high school. Many more events—including the annual Maine Festival, featuring state performing artists and craftsmen; the Bluegrass Festival; and the Maine Highland Games—are held at Brunswick's Thomas Point Beach. Thousands come to town for the annual Great State of Maine Air Show, usually held in July at the Brunswick Naval Air Station.

The Harpswells, three fingerlike peninsulas are Brunswick's arms into Casco Bay. One of these peninsulas includes the fishermen's haven of Bailey Island, known for its seafood restaurants, at the very end of Route 24.

In spring, the pleasant contrast of a few peaceful hours in Brunswick and the bustling shops in Freeport makes for a full and varied day—and leaves time for further exploration in Bath on Sunday.

Bath and boats have been synonymous ever since 1607, when the first vessel, the 30-ton *Virginia,* was launched here. More than 4,000 other ships have followed. The sign over the gates of the Bath Iron Works (BIW), proclaiming "Through these gates pass the world's best shipbuilders," is no idle boast for a company that celebrated its 110th birthday in 1994 and has many current employees who come from a long line of shipbuilding ancestors. Bath-built boats, from sleek racing yachts to military vessels, have long been valued all over the world for their fine craftsmanship. During World War II, 82 U.S. destroyers were built at BIW, more boats than were built by the entire empire of Japan. The Bath Iron Works still makes commercial boats and boats for the U.S. Navy.

The Maine Maritime Museum, on the shore of the Kennebec River just below BIW, celebrates this long seafaring heritage in a living museum complex that also includes an internship program that helps keep the art of building wooden boats alive. In warm weather, you can see several parts of the Maritime Museum by boat along the Kennebec River.

Park at the Visitors' Center on Washington Street at the Percy and Small Shipyard, beyond Bath Iron Works, and begin by touring the only surviving shipyard in America where large wooden sailing vessels were constructed. One, the six-masted *Wyoming,* was the largest wooden sailboat ever built in the United States.

Signs in the buildings and shops explain the steps in creating a boat, from laying out patterns and cutting frames to sailmaking and caulking. The Marine History Building uses hands-on, multimedia galleries and exhibits to show the close relationship between the people of Maine and the sea, and the L. L. Bean–sponsored lobstering exhibit building lets you walk down a mock pier and see staged "workers" preparing lobster meat in a canning room. You can watch a video that takes you through the day of a Maine lobsterman while you are perched on the gunwale of a lobster boat, and you can handle a live lobster during weekly presentations of lobster lore and life. The grounds are open for picnicking, and kids can play in a giant ship sandbox—complete with a crow's nest.

A drive inland along Washington Street puts you in the heart of Bath's historic district, past Federal, Greek, Gothic Revival, and Italianate mansions once owned by wealthy shipbuilders and sea captains. Several nice inns are in the district. Besides the mansions, have a look at the restored nineteenth-century Front Street, with its brick sidewalks and old-fashioned lampposts, starting with the attractive City Park. The statue in the pond is appropriately known as *Spirit of the Sea.* At the top of Front Street is City Hall and the Old Customs House, and Waterfront Park will give you a view of the river. If the weather is mild, Popham Beach and Reid State Park, two of Maine's best white-sand beaches, are nearby. You can also see the thousands of migratory birds and waterfowl that congregate at Merrymeeting Bay, visit the Swan Island State Park Wildlife Area, or hike through Morse Mountain's coastal wilderness. With museum, town, and surroundings, you can easily fill a full day in Bath, and the Chocolate Church for the Arts offers all kinds of evening entertainment throughout the year.

End the day with a Maine seafood dinner and you've completed your three Bs tour, perhaps with a bonus B to take home—all those bargains you picked up in Freeport.

And in case you want one last shot, remember that L. L. Bean will be open no matter how late you linger over dessert.

Area Code: 207

DRIVING DIRECTIONS   Freeport is on I-95, 20 miles north of Portland. It is 125 miles from Boston, 335 miles from New York, and 225 miles from Hartford. Follow U.S. Route 1 north for Brunswick and Bath.

PUBLIC TRANSPORTATION   Greyhound bus service to Brunswick; nearest air service is Portland Jetport.

ACCOMMODATIONS   **Harraseeket Inn,** ask about special packages, 162 Main Street, Freeport 04032, 865-9377, luxury inn in two buildings circa 1798 and 1850, antiques, canopy beds, fireplaces, M–EE, CP • **Isaac Randall House,** Independence Drive, Freeport 04032, 865-9295 or (800) 865-9295, 1823 farmhouse in wooded setting, informal eclectic country decor with colorful Southwestern accents, within walking distance to shops, M, CP • **Brewster House,** 180 Main Street, Freeport 04032, 865-4121 or (800) 865-0822, simple country decor in a Queen Anne Victorian, two blocks from L. L. Bean, I–M, CP • **181 Main Street,** at that address, Freeport 04032, 865-1226 or (800) 235-9750, handsome 1840 home, Colonial decor, convenient, M, CP • **Porter's Landing,** 70 South Street, Freeport 04032, 865-4488, renovated 1870 carriage house, quiet setting away from traffic, M, CP • **Captain Daniel Stone Inn,** 10 Water Street, Brunswick 04011, 725-9898, attractive and comfortable small hotel, M–E, CP • **Brunswick Bed and Breakfast,** 165 Park Row, Brunswick 04011, 729-4914, pleasant home near the college, fine collection of quilts, I–M, CP • **Harpswell Inn,** 141 Lookout Point Road, Harpswell (peninsula adjoining Brunswick) 04079, 833-5509, expansive home and newly restored carriage house, M–E, CP • **The Inn at Bath,** 969 Washington Street, Bath 04530, 443-4294, 1830 home decorated with great taste, M, CP • **1024 Washington,** at that address, Bath 04530, 443-5202, elegant small Victorian, some working fireplaces, I–M, CP • **Packard House,** 45 Pearl Street, Bath 04530, 443-6069, 1790 Georgian home, I–M, CP • **Fairhaven Inn,** North Bath Road, Bath 04530, 443-4391, country setting, good value, I–M, CP • **Popham Beach Bed and Breakfast,** HC31, Box 430, Popham Beach, Phippsburg (peninsula adjoining Bath), 04562, 389-2409, picturesque restored 1883 Coast Guard station directly on the beach, open May through October, M–E, CP.

DINING   **Jameson Tavern,** 115 Main Street, Freeport, 865-4196, historic 1779 tavern, M • **Harraseeket Lunch and Lobster Company,** South Freeport Harbor, 865-4823, lobster pound on the docks, usually open from mid-May, super, I–M • **Harraseeket Inn** (see above), formal dining room, M–E; or tavern menu, I–M • **Fiddlehead Farm,** 15 Independence Drive, Freeport, 865-0466, cozy farmhouse, excellent food but open for breakfast and lunch only, I • **The Great Impasta,** 42 Maine Street, Brunswick, 729-5858, tasty northern Italian, good value, I–M • **Richard's,** 115 Maine Street, Brunswick, 729-9673, German-American, M • **Cook's Lobster House,** 833-6641, and the **Original Log Cabin,** 833-5546, both on Route 24 on Bailey Island, are informal places to savor Maine lobster dinners, both I–E, depending on lobster prices • **Jack Baker's Oceanview Restaurant,** Route 24, Bailey

Island, 833-5366, a bit more ambience with your seafood, I–E •
Kristina's, 160 Center Street, Bath, 442-8577, eclectic menu, attractive
dining room, I–M • **The Osprey,** Robinhood Center, Riggs Cove (off
Route 127), Georgetown, 371-2530, nautical decor, fine American
menu, open from mid-May, M–E • **New Meadows Inn,** Bath Road,
West Bath, 443-3921, shore dinners, lobster, I–E.

SIGHTSEEING   **L. L. Bean Outdoor Discovery Courses,** Main
Street, Freeport, (800) 341-4341, courses in paddling, fly-fishing,
cycling, and other outdoor skills • **Wolfe's Neck Woods State Park,**
Wolfe's Neck Road, Freeport, 865-4465. Hours: open daylight hours
for nature trails, hiking, picnicking; programs in summer. Free. • **Mast
Landing Sanctuary,** Upper Mast Landing Road, Freeport, 781-2330.
Hours: open daylight hours, $2\frac{1}{2}$ miles of trails. Free • **Winslow Memorial Park,** Staples Point Road, South Freeport, 865-4198. Hours:
Memorial Day through September, beach, picnicking. Free • **Atlantic
Seal Cruises,** Town Wharf, South Freeport, 865-6112, variety of
cruises emphasizing seals and shorebirds, lobstering demonstrations;
phone for current offerings • **Freeport Sailing Adventures,** PO Box
303, Freeport, 865-6399, sails on Casco Bay aboard a 44-foot yacht;
phone for information • **Maine Maritime Museum,** 243 Washington
Street, Bath, 443-1316. Hours: daily, 9:30 A.M. to 5 P.M. $$$, family
rates • **Bowdoin College,** Brunswick, 725-3100. Guided tours from the
Admissions Office, Chamberlain Hall, off South Street; phone for cur-
rent schedule. Free • **Bowdoin College Museum of Art,** Walker Art
Building, 725-3275. Hours: September to June, Tuesday to Saturday,
10 A.M. to 5 P.M., Sunday, 1 P.M. to 5 P.M. Free • **Peary-MacMillan Arc-
tic Museum,** Hubbard Hall, 725-3416, same hours as Museum of Art.
Free • **Pejepscot Historical Society Museum,** 159 Park Row, 729-
6606. Hours: Memorial Day to Labor Day, Monday to Friday, 9 A.M. to
4:30 P.M., Saturday, 1 P.M. to 4 P.M.; rest of year, Monday to Friday only.
Free. The society also maintains the **Skolfield-Whittier House,** 161
Park Row. Hours: Memorial Day to Labor Day, 10 A.M. to 3 P.M., Satur-
day, 1 P.M. to 4 P.M. Guided tours, $$; and the **Joshua L. Chamberlain
Museum,** 226 Maine Street. Hours: Memorial Day through Labor Day,
Tuesday to Saturday, 1 P.M. to 4 P.M. $$.

INFORMATION   Freeport Merchants Association, Box 451, Free-
port, ME 04032, 865-1212; Chamber of Commerce of the Bath-
Brunswick Area, 59 Pleasant Street, Brunswick, 725-8797, or 45 Front
Street, Bath, 443-9751.

Antiquing in Old Connecticut

Nobody knows quite how it happens. First one antiques shop springs up, then another, and before you know it a whole town is wall-to-wall antiques.

There are a few such towns in New England—Sheffield, Massachusetts, and Searsport, Maine, among them—but none with choicer shops or scenery to offer than the historic town of Woodbury, Connecticut. Woodbury has become the "antiques capital" of the state, and in combination with its beautiful Colonial neighbor, Washington, it is a prime weekender's destination.

You'll need no guidebook to find the shops—Woodbury's long Main Street (along Route 6) is filled with them. They range from American Federal period furnishings at David Dunton to rustic Canadian pieces at Monique Shay to country French at Country Loft. British Country Antiques offers lots of pine and oak, painted armoires, antique bamboo, and other English specialties; Gerald Murphy has a nice mix of seventeenth- to nineteenth-century American and English country and formal; and Grass Roots offers a variety of dealers and moods. Linda Nelson Stocks offers four rooms of American furniture plus her original folk paintings and lithographs, and Hamrah's has the state's largest selection of antique Persian and European rugs. The names may change as shops change hands, but the variety and quality of the stores are constant.

The "most beautiful shop in Woodbury" award goes to Mill House, located a few miles outside town on Route 6. The main shop, a seventeenth-century gristmill, and several outbuildings along the Nonnewaug River hold a vast variety of eighteenth-century English and French furniture and accessories.

Between the Main Street shops you'll spy more Woodbury trademarks: the white spires of no fewer than four fine New England churches; and the 1754 Curtis House, the oldest hostelry in the state. Woodbury is also filled with early Colonial homes, the most notable being the Glebe House, which dates from the late 1600s and is credited as the birthplace of the American Episcopal Church. The lovely garden is the only one in America created by Gertrude Jekyll, the great English garden writer and designer, considered one of the most important women ever to work in the field of horticulture. Her 1927 plan, not used at that time, was found and carried out in 1987, and the blooms have grown lovelier each year.

When you've exhausted the shops or your spending money, follow Route 47 about eight miles north to Washington to discover one of the prettiest New England villages in this or any state. The home of two prestigious prep schools, Washington is a haven of old homes and old money. The big village green, dominated by the tall Congregational church and surrounded by glistening white Colonial homes set off with dark shutters, is all but perfect. Even the drugstore here is tucked into a Colonial home.

Though this is a very private town, there is enough to see and do to keep you happily occupied. The Gunn Museum, on the green, is filled with memorabilia from Washington homes and includes fine collections of clothing, dolls, textiles, and tools displayed in life-size vignettes.

The most unusual of Washington's sights takes you back even farther than Colonial times. The Institute for American Indian Studies promises and delivers "10,000 years in Quinnetukut" (Connecticut). The recently enlarged museum, one of the few devoted to early Indian life in this part of the country, aims to become a major center where the histories and cultures of New England's Native American populations can be shared. It is expanding and improving by the year. "As We Tell Our Stories," a fine exhibit, features tapes of actual Algonkian people interpreting their own history, including the memories of tribal elders. Other displays tell about some of the important elements in the lives of early natives—deer that furnished clothing, corn for nourishment, clay to make pots, baskets and wampum that were used for trade. One gallery is devoted to changing exhibits, including contemporary Indian art.

Outdoors is a reconstructed Algonkian village, a typical Indian encampment of the 1600s, with both reed- and bark-covered wigwams and a longhouse where a chief might have lived.

Films and other programs are scheduled for Saturday and Sunday afternoons, and there is an excellent gift shop.

Other local shops are clustered in Washington Depot, just a couple of miles away on Route 47. The Tulip Tree is filled to the brim with antique and fine reproduction furniture, lamps, and accessories, and Stocks in Trade specializes in country English and American furnishings, both new and antique. The Hickory Stick Bookstore also makes for fine browsing. The Pantry, also in Washington Depot, is a highly recommended stop for lunch. They also serve afternoon tea and make up elegant picnic lunches.

You have a choice of interesting places to stay in this area. If Colonial is your style, Woodbury offers the Merryvale Bed and Breakfast, an antique-filled 1789 home still boasting its original fireplaces and wide oak floorboards, and the Curtis House, a best bet for budget-watchers. It's a modest place, where you can sleep in a four-poster bed and dine in early American surroundings.

A few miles to the south, in Southbury, the Harrison Inn has modern and attractive resort facilities, including indoor and outdoor swimming, tennis, and golf.

If you are up for a splurge, consider the Mayflower Inn, in Washington, one of the poshest (and priciest) lodgings in Connecticut. Opened in 1992 after a restoration reputed to have cost $15 million, this is the very model of a country hotel, done with exquisite taste. The traditional gray shingle architecture of the original inn and several added buildings is known as "American Shingle Style," and it reflects New England, but the furnishings inside would be quite at home in the English countryside. The main sitting room is like a page from *House Beautiful,* with its velveteen upholstery and cozy clutter.

No two of the 25 guest rooms are alike. They are decorated in fine prints with coordinated stripes and solids and with lovely antiques. There are canopy beds, sleigh beds, and country iron headboards; some rooms have fireplaces, others have bay windows. Each room has a small library and exquisite accessories such as alarm clocks of English leather and Spode plates on the nightstands.

If you can't stay here, come for dinner. The food is excellent and the inn is worth seeing.

More tempting choices are found above Washington in New Preston, at Lake Waramaug. Boulders is the best of several excellent inns around the lake. The Birches Inn, recently refurbished, offers handsome rooms in the inn plus a boathouse with rooms directly on the lake. New Preston itself is developing into a quaint and busy shopping enclave offering antiques, art, and a variety of other wares.

You might spend Sunday just checking out the sights of the shops you missed or getting back to nature in the 95 acres of Lake Waramaug State Park or at the Flanders Nature Center, a 1,000-acre sanctuary with many lovely nature trails, in Woodbury. Or you can continue either antiquing or gazing at prize Connecticut architecture in two lovely towns nearby: Kent and Litchfield.

To get to Kent via a magnificent backcountry drive, route yourself from Washington south to New Milford on Route 109—uphill and downhill past white farms, red barns, stone walls, and split-rail fences. Signs reading FARM FRESH EGGS FOR SALE may tempt you to detour. At The Egg and I, country sausages, hams, and pork are the house specialties, and visitors are invited to tour the farm.

At Route 7, turn north and pass through the little town of Gaylordsville, where you may choose to stop again for the antiques stores. The Bittersweet Shop, a cooperative of 14 dealers, has everything from furniture to paintings to quilts.

In Kent there are many antiques shops and unique boutiques, as well as a number of art galleries, on or near Route 7. On Main Street, the Heron American Craft Gallery is always worth a stop, as are the Kent Art Association Gallery and the handsome Bacheller-Cardonsky Art Gallery, over the House of Books. The restored railroad station, known as Kent Station Square, is home to the Kent Antiques Center, with several dealers; and behind in an old railroad car is the Paris–New York– Kent art gallery, with top-quality art.

You'll see Kent Falls State Park right on Route 7 as you come into town, and if you want to stretch your legs, the easy trail up beside the falls will reward you with a series of scenic views, complete with roaring sound effects. Another very special stop in Kent is the Sloane-Stanley Museum, which contains the late artist Eric Sloane's collection of hand-crafted early American wooden tools, which are truly works of art.

If you prefer architecture to antiques, follow Route 109 north from Washington to Route 63 and Litchfield, a town that is on every list of the "most beautiful towns in America." Litchfield is considered by many to be the finest unrestored, unspoiled Colonial town in New England. This is a town for walking, and it's easy to see the sights since the magnificent homes are concentrated on two long blocks, North and South Streets, off the green.

Tapping Reeve opened the nation's first law school in his superb 1773 home on South Street with his brother-in-law, Aaron Burr, as his first pupil. Eventually, the pupils outgrew the house and a school building was erected in 1784. John C. Calhoun was a student here, lodging in the rectory next door and planting some of the elms that remain along the street.

Farther down the street is the 1736 home where Ethan Allen, Revolutionary War leader of the fabled Green Mountain Boys, is believed to have been born. Other significant buildings include the onetime residence of Oliver Wolcott Jr., now the town library, and the obligatory structure boasting "George Washington slept here"—in this case, the Elisha Sheldon Tavern.

The Historical Society has fine quarters on the corner of South and East Streets, and a stop will tell you a lot about Litchfield's development. You'll learn, for example, that this was also home to the Sarah Pierce Academy, the nation's first academy for women, conveniently located for socializing with Mr. Reeve's law students.

Litchfield has a growing number of art galleries, including the gallery of Frank Federico, who has won many awards. Troy Brook Visions Gallery, in Cobble Court, not far from town, offers the Shaker, mission-style, and traditional designs of Dan Gugnoni, a master furniture maker. For dining, the West Street Grill, a stylish bistro on the green, gets critics' raves for its innovative menu, and the same owners offer less formal Italian fare at Grappa, in Cobble Court.

Outside of town are two expert glass artists, Tony Carretta and Larry LiVolsi, who invite visitors into their studios to watch them create beautiful sculptures of glass.

If the day is fine, you might prefer to forget the shops and head for the White Memorial Foundation, the state's largest nature center and wildlife preserve, with almost every kind of outdoor activity plus Bantam Lake, 11 ponds, and the Bantam River. There are 35 miles of trails and a unique bird-watching facility as well as nature exhibits in the newly expanded Conservation Center—with lots of hands-on activities for children.

Another magnificent strolling place is Topsmead State Forest, a former estate whose grounds and gardens are now open to the public for hiking and picnicking with fabulous views of the Litchfield hills.

You need not be a real flower fancier to appreciate Litchfield's White Flower Farm. May and June are the peak bloom months for the eight acres of exotic display gardens in a nursery that is one of the nation's outstanding breeding grounds for perennial plants. Besides the gardens, there are 1,200 varieties of flowers in 20 acres of growing fields. Delphiniums are a specialty, as are tuberous begonias.

It is less than 25 miles between any two points in this area—Litchfield to Kent or either town from Woodbury or Washington—so you'll find it easy to spend several days in this beautiful section of old Connecticut enjoying the wealth of sights. But if you never manage to tear yourself away from Woodbury and the shops, you needn't apologize. You won't be the first to have fallen prey to the lures of the antiques capital of Connecticut.

<u>Area Code: Woodbury and Southbury, 203; Litchfield, Kent, Washington, and New Preston, 860</u>

DRIVING DIRECTIONS Woodbury is on Route 6, west of Waterbury, at exit 155 of I-84. It is about 140 miles from Boston, 85 miles from New York, and 45 miles from Hartford.

PUBLIC TRANSPORTATION Bonanza buses to Southbury, New Milford, or Kent.

ACCOMMODATIONS Ask about weekend and winter packages. **Heritage Inn,** Village Green, Heritage Road, Southbury 06488, 264-8200 or (800) 932-3466, M–E • **Curtis House,** Main Street, Woodbury 06798, 263-2101, I–M, CP • **Merryvale Bed and Breakfast,** 1204 Main Street South, Woodbury 06798, 266-0800, M, CP • **Mayflower Inn,** Route 47, Washington 06793, 868-9466, EE • **Boulders Inn,** Route 45, New Preston 06777, 868-0541, EE, MAP • **Hopkins Inn,** Hopkins Road, New Preston 06777, 868-7295, open May to October, I • **The Birches Inn,** 233 West Shore Road, New Preston, 06777, 868-1735, M–EE, CP • **Inn on Lake Waramaug,** New Preston 06777, 868-0563, mini-resort, rooms are in motel lodge, not the old inn, E–EE, MAP • **The Country Goose,** Route 7, Kent 06757, 927-4746, eighteenth-century Colonial, M, CP • **Chaucer House,** 88 North Main Street, Route 7, Kent 06757, 927-4858, small Colonial inn within walking distance of shops and Bonanza bus stop, M, CP • **Constitution Oak Farm,** 36 Beardsley Road, Kent 06757, 354-6495, a working farm in the country, I–M, CP • **Fife 'n Drum,** Route 7, Kent 06757, 927-3509, attractive rooms in lodge adjoining restaurant, M.

DINING **Carole Peck's Good News Café,** 694 Main Street South (Route 6), Woodbury, 266-4663, admired local chef, modern American food, art gallery, music on weekends, M • **Curtis House** (see above),

Woodbury, M • **The Olive Tree,** Routes 6 and 64, Woodbury, 263-4555, continental with a Greek flavor, M • **Mayflower Inn** (see above), Washington, M–E • **George Washington Tavern,** 21 Bee Brook Road (Route 47), Washington Depot, 868-6633, Colonial atmosphere, fish and chips, pot pie, and other pub fare, I–M • **Heritage Inn** (see above), Southbury, good bet for Sunday brunch, M–E • **Hopkins Inn** (see above), New Preston, Austrian owner and menu, excellent, M • **Boulders Inn** (see above), New Preston, attractive decor and setting, varied menu, M–E • **Le Bon Coin,** Route 202, New Preston, 868-7763, exceptional French bistro, M • **Doc's,** Route 45, New Preston, 868-9415, Italian, informal, gourmet pizzas, I–M • **Birches Inn** (see above), New Preston, former West Street Grill chef, M–E • **Café New Preston,** 18 East Shore Road, New Preston, 868-1787, cozy, Mediterranean dishes, M–E • **West Street Grill,** 43 West Street, Litchfield, 567-3885, contemporary American menu, excellent, M–E • **Grappa,** 26 Commons Drive, Litchfield, 567-1616, Italian specialties, gourmet pizza, I–M • **Toll Gate Inn,** Route 202, Litchfield, 567-4545, 1745 landmark, traditional menu, M–E • **Fife 'n Drum** (see above), known for its piano bar, M–E. *For lunch, tea, or a picnic to go:* **The Pantry,** Titus Square, Washington Depot, 868-0258.

SIGHTSEEING   Glebe House, Hollow Road (off Route 6), Woodbury, 263-2855. Hours: April to November, Wednesday through Sunday, 1 P.M. to 4 P.M. $$ • **Institute for American Indian Studies,** Curtis Road (off Route 199), Washington, 868-0518. Hours: April through December, Monday to Saturday, 10 A.M. to 5 P.M., Sunday, from noon; closed Monday and Tuesday, January through March. $$ • **Flanders Nature Center,** Flanders Road (off Route 6), Woodbury, 263-3711. Hours: trails open daily, dawn to dusk • **Gunn Historical Museum,** on the green, Washington, 868-7756. Hours: Thursday to Saturday, noon to 4 P.M. Free • **Sloane-Stanley Museum,** Route 7, Kent, 927-3849. Hours: mid-May to October, Wednesday to Sunday, 10 A.M. to 4 P.M. Adults, $$ • **Litchfield Historical Society Museum,** South Street, on the green, 567-4501. Hours: mid-April to mid-November, Tuesday to Saturday, 11 A.M. to 5 P.M., Sunday, from 1 P.M. $$; under 16 free; includes admission to **Tapping Reeve House and Law School,** South Street, Litchfield, 567-4501. Hours: (reopening summer 1988 after renovations) mid-May to mid-October, Tuesday to Saturday, 11 A.M. to 5 P.M., Sunday, from 1 P.M. $$ • **White Flower Farm,** Route 63 South, Litchfield, 567-8789. Hours: early April to mid-October, weekdays, 9 A.M. to 6 P.M.; rest of year, 10 A.M. to 5 P.M. Free • **White Memorial Foundation Center,** Route 202, Litchfield, 567-0857. Hours: grounds open daily; free. Museum open year-round, Monday to Saturday, 9 A.M. to 5 P.M., Sunday, noon to 4 P.M. $ • **Topsmead State Park,** Buell Road off East Litchfield Road (Route 118), Litchfield, 845-0226. Daylight hours. Free. *Litchfield glass artists (best to phone before stopping by):* **Tony Carretta,** 513 Maple Street, the Milton Barn, Litchfield, 567-4851; **Larry LiVolsi,** Lorenz Studio and Gallery, Route 109, Lakeside, 567-4280. Free.

INFORMATION Litchfield Hills Travel Council, PO Box 968, Litchfield, CT 06759, 567-4506.

Greeting Spring in Sandwich

The oldest town on Cape Cod is just about the loveliest.

Few places anywhere can match the charm and serenity of Sandwich. Beach-bound traffic tends to pass this by historic village, leaving it to those who like meandering down Colonial lanes, sitting beside a millpond, antiquing, or exploring gardens and fascinating little-heralded museums, one of them featuring a collection of famous Sandwich glass.

If you fit the bill, you'll find this special town at its very best late in May, when the wide lawns are still wearing fresh coats of green, and gracious homes and spired New England churches are framed by pastel clouds of crab apple, laurel, and dogwood blossoms. That's the time, too, when thousands of prize rhododendrons begin their annual seasonal spectacular at Heritage Plantation, a remarkable combination 76-acre showplace garden and museum complex.

Sandwich is also within easy reach of Sandy Neck, a 6½-mile barrier beach that is the most extensive conservation area outside the National Seashore, a world of gulls and dunes and marsh-side blueberry patches. So if the weather is right, you can add sunbathing and nature walks to your agenda.

There are two kinds of lodging right in the center of old Sandwich: the landmark Dan'l Webster Inn, on Main Street, or small bed-and-breakfast inns. The original historic inn, dating from 1692, is long gone, but the current Dan'l Webster is most attractive, though be forewarned that it often attracts tour groups for lunch. The choicest and quietest rooms are in the new wing or in the recently restored historic houses next door and across the street. Ask for a wing room looking out at the garden—or, if you want to splurge a bit, one of the handsome suites with fireplaces in the Fessenden House.

Of the bed-and-breakfast inns, the Captain Ezra Nye House, a 1792 home right across the street from the inn, is a top choice, and so is the elegant Victorian Isiah Jones Homestead, down the block. Six Water Street has a winning location right on the shoreline of Shawme Pond.

Outside of town, Wingscorton Farm Inn, a beautifully furnished 1758 Colonial off Route 6A, has acres of lawn and is a short walk to a private beach. Rooms in the house are suites, and there is a romantic carriage house for two on the grounds as well as a larger cottage ideal for families. This is a working farm on seven acres—complete with chickens, pigs, goats, horses, emus, alapacas, llamas, and a burro—so it can be a wonderful place for children.

For a room with a water view, Bay Beach is the place.

You'll probably want to begin your Sandwich stay just by taking a walk and enjoying the graceful ambience of the town, with its central green and millpond. Sandwich was founded in 1637 by ten men from Saugus, Massachusetts, who made their way to the top of Cape Cod and established a settlement they named after Sandwich, England. There are still many monuments to attest to this long history. The columned Sandwich Town Hall dates all the way back, and the Dexter Grist Mill, on Shawme Pond, near the center of town, is a restoration of the mill that operated here in 1640. Next door is the restored Hoxie House, one of the oldest homes on the Cape. It is open to the public in summer.

One of the local prides is the exquisite Wren-style steeple of the First Church of Christ, containing what is said to be the oldest church bell in America, dating to 1675.

Sandwich is only a village, so you'll have no problem finding your way along the central arteries, Main and Water Streets, or onto the side roads with their handsome homes. You'll find many worthwhile detours along the way.

Near the old mill and also on the pond is the Thornton Burgess Museum, dedicated to the author of the Peter Cottontail stories, who grew up in Sandwich. Web-footed creatures of all kinds stroll the lawns here, and you can visit Peter's own house.

One of the most historic buildings in town is the 1833 First Parish Meetinghouse, which currently houses the Yesteryears Doll Museum. The museum began in 1961 with the private collection of Mr. and Mrs. Ronald Thomas of Sandwich, who created the museum to house their lifetime of acquisitions. Many other dolls have been added over the years. There are dollhouses furnished in period style, miniatures, and other interesting toys on display as well. The gift shop is chock full of dolls, doll clothing, and accessories.

The main attraction in town for most people is around the corner at the Sandwich Glass Museum, where several rooms handsomely display a comprehensive collection of the renowned glassware that was made here from 1825 to 1888. Even if the name "Sandwich glass" means little to you, you'll recognize the "lacy" designs developed here that continue to influence our glassware patterns today. Though the museum seems small at first glance, it takes at least an hour to follow properly the interesting development of pressed glass, which proceeded from this factory's first experiments at mass production to the ornate pieces and glowing colors that were eventually produced by mid-century.

Among the more famous Sandwich pieces on exhibit are dolphin candlesticks in translucent and opaque colors, and the high-quality cut and engraved pieces that were made in the late 1860s and 1870s, when the Sandwich operation could no longer compete with larger factories and turned back to elegant hand-blown glassware.

This museum is a "sleeper," more interesting than you might have expected, and it may well leave you with a new interest in the craft of glassmaking. Don't be surprised if you are inspired to pick up a paperweight or some other unusual glass souvenir at the sales desk on your way out.

If you've taken your time, taken in the sights, and taken time for a leisurely lunch at the Dan'l Webster Inn, you may need no further activity for a pleasant Saturday than to browse the half dozen antiques stores, the art gallery, and the handful of tasteful gift shops in town, almost all near the middle of the village. Antiques buffs will want to note the annual Cape Cod Antique Dealers Association show and sale, held in early June at Heritage Plantation.

If you want to complete all the sights, take a brief driving tour to Old Cemetery Point, the town's first burying ground, dating back to 1683; the site of the original glass factory at Jarves and Factory Streets; and the old Quaker Meetinghouse and Graveyard, circa 1810, at Gilman and Spring Hill Road in East Sandwich. Also in East Sandwich, off Chipman Road, you can see the Thornton Burgess Briarpath, the original Peter Cottontail country, where there are now walking trails to let you follow in Peter's footsteps.

One other pleasant excursion is aboard the Cape Cod Scenic Railroad, a vintage train that runs from Sandwich to Hyannis, a $1\frac{3}{4}$-hour jaunt.

With the sights checked off and a good night's sleep, you'll be fresh for the new barrage of attractions awaiting at Heritage Plantation. This amazing complex is dedicated to the memory of Josiah K. Lilly Jr., described in the plantation brochure as "one of the most distinguished and unassuming twentieth-century American collectors."

What did Mr. Lilly collect? Name it. There are four separate buildings filled to the brim with his antique guns, military memorabilia and miniatures, vintage automobiles, paintings and American folk art, tools, crafts, and Currier and Ives lithographs. The museum buildings themselves are attractions. The car collection is housed in a round barn inspired by the Shaker structure in Hancock, Massachusetts. The Military Museum is in a hand-hewn building held together by oaken pins and hand-wrought iron, a reproduction of a Revolutionary-period structure called the Temple in New Windsor, New York. The Art Museum, overlooking Upper Shawme Lake, features a real old-fashioned 1912 carousel, still in perfect order to give visitors a nostalgic ride.

Just so as not to miss anything in the way of Americana, there's also a windmill transplanted from the nearby town of Orleans. And there are various galleries that feature changing art exhibits as well.

As if all that weren't enough, the Lilly family has located Heritage Plantation on the former estate of Charles O. Dexter, who gained distinction for hybridizing the now-famous Dexter rhododendrons. The annual blooming of thousands of rhododendrons and other flowering evergreens in May and June is an unforgettable spectacle. There are many other flower gardens, a daylily garden featuring 550 varieties, picnic grounds, a café, a garden shop, and several quiet nature trails on the grounds as well.

Bring along a picnic, and Heritage Plantation can easily occupy your whole day on Sunday. Or you might choose to end your weekend by taking an afternoon drive east on Route 6A, the old King's Highway, which goes through the Cape's attractive north shore towns. Since the water is colder and the beaches aren't quite as bountiful as those on the southern side of the peninsula, Route 6A has escaped the awful commercial buildup that has all but spoiled Route 28, across the way. The shaded drive through some of the old Colonial settlements such as Barnstable, Yarmouth, Dennis, and Brewster is scenic anytime, but without the summer traffic, you can really appreciate the lovely old homes along the way, many of them now housing antiques and crafts shops or converted into attractive inns.

If you drive straight through to Orleans and the intersection with the Mid-Cape Highway, the drive will take under an hour; if you stop to browse, it can take half a day. In the center of each town, you'll see a turnoff to the harbor and the beach, the chance to take a stroll or have a seafood dinner before you head home.

If you've given up on Cape Cod and its traffic and hassles, a springtime visit to Sandwich and its neighbors may change your mind. With its history intact and without summer crowds, it is easy to see why so many people fell in love with the Cape in the first place.

Area Code: 508

DRIVING DIRECTIONS Sandwich is the first town on the Cape after crossing the Sagamore Bridge, reached via the Mid-Cape Highway, Route 6, or Route 6A. It is 45 miles from Boston, 255 miles from New York, and 145 miles from Hartford.

ACCOMMODATIONS **Dan'l Webster Inn,** 149 Main Street, Sandwich 02563, 888-3622, M–E (ask about MAP and weekend plans) • **Isiah Jones Homestead,** 165 Main Street, Sandwich 02563, 888-9115, M–E, CP • **Captain Ezra Nye House,** 152 Main Street, Sandwich 02563, (800) 388-2278 or 888-6142, M, CP • **Wingscorton Farm Inn,** 11 Wing Boulevard (off Route 6A), East Sandwich 02537, 888-0534, suites in the main house, M, CP; carriage house, E, CP, cottage by the week only • **Bay Beach,** 1-3 Bay Beach Lane, PO Box 151, Sandwich 02563, 888-8813, excellent motel-style bed-and-breakfast inn on the water, open mid-May through November, E, CP • Some mid-Cape inns worth noting are the elegant Colonial **Wedgewood Inn,** 83 Main Street (Route 6A), Yarmouth Port 02675, 362-5157, M–E, CP • **Captain Freeman Inn,** 15 Breakwater Road, Brewster 02631, 896-7481 or (800) 843-4664, a Victorian with a pool and lavish suites, rooms, M–E, CP; suites, EE, CP; and the delightful **Isiah Hall Bed and Breakfast Inn,** 152 Whig Street, Dennis 02638, 385-9928 or (800) 736-0160, a country charmer off on a quiet road within walking distance of a beach, M, CP.

DINING **Dan'l Webster Inn** (see above), M • **Captain's Table,** 14 Gallo Road (at Town Neck Road), 888-8440, casual, overlooking marina and Cape Cod canal, entertainment on weekends, M • **Horizon's,** 98 Town Neck Road, 888-6166, informal dining facing the canal, pub/bar atmosphere, I–M • **Beehive Tavern,** 406 Route 6A, Sandwich, 833-1184, casual dining, I–M. *The following restaurants, all considered among the Cape's finest, are on or near Route 6A within a half hour's drive from Sandwich:* **Chillingsworth,** Route 6A, Brewster, 896-3640, often called the best on the Cape, prix fixe, EE; café menu, M • **Bramble Inn,** Route 6A, Brewster, 896-7644, prix fixe, EE • **High Brewster,** 964 Satucket Road, Brewster, 896-3636, E–EE. *Less pricey recommendations:* **Mattakeese Wharf,** Barnstable Harbor, 362-4511, seafood with a view, M • **Gina's by the Sea,** 134 Taunton Avenue, Dennis, 385-3213, M • **Brewster Fish House,** 2208 Main Street, 896-7867, M • **Abbicci,** 43 Main Street, Yarmouth Port, 362-3501, M–E.

SIGHTSEEING **Heritage Plantation of Sandwich,** Grove and Pine Streets, 888-3300. Hours: mid-May to mid-October, daily, 10 A.M. to 5 P.M. $$$$ • **Sandwich Glass Museum,** 129 Main Street, 888-0251. Hours: April 1 to October 31, daily, 9:30 A.M. to 4:30 P.M.; November, December, February, March, Wednesday to Sunday, 9:30 A.M. to 4 P.M. Closed January. $$ • **Yesteryears Doll and Miniature Museum,** Main and River Streets, 888-1711. Hours: May 15 through October, Monday to Saturday, 10 A.M. to 4 P.M. $$ • **Thornton W. Burgess Museum,** 4 Water Street, 888-6870. Hours: Monday to Saturday, 10 A.M. to 4 P.M., Sunday, 1 P.M. to 4 P.M. Donation • **Cape Cod Scenic Railroad,** 252

Main Street, Hyannis, 771-3788; scenic runs from Hyannis to Cape Cod Canal via Sandwich on vintage trains. Hours: Tuesday to Sunday, June through October; weekends only in May, November, December. Dinner runs offered. Phone for current schedule and rates.

INFORMATION   Cape Cod Chamber of Commerce, Routes 6 and 132, Hyannis, MA 02601, 362-3225.

 # City by the Sea: Portland, Maine

"I have this friend," the Portland native was telling us, "that everybody thought was crazy. Years ago he started buying wrecked-up buildings near the waterfront. People laughed at him and asked what on earth he was going to do with those old buildings."

The punch line, of course, is that the friend became a millionaire. The redevelopment of the waterfront, now a bustling area of attractive shops and restaurants known as the Old Port Exchange, led the way to a remarkable renaissance in Portland, Maine. It is a development that would have been hard to predict by anyone who knew the city a couple of decades ago.

Now young professionals from throughout New England are moving to this city that native Henry Wadsworth Longfellow once described as "the beautiful town that is seated by the sea." Portland is turning into an increasingly sophisticated and appealing place to live in and to visit, with a thriving arts community, a magnificent art museum designed by I. M. Pei, and some of the best food to be found north of Boston.

But it remains true that the first thing you notice in Portland is not buildings, but water. The city is on a peninsula with views of Casco Bay on three sides, the vistas made more dramatic because Portland is situated on a high crest of land. The proximity to shoreline, boat cruises, and the nearby rocky cliffs below Maine's most photographed and painted landmark, Portland Head Lighthouse, make visiting this city a double pleasure.

That the rebirth of Portland should have taken so long despite its fortunate location reflects how far the city had lagged. Once a prosperous shipping and shipbuilding port and the capital of Maine, it developed early in its history into a major center for importing molasses from the West Indies. The port continued to flourish until a devastating July 4 blaze in 1866 destroyed 1,800 buildings and left 10,000 people homeless. Though the city rebuilt quickly with the sturdy stone Victorian structures still evident today, it suffered a more serious setback in this century when the port declined, partly because of competition after the opening of the St. Lawrence Seaway.

In time, the deserted buildings near the harbor became havens for artists and craftspeople, who could get them for rock-bottom rents. They formed the Old Port Association, hoping to tempt browsers, stringing up their own lights and shoveling their own streets to make things more enticing, since the city no longer provided such services to the decaying area. That was the start of the recent revival, abetted by the Maine Way urban renewal program.

Meanwhile, downtown Portland underwent its own face-lift. Today, Congress Street, the main business thoroughfare, has been spruced up with brick sidewalks, old-fashioned street lamps, and a cleaning job that removed a century of grime from the old facades. New buildings abound, and Monument Square, at the corner of Congress and Middle, is now a plaza where colorful food carts offer everything from bagels to health food. Lunchtime entertainment adds to the square's lure as a local gathering place.

The liveliest activity in town is centered in the Old Port, between Monument Square and the wharves on Commercial Street. Here's where young people gather in trendy cafés and tourists shop the many offbeat stores—dozens of them—selling everything from pottery to antiques to clothing. The area continues to grow as more blighted blocks are restored, and it has become a showcase for crafts artisans from throughout northern New England.

Even with all these changes, Portland remains at heart a small city (population 65,000)—an inviting place where you can easily walk to all the sights.

The old face of Portland, part dowdy, part Old World charm, is still very much in evidence among the new buildings on Congress; a walking tour is an architecture buff's delight and a good place to begin your look at the city. The Convention and Visitors Bureau will supply you with free printed tours for different parts of the city. The Congress Street guide points up the contrasts now to be found on this street whose history spans more than two centuries.

At 425 Congress you'll find the Wadsworth-Longfellow House, circa 1785, crammed between stores and banks. The hostess-guided tour of the boyhood home of the famed poet and his family is a detour not to be missed by anyone interested in American literature or history. Farther on, the Federal-era First Parish Church is neighbor to the newer Casco Bank Building, and Beaux Arts and Queen Anne structures adjoin the ultramodern library—an unconventional yet somehow congenial blending of styles.

Switching over to the Old Port Exchange guide, you'll learn about the city's ups and downs as a shipping center, and the filling of land in the 1850s to form Commercial Street, which soon was lined with wharves and warehouses. Most of the major structures dating from the 1866 rebuilding are on Middle, Exchange, and Fore Streets, which offer another field day for architecture buffs. Custom House Wharf, home of Boone's, a local seafood landmark, and the departure point of the Casco Bay Line boat rides, hasn't been prettied up as much as the rest of the neighborhood, and it gives you an idea of what the entire area looked like not so long ago.

You'll probably not need the printed guide to notice one of the most intriguing new additions, the trompe l'oeil mural at Exchange and Middle by Portland artist Chris Denison, who transformed a blank brick wall into what looks for all the world like a period building. The open corner in front of the mural now serves as a gathering spot where informal summer concerts are held.

There's no question that you'll be tempted to interrupt your building gazing to look into the shops here, so allow plenty of time. Among the many crafts shops, look out for the Maine Potters Market, at 376 Fore Street, a cooperative displaying the work of a dozen of the state's artisans. A bounty of art galleries and antiques shops beckons as well in the Old Port and on Congress. Abacus, at 44 Exchange Street, is one of the prime stops for fine crafts. Shipwreck & Cargo, 207 Commercial Street, may be of special interest for its marine antiques, hardware, and salvage, and it sometimes yields rich finds for decorators and renovators. Names and owners do change, so check the current list of local antiques stores, available in most of the shops.

Between the landmarks and the looking, you can while away a very pleasant day in Portland, but before your energy flags, part of your day should be saved for the glorious Portland Art Museum. One prize permanent display here is the collection of Winslow Homer's donated by Charles Shipman Payson, the same patron who was principally responsible for the $11.6 million building. Joan Whitney Payson's European art collection, including works by Chagall, Degas, Gauguin, Monet, Picasso, and other masters, has also been installed here.

In addition, there are works by other artists—such as John Singer Sargent, Stuart Davis, Andrew Wyeth, and Edward Hopper—associated with Maine or Maine subjects, part of the growing State of Maine Collection. While the museum's own collection builds, it is working hard to bring in visiting shows of high caliber.

Perhaps the most stunning work of art here is the building itself, done in red brick and in shapes emphasizing circles, squares, and arches deliberately planned to work with the traditional architecture of the city and the adjoining original museum landmark buildings of the 1900s. It is rightfully one of Portland's prides.

If time permits, fans of the Victorian period will want to make a stop at the Victoria Mansion, an elaborate example of the most ornate styles of the era, and families will want to visit the Children's Museum of Maine, offering all kinds of hands-on fun and learning.

When hunger pangs strike, you're surrounded by tempting possibilities in Portland, and there is evening entertainment for every taste, from jazz in the Old Port to the Portland Symphony. Check also for performances by the Portland Ballet Company, the Portland Lyric Theater, and the Portland Stage Company. If you want really late entertainment, or if you have insomnia, remember that L. L. Bean is open all night in Freeport, just 15 minutes away.

Come Sunday, you might choose either to head for the wharf and board a cruise boat or to take a driving tour to see some of the city's prime water views. With planning, you can even manage both.

For the views, follow Congress Street east past the Portland Observatory and Monjoy Hill (once the site of a tent city of burned-out survivors of the 1866 fire) to the Eastern Promenade, overlooking Casco Bay. The homes here are bordered by a breezy park with benches where you can enjoy the sights. In the warmer months the 102 steps of the observatory, a historic 1807 octagonal signal tower, can be climbed for an even more panoramic perspective.

Fort Allen Park boasts a cannon straight from the USS *Constitution,* and the Eastern Cemetery, near Monjoy Hill on Congress and Washington, is a fascinating site dating back to 1639 that is full of centuries-old headstones embellished with angels and curlicues. The Western Promenade, another neighborhood of lovely homes, offers its own special view. On a good day you can see the White Mountains.

Back in town, follow State Street across the bridge to South Portland and watch for Route 77 signs to Cape Elizabeth. (Turn left at the first school if the sign is missing, as it was recently.) It will take you to Fort Williams Park and the famous Portland Head Lighthouse, built for George Washington in 1791 and even more imposing on its steep rocky perch than all those countless photos can convey. The museum in the former housekeepers' quarters tells the fascinating history of the lighthouse.

Farther on is Two Lights State Park, with 40 acres on the shore, and the Two Lights Lobster Shack, a prime stop for lobster or clams in a dining room or at outside picnic tables with ocean views. If the weather is conducive to beachcombing, drive farther on Route 77 to Crescent Neck Beach State Park or to Higgins Beach or to Scarborough Beach State Park in Scarborough. At Ferry Beach, off Route 207 in Prouts Neck, you can view the community whose rugged cliffs were the inspiration for many of Winslow Homer's works. The artist's studio remains here, much the way he left it, though it is not open to the public.

You can have your driving tour and still get back to Portland in plenty of time for an afternoon or sunset cruise from the wharf and a final seafood dinner—a fitting close for a visit to a city by the sea.

Area Code: 207

DRIVING DIRECTIONS I-95 and U.S. Route 1 both lead into downtown Portland, located on the southern Maine coast 109 miles north of Boston, 322 miles from New York, and 212 miles from Hartford.

PUBLIC TRANSPORTATION Portland is served by Delta, US Airways, United, and Continental Airlines, and by Greyhound and Concord Trailways buses. Downtown is easily manageable without a car.

ACCOMMODATIONS *Within walking distance of downtown sights are:* **Portland Regency,** 20 Milk Street, Portland 04101, 774-4200 or (800) 727-3436, restored armory building in Old Port, top choice, E • **Radisson Eastland Hotel,** 157 High Street, Portland 04101, 775-5411, gracious landmark, M–E • **Holiday Inn by the Bay,** 88 Spring Street, Portland 04101, 775-2311, M–E • **Westin Portland,** Park Avenue and Alder Street, luxury hotel opening late 1988; phone (800) 228-3000 for information • **Inn by the Sea,** 40 Bowery Beach Road, Cape Elizabeth 04107, 799-3134 or (800) 888-4287, mini-resort on the ocean, tennis, pool, E–EE. *Bed-and-breakfast inns:* **Pomegranate Inn,** 49 Neal Street, Portland 04102, 772-1006 or (800) 356-0408, extraordinary decor, filled with whimsy and charm, M–E, CP • **Inn at Park Spring,** 135 Spring Street, Portland 04101, 774-1059, 1835 town house, closest B & B to downtown, M, CP • **West End Inn,** 146 Pine Street, 04102, 772-1377, West End town house, circa 1871, M–E, CP • **The Danforth,** 163 Danforth Street, Portland 04102, 879-8755 or (800) 991-6557, 1821 mansion turned inn overlooking the harbor, fireplaces in every room, M–E, CP. *Budget motels:* **Econo Lodge,** 738 Main Street, Portland 04106, 774-5891, I–M • **Susse Chalet Motor Lodge,** 340 Park Avenue, Portland 04102, 871-0611, I–M. Many more hotels and motels are located south of town near the Maine Mall and the airport; write to Visitors Bureau (address below) for a complete list.

DINING *Seafood:* **Street and Company,** 33 Wharf Street, 775-0887, the freshest seafood, any way you like it, M • **Snow Squall,** 18 Ocean Street, South Portland, 799-2232, seafood on the waterfront, also grill specialties, M • **Newick's,** 740 Broadway, South Portland, 799-3090, try the heaping seafood platters, M • **Boone's,** 6 Custom House Wharf, Portland, 774-5725, part of the waterfront since 1896, lobster and seafood at fair prices, I–M • **DiMillo's Floating Restaurant,** 25 Long Wharf, Portland, 772-2216, locals say dining aboard ship is strictly for the tourists, but this is one of the busiest restaurants on the coast nevertheless, M–E • **Two Lights Lobster Shack,** at the entrance to Two Lights State Park, Cape Elizabeth, 799-1677. (Note: hours are 11 A.M. to 8 P.M. April to mid-October, to 8:30 P.M. July and

August.) Prices vary with the season's catch. *Italian:* **The Roma Café,** 769 Congress, 773-9873, longtime local favorite, often offers seasonal bargain twin lobster specials, M • **Perfetto,** 28 Exchange Street, 828-0001, popular, informal northern Italian, M • **Village Café,** 112 Newbury Street, 772-5320, an old-timer, reliable for home cooking, huge portions, reasonable, I–M. *Eclectic:* **Fore Street,** 288 Fore Street, 775-2717, soaring restored warehouse, open grill specialties, M • **Café Always,** 47 Middle Street, 774-9399, innovative New American menu, a longtime favorite, M • **Back Bay Grill,** 65 Portland Street, 772-8833, art deco mood, great mural of the city, sophisticated fare, M–E • **Tabitha Jean's,** 94 Free Street, 780-8966, contemporary menu and good reviews for a restaurant owned by the daughter of author Stephen King, M–E • **The Madd Apple Café,** 24 Forest Avenue, 772-6606, barbecue and southern specialties, informal, M–E • **Walter's Cafe,** 15 Exchange Street, 871-9258, busy, noisy, very popular spot for New American, open kitchen, I–M • **Zephyr Grill,** 653 Congress Street, 828-4033, informal offbeat decor, excellent and original menu, I–M • **Hugo's Portland Bistro,** 88 Middle Street, 774-8538, international dishes, lively, I–M • **Katahdin,** Spring and High Streets, 774-1740, funky, good home cooking, reasonable, I–M • **F. Parker Reidy's,** 83 Exchange Street, 773-4731, old-timer that remains popular, restored Victorian bank, steaks, seafood, lots of late-night activity, I–M.

SIGHTSEEING **Portland Museum of Art,** 7 Congress Street, 775-6148. Hours: Tuesday to Saturday, 10 A.M. to 5 P.M.; Sunday, from noon; Thursday and Friday, until 9 P.M. $$$; Friday from 5 P.M. to 9 P.M., free • **Wadsworth-Longfellow House,** 484-489 Congress Street, 879-0427. Hours: June to Columbus Day, Tuesday to Saturday, 10 A.M. to 4 P.M. $$ • **Victoria Mansion,** 109 Danforth Street, 772-4841. Hours: May through October, Tuesday to Saturday, 10 A.M. to 4 P.M.; Sunday, 1 P.M. to 5 P.M. $$ • **Children's Museum of Maine,** 142 Free Street, 828-1234. Hours: Memorial Day to Labor Day, Monday to Saturday, 10 A.M. to 5 P.M.; Sunday, noon to 5 P.M.; rest of year, closed Monday and Tuesday. $$; also, Friday 5 P.M. to 8 P.M., free • **Portland Observatory,** 138 Congress Street, 772-5547. Hours: open Memorial Day to Halloween whenever the flag is flying, generally Friday to Sunday, 1 P.M. to 5 P.M., also Wednesday and Thursday in July and August. $ • **Museum at Portland Head Light,** Fort Williams Park, 1000 Shore Road, Cape Elizabeth, 799-2661. Hours: June 1 to October 31, daily, 10 A.M. to 4 P.M.; guided tours at 11 A.M. and 2 P.M.; April and May, weekends only. $. *Boat trips:* The following offer a variety of cruises, including sightseeing and whale and seal watches; phone all for exact current offerings. **Casco Bay Lines,** Custom House Wharf, corner Commercial and Franklin Streets, 774-7871; **Bay View Cruises,** Long Wharf, 184 Commercial Street, 761-0496; **Mainely Tours,** 5½ Moulton Street, 774-0808; **Olde Port Mariner Fleet,** Long Wharf, Commercial Street, 775-0727; **MS Scotia Prince,** International Terminal, (800) 341-7540 or (800) 482-0955 in Maine, leaves Portland nightly for Nova Scotia, with cruises from 23 hours to several days available. Phone for current schedules and prices.

INFORMATION   Greater Portland Convention and Visitors Bureau, 305 Commercial Street, Portland, ME 04101, 772-5800.

Crafts Spectacular in the Pioneer Valley

You can hardly find a good orrery nowadays.

In case you don't know, an orrery is a mechanical reproduction of the solar system, named for Charles Boyle, the fourth earl of Cork and Orrery, who had the first known such contrivance made in about 1710.

Handmade orrerys were among the unexpected offerings a few years ago at the Craftfair of the American Crafts Council in West Springfield, Massachusetts—which just goes to prove that there's very little you can't find at this gathering of America's top craftspeople, a major event that is one of the largest of its kind in New England.

It is an appropriate location, since Springfield is part of the Pioneer Valley, a region that has grown into a crafts center in its own right. More than 1,500 artists and craftspeople live in the region, drawn by the combination of natural beauty and the rich cultural life supplied by five area colleges—Amherst, Mount Holyoke, the University of Massachusetts, Hampshire, and Smith. Northampton, the home of Smith College, is the lively center of things, a town filled with galleries, fine turn-of-the-century architecture, and a growing number of good restaurants.

Springfield's Craftfair will occupy a good part of a day. Some 300 artisans take part, selected by a jury of fine crafts artists. The artisans include potters; tin-, gold-, iron-, and silversmiths; candle molders; glassblowers; basket weavers; leather cutters; quilters; zither makers; wood carvers; weavers; and creators of wares so diverse as to defy description.

The event began in Vermont over three decades ago and kept outgrowing its sites, eventually moving to outdoor tents at the fairgrounds in Rhinebeck, New York. But by 1984 the crowds had grown so large that another move was necessary, and the big Eastern States Exposition Center in West Springfield won the prize. The Craftfair is bigger than ever now, with some 10,000 people turning out for the three-day event.

The displays offer everything from a ceramic toothbrush holder to a handmade rolling pin, from casseroles and canisters to large sculptures and exquisite furniture, with price tags anywhere from $25 to $25,000. In fact, if there is anything to complain about, it is the huge number of displays. Don't buy until you've covered everything; the perfect choice may be just around the corner.

There will be plenty of food stands to refuel your energy along the way, plus the traditional tavern and New England wine gardens on the center's grounds, which are also the annual site of the largest fall fair in New England.

When you've had your fill of browsing, you'll find plenty more to see and do in the Springfield area. This old New England town has recently spruced up its historic downtown around Court Square, a charming urban park, and is quite a pleasant place for a stroll and a bit of sightseeing.

You don't have to be a sports lover to enjoy Springfield's most colorful attraction, the Basketball Hall of Fame. The museum celebrates the sport that was born at Springfield College back in 1891. The lively exhibits are planned to get spectators involved in the game you can compare your own basketball skills to the skills of Hall of Famers in the Wilson Imgynation area or play against a star like Bill Walton in the exciting Elks Virtual Reality game.

Besides a host of exhibits—including Bob Lanier's gilded size-22 sneakers—you can see a movie that puts you smack in center court in the middle of the action, walk through an archway made of multicolored regulation sneakers, pass through a room hung with 300 colorful college jerseys, and even try your hand at shooting from the hall's most popular attraction, the Spalding Shootout, a moving sidewalk facing a battery of baskets. The game's great players and coaches are enshrined in the Honors Court, with medallions and a brief history of each man's career. They are also featured in action in exciting, lifelike stroboscopic photo images that illustrate the dynamics and grace of the sport. You can have your picture taken with a lifelike cutout of your favorite star.

Other highlights include a look at how uniforms and equipment have changed over the years and a peek at what it is like inside an actual locker room, with displays of the locker contents of some of today's superstars.

On the more cultural side, head for the complex known as the Quadrangle, where four museums are clustered around a green at State and Chestnut Streets. The George Walter Vincent Smith Art Museum offers European and Oriental decorative arts, the Connecticut Valley Historical Museum features period rooms and antiques plus collections of glass, pewter, and silver, and the Museum of Fine Arts has paintings and sculpture by American and European artists. The Springfield Science Museum features an African hall and a dinosaur hall, exhibits on early aviation, and a planetarium, along with nature exhibits.

The Springfield Armory, the inspiration for Longfellow's poem *The Arsenal at Springfield,* is a National Historic Site, with a unique collec-

tion of small arms through the centuries. And if you want to stroll an
urban pocket of choice Victoriana, walk over to Mattoon Street, two
blocks east of Main. The tree-shaded, cobblestone block with its old-
fashioned streetlights also has been listed on the National Register of
Historic Places.

Springfield has its share of hotels and motels, in the city or in West
Springfield, convenient to the Craftfair, but you might well prefer to
move on to the charming small towns that are home to its well-known
"Five Colleges." Two good reasons to be here are the attractive bed-
and-breakfast inns in the area and the variety of restaurants, from old
New England to trendy ethnic.

You also get a cross section of architecture on these handsome campuses. In Amherst, there's Amherst College, with its traditional halls of
ivy and its picture-book green, plus the mammoth, modern University
of Massachusetts and the rustic buildings of Hampshire College. Old
and new manage to mix nicely along the quadrangles of Smith, in
Northampton, and Mount Holyoke, in South Hadley. Both of these fine
women's colleges, along with Amherst, offer excellent art galleries on
campus.

Hampshire College has a unique offering, the National Yiddish Book
Center, an institution formed with a mission to preserve this vanishing
classic literature. The striking $7.9 million building, opened in 1997, is
designed to resemble a 19th-century Eastern European shtetl. A series
of exhibition rooms trace the history of Yiddish culture and many special programs are offered, including translations of Yiddish short stories
that are broadcast over National Public Radio.

Northampton's Main Street is the place for gallery hopping as well
as admiring architecture. Listed on the National Register of Historic
Places, the street offers a sampling of Victorian styles. The library holds
memorabilia of former resident Calvin Coolidge. Up the hill, at the top
of Main Street, Smith campus highlights include a stroll along Paradise
Pond, a stop to see the rare plants at the Lyman Plant House, and a look
into the Museum of Art for works by Picasso, Degas, Seurat, and other
masters.

One unique attraction on Main Street is the Words and Pictures
Museum, a project of the locally based creators of the Ninja Turtles. It
features sequential art, comic books, and graphic novels. You can
become a comic book artist yourself, playing with the words and pictures that tell your story.

For a look into the past, visit Historic Northampton, three homes
spanning the years from 1730 to 1813 plus a modern education center.
The museum's wide-ranging collections include more than 10,000 photographs, documents and manuscripts from the seventeenth to the twentieth centuries, fine art, furniture, ceramics, glass, metal, tools, and a
fine collection of textiles and costumes.

Neighboring towns have their own attractions. Deerfield, just a few miles north of Northampton, is one of the loveliest old New England towns and offers more than a dozen beautifully furnished museum-homes (see page 204 for more details). The 1813 Dickinson Homestead, in Amherst, where Emily Dickinson was born and lived most of her life, will surely interest those who admire her poetry. And Skinner State Park, in Hadley, the town between Northampton and Amherst, offers hiking trails and fabulous views from its summit. This is the vista that caused Swedish singer Jenny Lind to declare the Pioneer Valley "the Paradise of America." In June, masses of flowering mountain laurel add to the beauty of the park.

For shopping, Northampton is definitely the place. Thorne's Marketplace, at 150 Main, is a period department store that was transformed into boutiques and restaurants without losing the curved stairways, high tin ceilings, and shining wood floors of the original building. There are four antiques shops, including the multidealer Antique Center of Northampton, within a few yards of each other on Market Street.

But fine crafts are the real lure in this artisans' haven, and more than a dozen galleries beckon to show off their work. Some choice stops are Pinch Pottery, 179 Main, where Leslie Ferrin's creative ceramics, including some wonderfully whimsical teapots, are featured, and the Don Muller Gallery, 40 Main, with a spectrum of crafts. Even the contemporary showcases here are handmade. Silverscape Designs, 1 King Street, features work by dozens of jewelry artisans, and other crafts as well, housed in a dramatically restored bank with a glowing stained glass skylight and the original marble and brass teller's booth intact. Skera, 221 Main Street, offers wearable art—beautiful handmade clothing. The rest of the galleries include everything from handwoven contemporary rugs to American Indian art to handblown goblets.

It's a weekend to send you home with a new appreciation of the fine craftspeople who are keeping the artistry of American handcrafts alive and well. And if you don't return with an original souvenir, it certainly won't be for lack of choice. You might even turn out to be the first person on your block who owns an orrery.

Area Code: 413

DRIVING DIRECTIONS Springfield can be reached via I-91 from north or south and from east or west via the Massachusetts Turnpike, I-90. The Eastern States Exposition Center is off I-91 at exit 3. Northampton is 20 miles farther north off I-91. Springfield is about 90 miles from Boston, 150 miles from New York, and 26 miles from Hartford.

PUBLIC TRANSPORTATION Amtrak serves Springfield and may be offering special fares to the Craftfair with bus shuttle service from the station. Several major airlines fly into Bradley International Airport, which serves Hartford-Springfield; Greyhound, Peter Pan, and Vermont Transit provide bus service.

ACCOMMODATIONS   Hampton Inn, 1080 Riverdale Street, West Springfield 01089, 785-5365, I–M • **Days Inn,** 437 Riverdale Street, West Springfield 01089, 785-5365, I–M • **Springfield Marriott Hotel,** 1500 Main Street, Springfield 01115, 781-7111, E • **Sheraton Springfield Monarch Place,** 1 Monarch Place, Springfield 01104, 781-1010, M • **Lord Jeffrey Inn,** on the Common, Amherst 01002, 253-2576, the classic college inn, M–E • **Hotel Northampton,** 36 King Street, Northampton 01060, 584-3100, refurbished 1927 town landmark, centrally located, M–EE • **Autumn Inn,** 259 Elm Street, Northampton 01060, 584-7660, pleasant motel near Smith campus, M • **The Inn at Northampton,** U.S. Route 5 and I-91, Northampton 01060, motel with indoor and outdoor pools, tennis court. See also Deerfield listings, page 210. *Bed-and-breakfast inns:* **The Saltbox,** 153 Elm Street, Northampton 01060, 584-1790, charmingly furnished 18th century home across from Smith College campus, M, CP • **Clark Tavern Inn,** 98 Bay Road, Hadley 01035, 586-1900, authentically restored and furnished early 1700s Colonial, pool and lovely grounds, M, CP • **Allen House,** 599 Main Street, Amherst 01002, 253-5000, meticulously restored 1886 Victorian with period furnishings, I–M, CP • **Black Walnut Inn,** 1184 Pleasant Street, Amherst 01002, stately Federal-style brick home, circa 1821, good facilities for families, M, CP • **Hannah Dudley House,** 114 Dudleyville Road, Leverett, 01054 (12 miles from Amherst) 367-2323, 1797 homestead with six fireplaces, expansive wooded grounds, ponds, E, CP.

DINING   *Springfield:* Storrowton Tavern, 1305 Memorial Avenue, Eastern States Exposition Grounds, Exposition Road (off Route 147), West Springfield, 732-4188, 1795 tavern, M–E • **Hofbrauhaus,** 1105 Main Street, West Springfield, 737-4905, long-established German, Old World atmosphere, M–E • **Student Prince and Fort,** 8 Fort Street, Springfield, 734-7475, German, with interesting collection of beer steins, I–M • **Tavern Inn Restaurant,** 91 West Gardner Street, Springfield, 781-2882, near the Basketball Hall of Fame, sports decor, I. *Northampton:* **Green Street Café,** 64 Green Street, 586-5650, bistro with European flavor, original art on the walls, fine American menu, M–E • **Eastside Grill,** 19 Strong Avenue, 586-3347, Cajun specialties, very popular, I–M • **Spoleto,** 50 Main Street, 586-6313, creative Italian, I–M • **Wiggins Tavern,** Hotel Northampton (see above), 200-year-old tavern, New England specialties, M–E • **Spaghetti Freddy's at the Depot,** 125A Pleasant Street, 586-5366, in the restored Victorian train station, good pasta at good prices, I–M • **Fitzwilly's,** 23 Main Street, 584-8666, longtime local gathering spot in the building where Calvin Coolidge practiced law, I–M • **India House,** 45 State Street, 586-6344, tandoori specialties, I • **Paul and Elizabeth's,** 150 Main Street (in Thorne's Market), 584-4832, local vegetarian favorite, I–M • **La Cazuela,** 7 Old South Street, 586-0400, Mexican and Southwestern dishes, I–M • **The Northampton Brewery,** 11 Brewster Court, 584-4176, brew-pub in a former stable, very popular, I–M. *Other Choices:* **Lord Jeffrey Inn** (see above), formal atmosphere, M–E • **Judie's,** 51 North Pleasant Street, Amherst, 253-3491, pleasant, informal, almost everyone's favorite spot in town, M • **La Cucina Di Pinocchio,** 20 Boltwood Walk, Amherst, 256-4110, excellent northern Italian, wide menu, I–M • **Seasons,** 529 Belchertown Road, Amherst, 253-9909, airy former barn, country views, eclectic menu, M • **Squires' Smoke and Game Club,** 132 Main Street (Route 9), Williamsburg (about six miles west of Northampton), 268-7222, smoked and grill specialties in a former factory on the Mill River, M–E • **Yankee Pedlar Inn,** 1866 Northampton Street, Holyoke, 532-9494, Colonial ambience, longtime favorite in the area, M • **The Log Cabin,** Route 141, Easthampton Road, Holyoke, 536-7700, rustic setting and fine views, continental and American dishes, M. For lunch in Amherst, try **The Black Sheep Deli,** 79 Main Street; in Northampton, try **Curtis & Schwartz,** 116 Main Street, or the **Coolidge Park Café,** at the Hotel Northampton. See also Deerfield listings, page 210.

SIGHTSEEING **American Craft Council Craftfair,** Eastern States Exposition Center, West Springfield, 736-3003, usually mid-June; for current dates and rates, contact American Craft Enterprises, 21 South Eltings Corner Road, Highland, NY 12528, (914) 883-6100 or (800) 836-3470 • **Basketball Hall of Fame,** 1150 West Columbus Avenue, 781-6500. Hours: daily, 9 A.M. to 5 P.M., July to Labor Day, to 6 P.M. $$$$ • **Springfield Library and Museums,** the Quadrangle, State and Chestnut Streets, 739-3871, four museums. Hours: Wednesday to Sunday, noon to 4 P.M. $$ • **Springfield Armory National Historic Site,** One Armory Square, 734-8551. Hours: Memorial Day to Labor Day, Tuesday to Sunday, 10 A.M. to 5 P.M.; rest of year, Wednesday to Sunday, 10 A.M. to 5 P.M. Free • **Mead Art Gallery,** Amherst College, 542-2335. Hours: Monday to Friday, 10 A.M. to 4:30 P.M.; weekends, 1 P.M. to 5 P.M.; closed in August. Free • **Smith College Museum of Art,** Elm Street, Northampton, 585-2760. Hours: September through June, Tuesday, Friday, and Saturday, 9:30 A.M. to 4 P.M., Wednesday and Sunday, noon to 4 P.M., Thursday, noon to 8 P.M.; July and August, Tuesday to Sunday, noon to 4 P.M. (hours change, best to confirm). Free • **Words and Pictures Museum,** 244 Main Street, Northampton, 586-8545. Hours: Tuesday to Sunday, noon to 5 P.M. $$ • **Historic Northampton,** 46 Bridge Street, Northampton, 584-6011. Hours: tour of three historic homes, March through December, Wednesday to Sunday, noon to 4 P.M. $$ • **Skinner State Park,** Route 47, Hadley, 586-0350. Hours: daily, dawn to dusk. Summit House open weekends May to October • **His-**

toric Deerfield, PO Box 321, Deerfield, MA 10342, 774-5581. Hours: daily, 9:30 A.M. to 4:30 P.M. $$$$ • **Dickinson Homestead,** 280 Main Street, Amherst, 542-8161. Hours: May to October, Wednesday through Saturday, tours by advance reservation offered every 45 minutes from 1:30 P.M. to 3:45 P.M.; March, April, November, to mid-December, Wednesday and Saturday only. $$ • **National Yiddish Book Center,** Weinberg Building, Hampshire College, Amherst, (800) 535-3595. Hours: Daily except Saturday, 10 A.M. to 3:30 P.M. Free.

INFORMATION Greater Springfield Convention and Visitors' Bureau, 34 Boland Way, Springfield, MA 01103, 787-1548 or (800) 723-1548; Greater Northampton Chamber of Commerce, 99 Pleasant Street, Northampton, MA 01060, 584-1900.

Savoring the Shore in Connecticut

Early in June, when ringing cheers send off the annual Yale-Harvard regatta on the Thames River in New London, the oarsmen will be following the same historic river route that once took clipper ships out to sea.

Connecticut's upper shoreline, the focal point for much of the state's early history, is a three-century treasury of seafaring lore from the days of masted schooners to today's nuclear submarines.

But despite its salty attractions and the presence of Mystic Seaport, America's prime maritime destination, much of the 40-mile shore area north of New Haven has remained surprisingly unspoiled. Quaint Old Lyme still owes as much of its flavor to its Colonial heritage as to its proximity to the sea. And such nautical lures as New London's Coast Guard Academy and Stonington's lighthouse and fishing fleet remain delightfully overlooked by tourist crowds.

Cruising the shore by land is a perfect outing for early June, when the old Ivy League rowing rivalry is replayed as it has been for well over 100 years. It is America's oldest intercollegiate event.

Typically, crew races are scheduled for three starting times in the afternoon, and spectators can cheer on the Crimson or the Blue from riverside viewing areas along the four-mile course. For those wishing a closer look at the excitement, there is an observation boat that offers brunch and Dixieland entertainment as well as a better view. Other festivities take place all day along the New London pier, the scene of many special events throughout the spring and summer.

The pier and its activity are signs of a city trying hard to recoup some of its illustrious past as a wealthy whaling outpost. Although New London has lost the glory of its early days, there are a few interesting sights to be seen here. A walking tour might well start at the city's pride, its lovingly restored nineteenth-century train station, designed by Henry Hobson Richardson, the architect of Boston's Trinity Church. The station stands opposite the pier, convenient for those who want to connect to ferries for Block Island or Fishers Island.

Nearby is the restored schoolhouse named for native son Nathan Hale, who taught here prior to enlisting in George Washington's army. It was moved to be accessible to visitors.

Also near the waterfront is a statue of another notable town resident, playwright Eugene O'Neill, shown here as a young boy. The Dutch Tavern, O'Neill's favorite bar, is on Green Street, just off State Street, New London's main street. His boyhood home, Monte Cristo Cottage, has been restored and can be toured. In summer, the Eugene O'Neill Theater Center, in nearby Waterford, presents play readings by promising new authors.

Next door to the O'Neill Center is Harkness Memorial Park, a 234-acre waterfront estate that hosts Summer Music, a wonderful program of classical and popular music with big-name performers. You can buy tickets for seats inside the sheltered tent or sit on the lawn and enjoy a picnic under the stars. A picnic buffet is served on the grounds but must be ordered in advance.

New London's other landmarks include the 1833 Customs House, America's oldest operating customs house, whose front door was once part of the frigate *Constitution*; it is undergoing a major restoration by New London's Maritime Society. More sights to see are the Shaw-Perkins Mansion, U.S. naval headquarters for Connecticut during the Revolutionary War, and four columned whaling merchants' mansions known collectively as Whale Oil Row.

As you proceed south from Whale Oil Row, you'll come to Hempstead Street, with several fine old homes, including one of Connecticut's oldest, the 1678 Hempsted House, the only home that escaped the town's burning by the British in 1781.

New London's U.S. Coast Guard Academy, a cluster of handsome, traditional red-brick buildings on 100 acres high above the Thames, has inviting grounds, a well-endowed museum, and a multimedia center at river's edge that gives a comprehensive picture of the Coast Guard's role in our nation's history. The academy holds colorful formal dress parades in spring and fall; check for current dates.

There is a bonus for visitors when the *Eagle* is in port. The 295-foot square-rigger that led the nation's bicentennial parade of tall ships is a magnificent floating classroom for Coast Guard cadets each summer. When not at sea, it is usually at home in New London, available for free tours of the deck and the quarters of officers and crew.

Near the academy on Mohegan Avenue is the campus of Connecticut College, which includes the Lyman Allyn Art Museum, named in memory of a famous sea captain. It contains art, antiques, and a wonderful collection of dollhouses, dolls, and toys.

Also on the campus is the Connecticut College Arboretum, a particularly fine nature preserve, which offers 445 acres with hiking trails. Within the arboretum is the Science Center of Eastern Connecticut, a good bet for families for its exhibits, which include an observation beehive, reptiles, a science theater, a touch tank, and a picnic area.

Another favorite New London family attraction in summer is Ocean Beach Park, a beach with boardwalk games and rides. The small but imaginative Children's Museum of Southeastern Connecticut, in Niantic, below New London, is another pleaser, filled with hands-on exhibits, learning, and fun for everyone from toddlers to preteens. If the weather is fine, Rocky Neck State Park, in Niantic, provides a boardwalk and a half-mile crescent beach on Long Island Sound to be enjoyed by parents and kids alike.

Groton, just across the Thames from New London, is the home of the U.S. Navy submarine base, the largest of its kind in the world, providing yet another perspective on America's maritime traditions. The world's first nuclear submarine, the 320-foot *Nautilus,* was launched here in 1954. At the Historic Ship Nautilus Memorial, on the naval base, you can trace the progress of submarines from early days to the nuclear age and board that first nuclear-powered sub. Working periscopes, an authentic control room, and mini-theaters are part of the exhibits.

Fort Griswold State Battlefield Park, in Groton, marks some of the town's older historic moments. The park was the site of an important Revolutionary War battle in 1781, and the Memorial Tower and statue, on a hill overlooking the Thames, make an impressive picture. There is a small museum at the base of the tower, and the view from the top is worth every step of the climb.

New London and Groton can take one day or two, depending on your interest in nautical affairs. If you have never been to Mystic Seaport Museum, you really need another whole day for the feast of sights here: majestic wooden sailing vessels, a complete nineteenth-century village with working shops, museum buildings filled with rare boats, models of ships, figureheads, scrimshaw, marine art, and a please-touch children's museum filled with toys a sea captain's youngsters might have enjoyed.

There is much to see and do in Mystic, including a visit to the delightful penguin pavilion at the Mystic Aquarium. You may very well decide to save it for a weekend all its own.

In any event, do not omit the little towns beyond Mystic. Noank, jutting out into the west side of the Mystic River, offers spectacular views of Fishers Island Sound. The fine homes recall a time when this was a center for shipbuilding and lobstering. Later, it was an art colony, and galleries still display the work of local artists. Abbott's Lobster in the Rough here is a longtime summer favorite for outdoor dining on the shore.

Stonington, a tiny hamlet at the very edge of the shoreline, is for many the favorite destination along the shore. This wonderfully picturesque town has a Greek Revival center, a green surrounded by spired white churches, narrow streets lined with eighteenth- and nineteenth-century sea captains' homes, and a lighthouse dating to 1823 that houses a museum of village history. The view of Long Island Sound from the tower on a clear day is not to be missed.

Stonington's harbor is still crowded with working fishing boats, with many of the fishermen tracing their ancestry back to whalemen recruited in the Azores in the 1830s. Their old tradition of the blessing of the fleet continues here with a colorful ceremony in July.

North Stonington offers a unique dining opportunity, the chance to watch authentically costumed cooks preparing dinner over the open hearth at Randall's Ordinary. Their Colonial cookery is delicious, and the dinner is worth the drive. Guest rooms in the house and in the restored barn are equally authentic, though they may be a bit spare for some tastes.

Should you be feeling lucky, you can head farther inland from North Stonington for a change of pace at the Foxwoods Resort Casino, which is growing by leaps and bounds. You'll be amazed at the lavish facilities tucked away in the countryside in Ledyard, on the Mashantucket Pequot reservation. There's even a Las Vegas–style theater where big-name entertainers appear. A major Indian museum is slated to open on the grounds in 1998. Another chance to try your luck awaits on the other side of the Thames River at the newer Mohegan Sun Casino in Uncasville.

New London's best lodging is the Lighthouse Inn, the Victorian mansion of steel baron Charles S. Guthrie, near Ocean Beach Park. It has been renovated into an elegant enclave just a block from a private beach. Rich paneling and a carved spiral staircase lead to lavish guest rooms, including four huge front bedrooms with canopy beds and water views. There are rooms in an adjacent carriage house as well, and an excellent dining room. In town, the Radisson Hotel offers modern quarters within a short walk of the pier, and there is a Victorian bed-and-breakfast inn a short drive from the town's center.

If a Colonial inn is more to your taste, there are two good bets in Old Lyme, just a few miles down the shore, worthy stops for dinner as well as overnight. Whether you select the Bee and Thistle, a charming Colonial home, or the Old Lyme Inn, an 1850s mansion with an elegant French menu, you will find yourself in a very special town whose entire wide, shaded Main Street has been declared a National Historic District.

One of the finest residences on the street was the home of a pioneering American art colony. The columned Georgian mansion is known as the Florence Griswold Museum for "Miss Florence," who housed, fed, and nurtured a group of American Impressionist painters including Willard Metcalf and Childe Hassam, who developed the so-called ideal Lyme landscape that brought much attention to the area.

The house, now a National Historic Landmark, serves as headquarters for the Lyme Historical Society and contains paintings and panels left by the early artists, as well as collections of china, tools, and toys, and furnished period rooms, such as the front parlor, circa 1830. The famed dining room is lined with a double row of painted panels and furnished as it was when the artists took their meals there in the early part of this century.

The Old Lyme Art Association, next door, was founded in 1914 as a showcase for the many artists who continued to be attracted to the town, and it remains a prestigious gallery.

Another inviting lodging option a few miles down the coast, in Old Saybrook, is the Saybrook Point Inn, a stylish 62-room resort on the water with a spa and an indoor pool.

At the least, opt for lunch at the dock in Old Saybrook, watching the boats come and go. If all that nautical atmosphere makes you want to go farther out to sea, you'll find several options in the area, including shipping out on one of the windjammers, replicas of two-masted nineteenth-century schooners, that sail out of Mystic regularly for one-, two-, or five-day cruises.

Area Code: 860

DRIVING DIRECTIONS   All of the towns mentioned are on or near I-95 north of New Haven. New London is 113 miles from Boston, 125 miles from New York, and 45 miles from Hartford.

PUBLIC TRANSPORTATION   Amtrak goes to New London, Old Saybrook, and Mystic, but you'll need a rental car to get around once you arrive.

ACCOMMODATIONS   Lighthouse Inn, 6 Guthrie Place (off Pequot at Lower Boulevard, one-half mile east of Ocean Beach Park), New London 06320, 443-8411, M–EE, CP • **Radisson Hotel,** 35 Governor Winthrop Boulevard and Union Street, New London 06320, 443-7000, indoor pool, M–E • **Queen Anne Inn,** (with afternoon tea), 265 Williams Street, New London 06320,. 447-2600, Victorian B & B, M–E, CP • **Clarion Inn,** 1567 Kings Highway, Groton 06340, 446-0660, pleasant motel, indoor pool, M • **Sojourner Inn,** Route 184, Groton 06340, 445-1986 or (800) MY SUITE, all-suite motel with kitchenettes, good family choice, M–EE, CP • **Bee and Thistle Inn,** 100 Lyme Street, Old Lyme 06371, 434-1667, M–E, CP • **Old Lyme Inn,**

85 Lyme Street, Old Lyme 06371, 434-2600, M–E, CP • **Saybrook Point Inn,** 2 Bridge Street, Old Saybrook 06475, 395-2000, E–EE; ask about weekend packages. See pages 243–244 for Mystic listings.

DINING **Lighthouse Inn** (see above), elegant, with water views, E • **Timothy's,** 18 Bank Street, 437-0526, American and continental dishes, M–E • **Ye Olde Tavern Steak and Chop House,** 345 Bank Street, New London, 442-0353, old-timer, maritime decor, steak and seafood, I–E • **The Pocket,** 64 Bank Street, New London, 442-5711, good choice for lunch, I • **Diana,** 970 Fashion Plaza, Poquonnock Road, Groton, 449-8468, change of pace, Lebanese decor and menu, highly rated, M • **Mangia, Mangia at the Morton House,** 215 Main Street, Niantic, 739-9074, Italian, steaks and seafood, M • **Randall's Ordinary,** Route 2, North Stonington, 599-4540, authentic Colonial fireplace cookery. Be sure to reserve ahead; there is only one seating nightly, prix fixe, EE • **Bee and Thistle Inn** (see above), M–E • **Old Lyme Inn** (see above), M–EE • **Saybrook Point Inn** (see above), M–E • **Dock & Dine,** Main and College Streets, Saybrook Point, Old Saybrook, 388-4665, informal seafood spot, unbeatable water views, outdoor terrace in warm weather, M–E. Also see Mystic listings, page 244.

SIGHTSEEING **Yale-Harvard Regatta,** early June. Contact the tourism district office listed below for dates and current information on special events • **U.S. Coast Guard Academy,** Mohegan Avenue, New London, 444-8270. Hours: Visitors' Pavilion open May through October, daily, 10 A.M. to 5 P.M. Museum open year-round, Monday to Friday, 9 A.M. to 4:30 P.M.; Saturday, 10 A.M. to 5 P.M.; Sunday, 1 P.M. to 5 P.M. *Eagle* ship tours (when in port), Friday, Saturday, Sunday, noon to 5 P.M. Free. Write or call the academy for schedules for the *Eagle,* cadet dress parades, and Coast Guard Band concerts • **Shaw-Perkins Mansion,** 305 Bank Street, New London, 443-1209. Hours: May through October, Wednesday to Friday, 1 P.M. to 4 P.M.; Saturday, 10 A.M. to 4 P.M. $$ • **Nathan Hale Schoolhouse,** Union Plaza, New London, 443-8331. By appointment. Free • **Hempsted House,** 11 Hempstead Street, New London, 443-7949. Hours: May 15 to October 15, Thursday to Sunday, noon to 4 P.M. $$ • **Connecticut College Arboretum,** Connecticut College Campus, Williams Street, New London, 439-2140. Hours: daily during daylight hours; free tours, May through October, Sunday, 2 P.M. Free • **Science Center of Eastern Connecticut,** 33 Gallows Lane, New London, 442-0391. Hours: Tuesday to Saturday, 10 A.M. to 4 P.M. $$ • **Lyman Allyn Art Museum,** 625 Williams Street (near college), New London, 443-2545. Hours: September through June, Tuesday to Sunday, 1 P.M. to 5 P.M.; July to Labor Day, Tuesday to Saturday, 10 A.M. to 5 P.M., Sunday, 1 P.M. to 5 P.M. $$ • **Monte Cristo Cottage,** 325 Pequot Avenue, New London, 443-0051. Hours: Memorial Day to Labor Day, Tuesday through Saturday,

10 A.M. to 5 P.M.; Sunday, 1 P.M. to 4 P.M.; rest of year by appointment. $$ • **Ocean Beach Park,** Ocean Avenue, New London, 447-3031. Hours: Memorial Day to Labor Day, daily, 9 A.M. to 10 P.M. Parking: $ per hour, $$$$ maximum. Walk-in fees: nonresident adults and children, $ • **Harkness Memorial State Park,** 275 Great Neck Road (Route 213), Waterford, 443-5725. Hours: mansion has been closed for renovation; when completed, it will be open daily, Memorial Day to Labor Day, 10 A.M. to 5 P.M.; grounds open all year. Memorial Day to Labor Day parking fee, $$; rest of year, free. Summer Music Concert information: (800) 969-3400 • **Eugene O'Neill Theater Center,** 305 Great Neck Road, Waterford 06385, 443-5378. Performances in July and August; phone for schedules • **Historic Ship Nautilus and Submarine Force Museum,** U.S. Naval Submarine Base, Crystal Lake Road, Groton, 449-3174. Hours: May 15 to October 31, Wednesday to Monday, 9 A.M. to 5 P.M., Tuesday, 1 P.M. to 5 P.M.; rest of year, Wednesday to Monday, 9 A.M. to 4 P.M., closed Tuesday. Free • **Ft. Griswold Battlefield State Park,** Monument Street and Park Avenue, Groton, 445-1729. Hours: park open daily, dawn to dusk; museum and monument, Memorial Day to Labor Day, daily, 10 A.M. to 4 P.M., Labor Day to Columbus Day, weekends only. Free • **Groton Monument and Monument House,** Memorial Day to Labor Day, daily, 10 A.M. to 5 P.M.; Labor Day to mid-October, weekends only. Free • **Children's Museum of Southeastern Connecticut,** 409 Main Street, Niantic, 691-1255. Hours: Tuesday to Saturday, 9:30 A.M. to 4:30 P.M., Sunday, noon to 5 P.M.; also open Monday from Memorial Day to Labor Day and during school vacations. $$ • **Mystic Seaport,** 75 Greenmanville Avenue, Mystic, 572-5315. Hours: spring and fall, daily, 9 A.M. to 5 P.M.; summer months, to 8 P.M.; winter hours, daily, 10 A.M. to 4 P.M. $$$$$ • **Mystic Marinelife Aquarium,** 55 Coogan Boulevard, Mystic, 572-5955. Hours: daily, 9:00 A.M. to 5 P.M.; summer months, to 7 P.M. $$$$$ • **Florence Griswold Museum,** 96 Lyme Street, 434-5542. Hours: June to October, Tuesday to Saturday, 10 A.M. to 5 P.M.; Sunday, 1 P.M. to 5 P.M.; rest of year, Wednesday to Sunday, 1 P.M. to 5 P.M. $$ • **Lyme Art Association,** 90 Lyme Street, 434-7802. Hours: May to December, Tuesday to Saturday, noon to 4:30 P.M.; Sunday, 1 P.M. to 4:30 P.M.; call for schedule rest of year. $ • **Rocky Neck State Park,** Route 156, Niantic, 739-5471. Hours: daily, 8 A.M. to sunset; Memorial Day to Labor Day parking fee: weekdays, CT cars, $$; out-of-state cars, $$$; weekends, CT cars, $$$; out-of-state cars, $$$$$; rest of year, free. **Casinos: Foxwoods Resort Casino,** Route 2, Ledyard, (800) PLAY-BIG; **Mohegan Sun Casino,** Mohegan Sun Boulevard, Uncasville, 226-7711. *Boat trips:* Check current schedules and rates. **Captain John's Sportfishing Center,** 15 First Street, Waterford, 443-7259, deep-sea fishing, nature and lighthouse cruises; **Project Oceanology,** Avery Point, Groton, 445-9007 or (800) 364-8472, educational cruises aboard the Enviro-Lab; **Voyager Cruises,** Steamboat

Wharf, Mystic, 536-0416, sailing excursions; steamboat *Sabino* and schooner *Brilliant,* Mystic Seaport, 572-5315. **Windjammers:** *Mystic Whaler,* Mystic, (800) 697-8420; **Sylvina W. Beal,** Mystic, (800) 333-Mystic; **Voyager Cruises,** Mystic, 536-0416.

INFORMATION   Southeastern Connecticut Tourism District, PO Box 89, 470 Bank Street, New London, CT 06320, 444-2206 or (800) TO ENJOY.

Exploring Blooming Boston

Boston keeps getting better. From the cobbled streets of Beacon Hill to the gleaming marble of Copley Place, from the Victorian boulevards of Back Bay to the bustling waterfront, this is a town that has retained the best of the old while adding the new in a vibrant blend few cities can match.

No city offers more diversity. Some of 350-year-old Boston remains a citadel of conservatism—quiet charm and tradition, perfectly preserved red-brick town houses, fifth-generation Brahmins, tea at 4:00 P.M., and swan boats gliding on the lake in the Public Garden as they have since 1877.

Yet today's Boston is also nonstop action—sculls and sailboats on the Charles, joggers and skaters on the Esplanade, crowds converging on the food stalls in Quincy Market, shoppers nudging to get at the bargains in Filene's Basement.

It is the city of culture—of a world-renowned symphony and Museum of Fine Arts—and a maelstrom of rabid Red Sox and Celtics fans, Irish and Italian politicos, marathoners, camera-toting tourists, schoolchildren walking the red line of the Freedom Trail, plus thousands of young people who attend 150 area colleges and universities, giving the city eternal youth.

You can't really begin to know this complex city in a weekend, but you can sample its multiple pleasures more easily than you might imagine, because central Boston is essentially a compact, walkable area where a little foot power can take you a long way. Cars are only a nuisance, since the traffic is crowded and confusing.

So "pahk your cah," as the Bostonians really do say, stop at one of the Boston Common information booths on Tremont Street or at the Prudential Center to arm yourself with a city map and information, and plan a walking tour of the neighborhoods that will show you the fascinating facets of this urban gem. If your foot power lags, just board the

"T," the efficient, easy-to-use subway system, or one of the sightseeing trolleys that make continuous loops of the city, letting you get off and reboard as often as you wish.

Boston Common, the oldest public park in America, is a beautiful introduction to the city's sights. In spring it is resplendent with magnolias in bloom.

You might begin by following Tremont Street west from the information booths, turning left on Park Street to Beacon Street and the State House, at the top of that bastion of old Boston, Beacon Hill. Samuel Adams laid the cornerstone for Charles Bulfinch's gold-domed architectural masterpiece.

To appreciate the ambience of the Hill, you need only stroll the cobbled, gaslit streets lined with rows of fine brick town houses with gleaming brass door knockers, overflowing flower boxes, and finely detailed ironwork. Take Joy Street and go left on Mt. Vernon to reach the perfect hushed pocket of the past called Louisburg Square. You can visit the inside of a typical upper-class home of the past at the Nichols House on Mt. Vernon Street.

A left turn on Pinckney behind Louisburg Square and a walk downhill will bring you to Charles Street, a choice row of antiques shops, cafés, and coffeehouses leading back to Beacon Street.

The corner of Beacon and Charles Streets is of special note, both as the departure point for the British on their fateful expedition to Lexington and Concord and as the very spot where Officer O'Malley held up traffic to make way for the eight ducklings of Mrs. Mallard on their way to the Public Garden in Robert McCloskey's timeless children's tale. A detour to see the garden in its springtime prime, with a ride on the famous swan boats on the pond, is highly recommended. A sculpture commemorates the famous ducklings.

Walk to the right for two blocks on Beacon beside the garden to Arlington and across the Arthur Fiedler Memorial Bridge to reach the Esplanade, then pause to watch the activity on the Charles River and the promenade beside it. The Hatch Memorial Shell is the site of summer serenades by the Boston Pops Orchestra, and the space around it is a spot favored by joggers, skaters, and people watchers. You can see the domes of MIT just across the Charles in Cambridge, the town that is also the home of the splendid Harvard campus.

From here you can tour another handsome side of Boston by returning past Beacon to Marlborough or Commonwealth and turning right to follow the eight alphabetical streets from Arlington to Hereford through the Back Bay.

Boston was a lot hillier before the Back Bay was developed. Henry James once used the word *odiferous* to describe this 450-acre oozy swampland, which later was filled with soil leveled off from some of the hills. What emerged over a period of some 125 years was a model of nineteenth-century architecture in a green setting by Frederick Law Olmsted. Commonwealth, a parade of stately stone Victorian row houses with a wide grassy mall in the center, is the grandest street. Marlborough is simpler and greener, and some like it even better.

The alphabetical streets stop past Hereford at Massachusetts Avenue. A couple of blocks beyond is Kenmore Square, a gathering place for students from Boston University, which runs farther southwest along the river. To the east, near a park called the Fenway and Fenway Park, home to Boston's beloved Red Sox, are Simmons and Northeastern Colleges. The Boston Museum of Fine Arts, which houses one of the nation's outstanding collections of French Impressionist and American art, is in the same neighborhood. The Manets in the Impressionist Gallery are fabulous.

In this same area is the Isabella Stewart Gardner Museum, an extra-ordinary palazzo with a four-story, glass-enclosed courtyard built by an eccentric collector to hold her treasures, which include Italian Renais-sance masterpieces, Rembrandts, and works by Rubens, Degas, and Matisse.

Return on the other side of Commonwealth Avenue, away from the river, along Newbury and Boylston, Boston's traditional shopping streets. The Prudential Center, at Boylston and Hereford, was built over what was once the Boston trainyard and is now the Massachusetts Turnpike. There is lots of shopping here, including department stores like Lord and Taylor and Saks Fifth Avenue. The Prudential Tower Sky-walk offers a stunning 360-degree view of the city.

The "Pru" is now connected by overpass to the Hynes Convention Center and across busy Huntington Avenue to Copley Place, with a lineup of more posh stores. Walk through the Copley Place arcade and out through the Westin Hotel lobby and you will emerge on Copley Square, another city landmark, surrounded by the Boston library, Trinity Church, and one of the city's grande-dame hotels, the Copley Plaza. Don't fail to stop in the Public Library to see the art treasures and the glorious courtyard in this Beaux Arts treasure by the renowned architec-tural firm of McKim, Mead, and White. There is another soaring city view to be had at the top of the John Hancock Tower, off Copley Square.

From Copley Square, follow Dartmouth Street west two blocks to Newbury for the best of the shops and galleries, stretching four blocks back to the Public Garden at Arlington. The Louis of Boston store, in the former Museum of Natural History, is among the local landmarks, and its Café Louis is a chic stop for lunch or dinner. There are also many sidewalk cafés on Newbury to provide a resting place for weary sightseers. Sonsie and the Emporio Armani Express are cafés for those who want to see and be seen, better for people watching than dining.

At the corner of Newbury and Arlington, opposite the Public Gar-den, is the Ritz Carlton, a Boston landmark since 1927. The Ritz retains its attentive Old World service, and afternoon tea and the legendary lavish Sunday brunch are Boston traditions, along with dancing on the roof terrace.

But the title of "best in Boston" has passed on to the Four Seasons, located around the corner on Boylston Street and also facing the Public Garden. Newer and more lavish, this is the city's only five-diamond establishment, and it offers service that is both impeccable and friendly, along with every luxury from an indoor pool to free morning limousine service to downtown. The Aujourd'hui restaurant here is widely considered the city's best.

This is more than enough to fill a wonderful day, with stops at the many shops and sights along the way, but the Downtown Crossing must be squeezed in on Saturday if you want to have a look at another Boston institution, Filene's Basement. It is a 15-minute walk—or just a hop if you board the "T" at Arlington and Boylston. Get off at Park Street, turn right when you emerge, and cross Tremont to Winter Street and the stores. Filene's and Macy's are both one block away on the corner, where Winter and Summer Streets intersect with Washington—a pedestrians-only crossing that is the busiest intersection in New England. The scene is further enlivened by colorful wooden pushcarts filled with all kinds of wares and by impromptu entertainment by street musicians.

The famous Filene's bargain basement is nothing like the clones that have appeared in other cities. It is frequently a madhouse. The longer merchandise remains, the lower the markdown; aficionados watch the action day by day like brokers on Wall Street, waiting for the perfect moment to buy. On any given day, a new batch of bargains may arrive —anything from designer clothing to Oriental rugs—to be fought over by eager customers. There are few dressing rooms, so many customers simply try on merchandise on the selling floor. Even if you don't want to participate, it is definitely a major only-in-Boston sight.

On Washington Street to the right of all this shopping activity is the "combat zone," Boston's adult entertainment district. Go left on Washington, and at the corner of School Street you will run right into history: the Old South Meeting House, a center of pre-Revolutionary agitation; the Old Corner Bookstore, once a gathering place for Emerson, Hawthorne, and other literary greats; the old City Hall and the Old State House, the seat of Colonial government.

Less than a block away on the left is the Government Center, a curving red-brick plaza and its showpiece, the Boston City Hall. When it was completed in the late 1960s and early 1970s, some considered the center controversial for its modernity; others find that it blends pleasingly with its historic neighbors. You be the judge.

You can combine this last group of historic sites with a leisurely look at the waterfront and the North End on Sunday, either by following the orderly red lines of the Freedom Trail—the road marking events leading up to the American Revolution—or by making your own way and watching for the sights. On your own, start at the Government Center. A walk down the steps and across the street will bring you to Faneuil Hall, site of many town meetings at which impassioned patriots planned their fight for liberty.

Beyond is the Faneuil Hall Marketplace, composed of three long buildings. You can literally eat your way through the domed Quincy Market, in the center, which is filled with a heavenly assortment of food stands offering just about every edible you can imagine. The food market is flanked by cafés and the North and South Market buildings, with dozens of shops plus lots of pushcart wares, a flower market, and the Haymarket, an open-air produce exchange. All of this occurs in a festive setting of cobbled walks, bright banners, and clowns, mimes, and musicians that attracts more than a million people a month. You'll find plenty of places here for a pleasant brunch, or you can do-it-yourself at the various food stands.

On the booming Boston waterfront, there are many things to see and do, including the fun-filled New England Aquarium and cruises in the harbor. For more details on some of the harbor attractions and other city sights, see "Bringing the Kids to Boston," page 232.

To complete a look at the city, you'll want to proceed beyond Quincy Market via a pedestrian tunnel under the Fitzgerald Expressway at Hanover Street and into the North End, Boston's "Little Italy." (The expressway will be disappearing in the next few years in a major redevelopment plan, the $5 billion Central Artery Project that will include an eight- to ten-lane underground expressway and a four-lane tunnel connecting directly to Logan Airport; meanwhile, expect extensive construction.)

There is a European feeling to the North End's old residential area of brick houses and narrow streets, and dozens of tempting stops in Italian bakeries, coffee shops, and restaurants. A few blocks from the start of Hanover Street, a right on Richmond will bring you to the Paul Revere House, and a few blocks farther is the Old North Church, the city's oldest, where lanterns in the steeple were the signal for Revere's famous ride.

If you follow the Freedom Trail all the way to Charlestown, you can board "Old Ironsides," otherwise known as the USS *Constitution*, the oldest commissioned warship afloat in the world, and wind up at the site of Bunker Hill, the first battle of the Revolution, marked by a 220-foot monument with a stunning view of the city from the top. Going from the Old North Church to Bunker Hill will add $2\frac{1}{2}$ miles to your route.

Having seen most of central Boston, you still haven't explored its cultural treasures, such as the Museum of Fine Arts or the Isabella Stewart Gardner Museum, the excellent Museum of Science, and the special architecture of the Christian Science Center. Nor have you paid a visit to Cambridge, or visited the very moving Kennedy Memorial

Library Museum on Dorchester Bay, or had the unforgettable experience of hearing the fanatic fans at Fenway Park. And one weekend can't begin to take in all the nighttime attractions—theater, ballet at the handsomely restored Wang Center for the Performing Arts, symphony and opera, sports, and all the other forms of music and entertainment that a city full of sophisticates and college students regularly attracts.

There is always something more to do in Boston, and in recent years, something new to see, almost every time you go back. But chief among its pleasures is the activity that never palls no matter how many times it is repeated—strolling the neighborhoods that preserve the past in a blooming contemporary city.

Area Code: 617

DRIVING DIRECTIONS   From north or south, take I-93/3 or I-95; also from the north, Route 1, 1A, or 128. From the west, take I-90, the Massachusetts Turnpike, or Route 2, 9, or 20. Boston is 98 miles from Hartford and 208 miles from New York.

PUBLIC TRANSPORTATION   Boston can be reached by Amtrak, most major bus lines, and most airlines. Cars are only a nuisance in the city. Cabs, subways, a water ferry, and shuttle buses serve the airport, and the downtown transit system is excellent. For Airport Water Shuttle information, call 439-3131 or (800) 23-LOGAN.

ACCOMMODATIONS   So many possibilities, so few low prices! Almost all hotels do offer weekend packages at greatly reduced rates. This is a selective listing in descending order of price. When you inquire about current packages, find out whether parking is included—parking can cost $20 a day! *The luxury choices:* **Four Seasons Hotel,** 200 Boylston Street, 02116, 338-4400 or (800) 332-3442, elegant top choice, admirable service, health club and pool, EE • **Ritz Carlton,** 15 Arlington Street, 02117, 536-5700 or (800) 225-7620, still the epitome of Boston graciousness, EE • **Le Meridien,** 250 Franklin Street, 02110, 451-1900, stunning hotel in old Federal Reserve Bank building, EE. *On the waterfront:* **Boston Harbor Hotel,** 70 Rowes Wharf, 02110, 439-7000 or (800) 752-7577, posh, formal, great views, EE • **Bostonian,** Faneuil Hall Marketplace, 02109, 523-3600 or (800) 343-0922, tasteful, EE • **Marriott Long Wharf,** 296 State Street, 02109, 227-0800, striking contemporary, E–EE. *Back Bay:* **Colonnade,** 120 Huntington Avenue, 02116, 424-7000, small, low-key, elegant, EE (excellent weekend rates) • **Copley Plaza,** 138 St. James Avenue, Copley Square, 02116, 267-5300 or (800) 826-7539, nicely restored landmark, sometimes busy with conventions, E–EE • **Copley Square,** 47 Huntington Avenue, 02116, 536-9000 or (800) 225-7062, E • **Boston Park Plaza,** 64 Arlington Street (at Park Plaza), 02117, 426-2000 or (800) 225-

2008, big, convenient, good weekend packages, M–EE • **Newbury Guest House,** 261 Newbury Street, 02116, 437-7666 or (800) 437-7668, town houses converted to inn, modest but good price and location, M–E, CP • **Copley Inn,** 19 Garrison Street, 236-0300 or (800) 232-0306, small, modest, kitchenettes, well located and priced, M • **Elliot and Pickett Houses,** 6 Mt. Vernon Place, 248-9707, guest houses in 1830s town houses in fine Beacon Hill location, help-yourself breakfasts, shared and private baths, great value, M • **Howard Johnson** has three city locations, all M–E, not great but with reasonable weekend packages: **57 Park Plaza Hotel,** 200 Stuart Street, 02116, 482-1800, pool; **Howard Johnson Motor Lodge Fenway,** 1271 Boylston Street, 02215, 267-8300, and **Howard Johnson Hotel-Kenmore,** 575 Commonwealth Avenue, 02215, 267-3100. Really limited budgets call for motels in outlying areas, such as **Susse Chalet Inn Boston/Neponset,** 800 Morrissey Boulevard, Neponset 02122, 287-9200, M • **Days Inn-Newton,** 399 Grove Street, Newton 02162, 527-9000, I–M • **American Youth Hostels,** 12 Hemenway Street, 536-9455, dorm accommodations, I. *Bed-and-breakfast reservation services:* Many choices in Boston; see full listing on page xii.

DINING *Gourmet choices:* **Aujourd'hui,** Four Seasons Hotel (see above), superb, EE • **Ritz Carlton Dining Room** (see above), famous Sunday brunch, EE • **L'Espalier,** 30 Gloucester Street, 262-3023, romantic, top-rated food, prix fixe, EE • **Julien,** Le Meridien (see above), Old World ambience, continental menu, EE • **Seasons,** Bostonian Hotel (see above), EE • **Rowe's Wharf,** Boston Harbor Hotel (see above), elegant American menu, harbor views, M–EE • **Biba,** 272 Boylston Street, 426-7878, owner Lydia Shire is a culinary star, uniquely colorful decor, M–EE • **Hamersley's Bistro,** 553 Tremont Street, 423-2700, "nouvelle American," very popular, M–EE • **Café Louis,** 234 Berkeley Street, 266-4680, handsome decor, contemporary French cuisine, E–EE • **Ambrosia on Huntington,** 116 Huntington Avenue, 247-2400, French-Asian blend in a splendid setting, M–EE. *More locally recommended choices:* **Icarus,** 3 Appleton Street (South End), 426-1790, innovative American cuisine, live jazz in the bar, M–EE • **Grill 23,** 161 Berkeley Street, 542-2255, power scene, steaks-martinis-cigars crowd, M–EE • **Capital Grille,** 359 Newbury Street, 262-8900, more men's club ambience and thick steaks, M–E • **Hungry I,** 71½ Charles Street, 227-3524, French, romantic quarters in Beacon Hill town house, M–E • **Pignoli,** 79 Park Plaza, 338-7500, Lydia Shire's newest venture, "new Italian," M–E • **Ristorante Toscano,** 421 Charles Street, 723-4090, fine northern Italian, M–E • **Galleria Italiana,** 177 Tremont Street, 423-2092, much praised Italian, cozy, popular for breakfast and lunch as well as pre-theater dinner, M • **Elephant Walk,** 900 Beacon Street, 247-1500, highly rated French and Cambodian food, I–M • **Lala Rokh,** 97 Mt. Vernon Street, 720-5511, change-of-pace Persian cuisine, attractive intimate quarters, M • **Cottonwood Café,** 222 Berkeley Street, 247-2225, Southwestern fare, popular Boston version of a Cambridge favorite, M • **Skipjack's,** 199 Clarendon Street, 536-3500, casual, good seafood at reasonable prices, M • **Brew Moon Restaurant and Microbrewery,** 115 Stuart Street, 523-6467, cutting edge food to pair with excellent beers, I–M. *South End choices (this gentrifying neighborhood attracts a hip, young crowd):* **Jae's Café and Grill,** 520 Columbus Avenue, 421-9405, excellent Asian specialties, I–M • **Mistral,** 221 Columbus Avenue, 867-9300, former Aujourd'hui chef is a hit in smashing new quarters, M–EE • **Claremont Café,** 535 Columbus Avenue, 247-9001, informal bistro, eclectic menu, M. *North End Italian choices:* **Pomodoro,** 319 Hanover Street, 867-4348, creative menu, lots of fans, I–M • **Felicia's,** 145A Richmond, 523-9885, old-timer, basic red-sauce Italian, I–M • **Mama Maria's,** 3 North Square (at Little Prince Street), 523-0077, intimate, upscale, M–E • **Giacomo's,** 355 Hanover, 523-9026, long lines for seafood and other spicy Italian specialties; second location at 431 Columbus Avenue, 536-5723, I–M • **Daily Catch,** 323 Hanover Street, 523-8567 (also 261 Northern Avenue, Boston Fish Pier, 338-3093), Sicilian seafood specialties, M. *For cappuccino, gelati, etc.:* **Café Paradiso,** 255 Hanover Street, 742-1768 • **Caffe Vittoria,** 296 Hanover Street, 227-7606. *Some longtime institutions:* **Locke Ober,** 4 Winter Street, 542-1340, Old World ambience since 1875, traditional continental menu, E–EE • **Legal Seafoods,** Copley Place and two locations on Stuart Street behind Park Plaza Hotel (see above), great seafood but almost too popular—be prepared for a long wait, M–E • **Durgin Park,** 340 North Market Street, Faneuil Hall Marketplace, 227-2038, roast beef and baked beans family-style in hectic but historic surroundings (don't go to the one in Copley Place—it's not the same experience), M • **Ye Olde Union Oyster House,** 41 Union Street, Quincy Market, 227-2038, oldest in the city, established 1826, tourist mecca, go for oysters and chowder, M. *Budget choices:* **Omonia,** 75 South Charles Street, 426-4310, Greek, I–M • **Piccola Venezia,** 63 Salem Street, 523-9802 (or 263 Hanover Street, 523-3888), homestyle traditional Italian, I • **Jacob Wirth,** 33-37 Stuart Street (across from the Wang Center), 338-8536, no-frills German, same spot since 1868, I • **Blue Diner,** 150 Kneeland Street, 338-4639, wide-ranging menu, open all night, I–M • **Blue Wave,** 142 Berkeley Street, 424-6664, cheerful, noisy, cheap, M. **For lunch: Isabella Stewart Gardner Museum** (see under Sightseeing), a superb setting for lunch, terrace in warm weather, I (no museum admission required). *Dancing and romancing:* The most romantic spot in town for dancing and a city view is the **Customs House Lounge, Bay Tower Room,** 60 State Street, 723-1666. Skip the expensive dinner; come for drinks and the view. *Outside the city:* Several top local favorites are out of the city center; people with a car may want to try the following: **Olives,** 10 City Square, Charlestown, 242-

1999, raves for Mediterranean fare and gourmet pizzas, M–E • **Figs,** 67 Main Street, Charlestown, 242-2229, another winner for pasta and pizza, I–M • **Dali,** 415 Washington Street, Somerville, 661-3254, colorful Spanish, tapas, I–M. See also Boston family dining, page 236, and Cambridge, pages 297–298.

SIGHTSEEING   Boston National Historical Park Visitors Center, 15 State Street, 242-5642. Hours: daily, June to August, Monday to Friday, 8 A.M. to 6 P.M., Saturday and Sunday, 9 A.M. to 6 P.M.; rest of year, to 5 P.M. Information on the Freedom Trail—free ranger-led, 90-minute guided walking tours offered regularly; check current schedule • **Old State House,** 206 Washington Street (at State Street), 720-3290. Hours: daily, 9:30 A.M. to 5 P.M. $ • **State House,** Beacon and Park Streets, 727-3676. Hours: Monday to Friday, 9 A.M. to 5 P.M.; guided tours, 10 A.M. to 4 P.M. Free • **Nichols House Museum,** 55 Mt. Vernon Street, 227-6993. Hours: May to October, Tuesday to Saturday, 12:15 P.M. to 4:15 P.M.; February to April and November and December, Monday, Wednesday, and Saturday, 12:15 P.M. to 4:15 P.M. $$ • **Prudential Tower Skywalk,** 800 Boylston Street, 859-0648. Hours: daily, 10 A.M. to 10 P.M. $$ • **John Hancock Observatory,** St. James Avenue and Trinity Place, 572-6429. Hours: May to October, Monday to Saturday, 9 A.M. to 10 P.M., Sunday, 10 A.M. to 10 P.M.; rest of year, Monday to Saturday, 9 A.M. to 10 P.M., Sunday, noon to 10 P.M. $$ • **Museum of Fine Arts,** 465 Huntington Avenue, 267-9300. Hours: Tuesday to Sunday, 10 A.M. to 4:45 P.M., Wednesday to 9:45 P.M.; Thursday and Friday, west wing only to 9:45 P.M. $$$$; pay what you wish on Wednesday after 4 P.M. • **Isabella Stewart Gardner Museum,** 280 The Fenway, 566-1401. Hours: Tuesday to Sunday, 11 A.M. to 5 P.M. $$$$; under 12, free • **John Fitzgerald Kennedy Library Museum,** I-93 South, exit 17 (at Columbia Point, Dorchester), 929-4523. Hours: daily, 9 A.M. to 5 P.M. $$$ • **Paul Revere House,** 19 North Square, 523-2338. Hours: April 15 to October 31, daily, 9:30 A.M. to 4:15 P.M.; rest of year, closed Monday. $ • **USS** *Constitution,* Charlestown Navy Yard (part of Boston National Historical Park), Charlestown, 242-5670. Hours: guided ship tours daily, 9:30 A.M. to 3:50 P.M.; self-guiding top deck tours 3:50 to dusk. Free • **USS** *Constitution* **Museum,** 426-1812. Hours: late June to Labor Day, daily, 9 A.M. to 5 P.M.; March to late May and September through November, 10 A.M. to 5 P.M.; rest of year, to 4 P.M. $$. *Harbor cruises:* Check for current schedules and prices. **Boston Harbor Cruises,** One Long Wharf, 227-4321; **Bay State Cruise Company,** 67 Long Wharf, 723-7800; **Boston Duck Tours,** 101 Huntington Avenue, 723-DUCK; **New England Aquarium Whale Watch & Harbor Cruises,** Central Wharf, 973-5281; **Odyssey Cruises,** 60 Rowes Wharf, 654-9700, dinner cruises. *Walking tours:* **Boston by Foot,** 77 North Washington Street, 367-2345, May to October; phone for current offerings. *Trolley tours:* Phone for current information. **The Boston**

Trolley/Blue Trolley Tours, 269-3616; **Old Town Trolley Tours,** 269-7150. For more Boston attractions, see pages 236–237.

ENTERTAINMENT   Bostix Ticket Booth, Faneuil Hall Marketplace, 723-5181, half-price theater, music, and dance tickets on day of performance. Hours: Tuesday to Saturday, 11 A.M. to 6 P.M.; Sunday, noon to 4 P.M.

INFORMATION Boston Common Visitor Information Booth, Tremont Street and Prudential Center Visitors' Center, both open daily, 9 A.M. to 5 P.M. For written information, contact Greater Boston Convention and Tourist Bureau, Prudential Plaza, PO Box 490, Boston, MA 02199, 536-4100 or (800) 888-5515.

Summer

Overleaf: *Boating in Newport, Rhode Island. Photograph by John T. Hopf, courtesy of Newport County Chamber of Commerce.*

Flying High in Quechee

They celebrate Father's Day with a whoosh in Quechee, Vermont.

For more than a decade now, by 6:00 P.M. on the Friday of that weekend in June, the village green is crowded with people waiting to see the season's most colorful send-off.

By then, the green already has been transformed into a patchwork of striped and star-spangled giant balloons, waiting to soar on the favorable evening breeze. One by one, the balloons are filled with flaming gusts of hot air. First they grow big and round, then they stand erect, and eventually they sail aloft to the loud cheers of admiring bystanders.

It was an inspired idea to stage an annual balloon festival on this classic New England green. Colorful hot-air balloons astride the wind always cause people to gaze with pleasure and a bit of envy, but there is something special about the combination of the bright soaring balloons and the pastoral hills and farms that makes it well worthwhile to make the trip to Quechee—and to bring along several rolls of film.

Since the winds are also right at 6:00 A.M., early risers can see the spectacle repeated on Saturday. Even those who watch the Friday night liftoff are likely to return on Saturday morning to get another angle with their cameras or to watch their favorite balloon make a new ascent. And in case they still miss the perfect shot, there's always Saturday night, Sunday morning, and Sunday evening to try, try again.

If you become curious about what it takes to get the balloons aloft or how they ever get down again, the festival program will fill you in on everything—riding the wind and handling propane tanks, tether ropes, and burners—so you'll learn just how it's done.

Between launchings, the green is filled with down-home music and entertainment, dozens of crafts booths, and food stands, all adding further to the air of gaiety inspired by the balloons. The smell of chicken barbecuing on the outdoor grills may well tempt you to stay here for lunch or return for an economical outdoor dinner.

The festival takes place in a tiny town that is photogenic even without benefit of balloons. Quechee is best known for the river gorge that can be seen east of the village, on Route 4 on the way to Woodstock. Not all visitors make the detour into the village across a picturesque covered bridge, where the Ottauquechee River provides the town with a scenic natural backdrop of swirling downhill rapids and a waterfall.

To miss Quechee means missing a fascinating mill restoration, historic homes, some fine country inns, and a tasteful, tucked-away condominium community that provides all kinds of recreational facilities. Concerts and Saturday afternoon polo matches are other Quechee summertime lures.

If you stay at the Quechee Inn at Marshland Farm, you'll be within walking distance of the green but safely away from the crowds. The two-story inn was the 1793 home of Col. Joseph Marsh and one of Vermont's most distinguished families, whose members included a governor, a university president, and a U.S. ambassador to Italy. The brick-floored, timbered living room, equipped with a bar, offers a comfortable sitting area; there's a pleasant outdoor terrace and lawn for sunning, and an attractive Colonial-style dining room.

Bikes, canoe rentals, and a fly-fishing school are available right at the inn, and guests also have access to the clubhouse, pools, a sandy lake beach, a children's recreation area, a golf course, and the tennis, squash, and racquetball courts of Quechee Lakes, a resort community on 6,000 acres of woods and meadows in the nearby hills. It's also possible to rent one of the attractive condominiums or homes here and move in for a weekend or longer.

Another quite elegant little lodging, in the village, is the Parker House Inn, a handsome Victorian house recently redone with flair. Across the street is the Country Garden Inn, an elaborately decorated bed-and-breakfast home with antiques and an Oriental rug in every room, nice gardens, and a greenhouse breakfast room that doubles as a tearoom in the afternoon. Both these inns provide guest privileges at Quechee Lakes.

The Quechee Bed & Breakfast Inn is another attractive choice, though it is on busy Route 4 rather than in town. It will please antiquers who want to spend time at the three-story Antiques Collaborative, just across the road in Waterman Place.

Another happy choice is the Applebutter Inn, a warm and friendly place that is a few miles down the road off Route 4 tastefully furnished with country antiques.

The prime sightseeing attraction in town is the workshop and gallery of glassblower Simon Pearce, an Irishman who took over the old red-brick woolen mills on the dam in Quechee and harnessed the hydro-electric power to provide energy for his glass furnace. Pearce and his workers still make every piece painstakingly by hand, and the public is welcome to watch them at their labors—as well as to inspect the hydro-electric plant.

The showroom and shop are stunning, with great arched windows looking out on the river. In addition to Pearce glassware, pottery, and handwoven Irish woolens, a few antiques are for sale. Bargain hunters can also find reduced prices on some of the Pearce glasses and pitchers, though the price for "seconds" of such meticulously made items is still high. There is also an excellent restaurant where you can have lunch or dinner with a river view.

Farther west on Route 4, heading toward Woodstock, you'll find Scotland by the Yard, which offers tartan and tweed fabrics and handsome woolen clothing and sweaters. Continue into Woodstock and you'll have your fill of shops and restaurants. For more on Woodstock, see pages 3–8.

If you need further diversions, you can see polo played every Saturday at the Quechee Polo Club. For evening activity, take a drive across the Connecticut River to Hanover, New Hampshire, where something is almost always scheduled at Dartmouth's Hopkins Center.

Add the sporting possibilities and the color of the balloons to the peace of the countryside around Quechee, and you need little more to lift the summer season to a soaring start.

Area Code: 802

DRIVING DIRECTIONS   Quechee is located four miles from I-89 on Route 4, midway between Woodstock and White River Junction, Vermont. It is about 143 miles from Boston, 255 miles from New York, and 161 miles from Hartford.

PUBLIC TRANSPORTATION   Air service to Lebanon, New Hampshire, 7½ miles; Amtrak train service to White River Junction, 7 miles.

ACCOMMODATIONS   The Quechee Inn at Marshland Farm, MAP, Clubhouse Road, Quechee 05059, 295-3133, E–EE • **Quechee Lakes Real Estate Center,** Route 4, Box 385, Quechee 05059, 295-7525 or (800) 745-0042, one-bedroom units, E; larger condos, E–EE • **Parker House Inn,** Quechee Village 05059, 295-6077, attractive small Victorian inn, E–EE, MAP • **Country Garden Inn,** 37 Main Street, Quechee 05059, (800) 859-4191, M, CP • **Quechee Bed & Breakfast Inn,** Route 4, Quechee 05059, 295-1776, 1795 Colonial home, M–E, CP • **Applebutter Inn,** Happy Valley Road (just off Route 4), Taftsville 05073, 457-4158, lovely small inn just a few miles from Quechee, I–M, CP. Also see Woodstock listings on page 7 and Hanover listings on page 249 for additional lodging and dining suggestions.

DINING   Simon Pearce Restaurant, The Mill, Quechee, 295-2711, top choice, lunch, I; dinner, M–E • **The Quechee Inn at Marshland Farm** (see above), pleasant atmosphere, E, • **Parker House Inn** (see above), varied menu, on the formal side, M–E.

SIGHTSEEING   Quechee Balloon Festival, Village Green, Quechee, usually Father's Day weekend in mid-June, sponsored by Quechee Chamber of Commerce. Admission, $$. Call for schedules, information.

INFORMATION   Quechee Chamber of Commerce, PO Box 106, Quechee, VT 05059, 295-7900 or (800) 295-5451.

A Summer Fling in Connecticut

Come early July each year, a steady procession of cars can be seen bypassing beach and barbecue to head for a park in Norwalk, Connecticut.

Their destination? The Round Hill Scottish Games, a colorful Connecticut summer event that celebrated its 75th birthday in 1997. The games draw more than 700 contestants, from seven to seventy to take part in the piping, dancing, and sporting competitions that have been part of Scottish tradition for as long as anyone can remember.

Traditionally held near the Fourth of July holiday, it's not the usual Independence Day festivity, nor is this suburban commuter territory in Fairfield County an area you might ordinarily choose for a getaway destination. Yet it offers all the elements for a uniquely pleasant outing, with both beach and wooded beauty at hand, plus good shopping, summer theater, and a number of excellent restaurants nearby. If you know where to look, you may even find some old New England atmosphere here in the suburbs.

The games, which draw thousands of spectators each year, are patterned after the famed Highland Games in Scotland. The event originated early in the century in nearby Greenwich when a group of Scottish emigrants from the area joined forces to provide an occasion to wear their native Highland dress and preserve a bit of their heritage for their children. In the early years, proceeds were used to help other newly arrived Scots in this country.

Word of the occasion spread, the participants began to multiply, and the spectacle became such an attraction that the Round Hill Scottish Games Association was formed in 1923 to oversee the event and to disperse the profits to a number of charities. The location has been moved several times to accommodate ever-growing crowds.

There are three categories of events taking place all at once, giving something of the feeling of watching a three-ring circus. Athletic competitions such as track events and soccer are brought to a climax by the incredible "tossing of the caber."

A caber, measuring 16 feet in length and weighing over 150 pounds, looks much like a telephone pole. Legend has it that caber tossing dates back to the days before bridges were built, when brawny Scottish lads made their way across the waters by uprooting a tree and tossing it across the stream as a walkway. Today, heaving the heavy pole is a feat to try even the halest, and many contestants find they can hardly *lift* the caber, much less toss it anywhere. Their feeble efforts are greeted by hoots of laughter from the high-spirited holiday crowd.

Yet each year a few stout lads emerge who seem to have inherited the prowess of their ancestors, and a husky contender inevitably comes forward to give the king-size missile a prodigious toss that sets off wild cheering from the sidelines.

While the sportsmen are having at each other, more than a hundred dancers are competing in another area of the grounds. The dancers, gaily decked out in plaid knee socks, kilts, tunics, and caps, are judged by their skill in executing the carefully prescribed steps of dances such as the highland fling, the sailor's hornpipe, and the sword dance. The littlest contestants begin in the morning, followed by big brothers and sisters, and finally the adults. Many spectators seem to remain mesmerized for hours watching the graceful dancers perform their nimble steps.

To give stamina to the bystanders, refreshment stands are strategically placed on the grounds. These stands serve regional fare such as Scottish meat pies or fish and chips as well as an all-American menu of hot dogs and Cokes. There are souvenir stands as well, with tiny plaid tams for the tots, Celtic jewelry and other crafts, and a selection of beautiful wool tartan plaids of the clans for sale by the yard.

Last and far from least of the events is the bagpipe competition, with pipers and drummers in full regalia performing individually as well as in groups. The bagpipe bands in their colorful plaids come from all over the Northeast and as far away as Canada and Bermuda.

The pipers and bands march one by one to perform the specified categories of music: a march, a reel, a strathspey, and the tongue-twisting piobaireachd. Then, when the judging is done and the winner has been declared, the musicians mass for one last spectacular parade across the grounds, an unforgettable finale of sound and color.

For those who are making a weekend of it, Norwalk has some unexpected pleasures to offer. Silvermine Tavern is no longer the stagecoach stop it was in 1767, but an inn with great early American charm in a picture-book location overlooking a waterfall and a duck-dotted pond. Be sure to ask for one of the three choicest rooms—the ones that have balconies overlooking the falls. Even if you don't stay here, do have at least one meal—not so much for the food as for the cozy, low-ceilinged dining room filled with antique tools and the deck overlooking the ducks and geese on the pond. It's a perfect choice for Sunday brunch, a generous buffet spread.

The Silvermine section of Norwalk, a pre-Revolutionary township settled beside the Silvermine River, is picturesque country. It emerged as a noted artists' colony when sculptor Solon Borglum set up a studio here in 1895 and other artists soon followed suit. In 1922, a group got together to buy land and an old barn just across from the tavern and formed the Silvermine Guild of Artists. It is both school and gallery, with changing exhibits and a permanent section of original art and handcrafts for sale, many at reasonable prices. Silvermine Guild is also the scene of a summertime chamber music series.

The main part of Norwalk is also quite old, dating to 1649, but other than the village green you wouldn't know it today, since a British assault during the Revolutionary War all but wiped out the town. However, there are a couple of ancient cemeteries remaining for grave-rubbing buffs; one on Gregory Boulevard dates back to 1652.

South Norwalk, a formerly run-down area now known locally as SoNo, has had a face-lift that includes brick sidewalks and antique street lamps. Washington Street, the two-block heart of the area, features many interesting shops for browsing, as well as some excellent dining.

The major sightseeing attraction in SoNo is the Maritime Aquarium, located in a restored nineteenth-century factory building on five acres of Norwalk waterfront. This is part aquarium, part giant-screen IMAX theater, and part Maritime Hall, the latter a lively look at the ecology and maritime history of Long Island Sound told with hands-on exhibits and displays of classic boats. The aquarium is small in scale but includes some fascinating creatures such as stingrays and sharks, and has unique features such as a jellyfish exhibit, frisky otters in a woodland shoreline habitat display, and a "touch tank" where you can handle starfish and other denizens of the sea. Harbor seals cavort in a tank that allows them to swim indoors or out. There are interesting changing exhibits as well.

Those who want to learn more about marine life close up can sign on for guided three-hour study cruises aboard the research vessel *Oceanic*.

Another maritime pleasure in Norwalk is boarding a ferry for the 30-minute cruise to serene Sheffield Island, where you can tour a tiny 1868 lighthouse and explore a small wildlife sanctuary. If you bring a picnic lunch, you can stay a while and enjoy feeling away from it all, then board a later boat back.

Quite a different South Norwalk attraction is the New England Brewing Company, maker of Atlantic Amber and other brands. It is at once a pub, a brewery, and a mini-brewery museum where free tours of the brewing process are offered.

Another sightseeing gem, in the center of Norwalk, is the Lockwood-Mathews Mansion Museum. Legrand Lockwood was a poor boy who lived out the fantasy of becoming rich and returning to show off for the hometown folks. A quarter of a century before the Vanderbilts and the Astors began building their opulent "cottages" in Newport, Lockwood came back to his native Norwalk to build a 60-room mansion the likes of which had never been seen in this area. For the then-exorbitant sum of $2 million, he brought in European architects to create sweeping staircases, a three-story skylit octagonal rotunda, frescoes, inlaid woods and marbles, carved cherubs and nymphs, and such revolutionary modern devices as a hot-air furnace, hot and cold running water, and 14 full baths. A children's theater was tucked away under the eaves; wine cellars and two bowling alleys were built in the basement. In 1873 the *New*

York Sun pronounced Mr. Lockwood's dream house "perhaps the most perfect and elegant mansion in America."

Though it later came on hard times, the mansion was saved by a group of local preservationists, and the restoration became a community project supported by many volunteers and the Norwalk Junior League. It is well on the way back to its former magnificence, and it's well worth a visit.

Antiquers should head north on Route 7 beyond the Merritt Parkway and go beyond the newer shopping centers to the road that used to be known as "Antique Row." Watch on the right for the sign to Cannondale Village, a onetime railroad crossing that has been restored into a shopping complex. Detour on Route 33 for more antiques, country scenery, and a visit to Ridgefield, a delightful Colonial town with an avant-garde art museum and a Revolutionary War tavern for touring. It's a good plan to time your arrival to include lunch or dinner, since Ridgefield is known for its excellent restaurants.

A different detour off Route 7, to Route 102 West, takes you to the Weir Farm National Historic Site. This was once the home and studio of artist J. Alden Weir, an important member of the American Impressionist movement in the late nineteenth century. His floral paintings are considered among the finest still lifes produced in this country, and many of his paintings were inspired by the surroundings of his 57-acre summer home. The farm is one of only two historic sites in the United States celebrating American art. Guided walking tours are offered on Saturday and Sunday at 2 P.M.

If chic boutiques are more to your taste than antiques shops or artists, you may prefer to make your way to Westport, Norwalk's eastern neighbor on Long Island Sound. It is home to countless advertising and entertainment biggies and has many interesting shops to explore along its two-block Main Street as well as in small complexes running for several miles along U.S. Route 1, known in town as State Street.

Westport lodgings are more expensive, but they are choice. One possibility is a former country club on the sound, the Inn at Long Shore, now part of a town recreational center with attractive Colonial-decor guest rooms upstairs in the clubhouse and tennis courts and a golf course right outside the door. Or, if you want to splurge, the Inn at National Hall is an elegant rebirth of a venerable building on the banks of the Saugatuck River near the center of town. It is now one of the select properties of the prestigious Relais & Châteaux group.

If you don't want to miss out on the beaching most people associate with a summer weekend, you can visit Westport's Sherwood Island, a state park with more than a mile and a half of sandy beach on the sound and facilities for cookouts and picnicking. Though it shares the pebbles that plague sound beaches, it is one of the best on the Connecticut shore.

Any of the back roads off Route 33 in Westport heading north to the

Merritt Parkway will take you into magnificent wooded residential sections that are a sightseeing tour in themselves, and if you want to get a little closer to nature, Westport's Nature Center for Environmental Activities has wooded trails through a 53-acre sanctuary.

Come evening, Westport has more than its share of fine dining, and this is also the home of one of America's oldest summer theaters, the Westport Country Playhouse, where you'll most likely find the biggest names among the performers out on the summer circuit. And free concerts from jazz to rock to symphony are scheduled almost every summer night at the Levitt Pavilion, on the banks of the Saugatuck River near the middle of town.

What with beaching, browsing, and the sophisticated cuisine these wealthy commuter communities enjoy, you're likely to find that your days in Fairfield County will whiz by. Taken together with the Scottish Games and the annual Fourth of July fireworks at Norwalk's Calf Pasture Beach, it makes for a sparkling summer weekend.

Area Code: 203

DRIVING DIRECTIONS   Norwalk and Westport are reached via I-95, the Connecticut Turnpike, or Route 15 (the Merritt Parkway). Norwalk is 160 miles from Boston, 50 miles from New York, and 60 miles from Hartford.

PUBLIC TRANSPORTATION   Metro North train service to Norwalk and Westport.

ACCOMMODATIONS   **The Inn at Long Shore,** 260 Compo Road South, Westport 06880, 226-3316, M; suites, E • **Inn at National Hall,** 2 Post Road West, Westport 06880, 221-1351, EE, CP • **Silvermine Tavern,** Silvermine and Perry Avenues, Norwalk 06850, 847-4558, M, CP • **Norwalk Inn,** 99 East Avenue, Norwalk 06851, 838-5531, more motel than inn, but centrally located and reasonable, outdoor pool, I–M • **Four Points Hotel by Sheraton,** 426 Main Avenue (Route 7), Norwalk 06851, 849-9828, M • **Courtyard by Marriott,** 474 Main Avenue (Route 7), Norwalk 06851, 849-9111 or (800) 321-2211, M • **Westport Inn,** 1595 Post Road East, Westport 06880, 259-5236, motor inn, indoor pool, M–E.

DINING   *Westport:* **The Restaurant at National Hall,** Inn at National Hall (see above), attractive setting, eclectic and elegant menu, E–EE • **Sole E Luna,** 25 Powers Court, 222-2827, much lauded northern Italian, M • **Café Christina,** 1 Main Street, 221-7950, friendly European café in the old library, M–E • **Tavern on Main,** 146 Main Street, 221-7222, updated New England fare, cozy, top reviews and a great spot for celebrity watching, M • **Meeting Street Grill,** 1563 Post

Road East, 256-3309, American fare, lively ambience, M–E • **Da Pietro's,** 36 Riverside Avenue, 454-1213, excellent northern Italian food, some find the quarters cramped, M–E • **Spazzi,** 1229 Post Road, Fairfield, 256-1629, popular and trendy Italian in the town just beyond Westport, M. *Norwalk:* **Pasta Nostra,** 116 Washington Street, South Norwalk, 854-9700, tiny and usually packed for excellent pasta, M–E • **Cote d'Azur,** 86 Washington Street, South Norwalk, 855-8958, cozy French café, M • **Amberjack's Coastal Grill,** 99 Washington Street, South Norwalk, 853-4332, dining in a former bank, trendy California menu, seafood is a specialty, M • **Rattlesnake Southwestern Grill,** 2 South Main Street, South Norwalk, 852-1716, now a chain of Tex-Mex fare and reptilian decor; the bar is shaped like a snake, I–M • **Brewhouse Restaurant,** New England Brewing Company, 13 Marshall Street, 866-1339, brew-pub and brewing museum, interesting three-course dinners paired with beer, free tours of brewery, I–M • **Tra-Peze Bistro and Bar,** 18 South Main Street, 853-2123, solid all-American fare, M • **Maria's Trattoria,** 172 Main Street, 847-5166, good southern Italian home cooking, very popular—can get crowded, I–M • **Meson Galicia,** 10 Wall Street, 866-8800, attractive café in old trolley barn building, well-prepared Spanish specialties, M–E • **Silvermine Tavern** (see above), M–E • **Sunset Grille,** 52 Calf Pasture Beach (at Cove Marina), 866-4177, well prepared (and simple) fish is the feature, M. *Ridgefield:* **Stonehenge,** Route 7, Ridgefield, 438-6511, attractive setting, M–E, fine dining; or prix fixe, EE • **The Inn at Ridgefield,** 20 West Lane, Ridgefield, 438-8282, Colonial decor, E, nouvelle menu; or prix-fixe menu, EE.

SIGHTSEEING **Round Hill Scottish Games,** Cranbury Park, Norwalk, 854-7806. Annual event, usually held the weekend of the Fourth of July, starting at 9 A.M. and continuing all day. Phone for current dates and information. $$$ • **Maritime Aquarium at Norwalk,** North Water Street, 852-0700. Hours: daily, 10 A.M. to 5 P.M., to 6 P.M. in summer. Admission for Maritime Hall and Aquarium, $$$; IMAX theater, $$; combination ticket, $$$$ • **Lockwood Mathews Mansion Museum,** 295 West Avenue, Norwalk, 838-1434. Hours: Tuesday to Friday, 11 A.M. to 3 P.M.; Sunday, 1 P.M. to 4 P.M. $$; under 12, free • **Silvermine Guild Arts Center,** 1037 Silvermine Road, New Canaan, 966-5617. Hours: Tuesday to Saturday, 11 A.M. to 5 P.M.; Sunday, 1 P.M. to 5 P.M. Donation • **Weir Farm National Historic Site,** 735 Nod Hill Road, Wilton, 834-1896. Hours: April to November, Wednesday to Sunday, 8:30 A.M. to 5 P.M.; guided tours Saturday and Sunday at 2 P.M.; December to March, Wednesday to Friday, 8:30 A.M. to 5 P.M. Free • **Nature Center for Environmental Activities,** 10 Woodside Lane, Westport, 227-7253. Hours: Monday to Saturday, 9 A.M. to 5 P.M.; Sunday, 1 P.M. to 4 P.M. $ • **Westport Country Playhouse,** 25 Powers Court, Westport, 227-4177. June through mid-September. Check current season's offerings • **Levitt Pavilion for the Performing Arts,** Jessup Road, Westport, 226-7600. Phone for current listing of free summer programs, held late June through August. *Sheffield Island cruises:* **Norwalk Seaport Association,** 132 Water Street, South Norwalk, 838-9444 or (888) 701-7785. Schedules vary with the seasons. Phone for current times and rates. *Study cruises:* **Maritime Aquarium at Norwalk,** 852-0700, ext. 206. Three-hour outings, July through October, aboard the R/V *Oceanic* to study marine life in Long Island Sound. Winter cruises in January through March watch for harbor seals. Phone for times, prices.

INFORMATION Coastal Fairfield County Convention & Visitors Bureau at Merritt View, 383 Main Avenue, Norwalk, CT 06851, 840-8700. Tourist information: 854-7825 or (800) 866-7925. A Tourism Information Center is located at I-95 exits 15S/14N.

Scenery by the Sea in Ogunquit

Families love Ogunquit. So do singles, lovers of the opposite and the same sex, photographers, artists, nature seekers, theatergoers, weekenders without cars, teenagers, toddlers, and great-grandparents.

When you see the powdery three-mile stretch of beach curving into a backdrop of rugged cliffs, you'll know instantly why Ogunquit draws such a mélange of fans. The site the Indians called "Beautiful Place by the Sea" is aptly named, and the bountiful beach is a special treasure in Maine, a state whose rockbound coastline yields few such open spaces.

The beach alone explains why Ogunquit has been a popular vacation haven for 100 years, ever since a bridge was built in 1888 across the river that once divided the shore from the town. But Ogunquit has also made the most of its cliffs, topping them with a magnificent winding path called the Marginal Way, which meanders in and out of the bayberries and brush for a scenic mile of strolling, with unparalled views of the crashing sea beyond. It is a walk that never palls no matter how many times it is repeated.

Follow the Marginal Way to its end and you come to another facet of this delightful town. Perkins Cove is a picturesque little harbor that was discovered more than half a century ago by artists and craftspeople. Now the onetime fishermen's shanties are filled with shops, restaurants, and galleries.

The Ogunquit Playhouse, on Route 1, is another longtime resident, a mainstay on the summer circuit since 1933. And to further add to Ogunquit's special pleasures, you don't need a car here—in fact, you're almost better off without one, since parking spaces are at a premium and weekend traffic is a pain. Almost everything is walkable, and should your energy flag, all you need do is hop aboard one of the town's old-fashioned trolley buses, which make the rounds from 8:00 A.M. to midnight during the season.

It's hardly a surprise to learn that the beach is busy on weekends, particularly near the most popular entry, at Beach Street, where there are snack bars and dressing rooms. Both the footbridge at Ocean Street (off U.S. Route 1 north of the village) and the Moody Beach entrance (on Ocean Avenue via Bourne Avenue) are less congested. Happily, however, if you are willing to walk a bit, no matter where you enter you can still find plenty of space to plant your blanket and sit back to people-watch, a particularly colorful pastime given the mix of beachgoers.

You hardly need an itinerary for Ogunquit. When you've had enough sun (or if the unthinkable happens and it rains), just head down Shore Road to Perkins Cove, checking out the crafts and clothes along the way. Candles, cuddly stuffed animals, custom-designed jewelry, and hand-blown glass are among the varied offerings in the slew of shops in town.

There are many art galleries to choose from, including the Ogunquit Art Collaborative Gallery, which offers concerts, films, and lectures as well as exhibits. The Ogunquit Museum of American Art is exceptional, a handsome building of stone and wood with many windows to bring in the view of the rocky cove and meadows outside, and a lovely sculpture garden and lawns that make the most of the setting. The five galleries include works by Reginald Marsh and Charles Burchfield.

Antiquers will want to visit the Blacksmith's Mall, on Main Street (Route 1), with dozens of antiques-and-collectibles dealers, and will find many more shops along Route 1 between Ogunquit and Wells, including MacDougall-Gioet, another co-op with many dealers specializing in country furniture. Bargain hunters should head to the outlet malls to the north in Wells or to the south in Kittery. Families will enjoy River Lily Farm, where visitors can pick their own fruits, flowers, and vegetables and enjoy hayrides on the farm. And should you have a yen to get out to sea, Finestkind offers lobstering trips, sightseeing cruises, and sailing trips from Perkins Cove.

Where to stay in Ogunquit really depends on your personal preferences and pocketbook, for there's everything from guest house to motel to low-key resorts, all convenient to the beach. On the upscale end of things, Hartwell House has beautifully furnished accommodations. Many rooms in the main house have French doors leading to private balconies. The pretty, cozy Trellis House is among my favorites of the smaller B & B inns because of the convenient yet quiet location on a lane just off busy Shore Road.

Among the many dining options, Arrows is the current gourmet choice. If you are thinking about Maine lobster, head for the Ogunquit Lobster Pound, where you pick your own dinner to be cooked on the coals outdoors.

You might prefer to be able to visit during the week when the many Boston families who flock here on Saturday and Sunday have returned home, but somehow Ogunquit is a town that even weekend crowds can't spoil. Walking the expanses of beach or contemplating the waves from the Marginal Way, the rest of the world recedes before the splendor of this "Beautiful Place by the Sea."

Area Code: 207

DRIVING DIRECTIONS Take I-95 to U.S. Route 1, or simply follow Route 1, which becomes Main Street in Ogunquit. Ogunquit is 70 miles north of Boston, 40 miles south of Portland, 275 miles from New York, and 170 miles from Hartford.

PUBLIC TRANSPORTATION Air service to Portland, about 30 minutes north, and to Portsmouth, 20 minutes south of Ogunquit. Amtrak serves Wells, which is about 10 minutes north of Ogunquit. During the season, the Coastal Connection—a local bus service—connects Kittery, York, Ogunquit, Wells, Kennebunkport, and Kennebunk; phone 282-5408 for information.

ACCOMMODATIONS Ogunquit zip codes are all 03907. Rates given are for high season. *A few choice bed-and-breakfast picks:* **Hartwell House,** 110 Shore Road, Ogunquit, 646-7210, M–E, CP • **Trellis House,** 2 Beachmere Place, Ogunquit, 646-7909, M, CP • **The Morning Dove,** 30 Bourne Lane, 646-3891, 1860s home, gardens, ask for Grandma's Attic, I–M, CP • **Puffin Inn,** 233 U.S. Route 1, 646-5496, charming decor, though on busy road—ask for a room facing the rear, M, CP • **The Ogunquit House,** 7 King's Highway, 646-2967, restored 1880 schoolhouse, also cottages, M, CP • **Pine Hill Inn,** Pine Hill Road, PO Box 2336, 361-1004, tasteful Victorian, nice screened porch, M, CP. *Motel-resorts on the water:* **Sparhawk,** Shore Road, 646-5562, tennis, pool, E, CP • **Norseman Motor Inn,** Ogunquit Beach, 646-7024, directly on the beach, M–E • **Sea Chambers,** 37 Shore Road, 646-9311, tennis, pool, M–E, CP • **The Aspinquid,** Beach Street, 646-7072, motel units and efficiencies, tennis, pool, M–EE • **Cliff House,** Bald Head Cliff, Shore Road, 361-1000, classic resort recently remodeled, motel-type rooms, spectacular view, but far from town, E–EE.

DINING **Arrows,** Berwick Road, Ogunquit, 361-1100, sophisticated cuisine in a 1765 farmhouse, E–EE • **98 Provence,** 104 Shore Road,

646-9898, French country fare, charming decor, M–E; also great breakfasts, I • **Diane's,** 111 Shore Road, 646-9703, continental, quaint atmosphere, M • **Hurricane,** Oarweed Lane, Perkins Cove, 646-6348, trendy favorite, M–E • **Barnacle Billy's,** Perkins Cove, 646-5575, informal, nautical, outdoor deck, very popular, I–M • **Jonathan's,** 2 Bourne Lane, 646-4777, gardens, an aquarium, wide-ranging menu, entertainment, popular concerts upstairs, I–M • **Gypsy Sweethearts,** 18 Shore Road, 646-7021, creative dishes, reasonably priced, M; also known for breakfast, I • **The Old Village Inn,** 30 Main Street, 646-7088, seafood, continental menu, perennial favorite in one of the town's oldest buildings, circa 1833, M–E • **Clay Hill Farm,** Agamenticus Road, 361-2272, gracious country setting (car essential), M–E • **Poor Richard's Tavern,** Shore Road, 646-4722, country inn decor, homey New England fare, I–M • **Lobster Shack,** end of Perkins Cove, 646-4022, the name says it, rustic with water views, open mid-May to mid-October, I–M • **Ogunquit Lobster Pound,** Route 1 (north of the village), 646-2516, open early May to Columbus Day, I–M • **Wells Diner,** Route 1, Wells, 646-4441, a classic diner with great home cooking, legendary chowder, I.

SIGHTSEEING   The Ogunquit Museum of American Art, Shore Road (at Narrow Cove), 646-4909. Hours: July through September, Monday to Saturday, 10:30 A.M. to 5 P.M., Sunday from 2 P.M. Donation • **Ogunquit Arts Collaborative Gallery,** Shore Road and Bourne Lane, 646-8400. Hours: June to Columbus Day, Monday to Saturday, 11 A.M. to 5 P.M., Sunday from 1 P.M. Gallery free. Ask for film and concert schedules • **Ogunquit Playhouse,** Route 1 (south of the village), 646-5511. Open late June through August; check for current offerings. *Boat trips:* Usually May through October; phone for current schedules, rates. **Finestkind Scenic Cruises,** Barnacle Billy's dock, Perkins Cove, 646-5227, variety of cruises including lobstering • **Deborah Ann,** Perkins Cove, 361-9501, whale-watching cruises.

**INFORMATION   **Ogunquit Chamber of Commerce, Box 2289, Ogunquit, ME 03907, 646-2939. Information Bureau: 646-5533.

On Top of the World at Mt. Washington

The first scientists who set out to measure Mt. Washington back in 1784 calculated that the peak was some 10,000 feet high. They were a wee bit off the mark—the actual height is 6,288 feet—but it's easy to understand their error.

The White Mountains of New Hampshire have a majesty beyond their actual measure. Unlike the soft green mountains next door in Vermont, these highest mountains in the Northeast are rugged granite peaks, stark and grand. The view from Mt. Washington, the highest of them all, was aptly described by P. T. Barnum as "the second greatest show on earth."

Ever since one Darby Field became the first to climb Mt. Washington back in 1642, adventurers have found the mountain an irresistible lure. Scores of hikers take up the challenge or head for some of the other magnificent trails in the surrounding Presidential Range—Mts. Adams, Jefferson, Monroe, and Eisenhower, to name a few—New England's prime hiking territory. Many hikers stay in the Appalachian Mountain Club Lodge, at Pinkham Notch, or take advantage of the club's many guided walks and workshops.

But you needn't be an alpine climber to enjoy the Mt. Washington Valley. Since the first carriage roads were cut through the mountain passes in the early nineteenth century, increasing numbers of people have come every year just to be inspired by the views. Painters such as Thomas Cole and writers like John Greenleaf Whittier were among the early visitors.

These days you can scale the mountain by railway or by car as well as on foot, browse in scores of outlets, and enjoy a number of fine inns—all enhanced by the ever-present mountain views.

When it comes to settings, there are few hotels anywhere to rival the Mt. Washington, built in 1902, with no expense spared to make it one of the nation's premier resorts. Now rescued from recent financial troubles, the grand hotel still awes first-time visitors with the unforgettable image of the giant, gleaming white, twin-towered, red-roofed hotel, set against the mountains like a fairy-tale palace. There are two golf courses with breathtaking mountain views, 12 clay tennis courts, lovely bridle paths, pools, and playgrounds—everything for a well-rounded vacation.

If old-fashioned grandeur is not your style, there are alternatives for almost every taste. Since these mountains are so special, my favorite places are the ones that let you gaze at them. These lodgings come both grand and modest. The White Mountains Hotel is a new resort but built with a gracious old look, and it has an unbeatable location—right at the base of Cathedral Ledge. The vistas from the dining room and the golf course are fantastic. Snowvillage Inn is off by itself on a hilltop. It has the feel of an alpine resort, serene and informal, and boasts a grand perspective on the Presidentials. The Darby Field Inn, named for that pioneering climber, is a cozy farmhouse set by itself on Bald Hill, 1,000 feet above the valley.

Outside Jackson, one of the loveliest villages in the area, Nordic Village offers spacious condominiums; ask for the top level for the best views. In the town, on the way to Black Mountain, is Paisley and Parsley, a tastefully decorated small bed-and-breakfast home with picture-book vistas from the picture window.

And then there is Notchland Inn, set by itself at the entrance to Crawford Notch. This inn is an old granite-and-timber home with a parlor designed by Gustav Stickley, a founder of the arts and crafts movement. It is nicely renovated with lots of fireplaces and pleasant sitting areas. The owners have horses and a couple of llamas on the extensive grounds, as well as 8,000 feet of Saco River frontage, two prize swimming holes, and a hot tub in a gazebo by the pond.

Some equally appealing lodging choices without a view are listed at the end of this chapter.

The first order of business for most Mt. Washington visitors is simply to see the scenery, and Routes 16 and 302, which intersect in North Conway, lead to the best of it.

Wait for the clearest and calmest of days before you head for Mt. Washington itself. Bring along a sweater, because the summit tends to be windy and foggy much of the time. In fact, the highest wind ever recorded, 231 miles per hour, was measured at the weather station here.

The eight-mile auto toll road to the top, reached off Route 16 above Jackson, is the quick way up, with beauty filling every mile as you pass through lush greenery and wildflowers on your way above the timberline to the stark granite peak. You can do it in your own car, with an audio cassette tour that comes with the price of admission, or take a van for a guided tour.

Allow about three hours for the 3½-mile round-trip ride on the steam-powered Cog Railway, the world's first mountain-climbing railway, built in 1869. It takes off from Route 302, east of Twin Mountain, and chugs its way slowly up a right-of-way with plenty of steep grades to take your breath away. If you want an aerial view of things, the gondola at Wildcat Mountain, at Pinkham Notch, or the chairlift at Attitash Bear Peak will fill the bill.

Down in the valley, the most dramatic scenery is at the various "notches," the passes between the mountains. A hike, however short, is strongly recommended. You can pick up trail maps and information at the Appalachian Mountain Club headquarters on Route 16, at Pinkham Notch, and at the Crawford Notch State Park headquarters on Route 302, near the Mt. Washington Hotel.

Crawford Notch is where White Mountains tourism began—and according to legend, it is where the Presidentials acquired their names. Soon after the first carriage road went through, the region's most noted climber, innkeeper Ethan Allen Crawford, led a hiking party bearing a barrel of rum to Mt. Washington's bare and windy summit. There, raising their mugs in turn to surrounding peaks, they named the mountains as they toasted America's presidents. A marker shows the site of Crawford's inn, now vanished along with most of the other big turn-of-the-century wooden hotels.

If you are looking for a picnic spot, Echo Lake State Park, near North Conway, offers swimming and picnic grounds along with a scenic road to Cathedral Ledge and a panoramic look at the mountains and the Saco River Valley. There are two easy hikes here with rewarding vistas. Diana's Bath is a half-mile path leading along waterfalls. It is reached from the parking area off West Side Road, just north of North Conway. The Black Top path is found at the top of Hurricane Mountain Road, a scenic drive in itself. It is an undemanding walk along the summit with wonderful views.

Mountain bikers will find lift-served trails at Attitash Bear Peak, Bretton Woods, and Cranmore and Loon Mountains. Canoers should note that Saco Bound, on Route 302 in Center Conway, specializes in canoeing and kayaking and offers rentals as well as lessons and guided canoe and raft trips on the river.

When you are ready for more worldly pursuits, you'll find North Conway a lively center for the region. You can hardly call it unspoiled, but it manages to remain a pleasant town despite a main street that is a mélange of motels, shops, fast-food stops, and restaurants. Art galleries, antiques, a quilt shop, jewelry artisans, Scottish and Irish sweater shops, and clothing boutiques are all part of the eclectic mix. Two special stops are the League of New Hampshire Craftsmen shop, with fine crafts by the state's most talented artisans, and the Hand Crafter's Barn, across the way, with folksier collectibles.

The east end of town has become nirvana for bargain hunters, with more than 100 manufacturers' outlets. They include Anne Klein, Polo/Ralph Lauren, L. L. Bean, Donna Karan, Liz Claiborne, and Timberland, to drop just a few brand names. People may grumble about the traffic jams, but there are savings to be had here, and the shops certainly take care of the problem of what to do on a rainy day. If you pick up a good local map, you'll find that you can avoid some Main Street traffic by taking parallel roads.

The valley is rich in activities as well as scenery in the summer. The annual Arts Jubilee, usually July 4 through August, brings a series of free concerts and entertainment to Schouler Park, in North Conway, and arts-and-crafts shows featuring local crafters are regular events throughout the region.

If the kids are along, you can take them to the alpine slide or the water slide at Attitash Bear Peak, and to Heritage New Hampshire, a sound-and-light journey depicting everything from a voyage from England in 1690 to a train ride through Crawford Notch in 1910. From Heritage they'll probably beg you into Story Land, next door, where there are rides and life-size depictions of children's stories. Neither attraction is cheap, and neither is a must—just a way to keep everyone occupied should you need activities for restless small fry.

A final not-to-be-missed attraction won't cost you a cent. The Kancamagus Highway, Route 112 between Conway and Lincoln, runs for 32 magnificent miles right through the heart of the White Mountain National Forest. Created by the U.S. Forest Service to provide both scenery and access to beautiful wilderness through picnic areas and hiking trails, and named a National Scenic Byway, it is one of the region's real treasures. You'll see waterfalls like Lower Falls, Rocky Gorge, and Sabbaday Falls from the road; the small beaches near Lower Falls and the pool above Rocky Gorge are popular swimming places should the day be fine.

If you want to stretch your legs, detour for Champney Falls, a pleasant hour's walk from the trailhead off the highway.

You can take the highway around the mountains to see some of the wonders on the other side, such as Franconia Notch with its famous Flume and the Old Man of the Mountain.

Or maybe just save Kancamagus for a last drive and go home savoring some of the best scenery New England has to offer.

Area Code: 603

DRIVING DIRECTIONS   North Conway, the center of activity in the Mt. Washington Valley, is at the intersection of Routes 16 and 302. Coming from the south, take I-93 North to Route 3 East to Route 302, or take I-95 to Route 16 North. From east or west, take Route 302. North Conway is 140 miles from Boston, 350 miles from New York, and 245 miles from Hartford.

PUBLIC TRANSPORTATION   Concord Trailways bus service to Conway and Jackson; air service to Portsmouth (1½ hours) or Manchester (2 hours), New Hampshire, or to Portland, Maine (1½ hours).

ACCOMMODATIONS   *For mountain views:* **Mt. Washington Hotel,** Bretton Woods 03575, 278-1000 or (800) 258-0330 outside New Hampshire, E–EE, MAP, many packages available • **White Mountains Hotel and Resort,** at Hale's Location (off West Village Road), North Conway 03860, 356-7100 or (800) 533-6301, winter and spring, M, CP; summer and fall, M–E • **Snowvillage Inn,** Snowville 03849, 447-2818 or (800) 447-4345, E–EE, MAP • **Darby Field Inn,** Bald Hill, Conway 03818, 447-2181 or (800) 426-4147, M–E, CP, or E–EE, MAP • **Nordic Village,** Route 16, Jackson 03846, 383-9101 or (800) 472-5207, spacious units with kitchens are a good value, ask for higher condo units for best views, M–EE • **Paisley and Parsley,** Box 572, Route 16B, Jackson 03846, 383-0859, M, CP • **Notchland Inn,** Hart's Location (off Route 302), Bartlett 03812, 374-6131, E–EE, MAP. *Other good choices:* **Stonehurst Manor,** Box 1900, North Conway 03860, 356-3113 or (800) 525-9100, gracious estate, M–E, MAP also available • **Christmas Farm Inn,** Box 176, Jackson 03846, 383-4313, E, MAP • **Inn at Thorn Hill,** Jackson 03846, 383-4242, gracious home with excellent dining room, E–EE, MAP • **Wentworth Resort Hotel,** Jackson 03846, 383-9700, old-time resort, nicely refurbished, golf and tennis, E–EE, MAP • **Nestlenook Farm,** Dinsmore Road, Jackson Village, 03846, 383-9443 or (800) 659-9443, romantic Victorian, canopy beds, fireplaces, some Jacuzzis, pool, farm animals, hiking, boating, E–EE, CP • **Forest Inn,** Route 16A, PO Box 37, Intervale 03845, 356-0772, homey and welcoming inn away from traffic, 25 wooded acres with trails, pool, M–E, CP • **Buttonwood Inn,** Mt. Surprise Road, PO Box 3297, North Conway 03860, 356-2625, B & B convenient to town, tucked on five private acres, I–E, CP • **Village House,** PO Box 359, Jackson 03846, 383-6666, comfortable century-old village inn, pool and tennis, spacious quarters with kitchens in converted barn for families, many weekend packages, M, CP • **Nereledge Inn,** River Road, North Conway 03860, 356-2831, comfortable inn for families, outdoors enthusiasts, headquarters for rock climbing and fly-fishing instruction, I–M, CP • **The Farm by the River,** 2555 West Side Road, North Conway 03860, 356-2694, picture Grandma's house, circa 1785, on 65 acres bordering a river, I–M, CP; suites, M–E, CP • **Cranmore Mountain Lodge,** 859 Kearsage Road, North Conway 03860, 356-5502, modest old-fashioned country inn, pool, guest privileges at Mt. Cranmore Racquet Club, walking distance to town, I–M, CP • **Covered Bridge House,** Route 302, Glen 03838, 383-9109 or (800) 232-9109, small cheerful Colonial with river frontage, children welcome, I, CP • **Admiral Peary House,** 9 Elm Street, Fryeburg, ME 04037, (207) 935-3365 or (800) 237-8080, spacious and attractive quarters in a quiet town just 6 miles from North Conway, tennis court, billiard room, outdoor hot tub, M, CP. *Away from it all:* **Philbrook Farm Inn,** North Road, Shelburne 03581, 466-3831, old-fashioned farm setting, hiking, swimming, riding, M, MAP • **Stafford's in the Field Inn,** Chocorua 03817, 323-7766, simple farm ambience, sophisticated fare, M–EE, MAP.

DINING **The 1785 Inn,** Route 16, North Conway, 356-9025, exceptional food and setting, M–E • **The Bernerhof,** Route 302, Glen, 383-

4414, excellent Swiss fare, M • **Inn at Thorn Hill** (see above), prix fixe, M–E • **Stonehurst Manor** (see above), pasta to paella, M–E • **Notchland Inn** (see above), prix fixe, five-course dinners, E • **Thompson House Eatery** (T.H.E.), Routes 16 and 16A, Jackson, 383-9341, farmhouse setting, inventive menu, M • **Wildcat Inn & Tavern,** Jackson Village, 383-4245, rustic charm, some of the area's best dining, M–E • **Bellini's,** Seavey Street, North Conway, 356-7000, Italian, I–M • **Shalimar,** 27 Seavey Street, North Conway, 356-0123, a surprise in these parts, an Indian restaurant that gets high marks from everyone, I • **Darby Field Inn** (see above), continental menu, M–E • **Mt. Washington Hotel** (see above), prix fixe, main dining room, EE • **Ledges,** White Mountains Hotel (see above), great views, E • **Stafford's in the Field Inn** (see above), prix fixe, take a country drive for a legendary dinner, reservations essential, EE • **Fabyans Station,** Route 302 (adjacent to Cog Railway), 278-2222, casual dining in a restored railroad station, I–M. *Lively informal dining:* **Horsefeathers,** Main Street, North Conway, 356-2687, I–M • **Red Parka Pub,** Route 302, Glen, 383-4344, I–M.

SIGHTSEEING **Appalachian Mountain Club** (AMC), Pinkham Notch Camp, 466-2727, evening programs, workshops, guided hikes. Call for current schedules • **Mt. Washington Cog Railway,** Route 302, Twin Mountain, 278-5404 or (800) 922-8825 outside NH. Hours: early May to late October. Mid-June to Labor Day, trains depart daily on the hour, 8 A.M. to 4 P.M.; hours vary in spring and fall, so best to check; reservations advised. Adults, $39; children, $26 • **Mt. Washington Auto Road,** Route 16, Pinkham Notch, 466-3988. Hours: mid-May to late October, daily, 7:30 A.M. to 6 P.M., weather permitting; shorter hours in spring and fall. Car and driver, $$$$$; each additional adult passenger, $$$; children, $$; under 5, free; guided tour additional, $$$$$ per person • **Wildcat Mountain Gondola Tramway,** Route 16, Pinkham Notch, 466-3326. Hours: June 15 to late October, daily, 10 A.M. to 4:45 P.M.; Memorial Day to mid-June, weekends only. $$$$ • **Attitash Bear Peak Alpine Slide, Water Slide, Chairlift,** Route 302, Bartlett, 374-2368. Hours: mid-June to Labor Day, daily, 10 A.M. to 6 P.M.; late May to mid-June and September to mid-October, 10 A.M. to 5 P.M. Single rides, $$$; combination rides, $$$$$ • **Heritage New Hampshire,** Route 16, Glen, 378-9776. Hours: mid-June to Labor Day, daily, 9 A.M. to 6 P.M.; mid-May to mid-June and Labor Day to mid-October, 9 A.M. to 5 P.M. $$$$ • **Story Land,** Route 16, Glen, 383-4293. Hours: mid-June to Labor Day, daily, 9 A.M. to 6 P.M.; September through Columbus Day, weekends only, 10 A.M. to 5 P.M. Adults and children, $$$$$. *Hiking, biking:* For a free leaflet on hiking and mountain biking, and for trail maps for trails at state parks throughout New Hampshire, contact the New Hampshire Division of Parks and Recreation, Trails Bureau, PO Box 1856, Concord, NH 03302, 271-3254.

INFORMATION   White Mountains Visitors Bureau, PO Box 10, North Woodstock, NH 03262, 745-8720 or (800) 346-3687; Mt. Washington Valley Chamber of Commerce, Route 16, PO Box 2300, North Conway, NH 03860, 356-5701 or (800) 367-3364. The Chamber of Commerce offers free room reservation service.

Looking for the Real York

Pick your favorite York—historic village, beach resort, yachting port, or rocky Maine peninsula.

Some years ago, each one was a separate village, and the villages were known respectively as York Village, York Beach, York Harbor, and Cape Neddick. Though officially they've been combined into a single community, they are still commonly called "The Yorks," plural because each part has such a distinct personality. Together, they offer a mini-sampler of the Maine coast, each part with its own appeal and its own appealing lodgings.

For history buffs, York Village is the chief lure. The onetime Indian settlement of Agamenticus has the distinction of being not only the oldest surviving English settlement in Maine, dating back to 1624, but America's first chartered city, established in 1642. Its name at that time was Gorgeana, after Sir Ferdinando Gorges, an English soldier and mariner who was then proprietor of the Province of Maine.

It was given the name York and reduced to mere township when it was seized by Massachusetts along with the whole Province of Maine in 1652. In spite of frequent Indian attacks that threatened its existence in the 1600s, York survived and by the eighteenth century had become a prosperous provincial capital and an important way station between Portsmouth and points east. Its wharves and warehouses bustled with treasures from the lucrative West Indies trade.

One of the warehouses on the York River was owned by John Hancock, the well-known signer of the Declaration of Independence. It has been restored and is now maintained by the Old York Historical Society as a museum displaying tools of Colonial times as well as ship models and other relics of York's seafaring days.

As York diminished in commercial importance late in the nineteenth century, it gained new prominence as a seaside resort. Many wealthy easterners, including one Samuel Clemens (better known as Mark Twain), bought up the fine Colonial residences of the village as summer homes. A number of the historic houses in town never changed hands, however, and even today are still occupied by descendants of their builders, making York Village something of a living museum with an unusual sense of its past and a determination to preserve it.

More than half a dozen buildings in the village now constitute Historic York and are open to the public. One of most fascinating is the 1719 Old Gaol, one of the oldest remaining public buildings in the country. Stone dungeons with walls three feet thick and separate cells for criminals, women lawbreakers, and debtors were actually part of the jailer home. Kids love poking through the cells and peeking through the window in the children's bedroom, through which the prisoners were passed their meals. Almost everyone poses for souvenir snapshots outside, sticking head and arms through the openings of the pillory where minor offenders were held in public view as punishment for their misdeeds.

Another interesting stop is the Emerson-Wilcox House, which has served as home, tavern, and post office over its 200-year history. Now it offers period rooms, a chimney passage, and some exquisite eighteenth-century crewel bed hangings.

Other stops with tales of the past to tell are the 1745 Old School-house, where children learned navigation, bookkeeping, and surveying along with their three Rs; and Jefferds' Tavern, where weary stagecoach passengers found refreshments after their dusty ride in the late 1700s. The tavern is now the visitor center for the Old York Historical Society.

Over the course of the summer you can see all kinds of Colonial crafts demonstrations in Historic York's properties, including the making of candles, clothing, soap, cheese, and natural dyes. Fishermen's crafts such as net tying and crafting lobster traps are shown at the Hancock Wharf, and demonstrations of cooking on the open hearth are given at Jefferds' Tavern.

A walking tour will take you to all of these attractions and more—the restored Elizabeth Perkins House, the Old Burying Ground, the green, handsome private homes, and a couple of fine New England churches. The Olde Church, in the center of the village, is now head-quarters for York Handcrafters, with a variety of handmade gifts.

Route 1 also has a couple of interesting shopping stops, such as the York Antiques Gallery, where many dealers display their wares, the Diana Card collection of folk art, and the Woods to Goods store, a unique outlet for carved ships, toys, and frames made by inmates in Maine prisons—some very fine work sold at reasonable prices.

If York Village has the monopoly on local history, Nubble Light, on Cape Neddick, takes the prize for scenery. From the south, follow Route 1A past Long Sands Beach to Nubble Road; from the north take Route 1A to Broadway to reach the lighthouse that is one of Maine's most photographed landmarks. You'll understand why when you see its site—a spectacular rocky promontory over the sea—which epitomizes this coast's special character.

Continuing on Route 1A north past Short Sands Beach, you'll find

Cape Neddick Harbor, fed by York's second river, the Cape Neddick. The small beach at the river's mouth is sheltered, a good place for small children or picnickers.

Make a left turn off Route 1 up Mountain Road to see yet another side of York's appeal, the Agamenticus Wilderness Reserve. This 1,000-acre tract across the top of three major hills offers wooded trails for hiking, biking, or horseback riding; a variety of wildlife; picnic grounds; and lovely vistas. A full-service riding stable and mountain bike rentals are available to make the most of the area.

York Beach, with its two main town beaches, is most likely to appeal if you like a lot of action and people around, or perhaps if you have children, especially teenagers. The town of York Beach is filled with tourist shops, eateries, and an amusement park. It won't appeal to all tastes, but it does offer the advantage of varied activities within walking distance of lodgings, so it's easy for you and your teens to go off in different directions.

There are some reasonably priced Victorian rooming houses in this area, and a growing number of inns and resort lodgings throughout the villages. The new View Point, atop Nubble Road, can't be beat for views, but there are particularly choice lodgings in the remaining section, York Harbor.

York Harbor has its own beach, pebbly but more peaceful than the others. But mainly this is boating territory, and the picturesque harbor is filled with craft of all kinds, from sleek yachts to fishermen's dories. The inns make the most of the scene. At Dockside Guest Quarters, you can sit on the porch and watch skippers navigating around the tricky 90-degree turn where the York River flows into the sea. The Maine House here dates from the late 1800s and retains the flavor of a sea captain's home; it's filled with model sailboats, paintings of clipper ships, and scrimshaw—and with bookcases lined with books on lighthouses and sailing. Five rooms are in the house; the rest, with private decks or balconies, are in pine cottages along the shore.

Edwards' Harborside Inn, is a comfortable lodging with a sunporch, overlooks the harbor and gives you a good view of the lobster boats setting out; and Stage Neck Inn, on a spit at the entrance to the harbor, is surrounded by water. The latter is a full-scale resort with tennis, boating, and an 18-hole golf course. York Harbor Inn lacks a direct water view but makes up for it with a lot of early American charm.

From Stage Neck Road you can take a scenic stroll along the Fishermen's Walk, which runs along the shore of York Harbor. The path goes by the historic Sayward-Wheeler House, which is open to the public; crosses Route 103; and continues across the Wiggley Bridge, a small suspension footbridge, and through the Steedman Woods to Lindsay Road, near the George Marshall Store, an art gallery featuring special exhibits by the Old York Historical Society.

What with beaches and boats and all the Yorks to explore, you may not need further activities; but if you have a long weekend, there's a lot to see and do just south of York in Kittery and then just over the bridge in Portsmouth, New Hampshire, only 12 miles away.

Kittery's Fort McClary State Memorial, with its restored hexagonal blockhouse, is high on the list. The Kittery Naval Museum and a number of historic homes—including the exquisite Lady Pepperell House and the John Bray House, the oldest dwelling in Maine—are also of interest in this once-wealthy shipbuilding town. Kittery's current big attraction is a slew of outlet stores for bargain shoppers—they stretch for miles along Route 1.

Portsmouth deserves at least half a day just for Strawbery Banke, an outdoor museum of more than 40 buildings representing early American life in a seacoast village. Some of the buildings are fully restored and furnished; others hold exhibits.

Unlike other restorations that re-create only the early settlement, this village portrays life as it has changed over the years, a fascinating approach. The Drisco House, for example, is furnished on one side as it might have looked in 1790, on the other as it would have been in the 1950s. Furnishings in other homes range from the 1770s to 1908. The newest addition, opened in 1994, the Abbott Corner Store and Kitchen, revives the 1940s, including the ration stamps needed to buy products during World War II, which probably seems like ancient history to the schoolchildren touring the complex. This village from the past also ties itself firmly to the present by giving working space to contemporary craftspeople in some of its historic houses.

Other interesting exhibits reveal the construction techniques of the eighteenth century and the architectural analysis that goes into the process of restoration. There are many more fine homes to be seen in Portsmouth, one of them the former residence of naval hero John Paul Jones, and there's a wealth of interesting shops to explore. Portsmouth Harbor cruises and outings to the Isle of Shoals and Star Island are also highly recommended. There are nightly dinner cruises, too, and weekend evening cruises with dancing and entertainment.

None of these will ease the task of selecting your favorite York—but they may just add to your conclusion that Maine's southernmost coastal resort area has multiple reasons for a visit.

Area Code: 207

DRIVING DIRECTIONS   York is on Route 1A, off U.S. Route 1, on the southern coast of Maine; take the York exit of I-95, the Maine Turnpike. It is 62 miles from Boston, 267 miles from New York, and 157 miles from Hartford.

PUBLIC TRANSPORTATION   Air and bus service to nearby Portsmouth, New Hampshire; C & J Trailways provides bus service from Boston to York during the summer season; limousine service also is available from Boston and Portland airports.

ACCOMMODATIONS **Dockside Guest Quarters,** PO Box 205, York Harbor 03909, 363-2868, M; suites, I • **Edwards' Harborside Inn,** Stage Neck Road, PO Box 866, York Harbor 03911, 363-3037, M –E, CP; suites, E–EE, CP • **York Harbor Inn,** Route 1A, PO Box 574, York Harbor 03911, 363-5119 or (800) 343-3869, M–E, CP • **Stage Neck Inn,** PO Box 97, York Harbor 03911, 363-3850 or (800) 222-3238, E–EE • **View Point,** 229 Nubble Road, York Beach, 363-2661, luxury contemporary cottage suites with kitchens, great ocean views, E–EE • **Union Bluff Hotel,** Beach Street, York Beach, 363-1333 or (800) 833-0721, spruced-up old-timer across the road from a quiet spot of beach, M–E. *Bed-and-breakfast inns:* **Riverbank Cottage,** 11 Harmon Park Road, York Harbor 03911, 363-8333, charm, quiet location, harbor views, M, CP • **Tanglewood Hall,** 611 York Street (Route 1A), York Harbor 03911, 363-7577, spacious, gracious Victorian with a big wraparound porch, M, CP • **Wooden Goose Inn,** Route 1, Cape Neddick, 03902, 363-5673, lavish decor, antiques in every nook and cranny, sumptuous breakfasts and afternoon tea, closed in July, M, CP; also very special three-day dinner packages, EE • **Inn at Harmon Park,** 415 York Street, York Harbor, 363-2031, long-established, comfortable Victorian near the water, M, CP • **Cape Neddick House,** 1300 Route 1, Cape Neddick 03902, 363-2500, delightful 1885 Victorian farmhouse with hospitable hostess and a back porch facing ten acres of woodland, I–M, CP • **Willows Inn,** Long Beach Avenue, York Beach 03910, 363-8800, Victorian home on the beach, M–E, CP.

DINING **Cape Neddick Inn and Gallery,** Route 1, Cape Neddick, 363-2899, dine amid paintings and sculptures, a best bet, M–E • **York Harbor Inn** (see above), ocean views, M • **Dockside Dining Room** (see above), more views, M • **Lighthouse Restaurant,** Nubble Road, 363-4054, unbeatable location, seafood with panoramic views, I–E • **Chef Mimmo's,** Route 1A, York Beach, 363-3807, very good Italian food in an unlikely location—the middle of the action at York Beach, crowded, M • **Fazio's,** 38 Woodbridge Road, York, 363-1718, locally recommended Italian, I–M; also connected to **La Stalla** pizzeria, I • **Cape Neddick Lobster Pound Harborside Restaurant,** Route 1A, 363-5471, informal spot for lobster and more, nice location on Cape Neddick Harbor, I–M • **Foster's Down East Lobster & Clambake,** Axholme Road (off Route 1A), 363-3255, lobster pound and fish market, I–M. Also see Portsmouth listings, pages 252–253.

SIGHTSEEING *Historic York:* Old York Historical Society, 207 York Street, 363-4974. Mid-June to September, Tuesday to Saturday, 10 A.M. to 5 P.M., Sunday, 1 P.M. to 5 P.M. Tours from Jefferds' Tavern, off Route 1A facing the Old Burying Ground. Combined admission, $$$; individual properties, $ • **Sayward-Wheeler House,** 79 Barrell Lane Extension, York Harbor, 436-3205. Hours: June through mid-October, Wednesday to Sunday, noon to 5 P.M. $$.

INFORMATION   The York Chamber of Commerce, 599 U.S. Route 1, Box 417, York, ME 03909, 363-4422.

Away from It All on Block Island

It's more than the 12-mile distance to the mainland that separates Block Island from the rest of the world. Block Island is a trip to yesterday.

Despite the ferry boats that bring more visitors every year, this exquisite island somehow manages to retain its wild beauty and the look and serenity of a time long gone by. Around every bend, flower-splashed meadows and pond-dotted moors come into view, open and inviting, with little but crisscrossing stone fences and an occasional weathered clapboard home to show that anyone has been there before you.

The beaches bend for miles around the edges of the island: some of them are easily accessible, some can be reached only by narrow sandy paths descending bluffs that lower as much as 200 feet above the ocean. The tallest of the cliffs, known as Mohegan Bluffs, is as spectacular a sight from below as from the top, where you can see forever out to sea.

Bicycles outnumber cars 100 to 1 here, adding to the tranquility. The islanders were so upset by the intrusion of mopeds that they once threatened to secede from Rhode Island if a law was not passed banning the hated motorbikes from their quiet lanes. At present there is a compromise, with mopeds not allowed on dirt roads.

Though some of the old Victorian hotels have been spruced up in recent years, there's been no attempt to build resorts or amusements on Block Island, so the visitors who board the ferryboats from Rhode Island, Connecticut, and Long Island are precisely those who want to get away from all that. Even a weekend visit is enough to leave you refreshed, better able to cope with the pressures of the real world when you get back.

Most of the boats arrive at the pier in Old Harbor opposite a row of century-old, gingerbread-trimmed Victorian hotels now listed on the National Register of Historic Places. The most impressive is the spanking white National Hotel, meticulously restored to its original 1888 lines and resplendent with its dark green shutters, shiny black mansard roof, and elaborate cupola.

Lodgings on Block Island fall into two basic categories: the big wooden hotels that have been here for 100 years or more; and the newer, more intimate inns. Though some of the old hotels have nicely refurbished their rooms, few Block Island lodgings are fancy places by mainland standards, and most island lovers like it just that way.

For faraway views, you'll want to climb the hill up Spring Street to the Spring House or to the neat and trim 1661 Inn, where a seat on the porch or the deck can keep you mesmerized for hours—gazing at that deep and unbelievably blue sea. The rooms here vary from tiny to enormous, with the bigger and costlier ones offering private decks with views. The Sea Breeze, next door, is also a prime cozy little complex with its own fine water views. The Atlantic Inn, not far away on High Street, is another old-time landmark offering ocean vistas.

Recently, many other attractive bed-and-breakfast inns have opened around the island. Rose Farm Inn and the Old Town Inn are among the nicest. The most unusual is the Sasafrash, a converted church filled with antiques. The best view without doubt belongs to the Old Weather Bureau Inn, which was actually once the island weather bureau and sits high on a hilltop with vistas on all sides. The Blue Dory, in town, wins for most stylish furnishings.

To get your bearings on a first visit, you'll want to circle the island, not too difficult a task since it is only seven miles long and three miles wide. There are a dozen taxis that will gladly take you around if you've wisely left your car on shore, and bike shops all over the place will equip you to pedal your own path, poking down those tempting side roads as you ride to the beach. It's easy to get by on foot as well, especially with the beaches as tempting rest stops all along the way. The Greenway, a network of trails, winds through park, conservancy, and private lands from the center of the island to the southern shore, and the Clayhead Nature Trails cover the north end.

The island is shaped like a lamb chop, with Old Harbor situated just where the meatiest portion might begin. Heading north, you'll come to Crescent Beach, which is really a whole string of beaches along the Atlantic Ocean, with the dunes growing steeper as you proceed farther north. Fred Benson Beach is the most crowded, since it has changing facilities and a lifeguard, but all it takes is a walk to find space to yourself.

The island is almost bisected at this point by the Great Salt Pond, with New Harbor sitting at the pond's most sheltered inland spot. Here's where the sailors and yachtsmen drop anchor at nearby marinas.

Continuing on the main (and only) roadway, Corn Neck Road, you'll come to Sandy Point with its historic 1867 granite lighthouse in the dunes and a wildlife sanctuary that is a favorite spring nesting ground for seagulls as well as one of the prime destinations for bird-watchers on the East Coast. The North Light lighthouse has been restored and was opened in 1993 as a museum.

Corn Neck Road was named for the crop grown here by the Narragansett Indians, Block Island's original inhabitants, who called their home "Isle of the Little God." They were spotted in 1524 by Giovanni da Verrazano, then again in 1624 by Adrian Block, the Dutchman for whom the island was named. He was probably the first—but by no means the last—to sail over by yacht from Long Island.

Settler's Rock, at Sandy Point, marks the arrival of the English, who created the first real colony on the island. Block Island abounds with legends of shipwrecks and tales of ghosts and eerie lights, all passed on by generations of seafaring residents.

Sandy Point and its environs are flat. As you turn back toward the south past Old Harbor, the hills begin, and the dips and turns on Spring Street, Southeast Light Road, and the Mohegan Trail yield glorious views on all sides. It's at the southernmost end of the island that you'll find the dramatic view from Mohegan Bluffs and the Southeast Light, a quaint brick building that has stood as a beacon to sailors for over 100 years. It had to be moved some 240 feet back recently to keep it safe from the eroding bluffs.

Stairs in the sea grass make it easy to descend to the rocky beaches below to gaze back at the bluffs and perhaps find a suitable perch on sand or rocks for basking on the beach.

The main road cuts back inland past Rodman's Hollow, another of the island's five wildlife refuges, a great natural ravine left by a long-ago glacier. Once again, many paths wind through the meadows and marshes to the sea.

Once you've found your favorite spots, you'll likely want to spend most of your time occupying them and enjoying the beauty around you. If you want more activity, you can rent a sailboat at the Block Island Club, charter a fishing boat at the dock in Old Harbor, take out a canoe or a kayak from Orvis's Oceans & Ponds, or take a guided trail ride on horseback at Rustic Rides Farm.

Shopping is not a major occupation on Block Island, but there are some small, worthwhile stops in Old Harbor. They start right on Water Street across from the docks and continue around the corner on Dodge Street. The Star Department Store is Block Island's general store, with everything from beach umbrellas to clothing. Spring Street Gallery, a special stop, is a cooperative showing art, jewelry, stained glass, and quilts by local artists.

When the sun begins to set, one of the best views in town is off the deck at the Oar, at Block Island Boat Basin on New Harbor. For dining, there is no shortage of places to enjoy Block Island swordfish, bluefish, and the other fresh seafood that is a specialty at this fisherman's paradise. If you want evening action, go to Ballard's, a boatman's hangout that is by far the noisiest and most popular place around. The music here is strictly 1940s and '50s; younger action is at the Yellow Kittens Tavern, where there are live bands on weekends.

For an island souvenir, you might think of having Finn's Fish Market, in Old Harbor, pack up fresh fish or lobster for your trip home. It may prove some small consolation for having to leave this extraordinary getaway at sea.

Area Code: 401

TRANSPORTATION   By ferryboat, Block Island is 45 minutes from Port Judith, on the Rhode Island shore; two hours from New London, Connecticut; and about two hours from Montauk, on Long Island. There are also boats from Providence that stop at Newport on the way, a four-hour ride. For schedules and rates, contact Nelesco Navigation, Box 482, New London, CT 06320, or Interstate Navigation Company, Galilee State Pier, Point Judith, RI 02882, both reached at (401) 783-4613. Bonanza buses from Providence connect to local bus service in Galilee. Amtrak trains stop at Westerly, Rhode Island, where there is air service to the island via New England Airlines (a 12-minute flight), 596-2460 or (800) 243-2460. There are also flights from other points in the summer; check the chamber of commerce for the current schedules.

ACCOMMODATIONS   Expect minimum-stay requirements in season; all Block Island addresses are zip code 02807. Unless indicated, all lodgings are in Old Harbor. • **Spring House,** Spring Street, 466-5844, refurbished rooms, E–EE, CP • **Atlantic Inn,** High Street, 466-2006, nicely refurbished old-timer, hilltop with views, tennis and croquet courts, room 22 on top is prime, M–E, CP • **National Hotel,** Water Street, 466-2901 or (800) 255-2449, in-town landmark, nicely renovated, E–EE • **1661 Inn,** Spring Street, 466-2421 or (800) MANISSE, huge buffet breakfast and cocktails served on deck overlooking the water, rooms vary, some luxurious, E–EE, CP; some with shared baths, I–E, CP • **Manisses House,** Spring Street, 466-2421 or (800) MANISSE, same owners as 1661 Inn, elegant small restored hotel, but no views, M–EE, CP • **Sea Breeze Inn,** Spring Street, 466-2275, small complex with a variety of rooms, some with smashing views, M–E, CP • **Rose Farm Inn,** off High Street, Box E, 466-2021, very private location, big rooms, pretty decor in a Victorian farmhouse or the new Captain Rose House, M–E, CP • **Blue Dory,** Dodge Street, 466-2254, cozy inn and several adjoining buildings, wide variety of room sizes, elegant decor, walking distance to town, EE, CP • **Old Town Inn,** Old Town Road, PO Box 351, 466-5958, spacious and gracious, midway between Old Harbor and New Harbor, long hike but easy bike, M–E, CP • **Old Weather Bureau Inn,** Beach Avenue, Box 281, 466-9977 or (800) OFF-TO-BI, rustic decor, spectacular views, M–E, CP • **The Dewey**

Cottage, Ocean Avenue, 466-3155 or (800) 330-3155, fresh decor, one room with a whirlpool and a view, M–E, CP • **Sheffield House,** High Street, 466-2494, pleasant modest guest house, M–E, CP • **Barrington Inn,** Beach and Ocean Avenues, New Harbor, 466-5510, high on a knoll with wonderful views, M–E, CP • **The Sasafrash,** Center Road, PO Box 1227, 466-5486, unique, old church with soaring spaces, over-flowing with antiques, M, CP • **Gables Inn and Gables II,** Dodge Street, 466-2213, modest, old-fashioned guest houses near town, M.

DINING   **Atlantic Inn** (see above), four-course dinners, prix fixe, EE • **Hotel Manisses** (see above), attractive dining room with continental menu, M–EE • **Spring House** (see above), good reviews, attractive din-ing room, M–EE • **Winfield's,** Corn Neck Road, Old Harbor, 466-5856, intimate, special, M–E • **Dead Eye Dick's,** New Harbor, 466-2654, lively, waterfront deck, M • **Harborside Inn,** Water Street, Old Harbor, 466-5504, harbor view from the porch, M–E • **Eli's,** Chapel Street, Old Harbor, 466-5230, creative pastas, seafood, very popular, M • **Mohe-gan Café,** Water Street, Old Harbor, 466-5911, nautical decor, popular for lunch and dinner, I–M • **Ballards,** Old Harbor, 466-2231, a mad-house, but the best lobster prices in town, I–EE • **Finn's Seafood,** on the piers near Ballards, Old Harbor, 466-2473, informal, attached to fish market, best bet on the island for simply prepared fish at reasonable prices, I–M • **The Beachead,** Corn Neck Road, Old Harbor, 466-2249, everyone's favorite for burgers for lunch or light dinner; also chili, fish and chips, I • **The Oar,** Job's Hill (on West Side Road), New Harbor, 466-8820, pub overlooking Great Salt Pond for sunset watching, new owners are upgrading the casual menu, I–M.

SPORTS   **Oceans and Ponds, the Orvis Store,** Ocean and Connecti-cut Avenues, 466-5131, kayak and canoe rentals, charter fishing trips • **Rustic Rides Farm,** West Side Road, 466-5-60, horseback riding • **Block Island Club,** Corn Neck Road, 466-5939, sailboat rentals.

INFORMATION   Block Island Chamber of Commerce, Drawer D, Water Street, Block Island, RI 02897, 466-2982 or (800) 383-BIRI.

High Notes Near Mt. Monadnock

They call it the "Quiet Corner" of the state, a world of apple orchards, covered bridges, mountain views, and tiny towns untouched by time.

But come summer each year, New Hampshire's southwestern Monadnock region comes alive with music. You can follow the melody from town to town—Schubert in Peterborough tonight, Haydn at Jaffrey tomorrow, Mozart in Hancock the day after.

In all, more than 30 concerts, ranging from chamber music to recitals to orchestral works and opera, are held in the hamlets and villages in this green and rolling region during the annual six-week festival known as Monadnock Music. The major concerts are on weekends at the Peterborough Town House, and admission is charged. In addition, free concerts are held, moving from white-spired village church to meetinghouse in different small-town locales throughout the season, a perfect way to get acquainted with one of New England's least spoiled regions.

And these are just the beginning of the music. In 1992 the New England Marionette Opera, America's only opera company performed entirely with marionettes, debuted in its own specially constructed 135-seat theater in Peterborough. This delightful company presents classics from *Tosca* to *Porgy and Bess* performed to recorded music by lifelike, beautifully costumed 32-inch marionettes. The theater's OK (Opera for Kids) division includes an adaptation of Mozart's *Magic Flute,* and Menotti's *Amahl and the Night Visitors* is performed during the holidays. The company completed its first international tour in 1996 and will be at home in Peterborough until 1999.

The Apple Hill Chamber Players, artists-in-residence at Keene State College, perform in the Louise Shonk Keely barn, in Nelson, during the summer, and towns like Temple and Hancock have local bands that strut their stuff with concerts on the greens.

Besides this tuneful array, there is long-established summer theater in the area. The Peterborough Players have performed classics for over 50 years in a converted barn, and the American Stage Festival, in Milford, has been around since 1972. The Arts Center at Brickyard Pond, at Keene State College, also offers a variety of dance, music, and theater throughout the year.

The wonder is that the region remains relatively uncrowded, especially since Mt. Monadnock, the peak that Ralph Waldo Emerson called "the New Olympus," is, according to local authorities, the most-climbed mountain in North America.

Part of the reason is that an ascent to the 3,165-foot summit is an accomplishment within reach of even novice hikers, who can then enjoy the soaring view of six states that is worthy of a far loftier peak. On a really clear day, the White Mountains to the north, the Green Mountains to the west, and the tops of Boston skyscrapers to the east are all in sight.

The view of the mountain from below can be equally impressive, for it looms majestically out of all proportion to its size, visible from almost every town in the region. In the late nineteenth century, it attracted writers such as Emerson, Hawthorne, and Thoreau, who spent their summers here within sight of the inspiring peak. In the twentieth century, many of America's most famous writers, artists, and composers have come here to be inspired at the MacDowell Colony, the famous retreat on a 450-acre estate in Peterborough.

With all the music and theater in the area, the only problem you'll have filling your evenings in the Monadnock region is choosing among the many offerings.

By day the options are equally tempting. If you're at all active, you'll want to head for Mt. Monadnock. Stop at the State Park Visitor Center, in Jaffrey Center, to pick up a trail map and get some firsthand hiking pointers from the helpful staff members. There are 40 miles of trails and paths—from one to ten miles long and for every ability level.

Don't miss the early-to-mid-July riot of color at Rhododendron State Park, in Fitzwilliam. There are some 16 acres of the showy wild shrubs. The park offers a walking path around the entire glen, plus picnic grounds in shaded pine groves—and, of course, more of those ever-present views of Mt. Monadnock.

If you want to remain outdoors, there are many more parks to explore, and a number of local swimming holes. Among the highlights of the parks are the auto road to the summit of Pack Monadnock Mountain, in Miller State Park in Peterborough, and the swimming area on Otter Lake, in Greenfield State Park. The Wapack Trail, a skyline route along summits, provides breathtaking views from open ledges and rocky peaks. The 21-mile trail passes through New Ipswich, Temple, Sharon, Peterborough, and Greenfield, taking in several state parks.

There are also lakes and rivers for canoeing or sailing, and once you're armed with the necessary state fishing license, this is good country for anglers. Just stop at the Peterborough Information Center or ask —wherever you are staying—for directions to the nearest water. And this is excellent golfing territory, with five 18-hole golf courses available in the region. Those who want to be at the first tee bright and early can stay at Tory Pines Resort, in Francestown, which is built around a golf course.

If indoor diversions such as antiques and art galleries are more to your taste, you'll still not lack for choices. The best plan is to make a tour of the pretty little towns to see what each has to offer.

Peterborough is a handsome hub that is attracting many permanent residents. The Nubanusit River runs through the picturesque town center. The enormous granite slabs used to build the structures on Grove and Main Streets in 1847 have caused this area to be dubbed the "Granite Block." Farther on Grove, the Georgian red-brick buildings with photogenic white cupolas were built in this century, designed to complement the old. The Peterborough Library was the first free tax-supported public library in the country.

There are some intriguing small shops and galleries in town for browsing. The North Gallery, at Tewksbury, at the junction of Routes 101 and 123, has a nice selection of gifts, and the Sharon Arts Center, four miles south on Route 123, displays and sells fine crafts. Eastern Mountain Sports, headquartered in Peterborough, has an outlet store for its outdoor wear at Vose Farm Road, just off Route 202 north of town.

Drive south on Route 202, west on Route 124, and follow the signs to reach Fitzwilliam, a classic New England town, with a block-long green lined with fine white Colonial homes and choice antiquing, including the Fitzwilliam Antique Center, with 40 dealers.

If children are along, you may choose to drive west from Peterborough on Route 101 to Dublin and the Friendly Farm, where all kinds of lovable farm animals are in residence, ready to be fed and petted. Pretty Dublin is the home of both *Yankee* magazine and the area's best Italian restaurant, Del Rossi's Trattoria. Some of the best views in the region are found on Route 101 as it passes through Dublin and curves around Dublin Lake, with the mountain rising behind and to the west.

Drive north from Dublin on Route 137 for two more contenders for the "prettiest town" crown. Harrisville is one of the most perfectly preserved New England mill towns; the red-brick buildings around a group of ponds spilling into a waterfall attract both photographers and artists. Hancock boasts a Paul Revere bell in the steeple of the church, reputed to be the most photographed church in New England, and a charming historic inn, the 1789 Hancock Inn, New Hampshire's oldest.

Farther east is Francestown, another front-runner in the local town beauty derby, which has more antiques in its small town center. To the west is Keene, the "big city" of the area, with a population of over 22,000 people. Keene does not qualify as quaint, but it does offer good shopping at the Colony Mill Marketplace, where the Country Artisans Gallery showcases work by 300 craftsmakers and an antiques center includes over 100 dealers. You can see fine work from throughout New England at the Thorne-Sagendorph Art Gallery, at Keene State College.

If you're still searching for more to do, just about every little town has its own sights or historic house museum. Or you can check out the local covered bridges. Swanzey is the covered bridge capital, with four bridges within a five-mile area. Another place you may want to see is the Cathedral of the Pines, in Rindge. This is an outdoor shrine with a panoramic view and an altar honoring American war dead.

Hillsborough is to the north of Peterborough via Route 202, a bit out of the way but worth the drive. A notable home for president-watchers is the restored Franklin Pierce Homestead, in Hillsborough. And a unique inn sure to delight is the Inn at Maplewood Farm. If you turn on your radio here and hear that Martians are invading, you need not panic. It's only a replay of Orson Welles's original "War of the Worlds," one of hundreds of old radio classics that you can enjoy at this unique inn. Innkeeper Jayme Simoes is a vintage radio buff with a collection of over 1,000 cassettes that he rotates according to monthly themes, such as the Great Comedians, including Fred Allen and Jack Benny, or the Radio Gumshoes, featuring Ellery Queen and Sam Spade. The programs are broadcast on a low-power transmitter that can be heard only within the house.

Down the road a bit in the picture-perfect hamlet of Hillsborough Center is Gibson Pewter, with a talented father-son team practicing their craft in a barn workshop. Their contemporary pewter pieces are in the collection of the Boston Museum of Fine Arts, and when you see their beauty you'll likely want to collect a few for yourself.

Except for Keene, a small city, all the towns in the Monadnock region are tiny and little touched by time, and you'll hardly go wrong wherever you roam.

Nor are you likely to go wrong picking among the small country inns in the area. The Colonial John Hancock Inn is cozy and historic. The Amos A. Parker House is a sophisticated charmer that does justice to its pretty hometown of Fitzwilliam, and the Hannah Davis House, down the road, is another beautifully restored village home. The Benjamin Prescott Inn is a historic house in the country, with antiques and lots of nooks and crannies for exploring, and the Apple Gate is a welcoming small 1832 Colonial in the countryside, convenient to both Peterborough and the Sharon Arts Center.

For vistas, the Inn at Crotched Mountain is the unquestioned winner, and you'll know why as soon as you drive up the long hill and see the 40-mile view. There is one hazard, however: once you settle beside the pool with that scene in front of you, you may never be able to tear yourself away.

Area Code: 603

DRIVING DIRECTIONS   The Monadnock region is in the southwestern corner of New Hampshire. It can be reached from the west via I-91, taking the Route 119 exit to Hinsdale and on to Fitzwilliam; from the north, via I-89 to Route 202; from the south, via Route 2 to Route 202, which runs directly into Peterborough and Jaffrey. From the east, take Route 3 to Route 101 and go west to Route 202. The region is about 75 miles from Boston, 205 miles from New York, and 95 miles from Hartford.

PUBLIC TRANSPORTATION Vermont Transit bus service to Keene.

ACCOMMODATIONS **Amos A. Parker House,** Route 119, Fitzwilliam 03447, 585-6540, M, CP • **Hannah Davis House,** Route 119, Fitzwilliam 03447, 585-3344, M, CP • **John Hancock Inn,** Hancock 03449, 525-3318, M–E, CP • **Benjamin Prescott Inn,** Route 124 East, Jaffrey 03452, 532-6637, I–M, CP • **Apple Gate Bed and Breakfast,** 199 Upland Farm Road (and Route 123 South), Peterborough 03458, 924-6543, I, CP • **Inn at Maplewood Farm,** 447 Center Road, Hillsborough 03244, 464-4242, I–M, CP • **Inn at Crotched Mountain,** Mountain Road (off Route 42), Francestown 03043, 588-6840, pool and tennis, modest rooms, great view, I–M, CP • **Harrisville Squire's Inn,** Keene Road, Harrisville 03450, 827-3925, homey farmhouse on 30 acres, bike center, cross-country trails, I–M, CP • **Stepping Stones Bed and Breakfast,** RR1, Box 78, Wilton Center 03086, 876-3361, nineteenth-century home, artisan hostess, lovely gardens, good value, I, CP • **Final Folly Bed and Breakfast,** 203 Wilton Road, Wilton 03086, 1791 Colonial, nicely restored, I, CP • **Inn at New Ipswich,** Porter Hill Road, PO Box 208, New Ipswich, 30371, 878-3711, comfortable 1790 farmhouse, I, CP • **Tory Pines Resort,** Route 47, Francestown 03043, 588-6352, recommended for golfers, M–E, MAP.

DINING **Latacarta,** 6 School Street, Peterborough, 924-6878, interesting menu, most say best in the area, I–M • **Carolyn's Bistro,** 50 Depot Square, Peterborough, 924-2002, excellent for lunch as well as dinner, I–M • **Twelve Pine,** Depot Square, Peterborough, 924-6140, combination market and café, good lunch spot, I • **The Boilerhouse at Noone Falls,** Route 202 South, Peterborough, 924-9486, picturesque, views, I–M • **Fitzwilliam Inn,** on the green, Fitzwilliam, 532-8342, historic, cozy dining room, I–M • **John Hancock Inn** (see above), New England specialties, M–E • **Del Rossi's Trattoria,** Route 137, Dublin, 563-7195, Italian in a Colonial home, I–M • **Chesterfield Inn,** Route 9, Chesterfield, 256-3211, creative American cuisine in a 1700s farmhouse, M–E.

SIGHTSEEING **Monadnock Music,** PO Box 255, Peterborough 03458, 924-7610, six-week summer season, write for schedule and prices • **Peterborough Players,** Middle Hancock Road, PO Box 1, Peterborough, 924-7585, changing repertory, July and August only, call for details • **New England Marionette Opera,** Main Street, Peterborough, 924-4333, June through mid-December; prices vary, so it's best to check; all seats are reserved and advance reservations are recommended • **American Stage Festival,** Route 13 North, Milford, 673-7515. Check for this year's plays and prices • **Sharon Arts Center,**

Route 123, Sharon, 924-7256. Hours: Monday to Saturday, 10 A.M. to 5 P.M.; Sunday, from noon. Free • **The Friendly Farm,** Route 101, Dublin, 563-8444. Hours: May to Labor Day, daily, 10 A.M. to 5 P.M., weekends through mid-October. $$ • **Cathedral of the Pines,** Route 110, Rindge, 899-3300. Hours: daily, May 1 to October 31, 9 A.M. to 4 P.M. $$ per vehicle • **New Hampshire State Parks,** information for parks without a separate phone listing, 271-3556; unless noted, most parks have day's use fees—adults, $2.50; under 12, free; **Monadnock State Park,** Visitor Center off Dublin Road (Route 124), Jaffrey Center, 532-8862; **Rhododendron State Park,** Rhododendron Road, Fitzwilliam; **Miller State Park,** off Route 101, Peterborough; **Greenfield State Park,** off Route 136, Greenfield, 547-3497.

INFORMATION   Monadnock Travel Council, c/o Greater Keene Chamber of Commerce, 48 Central Square, Keene, NH 03431, 352-1303; Greater Peterborough Chamber of Commerce, PO Box 401, Peterborough, NH 03458, 924-7234; Information Center at the intersection of Routes 101 and 202, Peterborough.

Visiting Martha's Vineyard

If you're wealthy and/or a celebrity, chances are you have your own place on Martha's Vineyard, along with the likes of Carly Simon, Mike Wallace, William Styron, and Beverly Sills.

The next best thing to owning a place here is renting, with time to get into the rhythm of the island and discover its private places and pleasures. More than most places, the Vineyard has two personalities, public and private, and though it's a perfectly lovely spot for a weekend, be forewarned that you'll get only a superficial look at the reasons why so many people fall totally in love with this island.

First of all, Martha's Vineyard is by far the biggest of the major vacation islands on the New England coast—108 square miles, compared with roughly 30 for Block Island and 52 for Nantucket, its not-so-near neighbor off the Massachusetts shore. It takes a while to learn the ins and outs.

Martha's Vineyard is also quick to get to—just a 45-minute boat ride from Cape Cod. That attracts lots of summer vacationers, bringing the population from 10,000 people year-round to a summer glut of 100,000. Add hordes of day-trippers who want to see everything on a tour bus in a few short hours, and you can understand the problem.

But with all of that, the Vineyard still has magnificent beaches, seaside cliffs, woodlands, ponds, and wildlife preserves—and several diverse little towns to explore. What many people like best about the island is its ambience, an unusual blend of green country retreat and beach resort, with great sailing waters thrown in as a bonus.

Among the towns, Edgartown, with its handsome sea captains' homes, is the first pick for lodgings for most weekend visitors because it has the greatest variety of inns and restaurants, most within walking distance of town. Since shuttle buses make regular rounds from the ferry docks at Vineyard Haven and Oak Bluffs to the Court House in Edgartown, this is an easy place to visit without a car.

There are attractive choices in the other towns as well, and some people prefer to be "up island" in West Tisbury or Menemsha away from the crowds. Wherever you stay, to really see the variety of the island's offerings, if you don't have your own car, rent one, or rent a bicycle or moped when you get off the ferry. Like most islands, this is ideal biking country, though the hilly upcountry roads are not recommended for novices. There is a paved path for bicycles all the way from Oak Bluffs to Edgartown, and many miles of paths in the State Forest connecting Vineyard Haven, Oak Bluffs, Edgartown, and West Tisbury.

One of the first orders of business in understanding the makeup of Martha's Vineyard is a visit to each of its disparate communities. The island was dubbed Martha's Vineyard by an early explorer, Bartholemew Gosnold, who landed there in 1602 and named it to honor one of his daughters as well as the wild grapes he found growing in profusion.

The first permanent white settlement on the island came 40 years later at Edgartown, known then as Great Harbor. With its rich farms and whaling expeditions from its harbors, the island prospered until the Revolutionary War. In 1778 the British fleet arrived to burn ships and raid more than 10,000 sheep and 300 head of cattle from local farmers.

In the 1820s the whaling industry revived and fine homes in Edgartown were built by sea captains and merchants. Now a center for yachters instead of whalers, Edgartown still has the look of a nineteenth-century seaport. A walk around the little town, whose Water Street runs right beside the harbor, is a tour past spanking white Greek Revival homes that still display their dark shutters, fanlights, and "widow's walks," where worried wives watched for their husbands' safe return from the sea.

One of the houses on South Water Street belonged to Captain Valentine Pease, master of the ship on which Herman Melville made his only whaling voyage. Two other notable homes now serve as museums and another is the office of the *Vineyard Gazette*. The Federated Church, built in 1828, remains a landmark, along with the six-columned Old Whaling Church, which dominates Main Street and now serves as the local Performing Arts Center. Next door is the home of Dr. Daniel Fisher, once the richest man on the island, a physician who was also the largest manufacturer of spermaceti candles and who held the contract to supply all the nation's lighthouses with whale oil.

Behind the Fisher House is the oldest remaining residence, the 1672 Vincent House. The original brickwork, hardware, and woodwork have been preserved to allow visitors to see how buildings were constructed 300 years ago.

The Vineyard Museum is headquarters of the Martha's Vineyard Historical Society complex, with several properties. It includes the 1765 Thomas Cooke House, 12 rooms filled with antique furniture, scrimshaw, ship models, costumes, and gear used by whalers and early farmers. The Dale Huntington Library houses the Foster Maritime Gallery, exhibiting logbooks, charts, and more scrimshaw and ship models. The Captain Francis Pease House has three galleries devoted to island history plus a Native American Gallery.

Drive to the gingerbread cottages of Oak Bluffs to discover a totally different kind of island history. Just about the time the golden age of whaling was coming to an end, a new "industry" grew up: religion. It began in 1835, when the Edgartown Methodists held a camp meeting in an oak grove, which later became known as Wesleyan Grove, on the bluffs at the northern end of town. The meeting, with worshipers and preachers living in tents and speakers standing on a driftwood platform, became a yearly affair of growing popularity. By 1859 the Martha's Vineyard Camp Meeting had become the largest in the world, with 12,000 people attending. Within 40 years, crowds of 30,000 gathered regularly for Illumination Night, which marked the end of the summer season with mammoth Japanese lanterns and fireworks displays. The event is still celebrated each year in August.

According to island history, many who attended the meetings found the seashore and lovely surroundings "as uplifting as the call to repent" —and thus began Martha's Vineyard's new era as a summer resort. The tents gave way to wooden cottages, with the owners often trying to outdo one another in colorful Victorian gingerbread. Wesleyan Grove turned first into Cottage City, then, as tourism grew, into Oak Bluffs, a town of 1,000 cottages plus boardinghouses and stores.

Religion remained a drawing card. In 1879 a new steel tabernacle replaced the old circus tent. The building and the remaining old cottages give a unique flavor to the present town of Oak Bluffs. The town also claims to own the oldest carousel in the country, the Flying Horses, which delights children today as it did in the 1870s.

Ironically, pious Oak Bluffs, along with Edgartown, is one of the few places on Martha's Vineyard that offers bar service with meals. Otherwise, it's BYOB in island restaurants.

Continuing along the coast to Vineyard Haven, the commercial center of the town of Tisbury, will bring you to seafaring territory again and the busy dock where most of the island ferries pull in. The Seaman's Bethel, once a refuge for sailors far from home, has been restored and is now a museum of maritime mementos and history. The Town Hall, once a Unitarian church, is one of the island's handsome architectural legacies from whaling days. Follow Main Street to the West Chop Lighthouse for a scenic drive past some of Vineyard Haven's finest homes.

Back in town, follow State Road through wooded West Tisbury to North Road and into Chilmark, an area of rolling green hills and exceptionally private coastline that is a choice location for summer homes and a good spot for away-from-it-all inns. Watch for the turnoff to Menemsha, a tiny quintessential fishing village, and then follow Lighthouse Road to the brilliantly colored cliffs of Gay Head and its lighthouse. It is one of the first revolving lighthouses in the country, built in 1799. The Outermost Inn, in Gay Head, offers fantastic views from every room.

You can vary your route back by taking South and West Tisbury Roads into town. For a scenic detour off West Tisbury, take Deep Bottom for two miles and follow the sign to Long Point, a 580-acre preserve on the south shore with frontage on Tisbury Great Pond, as well as a couple of coves on the Atlantic and a half mile of South Beach.

Seeing the sights of Martha's Vineyard can fill a day, especially if you do it by bike. One highly recommended approach is to pack a picnic lunch and take time off for stops at a beach or walks through some of the nature preserves along the way.

Besides Long Point, there are Felix Neck, off the Vineyard Haven–Edgartown Road, and Cedar Tree Neck, on the north shore down Indian Hill Road off of State Road. These are places to see wildflowers, birds, and all manner of island pond life.

As for beaches, despite all those residents-only locations, there are many fine ones left from which to choose. One of the most beautiful of the public beaches is South Beach, also known as Katama Beach, on the south shore at Edgartown—three miles of powdery sand with surf on one side and protected salt pond on the other. East Beach, on Chappaquiddick, a small island off Edgartown, is part of the Cape Pogue Wildlife Refuge, which includes most of the barrier beaches forming the northeastern tip of Martha's Vineyard. Much of Chappaquiddick is an untouched wilderness of dunes, cedar thickets, salt marsh, and scrubby upland, accessible only on foot or in a four-wheel-drive vehicle. No tour groups to contend with here.

You'll find every kind of outdoor recreation on the island—tennis courts in Vineyard Haven, Oak Bluffs, Edgartown, and West Tisbury; and an 18-hole golf course in Oak Bluffs and a 9-hole course in Vineyard Haven. Fishing boats go out of all the main island docks, sailboats are for rent in Vineyard Haven, and boat rentals are available in Edgartown.

There are enough standard resort gift shops in island towns to keep die-hard shoppers occupied for a bit, and a dozen art galleries are spread around the island. Among the most interesting stops in Edgartown is the gallery on the main floor of the Charlotte Inn.

But shopping is the least of the reasons to come to Martha's Vineyard. Spend a weekend getting acquainted with the combination of country and seashore this lush island offers, its exceptional beaches and its unspoiled natural beauty, and you may well find you're one of the many who keep coming back for more.

Area Code: 508

TRANSPORTATION Passenger and car ferries to Martha's Vineyard run year-round from Woods Hole on Cape Cod (45 minutes); for information, contact Steamship Authority, PO Box 284, Woods Hole, MA 02543, 477-8600. Ferries for passengers only also operate in the warm months from the Cape Cod towns of Falmouth (35 minutes, 548-4800) and Hyannis (1 hour and 45 minutes, 778-2600), and from New Bedford, Massachusetts (1 hour and 30 minutes, 997-1688). There is bus service to Woods Hole from Boston and New York via Bonanza Bus Line, (800) 556-3815. Air service is provided by Cape Air, (800) 352-0714, and US Airways Express, (800) 428-4322. Woods Hole is 85 miles from Boston, 271 miles from New York, and 187 miles from Hartford. For other current ferry services and small airlines serving the island, contact the Martha's Vineyard Chamber of Commerce.

ACCOMMODATIONS **Charlotte Inn,** South Summer Street, Box 1056, Edgartown 02539, 627-4751, elegant, antiques-furnished 1820 home with gallery and fine restaurant downstairs, EE, CP • **Daggett House,** 59 North Water Street, Box 1333, Edgartown 02539, 627-4600, snug historic sea captain's home with garden on the harbor, and adjacent home, M–EE, CP • **Point Way Inn,** Main Street and Pease's Point Way, Box 5255, Edgartown 02539, 627-8633 or (800) 942-9569, warm ambience, pleasant decor, croquet on the lawn, M–EE, CP • **Shiverick Inn,** Pent Lane, Box 640, Edgartown 02539, 627-3797, formal, elegant, E–EE, CP • **Captain Dexter House,** 35 Pease's Point Way, Box 2798, Edgartown 02539, 627-7289, four-posters, pretty Laura Ashley decor, M–E, CP • **Colonial Inn,** North Water Street, Box 68, Edgartown 02539, 627-4711, 42-room old-timer with hotel services, inn ambience, M–E, CP • **The Arbor,** 222 Upper Main Street, Box 1228, Edgartown 02539, 627-8137, airy, attractive, good value, M–E, CP • **Katama Shores Inn,** Katama Road, Edgartown 02539, 627-4747, beach lovers' choice, motel decor but facing lovely South Beach, tennis, pool, some kitchens, M–EE • **Beach Plum Inn,** North Road, Box 98, Menemsha 02552, 645-9454, 1848 main house and a cottage complex, very private spot amid gardens overlooking the sound, E–EE, CP • **Menemsha Inn and Cottages,** Box 38, Menemsha 02552, 645-2521, secluded contemporary inn with water views, special, M–E, CP • **Lambert's Cove Country Inn,** Lambert's Cove Road, West Tisbury 02575, 693-2298, escapist's dream, charming farmhouse and cottages amid lawns, gardens, and an apple orchard, tennis, E, CP • **The Oak House,** Seaview Avenue, Box 299, Oak Bluffs 02557, 693-4187, oak paneling, gingerbread and Victoriana, M–EE, CP • **Inn at Blueberry Hill,** North Road, Chilmark, 02535, 645-3322, expanded farmhouse with lap pool, tennis, fitness facilities, shuttle bus to the beach, E–EE, CP • **Captain R. Flanders House,** North Road, Chilmark 02535, 645-3123, seventeenth-century home on 60 acres overlooking a pond, M–E, CP • **Outermost Inn,** 1 Lighthouse Road, Gay Head 02535, 645-3511, superb location on the cliffs, every room with ocean views, EE, CP • **Thorncroft Inn,** 278 Main Street, Box 1022, Vineyard Haven 02568, 693-3333, handsomely restored and furnished, working fireplaces, Jacuzzi, romantic, E–EE, CP • **Captain Dexter House,** 100 Main Street, Box 2457, Vineyard Haven 02568, 693-6564, attractive furnishings, walking distance to the ferry, M–E, CP.

LODGING RESERVATION SERVICE Martha's Vineyard and Nantucket Reservations, PO Box 1322, Vineyard Haven, MA 02658, 693-7200.

DINING **L'Etoille,** Charlotte Inn (see above), 627-8947, French, elegant and expensive, prix fixe, EE • **Savoir Faire,** Post Office Square, Edgartown, 627-9864, winning small café, creative menu, E–EE • **Starbuck's,** Harbor View Hotel, 131 Water Street, Edgartown, 627-7000, formal dining, lovely water views, E–EE • **Lattanzi's,** Post Office Square, Edgartown, 627-8854, Italian, cozy setting, M–EE • **Square-Rigger,** Upper Main Street at West Tisbury Road, 627-9968, informal, grilled seafood, M–E • **David Ryans,** 11 North Water Street, Edgartown, 627-3030, popular, lively café, eclectic menu, M–E • **The Wharf,** Main Street, Edgartown, 627-9966, informal, "pub grub" and seafood in former blacksmith shop, M–E • **O'Brien's Serious Seafood & Grille,** 137 Upper Main Street, Edgartown, 627-5850, eclectic fare, pleasant quarters in an old home, live music in the pub, M–E • **Main Street Diner,** Old Post Office Square (behind the post office), Edgartown, 627-9337, retro diner, home cooking, serves all three meals, I–M • **Lambert's Cove Country Inn** (see above), gourmet fare, country setting, by reservation only; M–E, notable Sunday brunch, M • **Home Port,** Menemsha Road, Menemsha, 645-2679, nautical, informal, on picturesque harbor, M–E • **Beach Plum Inn** (see above), exceptional setting, reservations essential, prix fixe, EE • **Outermost Inn** (see above), romantic, especially at sunset, reserve well ahead, E • **Louis' Tisbury Café,** 102 State Road, Vineyard Haven, 693-3255, tiny but highly regarded by island regulars, Italian, M–E • **Black Dog Tavern,** Beach Road, Vineyard Haven, 693-9223, informal, longtime waterfront gathering place, try the clam chowder, M • **Le Grenier,** Upper Main Street, Vineyard Haven, 693-4906, excellent French café, E–EE • **Stripers,** 26 Beach Road, Vineyard Haven, 693-8383, harbor views, fine seafood, good place for celebrity spotting, M–E • **Feast of Chilmark,** State Road, Chilmark, 645-3553, creatively prepared seafood, M–E; also popular for breakfast, I • **Red Cat,** 688 State Road, West Tisbury, 693-9599, hip hangout for all three meals, M–E, dinner; interesting tasting menu, EE • **Theo's,** The Inn at Blueberry Hill (see above), 645-3322, well regarded, prix fixe, EE • **The Oyster Bar,** 162 Circuit Avenue, Oak Bluffs, 693-3300, Soho by the sea, big open bistro, M–E • For night life, try **Hot Tin Roof,** Carly Simon's club at the airport, 693-1137.

SIGHTSEEING **Vincent House,** Main and Church Streets, Edgartown, 627-4440. Hours: Memorial Day to Columbus Day, daily, 10:30 A.M. to 3 P.M. $$ • **The Martha's Vineyard Historical Society/The Vineyard Museum and Oral History Center,** 59 School Street, Edgartown, 627-4441. Hours: mid-June to mid-October, Tuesday to Saturday, 10 A.M. to 5 P.M.; rest of year, Wednesday to Friday, 1 P.M. to 4 P.M., Saturday, 10 A.M. to 4 P.M. $$ • **Seaman's Bethel,** 15 Beach Road, Vineyard Haven, 693-9317. Hours: Monday to Friday, 9 A.M. to 1 P.M. Free.

INFORMATION Martha's Vineyard Chamber of Commerce, Beach Road, PO Box 1698, Vineyard Haven, MA 02568, 693-0085.

Moonlight and Mozart in Vermont

The sun was setting to the strains of Bach. As the concert played, listeners on the lawn were watching the big red ball dip behind the Adirondack Mountains across Lake Champlain, turning both sky and lake reflections into a progression of pink, rosy red, and smoky gray hues.

There are many summer music festivals in sylvan settings, and many are larger and more famous than the Vermont Mozart Festival. But few can rival the beauty or the intimacy of this very special event. Since 1974, the three-week festival beginning in mid-July has been a movable musical feast in and around Burlington, switching locations from estates bordering Lake Champlain to college campuses and churches to the ferryboat on the lake. In recent years, concerts have moved as far afield as the Trapp Family Meadow, in Stowe; the grounds of the Robert Frost Cabin, in Ripton; and the Basin Harbor Club resort, in Vergennes.

It is the lakeside lawn concerts, particularly those on the grounds of

Shelburne Farms, that provide the most memorable moments. The music and the change in scene from sunset to intermission views of moonlight on the water provide a rare harmony of sights and sounds.

And the music is top-rate, featuring the Vermont Mozart Festival Orchestra as well as visiting chamber music groups and top soloists. The high caliber of the musicians is even more evident because the audiences are small enough so that no amplification is necessary to come between listeners and performers. The popular concerts have inspired a winter chamber music series as well.

For anyone who loves music, the Mozart Festival is the perfect reason for a trip to Vermont's largest city. As an encore, you can cruise on the lake and get acquainted with one of New England's most remarkable collections of folk art.

Not that Burlington (population 40,000) feels anything like a big city. With Lake Champlain as its western border, the Adirondacks across the water, the Green Mountains to the east, and the University of Vermont and several smaller college campuses adding green space to the center, Burlington has the feel of a cosmopolitan college town blessed with enviable surroundings.

There is scant evidence these days that this is a town dating back to 1773. The heart of the downtown business area has been transformed into a pleasant, modern, four-block pedestrian mall known as the Church Street Marketplace, with colorful banners overhead and interesting shops, sidewalk carts, and open-air cafés along the way. This is one city whose downtown remains crowded and vibrant.

While there is a Radisson Hotel right off the Marketplace, some of the most interesting lodgings are located a few minutes' drive away from downtown. By far the most elegant is the Inn at Shelburne Farms, the exceptional manor house where the concerts are held and which is open to the public for lodging and dining. Reserve well in advance, and you'll find out how it feels to live like the lord of the manor.

On the outskirts of Burlington is the Inn at Essex, a new hotel complex in the Colonial country style, with an indoor pool and a special lure—a branch of the New England Culinary Institute, whose students provide outstanding fare in the inn's restaurants. One of the mansions in the university's neighborhood recently became the Willard Street Inn, the city's most appealing historic lodging.

Wherever you stay, you'll certainly want to take time for a look around the city. Burlington developed into a shipping center when the Champlain Canal, built in 1823, connected the lake to the Hudson River. Walk along the Battery and the King Street neighborhood, near the waterfront, to see the site of one of the earliest settlements, and then head for a stroll downtown. On the way you'll see a time line of Burlington history. Your discoveries will range from the 1798 Gideon King House, at 35 King Street, to Greek Revival homes of the 1860s, on Maple Street; from the 1928 City Hall, designed by the famous architectural firm of McKim, Mead, and White, to Burlington Square Mall, a high-tech center done by Mies van der Rohe in the 1970s. Another pleasant uphill stroll or drive is to the Hill section, through the Champlain College and University of Vermont campuses and prosperous residential neighborhoods dating back to the city's heyday.

The University of Vermont, incidentally, was founded by Ira Allen, brother of Revolutionary War hero Ethan Allen. Ethan's homestead is in Burlington and is open for tours, should you want to learn more about the state's most illustrious hero.

The mall that transformed Church Street back in 1982 houses dozens of merchants, from shops selling clothes, crafts, and books to Sweetwater's, a former bank converted into a restaurant. You'll have no trouble finding an outdoor café for lunch. Among the notable shops is a branch of the Vermont State Craft Center with work by 200 Vermont artisans. Adjoining the Marketplace is Burlington Square Mall, with more specialty stores.

Another interesting shop can be found a block west of Church Street on College Street. This shop, Bennington Potters North, comprises three floors stocked with pottery and all manner of attractive housewares. Cabot Creamery, maker of Vermont's best-known cheddar cheese, has a working creamery in town that offers observation windows for viewing the cheese-making process and free samples of the finished product.

Burlington has a number of shopping areas along Route 7 south of town heading toward Shelburne. Stop at the Vermont Teddy Bear Company and you can take a guided tour to see how the bears are crafted by hand.

If bargain hunting is your thing, a major outlet center—including names such as Jones New York and Nine West—is developing in Essex. Champlain Mill, in neighboring Winooski, is another kind of shopping mecca, offering all kinds of shops and crafts in an atmospheric restored mill. The Waterworks Restaurant here is a top choice for Sunday brunch on the deck overlooking the Winooski River rapids.

However, on a fine afternoon, you may well prefer more summery diversions, such as town beaches or boat rides on Lake Champlain, unusually scenic cruises thanks to the billowy mountain views on the far side. A bicycling and jogging path along Lake Champlain is accessible from the city's four lakeside parks.

Still another possibility is a tour of Shelburne Farms, principal site of the Mozart Festival concerts and well worth touring by day, when you can really see the grounds. The 1,685-acre farm is a rolling landscape of open fields and woodlands laid out by Frederick Law Olmsted, with striking views at every curve of the road through the property. It was the home of Dr. and Mrs. William Seward Webb, who had architect Robert

Henderson Robertson design their magnificent mansion in shingle, slate, and limestone to blend with the landscape. Both the mansion, whose porch serves as the main stage for the summer concerts, and the Coach Barn, where smaller concerts are held, are exceptional buildings. As mentioned, the Inn at Shelburne Farms also can be visited for dinner or an overnight stay.

The Webbs began their farm as an experimental agricultural show-place, and Webb descendants have continued it as a model of progressive cattle and dairy farming, as well as a demonstration bakery and cheese-making operation. No fossil fuel fertilizers, herbicides, or pesticides are used on the farm. The tour includes the manor house, the great barns and the dairy building, exhibits of Vermont agriculture, and a small store featuring farm products—including some of the tastiest Vermont cheese to be found. There are walking trails here, also, with stupendous water views. The latest addition is the Children's Farmyard, where youngsters can pet the animals.

You may well be back here on the lawn in the evening, since Saturday nights are usually reserved for concerts on the South Porch of Shelburne Farms.

When it comes to dinner, there are many excellent choices in the Burlington area. The names cited most frequently seem to be the lavish Inn at Shelburne Farms, Café Shelburne, and Pauline's.

On Sunday, drive back to Shelburne to see another of the Webbs' legacies, the Shelburne Museum. There is no way to take in all of this amazing complex of Americana in a day, for this is the nation's foremost showcase of folk art. The museum's founder, Electra Havemeyer Webb, was a pioneer collector of Americana and American folk art, and her interests were wide.

There are more than 40 buildings on the 45-acre site, which is probably best described as a "collection of collections." The beautifully landscaped grounds are set up like a New England village, and some of the buildings are simply homes furnished in period antiques. But within many of them are unmatched exhibits of quilts, decoys, cigar store Indians and carousel figures, weather vanes, trade signs, accessories, primitive drawings and paintings, and painted furniture.

There seems to be no end to the variety of displays—dolls and dollhouses, Toby jugs and lustre pitchers, clocks, valentines, penny banks and puppets, embroidery, scrimshaw, and so on—all in prodigious numbers. Among the more unusual exhibits are a 525-foot hand-carved model of a circus parade and the big-as-life SS *Ticonderoga,* the last vertical-beam sidewheel passenger steamer intact in the United States. You can go on board to see the handsome paneling and elegant interiors.

Meanwhile, the pleasant little town of Shelburne has some interesting shops to bring you back to reality, everything from a delightful country store to Crafts in Common, a showcase of handcrafts. Or you can continue driving south for another half hour or so to Middlebury, stopping on the way to see the Vermont Wildflower Farm, in Charlotte, at its late-July peak. Middlebury, a picture-book college town, is the original home of the Vermont State Craft Center at Frog Hollow, as well as the Vermont Folklife Center, where there are exhibits of traditional art from the state and the region. At 52 Seymour Street, you can also visit the bovine studio and shop of Woody Jackson, the man who made Vermont's black-and-white cows renowned.

Middlebury offers its own fine choices for dining. Swift House Inn, an 1815 estate, has traditional fare with a French influence; Woody's offers art deco decor, a creative menu, and a deck on the river; and the Dog Team Tavern, just off Route 7 about four miles north of Middlebury, is a traditional New England country inn with such regional specialties as sticky buns, country fried chicken, and baked ham with fritters. What nicer way to end a weekend in Vermont?

<u>Area Code: 802</u>

DRIVING DIRECTIONS Burlington is in northwestern Vermont. I-89 goes directly into the city, as does Route 7. It is 225 miles from Boston, 300 miles from New York, and 222 miles from Hartford.

PUBLIC TRANSPORTATION Burlington is served by several airlines, including United, Continental, and US Airways, as well as by Amtrak train service and Vermont Transit bus lines. Ferry service is available from New York State across Lake Champlain.

ACCOMMODATIONS **The Inn at Shelburne Farms,** Shelburne 05482, 985-8498, palatial, exceptional, open mid-May to mid-October, M–EE (less expensive rooms share bath) • **Willard Street Inn,** 349 South Willard Street, Burlington 05401, 651-8710 or (800) 577-8712, M–E, CP • **Radisson Burlington,** Burlington Square, Burlington 05401, 658-6500, downtown, M–E • **Sheraton Burlington Inn,** 870 Williston Road, South Burlington 05403, 862-6576, resort-motel near airport, tennis, indoor and outdoor pools, M–E • **Willow Pond Farm,** 20 Cheesefactory Lane, South Burlington 05403, 985-8505, contemporary bed-and-breakfast home on 200 acres of orchards and gardens, convenient for Shelburne, I–M, CP • **Marble Island Resort,** Malletts Bay, 150 Marble Island Road, Colchester 05446, 864-6800, intimate resort, beautiful views, golf, tennis, boating, good value, M. *Budget options:* **Econo Lodge,** 1076 Williston Road, South Burlington 05403, 863-1125 or (800) 446-6900, I–M • **Comfort Inn,** 1285 Williston Road, South Burlington 05403, 865-3400, I, suites, I–M • **Days Inn,** 1976 Shelburne Road (Route 7), Shelbourne, 985-3334, I, CP. *Within a half hour's drive:* **Inn at Essex,** 70 Essex Way, Essex Junction (just outside Burlington) 05452, 878-1100 or (800) 288-7613 outside Vermont, indoor and outdoor pools, M–E • **Strong House Inn,** 82 West

Main Street, Vergennes (22 miles from Burlington) 05491, 877-3337, lovely 1834 Federal-style mansion turned bed-and-breakfast inn, antiques, gardens, M, CP; suites, M–E, CP • **Swift House Inn,** Stewart Lane and Route 7, Middlebury 05733, 388-9925, Federal-style estate, some fireplaces, whirlpools, M–E, CP • **North Hero House,** PO Box 106, North Hero 05474, 372-8237, charming, away from it all in the Champlain Islands, beach, tennis, boating, I–M.

DINING   Café Shelburne, Route 7, Shelburne, 985-3939, intimate, country French, the top choice, M • **The Inn at Shelburne Farms** (see above), elegant, formal dining, E–EE • **Pauline's,** 1834 Shelburne Road (Route 7), South Burlington, 862-1081, creative menu, highly recommended, I, café; formal dining room, M–E • **Isabel's on the Waterfront,** 112 Lake Street, 865-2522, inventive menu in a restored warehouse, excellent for lunch, dinners or weekend brunch, I–M • **Five Spice Café,** 175 Church Street, Burlington, 864-4505, variety of Asian cuisines, I–M • **Leunig's Bistro,** Church and College Streets, 863-3759, in the Marketplace, new chef has upgraded to fine Mediterranean fare, also a good choice for lunch, I–M • **Sweet Tomatoes Trattoria,** 83 Church Street, on the Marketplace, 660-9533, pastas, wood-fired brick oven pizza, popular, I–M • **The Daily Planet,** 15 Center Street, Burlington, 862-9647, ethnic foods, funky, fun, I–M • **Mona's,** 3 Main Street, Burlington, 658-MONA, basic American fare, undoubtedly the best lake views in town, I–M • **Ice House,** 171 Battery Street, Burlington, 864-1800, go for drinks on the deck with lake views, M–E • **Sweetwater's,** 120 Church Street, in the Marketplace, Burlington, 864-9800, snacks to meals in a converted bank, big Sunday brunch, I–M • **Dockside,** 209 Battery Street, Burlington, 864-5266, seafood near the waterfront, I–M • **Waterworks Restaurant,** Champlain Mill, Winooski, 655-2044, overlooking rapids, good for brunch, I–M • **Butler's,** Inn at Essex (see above), chefs from New England Culinary Institute, M; NECI students also man the informal **Birch Tree Café** at the inn, I • **Swift House Inn,** Middlebury (see above), American fare, M–EE • **Woody's,** Bakery Lane, Middlebury, 388-4182, on the river, M • **The Dog Team Tavern,** off Route 7, Middlebury, 388-7651, sticky buns, relishes, New England dining, I–M.

SIGHTSEEING   Vermont Mozart Festival, Box 512, Burlington 05401, 862-7352, three weeks, mid-July to early August; write or phone for current schedule and concert prices • **Shelburne Museum,** Route 7, Shelburne, 985-3346. Hours: mid-May to late October, daily, 10 A.M. to 5 P.M.; rest of year, by appointment. $$$$$ (tickets are good for two consecutive days) • **Shelburne Farms,** Harbor and Bay Roads, Shelburne, 985-8685. Hours: late May to mid-October, 9 A.M. to 5 P.M.; guided tours periodically, 9:30 A.M. to 3:30 P.M.; Visitor Center open year-round, 10 A.M. to 5 P.M. $$$ • **Ethan Allen Homestead,** Route

127, Burlington, 865-4556. Hours: mid-May to mid-October, Monday to Saturday, 10 A.M. to 5 P.M.; Sunday, 1 P.M. to 5 P.M. $$ • **Cabot Creamery,** 128 Main Street, 563-2231. Hours: mid-June through October, tours daily, 9 A.M. to 5 P.M. $, under 12, free. • **Spirit of Ethan Allen Cruises,** Burlington Boat House, College Street, Burlington, 862-8300, summer day and dinner cruises aboard a paddle wheeler, varying schedules and rates; phone for information • **Lake Champlain Ferry,** King Street Dock, Burlington, 864-9804, one-hour trips across Lake Champlain, mid-May to late October; phone for current schedules and rates • **Vermont Wildflower Farm,** Route 7, Charlotte, 425-3500. Hours: May to late October, 10 A.M. to 5 P.M. $$, under 12, free.

INFORMATION Lake Champlain Regional Chamber of Commerce, 60 Main Street, Suite 100, Burlington, VT 05401, 863-3489.

Scaling the Heights at Acadia

Mother Nature created many wonders along the coast of Maine, but when she got to Mount Desert Island she pulled out all the stops.

The heart of this ultimate down east destination is Acadia National Park—32,000 spectacular acres that encompass everything from rugged rockbound coastlines to green hills, 26 lakes and ponds, and 18 mountains. One of the latter, Cadillac Mountain, is the highest point on the eastern seaboard.

Mount Desert (accent on the last syllable), a 16-by-13-mile retreat just across a causeway from the mainland, also includes Bar Harbor, once a mecca for the wealthy and now a thriving little waterside resort town of shops, restaurants, and lodgings, including lavish summer homes that have been transformed into attractive inns.

For boaters, or anyone who appreciates peerless water views, there is Somes Sound, which splits the far end of the island almost in half. This deep arm of the sea between mountainsides is the only fjord on the East Coast. The two sides provide ample coastline for scenic resorts in the peacefully removed fishing village of Southwest Harbor and in Northeast Harbor, a posh yachting town with just a bit more action. Northeast Harbor is closer to the park, but is still far away from Bar Harbor's busy streets.

As if all that weren't enough of a lure, these are also absolutely prime lobstering waters, and almost all the restaurants on Mount Desert, as well as a couple of very reasonably priced "lobster pounds," offer the very best of Maine's most famous culinary treat.

The focal point for visitors is Acadia, one of the nation's most popular national parks. To make the most of your visit, start at the Visitors' Center, just off Route 3 at Hull's Cove, north of Bar Harbor, for a film on the park, information, park maps, and schedules of the many activities conducted by park rangers during the summer months. These include nature walks, mountain hikes, sunset photo walks, and evening activities, which sometimes include walks to look at the starry heavens. Naturalist-guided sea cruises are a highly recommended way to appreciate and learn about your surroundings. You can also rent canoes for your own explorations or sign on at the National Park Outdoor Activity Center, in Bar Harbor, for a guided sea kayak tour.

Armed with maps, you're ready for the 27-mile Park Loop Road. Stopping points include Sieur de Monts Spring, featuring the Wild Gardens of Acadia, with their profusion of native wildflowers; and many viewpoints along Ocean Drive, where the road becomes one-way, a plan no doubt wisely devised to make it easier to admire the views and pull over to the lookouts without causing traffic problems. Crescent-shaped Sand Beach is a favorite sunning spot off the drive, and there is always a crowd at Thunder Hole, named for the deafening thump of the surf as it roars into a cavern carved into the cliffs by eons of waves.

When you get to Jordan Pond House, make a stop for a meal or the famous tea served with popovers on the lawn in midafternoon. The house is a contemporary edition of the landmark original that burned down. It is a handsome structure with glass walls that allow you to take in the noted view of the pond and of the two round peaks behind known as "The Bubbles." The melt-in-your-mouth popovers and the legendary homemade ice cream can be had with lunch or dinner as well as with tea—and they're worth a wait in line.

Near the end of the Park Loop is the side road to the top of Cadillac Mountain and awesome views from every side of the 1,532-foot summit. Because it is the first place where the sun reaches the nation each morning, the peak inspires some unique rituals, including the annual Fourth of July square dance at 12:01 A.M., followed by a sunrise breakfast.

Back on Route 3, heading toward Northeast Harbor, you'll come to Seal Harbor, another popular beach and a village that gained some note as the summer home of Nelson Rockefeller. It was his father, John D. Rockefeller Jr., along with Edsel Ford and some other early summer residents, who recognized the fragile beauty of the area and moved to preserve it for public use. They bought up nearly a third of the park's total acreage and turned it over to the federal government in 1919 as the basis for the first national park in the East.

Because cars were banned on Mount Desert for a time, the park contains some 50 miles of carriage roads—once the province of the horse-drawn carriages of the wealthy—which are now ideal for hikers, bikers, horseback riders, and cross-country skiers in the winter.

Route 3 ends in Northeast Harbor, a yachtsman's haven and an elegant summer colony of large "cottages," special inns, and exclusive village shops. Take a look at the Thuya Gardens, off Route 3, a mix of formal English flower beds and Japanese effects. The Asticou Gardens, at the junction of Routes 3 and 198, across from the Asticou Inn, are at their peak in June, but there are attractive native plants and a Japanese sand garden to be seen all summer.

The big Asticou Inn, with an incomparable view of the harbor, is the most elegant of all Mount Desert hotels, though the atmosphere is a bit staid. Two very pleasant smaller inns are found here also. The gracious, shingled Harbourside Inn, a welcoming place where the hostess takes particular pride in serving her guests homemade blueberry muffins for breakfast, offers big, comfortable, simply furnished rooms, many with working fireplaces. The Maison Suisse Inn, a nineteenth-century summer cottage right in the village, looks like a fairy-tale cottage set in a rustic garden. The furnishings are simple, the rooms are airy and spacious, and some provide private outdoor sitting areas. The rates include breakfast at the restaurant-bakery across the street.

To complete an island tour, follow Sargent Drive, an enclave of secluded, lavish summer homes that parallels Somes Sound, and at the end take Route 198, which curves around the head of the sound into Somesville, a well-preserved village of Colonial homes that is the island's oldest settlement. The drive south from Somesville on Route 102 along Echo Lake will bring you to Southwest Harbor, a shipbuilding and fishing village that is also a popular summer community with a handful of interesting shops. The Kingsleigh Inn is a pleasant stopping place right in the tiny village, with harbor views from the porch and from a panoramic third-floor suite with a turret. The rooms at the 100-year-old Claremont aren't anything special, but the location on Somes Sound most definitely is. A bit farther on is the Moorings, a snug and cozy berth with nautical motifs and a popular restaurant looking out on the harbor. Every kind of boat, including a canoe, can be rented right next door.

While you're in Southwest Harbor, take time for two special attractions that are easy to overlook. The first is the tiny Wendell Gilley Museum, showing off the work of a local artist who became known for his extraordinary wooden bird carvings. The second is the Southwest Harbor Oceanarium, a great place for kids, with its "touch tanks" and other hands-on exhibits, including phones where you can listen to the "songs" of whales.

Appropriately, one of the best lobster pounds in the area is nearby on the docks. At Beal's Lobster Pier you can buy fresh lobster at very reasonable prices, wait for your choice to be cooked, and eat it on the spot at outside picnic tables beside the water.

Fisherman's Landing, a similar establishment on the pier in Bar Harbor, offers a rustic enclosed eating pavilion. Fisherman's Landing closes by 8:00 P.M. (Beal's closes even earlier), so if you want a relatively inexpensive lobster feast, plan an early dinner.

"Bah Hahba," as the natives call it, can become clogged with tourists, but it is lively and offers visitors much to see and do within an easy stroll. It is filled with restaurants that offer fine dining as well as lobster specials, and there are enough shops to keep you browsing for quite a while. The Eclipse Gallery, on Mt. Desert Street, has handsome contemporary American crafts; and Island Artisans, on Main Street, and the Lone Moose, on West Street, feature work by Maine artisans.

Bar Harbor suffered a terrible fire in 1947 that destroyed a third of the fine old summer homes and ended its days as an elite resort. Many of the most gracious lodgings in town are in the remaining summer showplaces that line West Street and the shore path east of the municipal pier. Most exceptional are those with water views. The most spectacular is Breakwater 1904, a beautifully restored mansion directly on the water, where you can live like the upper chest of yesteryear. Among the more modest choices, the Manor House Inn, a three-story Victorian, has warmth and a convenient location within walking distance of town.

For more privacy, you can't beat the romantic Inn at Canoe Point, a small hideaway perched over the water at Hull's Cove near the park entrance.

There are a number of special events in the area during the summer. The Bar Harbor Music Festival and the Bar Harbor Festival of Chamber Music, featuring special musical events on various dates during July and August, have both been regular features for over 30 years. The local drama group is the Acadia Repertory Theater, which performs at the Masonic Hall in Somesville—a good evening out combined with an early lobster dinner at Beal's.

And should you want to get out on that deep blue water while you are here, you'll find a number of ways to do so. Besides the informative naturalist cruises sponsored by Acadia National Park, the Frenchman's Bay Company, next to the municipal pier in Bar Harbor, offers daily sightseeing cruises and deep-sea fishing boats. Sailing sloops go out from the Golden Anchor Pier, and the *Bluenose* ferry offers a daylong "Sea Fun" outing to Yarmouth, Nova Scotia, with all the meals and trappings of a lavish ocean cruise. There are still more cruises to view lobstering, seals, and osprey; whale-watching cruises; fishing charters; and a variety of ferryboat and mailboat cruises to nearby islands out of Northeast Harbor—plus the ferry to Swans Island out of Bass Harbor. The Island Information Bureau, on Route 3 just past the causeway leading to Mount Desert, and the Bar Harbor Chamber of Commerce Information Center, at the *Bluenose* ferry terminal on the harbor and on Main Street, will have all the current schedules.

If you find yourself facing a rainy day, don't despair. Take the opportunity to check out those museums in Southwest Harbor or to visit the other locations of the Oceanarium. At the Bar Harbor Oceanarium

Harborside Hotel & Marina
55 West St. - Downtown Bar Harbor
www.Barharborresorts.com

SCALING THE HEIGHTS AT ACADIA

137
SUMMER

you'll find live harbor seals in a 50,000-gallon tank. A licensed lobster-man is on duty to fascinate you and your youngsters with a zillion little-known facts about how these tasty crustaceans live and how they are caught. He illustrates his narrative with live lobsters, sometimes includ-ing a mother carrying several dozen babies on her bottom. Having learned about these creatures of the deep, you can see them being born at the Lobster Hatchery, where anywhere from 5,000 to 10,000 tiny newborns may be in residence.

The College of the Atlantic's Natural History Museum is another place where visitors get involved with hands-on exhibits and live talks. The Bar Harbor Historical Society, in the basement of the Jesup Memo-rial Library, displays photos and clippings of what it was like in the lav-ish old days of the grand hotels and steamers.

Sun is preferable, of course, to make the most of the natural beauty of the area, but whatever the weather, Mount Desert is an unbeatable destination. It's the place for unsurpassed down east scenery—and some of the best lobster dinners that Maine has to offer.

Area Code: 207

DRIVING DIRECTIONS   Take I-95 to Augusta, then Route 3 East to Mount Desert; or take the Maine Turnpike to Bangor, follow Route 1A to Ellsworth and then Route 3 across the causeway. On Mount Desert, Route 3 leads to Bar Harbor, Route 102 to Southwest Harbor, and Route 198/3 to Northeast Harbor. Bar Harbor is 276 miles from Boston, 482 miles from New York, and 372 miles from Hartford.

PUBLIC TRANSPORTATION   Air transportation to Hancock County Airport, 12 miles, and Bangor Airport, 50 miles. There is Grey-hound/Vermont Transit bus service from Boston to Bar Harbor.

ACCOMMODATIONS   **Inn at Canoe Point,** Hull's Cove 04644, 288-9511, romantic hideaway directly on the water, E–EE, CP • **The Breakwater 1904,** 45 Hancock Street, Bar Harbor 04609, 288-2313 or (800) 238-6309, luxurious showplace on the water, E–EE, CP • **Bal-ance Rock Inn,** 21 Albert Meadow, Bar Harbor 04609, 288-9900, another exceptional waterfront mansion, though additions have given it a more commercial feel, E–EE, CP • **Nannau,** Lower Main Street, Bar Harbor 04609, 288-5575, shingled shorefront estate with handsome William Morris decor, M–E, CP • **The Tides,** 119 West Street, Bar Har-bor 04609, 288-4968, suites facing the water, great location but so-so decor, M–EE, CP • **Ledgelawn,** 66 Mt. Desert Street, Bar Harbor 04609, 288-4596, grand manor and carriage house, pool, some fire-places, whirlpools, M–E, CP • **Manor House Inn,** 106 West Street, Bar Harbor 04609, 288-4759, turn-of-the-century ambience, warm decor, big porch, attractive additional cottage accommodations on grounds,

M–E, CP • **The Maples Inn,** 16 Roberts Avenue, Bar Harbor 04609, 288-3443, nicely decorated small in-town bed-and-breakfast, M, CP; suite, E, CP • **Ridgeway Inn,** 11 High Street, Bar Harbor 04609, 288-9682, small pleasant Victorian in town, M, CP; suites, M–E, CP • **Seacroft Inn,** 18 Albert Meadow, Bar Harbor 04609, 288-4669 or (800) 824-9694, modest rooms and efficiencies, quiet and convenient location near town, M • **Inn at Bay Ledge,** 1385 Sands Point Road, Bar Harbor 04609, 288-4204, very private clifftop lodge outside town, rustic feel, grand views, some Jacuzzis and fireplaces, swimming pool, E–EE, CP • **Harbourside Inn,** Northeast Harbor 04662, 276-3272, warm ambience, top choice in the price range, M, CP; suites, E, CP • **Maison Suisse Inn,** Main Street, Northeast Harbor 04662, 276-5223, charming outside, airy and comfortable within, M–E, CP • **Asticou Inn,** Northeast Harbor 04662, 276-3344, formal old-time resort-hotel, E–EE, MAP • **Kingsleigh Inn,** 373 Main Street, Southwest Harbor 04679, 244-5302, pleasant, small bed-and-breakfast near the harbor, M, CP; suites, E, CP • **The Claremont,** PO Box 137, Southwest Harbor 04679, 244-5036, landmark building and location, M, CP; E, MAP • **Moorings,** Shore Road, Manset, Southwest Harbor 04679, 244-5523, main house and motel on the water, no frills but good value, I–M, CP. *Motels on the water:* **Bar Harbor Inn,** Newport Drive, Bar Harbor 04609, 288-3351, refurbished motel by the sea, grand oceanfront lodge, pool, motel, E, CP; lodge, EE, CP • **Atlantic Eyrie Lodge,** Highbrook Road, Bar Harbor 04609, 288-9786, hilltop motel, water views, kitchens, good for families, E. For budget motels, call or write the Chamber of Commerce.

DINING **George's,** 7 Stevens Lane, Bar Harbor, 288-4505, long considered one of the best in town, lobster strudel a specialty, E, some game dishes; grazing menu, I–M • **Porcupine Grill,** 123 Cottage Street, Bar Harbor, 288-3884, trendy menu, attractive decor, very popular, M–E • **The Fin Back,** 78 West Street, Bar Harbor, 288-4193, intimate café, excellent chef, seafood specialties, M–E • **Cafe Bluefish,** 122 Cottage Street, Bar Harbor, 288-3696, dark wooden booths, antique books, mix-matched china, creative seafood, M • **124 Cottage Street,** at that address, Bar Harbor, 288-4383, popular for giant salad bar, varied menu, M • **Maggie's Classic Scales,** 6 Summer Street, Bar Harbor, 288-9007, informal, seafood, M • **Lompoc Café and Brewpub,** 36 Rodick Street, Bar Harbor, 288-9392, unusually interesting pub menu, I–M • **The Burning Tree,** Route 3, Otter Creek, 288-9331, chef-owned, wide variety of seafood, well recommended locally, M • **Jordan Pond House,** Park Loop Road, Acadia National Park, 276-3316, exceptional location, standard menu, I–M, best for lunch or tea, I; dinner, I–M • **The Bistro at Seal Harbor,** Main Street, Seal Harbor, 276-3299, charming small cafe, tasty seafood specialties, M–E • **Red-**

field's, Main Street, Northeast Harbor, 276-5283, imaginative menu, tops in the area, reserve well ahead, M–E • **The Claremont** (see above), come for the old-fashioned ambience and superb water view, M • **Preble Grille,** 14 Clark Point Road, Southwest Harbor, 244-3034, casual café, regional dishes with a Mediterranean accent, M. *For lobster-by-the-pound:* Prices vary by the season, but these are always the best values around. **Fisherman's Landing,** West Street (on the pier), Bar Harbor, 288-4632 • **Beal's Lobster Pier,** Clark Point Road, Southwest Harbor, 244-3202 • **Abel's Lobster Pound,** Route 198, Northeast Harbor, 276-5817 • **Oak Point Lobster Pound,** Route 230, Trenton, 667-8548, great views and great lobster • **Tidal Falls Lobster Pound,** Tidal Falls Road, Hancock, 422-6818, a drive, but a great location next to the falls.

SIGHTSEEING **Acadia National Park,** PO Box 177, Bar Harbor 04609, 288-3338. Hours: park open year-round; Visitors' Center, Route 3, Hull's Cove, open daily, July and August, 8 A.M. to 6 P.M.; May, June, September, October, 8 A.M. to 4:30 P.M. Park Headquarters, on Route 233, has information the rest of the year. Write for information, schedules. Admission to park: weekly pass per car, $$ • **Oceanarium and Lobster Hatchery,** Route 3 (as you come onto Mount Desert Island), Bar Harbor, 288-5005. Hours: Monday to Saturday 9 A.M. to 5 P.M. $$ • **Southwest Harbor Oceanarium,** Clark Point Road, 244-7330. Hours: July and August, Monday to Saturday, 9 A.M. to 5 P.M. $$ • **Wendell Gilley Museum,** Main Street and Herrick Road, Southwest Harbor, 244-7555. Hours: July and August, Tuesday to Sunday, 10 A.M. to 5 P.M.; rest of the year, 4 P.M. $$ • **Natural History Museum,** Turrets Building, College of the Atlantic, Route 3, Bar Harbor, 288-5015. Hours: June to Labor Day, daily, 9 A.M. to 5 P.M.$ • **Bar Harbor Historical Society,** Jesup Memorial Library, 34 Mt. Desert Street, Bar Harbor, 288-3838. Hours: mid-June through October, Monday to Saturday, 1 P.M. to 4 P.M. Free • **Thuya Gardens,** Route 3, Northeast Harbor, 276-3344. Hours: daily, 7 A.M. to 7 P.M. $.

INFORMATION Bar Harbor Chamber of Commerce, 93 Cottage Street, PO Box 158, Bar Harbor, ME 04609, 288-5103.

Supping with the Shakers in Hancock

Was it brown sugar? Honey? Maybe a touch of apple cider? No one at the long dinner table in the Believers Dining Room was sure of the secret ingredient in the old Shaker recipe. The guests knew only that cabbage, nobody's favorite vegetable, had been transformed into a treat that had everyone asking for more.

At the dinners held in summer and fall at Shaker Village, in Hancock, Massachusetts, you quickly discover that the industrious people who lived here a century ago definitely did not include good food among the worldly pleasures they disdained.

From their earliest years the Shakers paid careful attention to food and its preparation, and as the skill of the "Kitchen Sisters" became known, city excursionists began arriving to share the Shakers' dinners on weekends. They still do. The Saturday night programs called "An Evening at Hancock Shaker Village" give visitors the chance to sample menus that include traditional fare from the book *The Best of Shaker Cooking,* such as ham baked in cider, Sister Clymena's chicken pie, herbed rice, Eldress Bertha's summer squash casserole, and Sister Mary's zesty carrots. The Shaker chocolate pound cake is a favorite, along with the rich lemon cake with raspberry sauce, but even "green and red cabbage" takes on added flavor from the seasonings and the surroundings. The menus change each week, so if you've tasted one Shaker dinner, you definitely have not sampled them all.

Before dinner, guests are invited on a tour of the village with a guide in Shaker costume, and they are offered beverages in the 1830 kitchen, where they can inspect the laborsaving devices used by the clever Kitchen Sisters.

The dinners are an added treat in the Berkshire region of western Massachusetts, which regularly serves up one of New England's most overflowing platters of summer pleasures. The Boston Symphony concerts at Tanglewood, the dance festival at Jacob's Pillow, top-notch summer theater at Stockbridge and Williamstown, and the Shaker Village are only the start of a true smorgasbord of weekend delights.

With all of this, it should come as no surprise that summer reservations are hard to come by, and when the Boston Symphony arrives for the weekend, prices almost double. Even for the motels on Route 7, several months in advance is none too soon to secure a room. Because weekend rooms are at such a premium, if you'll settle for missing Tanglewood's major events, this is one area that is worth considering for a middle-of-the-week break.

The region known as "the Berkshires" actually runs from the southern to the northern border of Massachusetts on and around Route 7. Sheffield, the first of the towns, is an antiquers' haven. Next comes Great Barrington, a local commercial center that is gaining renown as a dining center, and Stockbridge, the quintessential New England village, immortalized by its most famous resident, Norman Rockwell. To either side are South Egremont, New Marlborough, Lee, Becket, and West Stockbridge, the first four slightly removed from the crush of summer visitors, the latter a tiny boutique-strewn village often filled with strollers.

Lenox, the home of Tanglewood, was known as the inland Newport for its fine summer homes occupied by both the wealthy and by literary greats of the last century. It is the most gracious of the towns. Farther on are Pittsfield, another shopping center, and Williamstown, the handsome hometown of Williams College, also known for the fine Clark Art Institute, with its Impressionist paintings and other noted collections. The Williams College Museum of Art is also quite exceptional.

There are dozens of lodgings in these towns for every taste and pocketbook—historic inns, resorts, and two particularly lavish retreats: Wheatleigh, where you'll enjoy all the luxury of an Italian palazzo built by a contessa; and Blantyre, a summer mansion that is every bit as regal as the name implies. And everyone seems to show up eventually for a drink on the porch or the patio of the wonderful old Red Lion, on a downtown corner in Stockbridge, a classic Colonial inn that is better recommended as a gathering place than a lodging.

The Apple Tree Inn, conveniently set at the gate of Tanglewood, shares with Wheatleigh the advantage of allowing guests to walk to the concerts. It's a benefit you'll appreciate more when you see the lines of traffic.

The Roeder House, in Stockbridge, is a beautifully furnished smaller inn. It has a pool, as does the warm and welcoming Weathervane Inn, a converted farmhouse in South Egremont, and the gracious mansion called Applegate, in Lee. Lenox offers lodgings in some of the former mansions and historic homes; the Williamsville Inn is a winning country setting, and the Historic Merrill Inn is a perfectly restored and handsomely furnished Colonial tavern that is one of the area's best values.

As you might expect in such a popular area, dining is fine, with a price range from modest to exorbitant—something for everyone.

With the basics out of the way, you can begin the difficult task of choosing among the rich arts offerings throughout the area. Tanglewood tops the list. It has been a major Northeast attraction since 1936, when it became the summer home of the Boston Symphony. The 6,000 seats in the open-air shed, which is noted for its acoustics, are frequently sold out; as many as 10,000 more people may congregate on the big lawn in back, enjoying elegant picnics along with a symphony concert under the stars. The Seiji Ozawa Hall, a 1994 addition, is a 1,200-seat theater that is an ideal home for chamber music and recitals. The full roster includes top pop music stars and the Boston Pops as well as the classics.

The grounds at Tanglewood can be seen best on Sunday afternoons, when visitors have a chance to stroll some of the 210 acres of William Aspinwall Tappan's former estate, past the formal gardens and the re-creation of the red house where Nathaniel Hawthorne once worked.

Tanglewood is not the only mecca for music lovers in the Berkshires. Some 150 voices accompanied by an orchestra are the feature at the Berkshire Choral Festival, held in a shed on the campus of the Berkshire School, in Sheffield; and Aston Magna presents early music on original instruments in the intimate setting of the St. James Church, in Great Barrington. The Berkshire Opera Festival performs at the Koussevitzky Arts Center at the Berkshire Community College, in Pittsfield. In the fall, Pittsfield also hosts the South Mountain chamber music concerts.

For fans of the dance, major troupes from around the world can be seen at the oldest event of its kind in the country, the Jacob's Pillow Dance Festival, in Becket. The Albany Berkshire Ballet also has a six-week summer season at the Arts Center in Pittsfield.

Theater buffs have the happy choice of the long-established and excellent Berkshire Theater Festival, in Stockbridge, with three arenas showing drama, musicals, and children's plays; or the highly acclaimed productions at the Williamstown Theater Festival. If the Bard's the thing, there is Shakespeare & Company, performing in a natural amphitheater on the grounds of the Mount, Edith Wharton's former estate, high above Laurel Lake. Wharton stories are dramatized in the intimate theater in the main house.

In addition to the arts, there are enough sightseeing attractions in the mountains and woodlands and lovely towns of the Berkshires to keep you busy even if you had nothing else to do. Priority goes to two special places. The first is the Norman Rockwell Museum, featuring the well-known illustrations of the artist in the town where he spent his last 25 years. The world's largest collection of his work can be seen in this stunning museum on a 36-acre former estate just outside Stockbridge. The museum inspires new appreciation for Rockwell's talents at mirroring changing American society. His studio has also been moved to this site. Not the least of the museum's pleasures are the grounds, which offer expansive views of the Housatonic River Valley and the Berkshire countryside.

The second is Hancock Shaker Village, the most elaborate of all the Shaker museums, where 20 buildings have been restored of the original 100 structures in a settlement that was established in 1790 and reached its height in the 1830s.

Here, you'll learn a lot about the ingenious Shaker people. The name "Shaker" came from the form of worship practiced by the United Society of Believers in Christ's Second Appearing. The "shaking" was the ecstatic response of worshipers to their perception of the presence of the divine spirit. The faith was founded on four fundamental principles: separation from the world, common property, confession of sin, and celibacy, meaning separation in living quarters but equality in privileges for the sexes.

The Shakers had a genius for finding the most functional way of doing things, exemplified by their classically simple tables and chairs and pegs, precursors of modern design. Their legacy to us includes the first packaged garden seeds and herbal remedies, and they often improved on the technology of the day with such practical innovations as the circular saw, the flat broom, and the clothespin.

The trilevel round stone barn in Hancock is the most striking reminder of Shaker ingenuity, with a shape as practical as it is beautiful, a design that enabled as many as 54 head of cattle to be fed by a single farmhand from a central core. Among the other buildings to be toured are the Brethren's and Sisters' shops, where you'll see the chair, broom, and oval box–making industries that were run by the men, and the dairy, medical department, and weaving facilities that were the province of the women. Craftspeople, on hand to demonstrate these various occupations, reproduce Shaker small goods, wooden objects, and furniture.

A variety of reproduction pieces is available at the museum shop, and homemade bread, preserves, and other foods made from Shaker recipes are for sale in the appropriately named Good Room, in the 1910 barn.

One of the most important buildings in the village is the 1830 Brick Dwelling, which housed 100 Shakers. In addition to retiring rooms, the building contained the meeting room used for weekday worship and the communal dining room, where dinners are now served. The building currently has a variety of room settings illustrating aspects of Shaker daily life, including cooking demonstrations in the original kitchen.

The grounds remain a working farm, where you can see historic breeds of sheep, cows, horses, and chickens, as well as tour an heirloom garden where nineteenth-century varieties of vegetables and herbs are grown using Shaker planting and cultivation methods. Children are introduced to life in a nineteenth-century Shaker community in the Discovery Room, where they can see demonstrations of crafts such as weaving and basketmaking and can try on Shaker clothing.

If your favorite sites are the shops, there are plenty of them to tempt you in the area. Lenox is of note for the Curtis House shops and the upscale shops on and off Church Street in the village. You can watch glassblowers practice their craft at the Berkshire Center of Contemporary Glass, a gallery in West Stockbridge. For bargain hunters, an outlet mall is located north of Lenox on Route 7. For those who like browsing art, the old mill spaces in Housatonic are being transformed into interesting galleries.

On a beautiful summer day, you might prefer to forget about sights or shops and enjoy a swim. Try York Lake, in New Marlborough; Benedict Pond, in Beartown State Forest near Great Barrington; or Pontoosuc Lake, on Route 7 south of Pittsfield, which offers boat rentals as well as a little beach.

For hikers there are several choices, including Monument Mountain, between Great Barrington and Stockbridge; 39 miles of the Appalachian Trail; and Mount Greylock, the highest in the state. Serious hikers or anyone who is on a budget and is willing to put up with spartan furnishings and shared rooms can stay on top of Mount Greylock in the Bascom Lodge, run by the Appalachian Mountain Club. The club sponsors many guided walks and programs. You can pick up a schedule at the Visitors' Center, just off Route 7 in Lanesboro, north of Pittsfield. The road is plainly marked.

Should you have the time, there are more places of interest to be visited, two of them monuments to famous sculptors. Chesterwood, an estate set beside the Housatonic River and overlooking the mountains in Stockbridge, was aptly described as "heaven" by its former owner, Daniel Chester French, the sculptor of the seated Lincoln figure at the Lincoln Memorial in Washington. Tyringham Art Galleries is a curiosity. The studio of Sir Henry Kitson, best known for his Minuteman statue in Lexington, it is a Hansel-and-Gretel affair appropriately called the Gingerbread House, with a "thatched roof" that is itself a sculpture weighing 80 tons.

Naumkeag, a Stockbridge mansion designed by Stanford White, is one of the grander homes in the area, with a fine garden; and Arrowhead, in Pittsfield, is of interest as the home where Herman Melville wrote *Moby Dick*. Flower lovers will also enjoy Bartholomew's Cobble, a 200-acre world of meadows and woods and wildflowers in Ashley Falls; and the Berkshire Botanical Garden, a 15-acre show garden in Stockbridge.

All these attractions simply can't be seen in one weekend, which is probably a very good thing. The Berkshire mountainsides are beautiful in autumn, offer skiing in the winter, and take on a special glow in the bloom of spring—which gives you lots of excuses to come back and see what you've missed.

Area Code: 413

DRIVING DIRECTIONS   Lenox, the heart of Tanglewood country, is on Route 7, about 150 miles from both Boston and New York, and 53 miles from Hartford. Hancock Shaker Village is about 15 minutes away, in Pittsfield; make a left turn off Route 7 in Pittsfield to Route 20, which takes you directly to the village.

PUBLIC TRANSPORTATION   Bonanza lines provides bus service to the area. Amtrak serves Pittsfield from Boston. Closest major airports are in Springfield, Massachusetts (70 miles away), or Albany, New York (37 miles). If you stay near Tanglewood, you can manage without a car, but you'll miss a lot of the sights.

ACCOMMODATIONS   Rates given are for weekends in July and August concert season and foliage season; all are less on weekdays and in September—and much less after October. All inns have minimum-stay requirements in season. **Apple Tree Inn,** 224 West Street, Lenox 01240, 637-1477, lovely hilltop location, M–EE, CP (less-expensive rooms are in a modern motel-lodge on the grounds) • **Birchwood Inn,** 7 Hubbard Street, Lenox 01240, (800) 524-1646, gabled 1757 white clapboard home overlooking the village, M–E, CP • **Cliffwood Inn,** 25 Cliffwood Street, Lenox 01240, 637-3330, antiques-filled Belle Époque Stanford White showplace, breakfast on the veranda overlooking the grounds and pool, M–E, CP • **Brook Farm Inn,** 15 Hawthorne Street, Lenox 01240, 637-3013, Colonial charm, poetry readings and concerts, pool, M–E, CP • **Walker House,** 24 Walker Street, Lenox 01240, 637-1271, art-filled, offbeat, and interesting, M–E, CP • **Garden Gables Inn,** 141 Main Street, Lenox 01240, 637-0193, cozy, Colonial decor, big pool, M–EE, CP • **The Roeder House,** Route 183, Stockbridge 01262, 298-4015, fine furnishings, antiques and good taste, pool, M–EE, CP • **Williamsville Inn,** Route 41, West Stockbridge 01266, 274-6118, country charm, pool, tennis court, M–E, CP • **Weathervane Inn,** Route 23, South Egremont 01258, 528-9580, attractive converted farmhouse, pool, M, CP; suites, M–E, CP; E–EE, MAP • **Historic Merrell Inn,** Route 102, South Lee 01260, 243-1794, authentically restored 1800 stagecoach inn, lovely furnishings and grounds, M, CP • **Applegate Bed and Breakfast,** 279 West Park Street, Lee 01238, 243-4451, Southern mansion transplanted to New England, pool, M–EE, CP • **The Inn at Richmond,** 802 State Road (Route 41), Richmond 01254, 698-2566, relaxed country inn adjoining scenic horse farm, M–E, CP • **Staveleigh House,** Route 7, Sheffield, 229-2129, convenient for antiquers, good value for all, M, CP. *The top of the line:* **Blantyre,** Route 20, Lenox 01240, 298-3806, EE, CP • **Wheatleigh,** West Hawthorne Road, Lenox 01240, 637-0610, E–EE CP. Also see Williamstown listings, page 257.

DINING   *Gourmet picks:* **Wheatleigh** (see above), continental-French, widely praised, prix fixe, EE (if you can't afford the dinner tab, consider the luxurious Sunday brunch, E) • **The Old Inn on the Green,** Route 57, New Marlborough, 229-3131 or (800) 286-3139, worth the long drive for five-course dinners in a candlelit eighteenth-century dining room, by reservation only, prix fixe, EE • **Blantyre** (see above), elegant dining, prix fixe, EE • **John Andrew's,** Route 23, South Egremont, 528-3469, many consider this pleasant, more down-to-earth restaurant the area's best, pizzas and pasta to formal dining, I–M. *More top choices:* **La Bruschetta,** 1 Harris Street, West Stockbridge, 232-7141, upscale Italian, M • **The Old Mill,** Route 23, South Egremont, 528-1421 restored gristmill, long a local favorite, M–E • **Williamsville Inn** (see above), continental, M–E • **Church Street Café,** 69 Church Street, Lenox, 637-2745, excellent bistro, good choice for dinner, or lunch, I–M • **Union Bar & Grill,** 293 Main Street, Great Barrington, 528-8226, Soho in the Berkshires, happening bar, eclectic menu, M–E • **Federal House,** Route 102, South Lee, 243-1824, formal dining, continental, M–E • **Lenox 218,** 218 Main Street, Lenox, 637-4218, northern Italian, attractive contemporary setting, M • **Castle Street Café,** 10 Castle Street, Great Barrington, 528-5244, bistro menu, well-regarded chef, M–E • **The Red Lion Inn** (see above), New England fare, best for people-watching, M–E, more formal dinner; breakfast and lunch, I. *Casual dining:* **Jack's Grill,** Main Street, Housatonic, 274-1000, informal, fun, good reviews, I–M • **The Dakota,** Route 7, Lenox/Pittsfield line, 499-7900, informal, rustic Western decor, popular, I–M • **Rosebourough Grill and Country Restaurant,** 90 Church Street, Lenox, 637-2745, pleasant café, varied menu, I–E • **The Orient Express,** off Main Street, West Stockbridge, 232-7110, Vietnamese, longtime area favorite, I • **Elizabeth's Café,** 1264 East Street (about a mile east of Route 7), Pittsfield, 448-8244, out-of-the-way find, delicious homemade Italian food, I–M. For Tanglewood picnics, call **Cheesecake Charlie's,** 637-3411, or **Moore Fine Food,** 637-0336. Also see Williamstown listings, pages 257–258.

SIGHTSEEING **Hancock Shaker Village,** Route 20 (at Route 41), Pittsfield, 443-0188. Hours: late May to late October, daily, 9:30 A.M. to 5 P.M.; April to late May and late October through November, daily, 10 A.M. to 3 P.M. $$$$$; **An Evening at Hancock Shaker Village,** tour, candlelight dinner, and entertainment, most Saturday nights, July to mid-October; reservations required. $38 • **Norman Rockwell Museum,** Route 183, Stockbridge, 298-4100. Hours: May to October, daily, 10 A.M. to 5 P.M.; November to April, weekdays, 11 A.M. to 4 P.M., weekends, 10 A.M. to 5 P.M. $$$$ • **Chesterwood,** Route 183 (two miles west of Stockbridge), 298-3579. Hours: May to October, daily, 10 A.M. to 5 P.M. $$$ • **Naumkeag Museum and Gardens,** Prospect Hill, Stockbridge, 298-3239. Hours: Memorial Day to Columbus Day, daily, 10 A.M. to 5 P.M. House and garden, $$$; garden only, $$ • **The Mount, Edith Wharton Restoration,** Plunkett Street, Lenox, 637-1899. Hours: June through October, daily, 10 A.M. to 2 P.M.; Saturday and Sunday only in May. $$$ • **Tyringham Art Galleries, Gingerbread House,** at Routes 102 and 20, Tyringham, 243-3260. Hours:

Memorial Day to Columbus Day, 10 A.M. to 5 P.M. $; under 12, free •
Arrowhead, 780 Holmes Road, Pittsfield, 442-1793. Hours: Memorial
Day to Labor Day, daily, 10 A.M. to 5 P.M.; Labor Day to October 31,
Friday to Monday, 10 A.M. to 5 P.M.; by appointment in winter. $$ •
Bartholomew's Cobble, off Route 7A, Ashley Falls, 229-8600. Hours:
grounds open year-round dawn to dusk; museum, April 15 to Novem-
ber 1, daily, 9 A.M. to 5 P.M. $$ • **Berkshire Botanical Garden,** Routes
102 and 183, Stockbridge, 298-3926. Hours: May through October,
daily, 10 A.M. to 5 P.M. $$; under 12, free. Also see Williamstown attrac-
tions, page 258.

PERFORMING ARTS   For all the following listings, it is best to
write or call for current schedules and prices, as they change from sea-
son to season: **Tanglewood,** West Street (Route 183), Lenox, 637-5165
or (800) 274-8499; before June, (617) 266-1942. Tickets also available
from Ticketmaster. Concerts July through Labor Day • **Jacob's Pillow
Dance Festival,** George Carter Road (off Route 20), Becket, 243-0745,
late June through August • **Shakespeare & Company,** the Mount,
Route 7, Lenox, 637-1199, late May through October • **Berkshire
Choral Festival,** Berkshire School, Sheffield, 229-3522, July and
August • **Berkshire Theater Festival,** Main Street, Stockbridge, 298-
5576, late June through August • **Williamstown Theater Festival,**
Adams Memorial Theater, Park and Main (intersection of Routes 7 and
2), Williamstown, 597-3400, July and August • **Aston Magna Founda-
tion,** 323 Main Street, PO Box 28, Great Barrington, 528-3595 or (800)
875-7156, July to early August • **Berkshire Opera Company,** 314
Main Street, Great Barrington, 528-4420 (performances in Pittsfield) •
Albany Berkshire Ballet, 51 North Street, Pittsfield, 445-5382 •
South Mountain Concerts, Routes 7 and 20, Pittsfield, 442-2106,
September to early October.

INFORMATION   Berkshire Visitors' Bureau, Berkshire Common,
Pittsfield, MA 01201, (800) BERKSHR or 443-9186 • Lenox Chamber
of Commerce, 75 Main Street, Lenox, MA 01240, 637-3646 or (800)
25-LENOX, information and lodging referral service.

Show-and-Tell at Lake Sunapee

I almost hate to write about New London, New Hampshire. After all, if too many people find out about this classy little college town at the top of Lake Sunapee, the congenial, low-key inns in town may be booked solid when I want to go back.

There's no problem, however, writing about the annual summer show of the League of New Hampshire Craftsmen Foundation, at Mount Sunapee State Park, because it is already one of the region's most eagerly awaited annual events, so popular that it has grown from a weekend affair to a full nine days.

Fine crafts seem to flourish best in the country, where artisans still take time and pains with handwork. In New Hampshire, a state that remains largely rural with lots of country to go around, the crafts tradition is strong and still growing. Much of the impetus is due to the efforts of the league, which began holding the nation's first crafts fair more than 60 years ago.

The host of white tents set up in front of the grassy ski slopes hold some 175 booths of juried fine crafts from a wide range of artisans— potters and silversmiths to basket makers and bird carvers. One of the most popular features of the fair is the "Living with Crafts" exhibit, in an adjoining building, a display showing off hand-crafted furnishings in model room settings, giving everyone new ideas and inspiration to take back home. The handmade furniture pieces, which include modern versions of the old cabinetmaker's work of art, the highboy, are real showstoppers—the priceless antiques of the future. In the same building is an exhibit of handcrafted clothing and accessories called "Craftwear."

But this lively affair is more than booths and displays. There are dozens of demonstrations by artisans and talented men and women from various craft guilds and organizations around the state such as Canterbury Shaker Village and the New Hampshire Farm Museum— perhaps a pewtersmith, a basket maker, or a seamstress turning flax into yarn at a spinning wheel—much to the delight of an audience of fascinated children. Both children and adults are welcome to take craft workshops as well as to watch others at work.

The kids have their own Children's Tent for creative workshops taught by master craftspeople plus other art activities. Many of them manage to coax their parents into a ride on the Mount Sunapee gondola, allowing everyone a bird's-eye view of the mountains and lakes of the area.

The big lake is Sunapee, and there's a public beach to make the most of it. It is pleasant, albeit crowded.

Boating is another favorite pastime. You can either rent your own small craft or go out for a two-hour cruise on the big MV *Mt. Sunapee II.* Dinner cruises, featuring buffet suppers and beautiful sunsets, are also offered on the MV *Kearsarge.*

Not far from Lake Sunapee State Park and on the shore of the lake is the Fells, the former home of John Hay, Abraham Lincoln's secretary and secretary of state under Theodore Roosevelt. Nearly 700 acres of grounds and woodland offer gardens, cool wooded walking trails, and the chance to tour the house on weekends and holidays. Much of the land is a National Wildlife Refuge.

The Sunapee area has a variety of lodgings away from the crowds. Dexter's Inn is a delightful hideaway, tucked high up on a hill with a choice of views—lake on one side, mountain on the other. There's a lot of emphasis on tennis here, and the pool is situated perfectly to make the most of the views.

The Inn at Sunapee is a homey farmhouse on a spectacular site with views of lakes and mountains; it also offers a pool and a tennis court. Another option, not far away, is the Follansbee Inn, a rambling old-fashioned 1840 inn with private frontage on Kezar Lake, in North Sutton. The most stylish inn in the area is Rosewood, a recently restored Victorian on 12 private acres where guests enjoy a three-course "candlelight and crystal breakfast." Rosewood sponsors a number of popular mother-daughter weekends in the off-season.

But, you can't really talk about the Sunapee area without mentioning New London, though many generations of Dartmouth students who made their way here to date the women at Colby-Sawyer College certainly will need no introduction to the town.

Don't expect anything big or flashy. The New London Barn Players have been resident summer performers here since 1933, but even so, New London is light-years away from being a tourist town—and that's part of its charm. The real pleasure of New London is simply strolling the pretty and unspoiled streets and savoring the relaxed small-town ambience that can make workaday pressures seem a faraway illusion.

The traditional red-brick buildings of the Colby-Sawyer campus are right in the center of things on Main Street, and they lead on to a row of handsome white Colonial homes and the requisite white-spired New England church. There are a few crafts and antiques shops for browsing, and the Artisans Workshop is worth a stop for arts and crafts exhibits. Baynham's has a potpourri of nice gifts, a 1950s soda fountain, and a pleasant café for lunch and light suppers.

Eventually you'll find your way to the New London Inn, either for a meal or for lodgings.

The inns in this town are not sophisticated resorts, they're homey and simple lodgings. The New London Inn is the most historic; the "new wing" was built in 1806; the rest of the building dates back to 1792. New owners have refurbished the venerable building, so it's looking better than ever. Guests at the inn are given passes to the residents-only beach at Little Sunapee, about a mile and a half away and much less crowded than the big beach at the big lake.

The Hide-Away Inn is just that—a cozy, rustic, wood-paneled retreat up the hill from Little Lake Sunapee. New, young owners have made the restaurant the best in town. Also hidden away is the Inn at Pleasant Lake, outside town, an eighteenth-century farmhouse with views of Pleasant Lake on one side and of Mount Kearsarge on the other, with guest privileges at the private beach club just across the way. There are new, young owners here as well, including a chef who was trained at the Culinary Institute of America.

Colonial Farm Inn has a highly praised dining room, attractively decorated rooms and an antiques shop on the premises, but it also has the disadvantage of being situated on the main highway. A busy road is also a drawback for Maple Hill Farm, but families will surely want to know about this relaxed, old-fashioned inn on the shore of Little Lake Sunapee, a place as homey as Grandma's farm, where families are welcome to join in gathering eggs in the barn and petting the baby lambs.

Golfers may want to check out the Fairway Motel, at the Lake Sunapee Country Club, which lets you stay within a putt of the starting green and offers tennis and a pool as well. Golfers may also want to visit the Country Club of New Hampshire, in North Sutton, rated as one of New England's best public courses.

The crafts fair, boating and swimming, a game of golf or tennis, some backroads exploring plus a stroll or two down New London's Main Street should easily fill a pair of peaceful country-style days. For more shopping, check nearby towns such as Georges Mill, where Prospect Hill has a big display of both antiques and replicas, or Andover, where Potter Place Gallery exhibits work by New England artists and artisans.

Evenings in the Sunapee area hold a choice of the New London Players or a half hour drive to Hanover for the Dartmouth Players Repertory Company or a host of attractions at the Hopkins Center.

A highly recommended end to the weekend is a detour north on Route 12A to Cornish and the Sunday afternoon concerts during July and August at Saint-Gaudens National Historic Site. This is the magnificent home, gardens, and studio of Augustus Saint-Gaudens, one of America's greatest sculptors, whose famous "Standing Lincoln" and many other works led the way toward realism in sculpture. Saint-Gaudens' graceful home, Aspet, circa 1800, is lovely; the many-acred grounds are even more spectacular, with a soaring view of hills and mountains beyond. The chamber music series is held in the sky-lit studio, but many people prefer staying out on the lawn to listen while they contemplate the beauty around them.

This area along the Connecticut River is well worth considering for an extended stay. Across a picturesque covered bridge from Cornish—in Windsor, Vermont—is the workshop and showroom of Simon Pearce, where you can watch glassblowers creating exquisite goblets and home accessories by hand. A restaurant, being added at press time, promises to be the best in the area.

Windsor is also home to a branch of the Vermont State Craft Center; to the Old Constitution House, where the state was born in 1777; and to the American Precision Museum, housed in a nineteenth-century armory, the place where the country's modern system of industrial design was born with the introduction of the concept of interchangeable parts. The museum includes the National Machine Tool Collection, a virtual historical record of America's manufacturing past and its influence on the world.

Driving south of Windsor on Route 5 in Ascutney, you can stop at the showroom of Claire Murray and perhaps pick up seconds of her beautiful hand-hooked rugs.

This area along the river offers some lovely lodgings. Lovers of Colonial homes will surely admire the Chase House, in Cornish, a beautifully restored national landmark. Built in 1775, the Federal-period house was once the home of Salmon Portland Chase, a chief justice of the Supreme Court and founder of the Republican Party. You can find his picture on the front of a $10,000 bill, if you happen to have one handy.

Farther north, Home Hill is a hideaway retreat with a pool and a highly regarded French restaurant, and to the south, the Maple Hedge Bed and Breakfast, in Charlestown, is a small bed-and-breakfast inn in a historic home, furnished with care by warm hosts.

On the Vermont side of the river, the Inn at Weathersfield boasts one of the state's most acclaimed dining rooms, with meals served by candlelight in a charming eighteenth-century setting. There are more finds in this area filled with unexpected pleasures—not the least of them the no-longer-hidden charms of New London.

Area Code: 603

DRIVING DIRECTIONS To reach the Lake Sunapee area from the east, take I-93 to I-89 North to New London, south on Route 11 to Mount Sunapee State Park. From the west, take I-91 to exit 8, go about 13 miles east on Route 103 to the park, then north on Route 11 to New London. New London is 110 miles from Boston, 260 miles from New York, and 150 miles from Hartford. Mount Sunapee Park is about 10 miles away.

PUBLIC TRANSPORTATION Vermont Transit bus service from Boston to New London.

ACCOMMODATIONS **New London Inn,** Main Street, New London 03257, 526-2791 or (800) 526-2791, I–M, CP • **Inn at Pleasant Lake,** Box 1030, Pleasant Street, New London 03257, 526-6271 or

(800) 626-4907, M, CP • **Hide-Away Inn,** Twin Lake Villa Road, New London 03257, 526-4861 or (800) 457-0589, M, CP • **Colonial Farm Inn,** Route 11, New London 03257, 526-6121 or (800) 805-8504, I–M, CP • **Maple Hill Farm,** 200 Newport Road, New London 03257, 526-2248 or (800) 231-8637, I–M, CP • **Fairway Motel,** Lake Sunapee Country Club, Route 11 East, New London 03257, 526-6040, I • **Dexter's Inn and Tennis Club,** Stagecoach Road, Sunapee 03782, 763-5571, pool and tennis, E, MAP • **The Inn at Sunapee,** Box 336, Sunapee 03782, 763-4444 or (800) 327-2466, I–M, CP • **Seven Hearths,** Old Route 11, Sunapee 03782, 763-5657 or (800) 237-2464, some rooms with working fireplaces, M–E, CP • **Rosewood Country Inn,** 67 Pleasant View Road, Bradford 03221, 938-5253 or (800) 938-5273, I–M, CP; suites, M–E, CP • **Follansbee Inn,** Route 114, PO Box 92, North Sutton 03260, 927-4221, I–M, CP • **Blue Goose Inn,** Route 103B (at Mount Sunapee State Park), Mt. Sunapee 03772, 763-5519, modest roadside farmhouse, closest lodging to the craft fair, I, CP • **The Chase House,** Route 12A, Cornish 03745, 675-5391, M, CP • **Home Hill,** River Road, Plainfield 03781, 675-6165, secluded estate, pool, tennis, golf, hiking trails, M–E, CP.

DINING   **New London Inn** (see above), American fare, I–M • **Hideaway Inn** (see above), one of the area's best, M • **Colonial Farm Inn** (see above), highly regarded locally, M • **La Meridiana,** Route 11, Wilmot (just east of New London), 526-2033, northern Italian, well recommended, I–M • **Inn at Pleasant Lake,** (see above), prix fixe, EE • **The Millstone,** Newport Road, New London, 526-4201, extensive menu, good Sunday brunch, I–M • **Peter Christian's Tavern,** Main Street, New London, 526-4042, informal, reliable, I–M • **Four Corners Grille,** Route 11 (at Route 114), New London, 526-6899, casual, burgers to full meals, great views of Mount Kearsarge, I–M • **The Inn at Sunapee** (see above), M • **Dexter's Inn** (see above), very popular, M • **Tommy's Anchorage,** Sunapee Harbor, 763-4777, light fare, deck on the harbor, M • **MV Kearsarge,** dinner boat, Lake Avenue, Sunapee, 763-5477; phone for current rates and schedules • **Home Hill** (see above), prix fixe, highly regarded French cuisine, EE • **Inn at Weathersfield,** prix fixe, Route 106, Weathersfield, VT (just south of Perkinsville) 05151, (802) 263-9217 or (800) 477-4828, four-star dining, EE.

SIGHTSEEING   **League of New Hampshire Craftsmen Fair,** Mount Sunapee State Park, Route 103, Newbury, NH; held annually in early August. $$$; 12 and under, free. For dates, contact the league at 205 North Main Street, Concord, NH 03301, 224-1471 • **Mount Sunapee State Park Beach,** 763-2356. Hours: mid-June to Labor Day and weekends in late May and early June, daily, 9:30 A.M. to 8 P.M. $; under 12, free with adult • **Mount Sunapee Chairlift Ride,** Mount Sunapee State Park, 763-2356. Hours: late June to Labor Day, daily,

11 A.M. to 6 P.M.; late May, September to mid-October, weekends only, 9 A.M. to 5 P.M. $$$ • **MV** *Mt. Sunapee II* sails from Sunapee Harbor mid-May to mid-October; call 763-4030 for current schedules and rates • **Saint-Gaudens National Historic Site,** Route 12A, Cornish, 675-2175. Hours: daily, 9 A.M. to 4:30 P.M. $$; under 17, free. Concerts held Sundays at 2 P.M. in July and August • **The Fells,** Route 103A, Newbury, 763-4789. Hours: daily, dawn to dusk; house tours, weekends and holidays, 11 A.M. to 5 P.M. $$. *Windsor, Vermont:* **Simon Pearce,** off Route 5 north of town, Windsor, 674-6280. Hours: daily, 9 A.M. to 5 P.M. • **The Old Constitution House,** Route 5, Windsor, 672-3773. Hours: late May through mid-October, Wednesday to Sunday, 11 A.M. to 5 P.M. $ • **American Precision Museum,** 196 Main Street (Route 5), Windsor, 674-5781. Hours: Memorial Day to November 1, Monday to Friday, 9 A.M. to 5 P.M., Saturday and Sunday, 10 A.M. to 4 P.M. $$.

INFORMATION Sunapee Vacation, PO Box 400, Sunapee, NH 03782, 763-2495 or (800) 258-3530 (out of state).

Smooth Sailing in Boothbay Harbor

Picture-postcard photographs of Boothbay Harbor, Maine, resemble paintings of a perfect seacoast village. Views from the land show shimmering light on the water, a montage of masts and deep blue sea studded with pine-rimmed islands. From the sea you can see the harbor backed by a row of wharves and tiny shops, with trim New England homes, church steeples, and green hills in the distance.

The pictures don't lie. This is as idyllic a spot as you'll find on the Maine coast—or any coast. It is also a lively community, full of crowds in summer, a town that can rightfully boast of being the "Boating Capital of New England." Boothbay becomes even more picturesque in late June during Windjammer Days, when a whole fleet of many-rigged tall ships makes a stately procession into the harbor. Parades, band concerts, and fireworks also mark the occasion.

But this is one place that needs no special occasion to make your visit an event. You need only board one of the many craft waiting in the harbor to appreciate just why this area is a perennial favorite for sailors and yachtsmen. The trip from Boothbay to Monhegan Island in particular is a not-to-be-missed experience for anyone who appreciates untouched natural beauty.

But first you'll want to settle on land, and that can be a pleasantly difficult decision. There are several parts to Boothbay, the village and three fingerlike peninsulas jutting out to sea. Each has its own attractions.

If you want to be within a five-minute walk of the village piers, shops, and restaurants but a bit removed from the bustle, head up the hill to the delightful little Anchor Watch, a bed-and-breakfast home with wonderful water views from three of its four rooms. Other bed-and-breakfast inns are in the village, though on busier streets.

East Boothbay, a quiet little village about three miles away, is home to a nicely restored 125-year-old country inn, the Five Gables, with a serene location and a wraparound porch with views of a picturesque cove. At the end of the peninsula is Ocean Point, with a classic rocky shoreline to explore. Ocean Point Inn is off by itself at the entrance to Linekin Bay, a complex of inn and lodge, motel and cottages, with its own dining room and a handy heated pool.

A five-minute drive west from Boothbay Harbor will bring you to Hodgdon Island Inn, a relaxing country inn on a cove, and once again, a swimming pool.

Spruce Point, a scenic rocky peninsula, also about five minutes' drive from the village, is the site of the area's most elegant resort, Spruce Point Inn, set on 100 wooded acres and offering a pool, tennis, a putting green, a marina, and sunset cruises. Guests can use the inn shuttle to get to town.

If you really want the sense of being away from it all, head across the bridge from Boothbay to Southport Island. Two rustic inns here have water views to stop you in your tracks. Don't expect fancy decor at Newagen Inn, but do expect an extraordinary site in the middle of a nature preserve jutting directly into the Gulf of Maine. Albonegon Inn (accent on the *nee*), a cozily cluttered little place, has an equally smashing site on its own tiny island off the mainland with a view of harbor islands, forested peninsulas, and the fisherman's passage that is the gateway to the Atlantic. These are places where you could easily settle in not just for a relaxing weekend but for a quiet, rejuvenating week or two, happily contemplating the view.

One thing to be done as soon as you get to Boothbay Harbor is to head straight for the wharf to make your reservation for an outing on the water. There is a wide choice of boats—more than 50 kinds of trips —from an hour's sail to a 41-mile cruise up the Kennebec River to see the ships being built at the Bath Iron Works.

Whichever you choose, you'll be gloriously out to sea among picturesque pine-covered islands and lighthouses, where ospreys soar and herons skim, dolphins and seals play, and (with a little luck) whales can be sighted in the distance.

For the most extraordinary trip of all, board the *Balmy Days* for Monhegan Island. Jamie Wyeth, one of the many artists who summer on Monhegan, described the island to a reporter as "like living on a ship, out of sight of land."

The living here is primitive—few telephones, little electricity—and that's just the way those who love the place want to keep it. Part of Monhegan's beauty is its wildness and the amazing variety of terrain—200-foot cliffs jutting into the sea, virgin forests, ponds and coves, and sighting places along the way for bird and seal watchers with binoculars in hand. The harbor seals are seen best at half tide on Seal Ledge, and sometimes they can be spied at Lobster Cove and off Fish Beach as well.

You'll be given a map as you come onto the island to guide your way. There are a few sights to visit—a museum, a lighthouse, and many artists' studios—but the island's most fabulous sight is itself. Walking trails are clearly marked on the map as to distance and difficulty. The Cathedral Woods are pleasant, cool, and shady, and are strewn with wildflowers, ferns, and "fairy houses" of sticks and bark, built (according to the guide) to entice woodland fairies to set up housekeeping. The most spectacular walks go straight across the top of the cliffs, offering overviews of waves crashing on rocky headlands, which may well remain your favorite memories of Maine.

Monhegan takes up an entire day. The *Balmy Days* ships out at 9:15, arrives at 10:50, and allows you four hours on shore before heading back for a 4:30 arrival in Boothbay Harbor. Lunch is available at both the island's laid-back hotels, the Island Inn and the Trailing Yew, and if you are so taken that you want to come back to stay a while, you can make your reservation now for the next season—the hotels are often booked a full year ahead.

You'll be back on the mainland in plenty of time to try one of the many restaurants for dinner and to make the rounds of the shops, most of which are conveniently open in the evening. If you wander the winding, narrow streets of town, you'll find some worthwhile stops tucked among the souvenir emporiums. McKown Street is a good bet for shops such as Abacus and Hand in Hand for fine American crafts. The Custom House, on Wharf Street, is known for its hand-painted blueberry pottery, and Gimbel & Sons, a country store, has a variety of gifts; it has been owned and operated by the Gimbel family for over 30 years.

There are many art galleries for pleasant browsing, including the community-supported Boothbay Region Art Foundation Gallery, on Townsend Avenue, which displays some of the better work of area artists in changing shows each season. Gleason Fine Art is housed in the Old Brick House, on Oak Street, circa 1807, built by a well-known early builder, John Leisman Jr., who had the bricks imported from England.

The other attractions in town are recommended only for a rainy day, though kids may enjoy the steam train ride at the Boothbay Railway Village or the chance to pet a fish at the small aquarium operated by the Department of Marine Resources.

The town of Boothbay Harbor extends across the river via a footbridge. The main incentive to cross over to the east side is dining.

Choices include the deck of the Rocktide with its postcard view of the harbor across the water, Brown's Wharf, or the Lobsterman's Co-op.

Evening entertainment is informal, mostly occasional live music in places such as the lounge at J. H. Hawk, a restaurant on Pier One. Carousel Music Theater provides Broadway revues, but remember that you're very far off-Broadway. And there's always the Dolphin Mini-Golf Course, on Route 27 in Boothbay, which includes its own New England lighthouse and covered bridge.

If you spend your Saturday at sea, you might relax on Sunday and enjoy the scenery, try another kind of boat excursion, check out the art, or perhaps make the half-hour drive to Pemaquid Point, another of those convoluted peninsulas that mark this part of the coast. This one is reached through the neighboring town of Damariscotta, back on U.S. Route 1.

One of the lesser-known gems of Maine's shoreline, Pemaquid Point is a prime example of that much-vaunted "rockbound coast," with a photogenic old lighthouse, a little fishermen's museum and art gallery, and shelves of granite descending into the sea that are especially fun for rock clamberers. The area around the lighthouse has been turned into a park, and the crescent-shaped beach around the bend is open to the public for a fee. The 1827 lighthouse offers one of the best perspectives on the pounding surf.

Not only is Pemaquid as dramatic a viewpoint as any you'll encounter on the coast, it offers a bonus for history and archaeology buffs at Fort William Henry, in the state park that has been developed near the beach. This is where England held off the French in four successive forts built between 1605 and 1729. The Old Fort House, built for the last battles, has been restored and shouldn't be missed, even if all you want to do is take a scenic snapshot.

North of the fort are the remains of a once-thriving settlement that existed as early as 1620. Archaeologists have unearthed many of the old cellars, including that of the Customs House, where clearance was required of all ships. Some 40,000 artifacts have been recovered, and a small museum at the Colonial Pemaquid State Historic Site holds the results of the digs—tools and pottery shards and all manner of possessions reflecting the lives of those who settled here over 350 years ago.

Also in Damariscotta is the restored St. Patrick's Church, the oldest surviving Catholic church in New England, complete with a Paul Revere bell in the tower and an adjacent old cemetery.

If you want to have a meal on Pemaquid Point, there's the Pemaquid Fisherman's Co-op, where you can eat your lobster and watch fishermen hauling in their catch, or Bradley Inn, a Colonial-style inn on Route 320. The inn is attractive and its Ships restaurant is something to keep in mind if you decide to come back to Pemaquid. Like Monhegan and Southport Island and the rest of the beautiful midcoast around Boothbay Harbor, it seems to beg for a longer visit.

Area Code: 207

DRIVING DIRECTIONS Boothbay Harbor is 12 miles off U.S. Route 1 in midcoastal Maine, 55 miles east of Portland. Turn south off Route 1 onto Route 27 about a mile north of Wiscasset and follow it into town. It is 164 miles from Boston, 374 miles from New York, and 264 miles from Hartford.

PUBLIC TRANSPORTATION Air service to Portland; taxi service is available from the airport into Boothbay. You can manage without a car if you stay right in town.

ACCOMMODATIONS Spruce Point Inn, Boothbay Harbor 04538, 633-4152, area's best resort, E–EE, MAP • **Ocean Point Inn,** PO Box 409, Shore Road, East Boothbay 04544, 633-4200, inn, motel, and cottage accommodations at the tip of a scenic peninsula, M–E • **Anchor Watch,** 3 Eames Road, Boothbay Harbor 04538, 633-7565, small charmer with great views, M, CP • **Water's Edge,** 8 Eames Road, Boothbay Harbor 04538, 633-4251, same special location facing the water, I–M, CP • **Albonegon Inn,** Capitol Island 04538, 633-2521, old-fashioned retreat, simple accommodations and a world-class view, I–M, CP • **Newagen Inn,** Southport Island, Cape Newagen 04552, 633-5558 or (800) 654-5242, wonderful location surrounded by water, M–E, CP • **Five Gables Inn,** Murray Hill Road, East Boothbay 04544, 233-4551 or (800) 451-5048, century-old summerhouse, quiet, scenic location, M–E, CP • **Admiral's Quarters,** Commercial Street, Boothbay Harbor 04538, 633-2474, modest in-town bed-and-breakfast inn, I–M, CP • **Captain Sawyer's Place,** 87 Commercial Street, Boothbay Harbor 04538, 633-2290, another pleasant bed-and-breakfast choice in town, I–M, CP • **Hodgdon Island Inn,** Barter's Island Road, Trevett 04571, 633-7474, old-fashioned inn, peaceful setting, pool, M, CP. *Among the nicest of the motels:* **Topside,** McKown Hill, Boothbay Harbor 04538, 633-5405, inn and motel just up the hill from town with water views, M • **Ocean Gate,** Southport 04576, 633-3321, M–E • **Lawnmeer Inn,** Southport 04575, 633-2544, I–M • **Rocktide,** East Boothbay 04538, 633-4455, M. *Monhegan Island:* **Island Inn,** Monhegan 04852, 596-0371, M–E. MAP • **Trailing Yew,** Monhegan 04852, 596-0440, M, MAP.

DINING Black Orchid, on the By-Way, Boothbay Harbor, 633-6659, Italian and seafood specialties, a cut above for this area, M–E • **Spruce Point Inn** (see above), sophisticated menu, overlooking the ocean, M–E • **Lawnmeer Inn** (see above), water views, seafood specialties, M • **Newagen Inn** (see above), simple decor, fabulous views, varied continental menu, M–E • **Tugboat Restaurant,** 100 Commercial Street, Boothbay Harbor, 633-4434, seafood, overlooking the harbor, M–E • **Harbour High,** 33 Oak Street, Boothbay Harbor, 633-3444, pleasant casual ambience, varied menu, I–M • **Chowder House,** at the footbridge, Boothbay Harbor, 633-5761, outdoor deck on the water, very informal, I–M also good for breakfast and lunch, I • **J. H. Hawk Ltd.,** Pier One, Boothbay Harbor, 633-3444, upstairs on the docks, nautical decor, burgers to Cajun, live entertainment, I–E • **No Anchovies,** Townsend Avenue, Boothbay Harbor, 633-2130, pasta and pizza, very popular, I–M • **Rocktide,** 45 Atlantic Avenue, east side, Boothbay Harbor, 633-4455, seafood, outdoor deck, great view, formal and informal dining; a free trolley runs to and from the village, I–M • **Christoper's 1820 House,** Route 96, East Boothbay, 633-6565, pleasant dining room, New England cuisine, excellent chef, water views, I–M • **Lobsterman's Wharf,** Route 96, East Boothbay, 633-3443, seafood, pasta dishes, waterfront deck, I–M • **Bradley Inn,** Pemaquid Point Road, New Harbor, 677-2105, nautical decor, excellent varied menu, I–M. *Lobster!* (Prices vary with the year, but always are less at these informal outdoor eateries.) **Boothbay Region Lobstermen's Co-op,** Atlantic Avenue, east side of the harbor, 633-4900, no-frills lobster at waterside picnic tables • **Robinson's Wharf,** Route 27 at the bridge, Southport, 633-3830, informal menu as well as lobster, I • **Cabbage Island Clambake,** Boothbay Harbor, 633-7200, includes cruise to Cabbage Island • **Pemaquid Fisherman's Co-op,** Pemaquid Harbor, 677-2642.

SIGHTSEEING **Boothbay Region Art Foundation Gallery,** 7 Townsend Avenue, Boothbay Harbor, 633-2703. Hours: Monday to Saturday, 11 A.M. to 5 P.M., Sunday, 2 P.M. to 5 P.M. Free • **Marine Resources Aquarium,** McKown Point Road, West Boothbay Harbor, 633-9542. Hours: Memorial Day to Columbus Day, 10 A.M. to 5 P.M. $ • **Boothbay Railway Village,** Route 27, Boothbay, 633-4727. Hours: mid-June to mid-October, daily, 9:30 A.M. to 5 P.M. $$$. *Boat trips:* **Argo,** Pier 6, 633-7200, sightseeing cruises daily in season • *Balmy Days II* to Monhegan, Pier 8, 9:30 A.M. daily, 633-2284, also harbor tours, supper cruises • **Cap'n Fish's Scenic Boat Trips,** Pier I, 633-3244, daily excursions, also sunset cruises, lobster fishing, whale, puffin and seal watches • **Miss Boothbay,** Pier 6, 633-6445, lobster boat cruises. *Sailboat cruises:* **Appledore,** Fisherman's Wharf, 633-6598, 65-foot windjammer • **Mary Eliza,** Boothbay Harbor Inn, 633-6302, 31-foot sloop • **Bay Lady,** Pier 8, 633-2284, smaller sailboat, 1½-hour sails • **Windbourne Cruises,** Ocean Point, East Boothbay, 882-1020, 40-foot sailboat. For any additions and for fishing boat schedules, contact the Chamber of Commerce.

INFORMATION Boothbay Harbor Region Chamber of Commerce, Route 27, Boothbay Harbor, ME 04538, 633-2353.

Discovering the Other Nantucket

The day-trippers hardly know it exists. For most of the passengers pouring off the ferry, Nantucket Island means the quaint cobblestoned village with its whaling captains' mansions, rose-covered cottages, shops, beaches—and crowds.

But just a few miles away there's another Nantucket, Siasconset and Wauwinet, two tiny settlements that still miraculously match one eighteenth-century visitor's description: "Perfectly unconnected with the real world and far removed from its perturbations." Visitors might be surprised to find that on an island known for its fine dining, the two most lauded restaurants are in these outposts, along with some of its poshest accommodations.

The better known of the two, universally called 'Sconset, is a beguiling village set between the cranberry bogs and the rose-grown bluffs overlooking the Atlantic. The miniature cottages winding along 'Sconset's lanes suggest its seventeenth- and eighteenth-century origins as a whaling outpost. They are fishermen's shanties that have been altered and added to over the centuries. Many are unique, built with used wood brought from town or retrieved from shipwrecks, giving rise to the town's nickname of "Patchwork Village."

'Sconset's special flavor began to attract visitors as early as the 1800s. By the end of the century, when the Nantucket Central Railroad extended its narrow-gauge tracks to provide a fast, 35-minute ride from town to the village, the passengers included a "who's who" of the American stage. Stars such as Lillian Russell and Joseph Jefferson came to vacation in what had become a summer haven for Broadway luminaries.

With the rise of Hollywood, the actors' colony moved westward, leaving 'Sconset's glorious beaches in peace. With the exception of one pleasant little café and a spot offering gourmet box lunches, the village square offers little more than basics—food, papers and magazines, liquor, and gasoline. It is marked by the antique water pump that once served the entire community.

Tucked behind hedges and a garden down the lane, however, is the Chanticleer, where chef Jean-Charles Berruet has held sway for more than two decades as the island's most lauded chef, creating delicacies such as scallops poached in Madeira sauce with truffles or *gratin de homard* in a lobster sauce with cognac. For lunch, tables are set in a vine-covered arbor outside.

Though many people rent houses here during the summer, there are few lodgings in 'Sconset for transient visitors, which is one reason the village retains its peaceful air. The Summer House, on a bluff at the southeastern edge of the island, is the best of the choices, offering cottage accommodations with access to the beach, plus its own pool and cheerful dining spaces. Rooms are furnished with English pine and come with personal marble Jacuzzis. The other possibility is Wade Cottages, a former estate perched on a magnificent seaside bluff. You can rent an entire cottage or a single room here; rooms that share baths are quite reasonably priced.

Wauwinet, Nantucket's other faraway retreat, is even less developed. It consists of miles of ocean and bayfront beach to tempt strollers, sun worshipers, and fishermen. There are a few houses, one hotel, and not another commercial establishment in sight.

Fishermen were originally attracted to Wauwinet because of the strand of land they dubbed "the haulaway," a strip separating the calm inner harbor from the open Atlantic where they could literally haul their dories across from one to the other. As in 'Sconset, the fishermen built huts that were expanded over the years, but this community soon centered on Wauwinet House, a rambling gray-shingled beach house opened by James Backus in 1897 to serve meals for fishermen on its big screened porch.

People began asking to stay overnight, and Wauwinet was soon a thriving summer hotel. It remained so over many years, turning into a no-frills haven for nature lovers and escapists.

Then new owners came in, renovated to the reported tune of $8 million, and the hotel was reborn as Nantucket's most exclusive retreat, now called simply "the Wauwinet." For those who can afford the tab, there's no better place to escape the crowds and still enjoy all the luxuries of civilization. The shingled facade is almost unchanged, but the interior of the hotel is now a stylish world of chintz and antique pine, stenciling, folk art, and faux ceiling clouds—all the accoutrements of country chic. Additional accommodations are in shingled cottages near the beach.

Amenities are legion, including daily cheese, port, and sherry tastings in the library; use of sailboats and rowboats and kayaks; tennis; croquet; mountain bikes; and free shuttle service into town. You can cruise the bay on the Wauwinet's custom launch or ask to be dropped off at a secluded cove for a private picnic.

The inn restaurant, named Topper's after the owner's dog, quickly rivaled the Chanticleer for the title of "best on the island" for its New American cuisine. Even the sumptuous breakfasts served to guests are extraordinary. Leave the calorie counter at home.

Those who stay in town and want to come to Wauwinet for lunch or dinner can do so via a free cruise on the *Lady Wauwinet,* a wonderful outing. The terrace is an unbeatable place for watching glorious island sunsets.

One thing that has not changed at Wauwinet is unending vistas of blue sea. With all the activities available, you can be happy here doing absolutely nothing—just appreciating the rare tranquillity ensured for years to come by the Backus' gift of more than 500 acres of surrounding land to the Massachusetts Trustees of Preservation.

Almost everyone eventually takes off along the four-mile curved beach to Great Point and its lighthouse, rebuilt after a storm and now solar-powered. The hotel offers guided walks for guests.

If you want more action, take the hotel shuttle, drive, or bike the eight miles or so and join the tourists on the cobbled lanes in Nantucket Village, where there are scores of restaurants, movies, nightlife, and plenty of shops to keep you occupied. The Whaling Museum is just the thing for a cloudy day, as are the elegant homes of the old whale-oil merchants. See page 20 for more about Nantucket sights, and visit the Chamber of Commerce for information on guided walking tours of the beautiful village.

When you've had your fill of sights, you can come back to 'Sconset or Wauwinet, leaving crowds and cares behind for the company of the gulls and the sea.

Area Code: 508

TRANSPORTATION   See page 24.

ACCOMMODATIONS   A three-day minimum may be required in season; all accommodations are less in spring and fall. • **Summer House Cottages,** Box 880, South Bluff, Siasconset, Nantucket 02564, 257-4577, late April to early October, EE, CP • **Wade Cottages,** Box 211, Siasconset, Nantucket 02564, 257-6308, late May to mid-October, M–EE, CP • **The Wauwinet,** Wauwinet, Nantucket 02584, 228-0145 or (800) 426-8718, early May to October, EE, CP.

DINING   **The Chanticleer,** Siasconset, 257-6231, open late May to mid-October, lunch served June through September, reservations essential, M–E; dinner, prix fixe, EE • **Topper's,** the Wauwinet (see above), M, lunch; dinner, EE • **Summer House** (see above), EE • **'Sconset Café,** Siasconset, 257-4008, highly regarded New American, serves all three meals, I, lunch; dinner, E, on the square • **Claudette's,** on the square, Siasconset, 257-6622, have a sandwich on the deck or take a box lunch to the beach, I. For additional Nantucket suggestions, see page 25.

SIGHTSEEING   See pages 25–26.

INFORMATION   Nantucket Island Chamber of Commerce, 48 Main Street, Nantucket, MA 02554, 228-1700.

Fall

Overleaf: *Autumn in Woodbury, Vermont. Photograph courtesy of Vermont Travel Division.*

Indian Summer in Kennebunkport

Kennebunkport, Maine, is picturesque . . . posh . . . and packed with people and cars in midsummer. There's good reason to head for this delightful seafaring town, but since its special pleasures are not limited to July and August, there's no reason to put up with the crowds.

Instead, mark Kennebunkport down for a warm Indian summer weekend after Labor Day. You can still live in a sea captain's mansion, see the lovely shuttered Colonial homes and enormous summer "cottages," walk the cliffs and the wide beaches, watch the foam spout at "Blowing Cave" and the sun set at Porpoise Point, and eat all the lobster you can hold—without having to fight for space to do it all.

Kennebunkport has always been a desirable place to be. Even Maine's Indians chose to set up their campgrounds along the beautiful beaches here, and countless artists and writers have been inspired by the views. Kenneth Roberts, a native, immortalized the town in his novel *Arundel* (the name of the village until 1821), and Booth Tarkington wrote his novels aboard his schooner *Regina,* which was moored on the Kennebunk River for years.

The village became a favorite summer resort for the wealthy in the late 1880s and has boasted prominent summer residents ever since.

In the 1700s, Kennebunkport grew into a port and shipbuilding center second only to Portland on the Maine coast. Eight hundred vessels were launched from here in less than 80 years. The unusual profusion of fine Colonial residences in the central Historic District is testament to the fortunes that were made in the shipbuilding trade.

Though there are excellent lodgings of every kind to be found, including some lovely spots on the water, one of the particular pleasures of Kennebunkport is to stay in one of the old mansions that now serve as elegant inns. The best known (and for good reason) is the Captain Lord Mansion, built by a wealthy shipbuilder who kept his carpenters occupied during the British blockade of the harbor in 1812 by putting them to work constructing the town's most imposing residence. And grand it remains, a three-story, creamy yellow clapboard, Federal-style structure with rows upon rows of tall shuttered windows and an octagonal cupola on top. The three-story stairway, many fireplaces, and ornate Victorian furnishings in the inn's 16 rooms are exceptional. The latest addition, the Captain's Suite, has a fireplace, a whirlpool for two, and a hydro massage shower.

Needless to say, your odds of getting a reservation are better off-season, but do write well ahead anyway.

If the Captain Lord is full, all is far from lost, for the 1813 Captain Fairfield Inn, just across the way, has also been beautifully restored, and it is a bit cozier in feel, thanks to particularly friendly innkeepers. The Inn on South Street is a most gracious smaller home, a Greek Revival Federal-style home built in the early 1800s and listed on the National Register of Historic Places. The house is filled with an exceptional collection of Orientalia.

The Lower Village, the heart of Kennebunkport, is a short stroll from any of these inns. It is a compact area that is best appreciated on foot. The 1824 South Congregational Church, across the way from the shopping area, with its 100-foot white steeple and weather vane–topped Christopher Wren cupola and belfry, is a quintessential New England sight and has the subject of many photographs.

Across the way, in the Temple Street Post Office, you can see a Gordon Grant mural depicting the harbor as it was in the old days, when the air was filled with the clang of shipbuilders' hammers and the cries of crews unloading cargo from around the world. Dock Square, where square-riggers were once moored, is no less busy today as a complex of weathered buildings housing all manner of shops and restaurants. The Dock Square Market Building, moved here in 1849, once housed a Baptist church and a school. The Bookport Building started life as a rum warehouse for Perkins' West India Goods. You'll find almost every kind of clothing and craft for sale here, though the emphasis is on fashions that are on the preppy side.

From Dock Square, walk down Ocean Avenue past more shops and turn left on Pearl Street, then right on Pleasant to view some of the finest of the sea captains' homes. Green and Maine Streets offer more architectural delights.

You'll find art galleries almost everywhere you go, since Kennebunkport remains a magnet for artists. The guide published by the Art Guild of the Kennebunks lists dozens of choices. Look for it in most of the galleries.

Return to Ocean Avenue and take a very long walk or a drive around rocky Cape Arundel and you'll begin to see what inspires the artists. The rugged coastline here is superb, and there's a bonus if you clamber down the rocks to Spouting Rock and Blowing Cave, where the waves perform a foaming, leaping dance in rhythm with the tide. Keep going and you'll see St. Ann's Episcopal Church, built of sea-washed stone, just beyond reach of the waves, with the ocean in sight beyond the altar of an outdoor chapel. When you spy the guards on duty, you'll know you've reached the Bush residence at Walker Point, the family compound of former president George Bush.

There is a beach off Ocean Avenue in town, but the better bet is Goose Rocks Beach, about a ten-minute drive along King's Highway off Route 9. The beach is near Cape Porpoise, whose pier is a center for

lobstering and much of the commercial fishing activity of Kennebunkport. It is a scenic spot for taking photos, especially near sunset.

One of the most delightful of Kennebunkport's small inns is the Inn
at Harbor Head, hidden away high on a hill overlooking Cape Porpoise
Harbor and the ocean beyond. Canopy beds, antique pine, and artistic
taste make each of the five bedrooms special.

Some of the best eating in town is also found at Cape Porpoise. For
lobster sans frills, there's Nunan's Lobster Hut; for more formal dining,
Seascapes offers both harbor views and creative menus. For true
gourmet fare back in town, the White Barn heads the list, with formal
menus served in a strikingly restored barn.

Another local eating experience that shouldn't be missed is breakfast
at the Green Heron, in town, a many-course delight with wonderful
fresh fruits and baked goodies that has become a local institution—as
the long waiting lines outside the inn on weekend mornings suggest.

If the shops and galleries pall and the weather isn't conducive to
beach walks, visit the Seashore Trolley Museum, one of the largest collections of electric and railway cars in the country, for a bit of nostalgia
and an old-fashioned trolley ride. If bargains are of more interest than
trolleys, head for Wells and its array of discount stores.

Another possibility is the short drive to Kennebunk to see another
magnificent early New England church, the First Parish Unitarian
Church, built in 1772. The Christopher Wren steeple was added when
the church was enlarged in 1803–1804, and a Paul Revere bell was
hung at the same time. Kennebunk's tiny Brick Store Museum, on the
main street, offers interesting exhibits from the town's early days,
including furniture, paintings, and ship models. Kennebunk lacks its
seaside sister's charm, but it does have some interesting historic homes
and some fine beaches of its own.

If the sun is shining, there are boats waiting to take you out to sea for
a scenic cruise, a fishing excursion, or whale watching in season, and
the neighboring Wells National Estuarine Research Reserve offers a
unique nineteenth-century saltwater farm, a Visitors Center, the Rachel
Carson National Wildlife Refuge, and seven miles of trails on its 1,600
acres. Guided walks are offered daily in summer and on weekends in
spring and fall.

In truth, though, it's hardly likely you'll stray far from Kennebunkport. Ensconced in your own sea captain's quarters with magnificent seascapes, historic homes, and half a hundred shops and galleries
just around the corner, why on earth would you want to leave?

Area Code: 207

DRIVING DIRECTIONS   Kennebunkport is on the southern coast
of Maine, about 25 miles below Portland. From I-95 or U.S. Route 1,

follow Route 35 east into town. Route 9, closer to the shore, also leads to Kennebunkport. It is 88 miles from Boston, 298 miles from New York, and 188 miles from Hartford.

PUBLIC TRANSPORTATION Greyhound bus service to Biddeford, 7 miles; nearest air service is Portland.

ACCOMMODATIONS **Captain Lord Mansion,** Box 800, Pleasant and Green Streets, Kennebunkport 04046, 967-3141, ultraluxurious sea captain's home, E–EE, CP (less from January 1 to April 30—and the rooms have fireplaces!) • **Captain Fairfield Inn,** Pleasant and Green Streets, Kennebunkport 04046, 967-4454, 1813 Federal mansion, warm ambience, great breakfasts, M–E, CP • **The Inn at Harbor Head,** Pier Road, Box 1180, Cape Porpoise, Kennebunkport 04046, 967-5564, exceptional location and decor, E–EE, CP • **The Inn on South Street,** Box 478A, Kennebunkport 04046, 967-5151, attractive nineteenth-century Greek Revival home, M–E, CP • **Old Fort Inn,** Old Fort Avenue, Kennebunkport 04046, 967-5353, secluded and rustic, with pool and tennis court, M–EE, CP • **White Barn Inn,** Beach Street, Kennebunkport 04046, 967-2321, inn and luxurious restored carriage houses, whirlpools, fireplaces, pool, member Relais & Châteaux, M–EE, CP • **1802 House,** Box 646A, 15 Locke Street, Kennebunkport 04046, 967-5632, cozy, quiet, Colonial ambience, M–E, CP • **Bufflehead Cove,** off Route 35, PO Box 499, Kennebunkport 04046, 967-3879, romantic rural location only a mile from town, serene water views, balconies, some fireplaces, whirlpools, E–EE, CP • **Inn at Goose Rocks,** Dyke Road, Goose Rocks, Kennebunkport 04046, 967-5425 or (800) 457-7688, wooded setting on marshes, near the beach, pool, M–E, CP • **The Colony,** Ocean Avenue and King's Highway, Kennebunkport 04046, 967-3331, big, staid classic seaside hotel in town, EE, MAP.

DINING **White Barn Inn** (see above), charmingly restored barn, exceptional fare, prix fixe, EE • **Grissini Trattoria,** 27 Western Avenue, 967-2211, very popular Italian bistro from the folks at the White Barn, I–M • **Kennebunkport Inn,** Dock Square, 967-2621, gracious dining room in old home, modern New England menu, M–E • **Cape Arundel Inn,** Ocean Avenue, 967-2125, water views and fine dining, continental menu, M–E • **Seascapes,** Cape Porpoise Harbor, 967-8500, elegant dining, views, M–E • **Salt Marsh Tavern,** 46 Western Avenue (Route 9), Kennebunkport, 967-4500, striking barn setting at the edge of the marsh, creative menu, M–E • **Breakwater Inn,** Ocean Avenue, Kennebunkport, 967-3118, harbor views, varied menu, I–M • **Windows on the Water,** Chase Hill Road, Kennebunkport, 967-3313, casual, screened terrace, outdoor dining in season, seafood specialties, I–E • **Tides Inn by the Sea,** 737 Goose Rocks Beach,

Kennebunkport, 967-3757, rustic setting overlooking the beach, interesting menu, M–E • **Arundel Wharf,** 43 Ocean Avenue, 967-3444, informal, harborfront, nautical decor, seafood, I–M • **Nunan's Lobster Hut,** Route 9, Cape Porpoise, 967-4435, informal lobster spot, I–M • **Cape Porpoise Lobster Co., Inc.,** 15 Pier Road, Cape Porpoise, 967-4268, lobster rolls, chowder, etc., I–M • **The Green Heron,** Ocean Avenue, 967-5353, for breakfast, I • **The Impastable Dream,** 17 Main Street, Kennebunk, 985-4290, local favorite for Italian, come early or late and stand in line, I–M • **Wells Diner,** Route 1, Wells, 646-4441, a classic diner with great home cooking, legendary chowder, I.

SIGHTSEEING **Seashore Trolley Museum,** Log Cabin Road, Box 220, Kennebunkport, 967-2800. Hours: Memorial Day to Labor Day, Monday to Friday, 10 A.M. to 3:30 P.M., Saturday and Sunday, 10 A.M. to 4:30 P.M. Shorter hours spring and fall, best to check. $$$ • **Brick Store Museum,** 117 Main Street, Kennebunk, 985-4802. Hours: museum, Tuesday to Saturday, 10 A.M. to 4:30 P.M., closed Saturday January to April; house, July through September, Tuesday to Friday, 1 P.M. to 4 P.M. $$, under 12, free • **Cape Arundel Cruises,** Arundel Shipyard, Route 9 (by the bridge), PO Box 840, Kennebunkport, 967-5595, phone for rates and schedules.

INFORMATION Kennebunk-Kennebunkport Chamber of Commerce, PO Box 740, Kennebunk, ME 04043, 967-0857.

Inns and Arts of Vermont

Inn fever is an epidemic that strikes thousands in New England, and it is highly contagious. You'll find victims in small towns and on back roads everywhere, ready to travel any lengths to track down a new and choice country inn.

If you share this delightfully incurable affliction, you'll find the southwestern corner of Vermont happy inn-hunting grounds. There are dozens of inns within a wiggly scenic rectangle roughly 30 by 25 miles, with Dorset, Bennington, Wilmington, and West Townshend as the corners. Many of these inns can rightfully be called exceptional, each in its own way, with something for everyone, budget to deluxe. Many have excellent restaurants, supplemented by additional fine dining throughout the region.

And to make the quest even more rewarding, this is a route rich in art, where you will find prize galleries as well as one of Vermont's major annual exhibitions, the month-long fall Stratton Arts Festival, plus other colorful fall art and crafts events. Add the scenery of an area with four ski mountains, lots of opportunity for hiking and canoeing, and more shops than can fit into a month of weekends, and you have a year-round destination that becomes unbeatable in foliage season. Just reserve early—rooms at the prize inns go fast.

The major commercial center is Manchester, a town that likes to call itself Manchester and the Mountains to underscore its role as the heart of this cluster of villages. Since it is within easy reach no matter where you choose to stay, Manchester makes an ideal starting point for an inns-and-arts tour.

There's plenty to see and do right here, and you'll find lots of information at the Visitors' Center in Manchester Center. You'll also find cars—long lines of them— clogging the intersections of Route 30, 11, and 7. The lure is Manchester Commons, a shopping complex that includes outlets for Polo/Ralph Lauren, Coach leather, Cole Hahn shoes, and many other upscale labels. Right across the street is Battenkill Plaza, where Anne Klein, Donna Karan, Ellen Tracy, and Van Heusen stores beckon. And the shops continue to march eastward farther and farther along Route 30, including a major new mall that includes Brooks Brothers, Armani, Esprit, and other fashionable names. Across the road is an outlet for Orvis, the outdoor outfitters whose headquarters are on Route 7A, farther south.

If shopping is not your sport, outdoor enthusiasts should note that there are three golf courses as well as public tennis courts in town, and more facilities not far away at Stratton Mountain. For more outdoor activity, bikes are for rent at Battenkill Sports, at the intersection of Routes 7/11/30 in Manchester Center, and there's plenty of hiking in the area, with both the Long Trail and the Appalachian Trail nearby. Stop at the U.S. Forest Service headquarters on the way to Bromley Mountain, north of Manchester on Routes 11 and 30, for maps and guidance.

Though many pleasant inns line Route 7A, the traffic has taken away the feeling of a country getaway. The best bet for a quiet spot is Manchester Highlands Inn, up the hill and serenely away from all the traffic on Route 30. This is a classic "painted lady" Victorian with comfortable decor and lots of public rooms plus a big lawn with a pool for relaxing. You can rock on the porch and watch the sun set over Mount Equinox.

Or head for Dorset, the northern tip of your driving tour, for a tranquil Colonial oasis or a romantic bed-and-breakfast inn. Barrows House is a world of its own, a collection of houses centered on a 1784 mansion, all set amid towering trees and well-groomed gardens. Guests here enjoy tennis courts, a pool, a croquet court, a gazebo for enjoying the setting, and an excellent restaurant.

You'll look hard to find a more charming stop than the Cornucopia of Dorset, located just down the block in a nineteenth-century home with a wonderful combination breakfast/sunroom. The room's decor is tasteful, the breakfasts are sumptuous, and the rates include afternoon tea.

The Dorset Inn, on the green right on the pretty little main street of town, is another very attractive possibility. It offers lots of Colonial atmosphere and a highly regarded dining room. Just across the road is the Dovetail Inn, a relaxed, reasonably priced Colonial-style bed-and-breakfast inn in a pair of the town's appealing old homes, highly recommended for those on a budget.

The fighting-mad Green Mountain Boys signed their personal declaration of independence in Dorset, an event remembered by a marker in the center of town. In the peaceful, moneyed Dorset of today, a more significant claim to fame may be what is reputedly the oldest nine-hole golf course in the country at the Dorset Field Club. The Dorset Playhouse is in residence through Labor Day, and the town has several stops for antiquers.

The Dorset Antique Center, on Route 30, offers a group of dealers with a variety of wares sharing a 200-year-old country farmhouse. A detour for apples will take you to Mad Tom's Orchard, in East Dorset, where you can pick your own apples to go with the Vermont cheese and maple syrup you'll probably acquire at a country store en route.

Returning to Manchester and heading south, take historic Route 7A to Manchester Village and the two main sightseeing stops in the region, both offering expansive hilltop views as well as a chance to get out and walk. The Southern Vermont Art Center, a gracious mansion on 407 sylvan acres, has changing exhibits of art, sculpture, and photography, and also offers nature walks, including a Botany Trail with 67 varieties of wildflowers. Fall brings an annual show of work by New England artists. Concerts are held throughout the year for every taste from classical to jazz. The Garden Café here is a highly recommended stop for lunch or brunch with a view.

Hildene is the Georgian mansion built by Robert Todd Lincoln, Abraham's son, and occupied by descendants of the Lincoln family until 1975. It is one of the most fascinating historic houses to visit. Guided tours include a demonstration of the mansion's 1,000-pipe Aeolian organ. Hildene sits on 412 acres with formal gardens and walking trails, and you can picnic here with the valley below spread in front of you in its best autumn colors. An Antiques Festival is held on the grounds in late September, and the first weekend in October brings an annual Foliage Craft Festival. If you come back in winter, there's excellent cross-country skiing on the grounds.

The American Museum of Fly Fishing is another local institution, of interest not only to the many who come to try their luck in the nearby Battenkill River, a noted trout stream. Masterworks of America's best fly-tiers are displayed, along with the tackles of such notable fishermen as Daniel Webster, Dwight Eisenhower, Andrew Carnegie, and Ernest Hemingway. Should you be inspired to improve or take up the sport, the Orvis store nearby is fly-fishing headquarters and holds teaching clinics regularly.

Manchester Village was a posh resort during the pre–Civil War days, when its Equinox House was a well-known summer retreat, and it still boasts the marble-slab sidewalks and handsome homes from those glory days. The village is looking very spiffy once again since restoration of the grand old hotel was completed, and there are now many upscale shops to tempt upscale visitors. The hotel offers golf, tennis, and a well-equipped spa.

Another restored old-timer is the Wilburton Inn, a Tudor-style summer estate built in the early 1900s, complete with mansion with cherry woodwork and stained-glass windows. The inn is totally private, with extensive grounds on a high knoll with soaring mountain views. The refurbished rooms are roomy, and many offer fireplaces, four-poster beds, whirlpool baths, and private decks. Outdoor amenities include tennis courts, a pool, and an extensive collection of contemporary outdoor sculpture. The food lives up to the extraordinary setting.

Two choice small inns are just a stone's throw from the Equinox. The Reluctant Panther Inn, a 150-year-old house easy to spot for its lavender paint, is country elegant and is an excellent dining choice. The 1811 House, which was actually built in the 1770s, is a showcase for period antiques and is surrounded by a nice lawn and gardens.

Farther down Route 7A, the Inn at Ormsby Hill is a showplace, with rooms that are among the most luxurious of any inn's, furnished to magazine cover perfection. There's a cozy sitting room with a fireplace and a dazzling dining room with a wall of windows looking out to the mountains. Innkeeper Chris Sprague, a talented chef, offers lavish breakfasts and the option of weekend dinners, for guests only, much like a private dinner party. She'll even provide a light, inexpensive meal if you arrive late on Friday night.

One of those ubiquitous country stores awaits on Route 7A in Arlington, as does a shop and museum featuring the works of Norman Rockwell, a onetime village resident. Follow the road to East Arlington for Candle Mill Village, a cache of shops in a former gristmill beside a waterfall. The neighboring East Arlington Antique Center has wares from 125 dealers in two historic buildings, and there's a pleasant restaurant in one building, the East Arlington Café, with good food at modest prices.

Take the road just opposite the columned Arlington Inn (a good bet for dinner) to the West Mountain Inn, a wonderful hideaway near the Battenkill River with warm country ambience and an unbeatable mountain view. Children will like the resident llamas and goat; trout fishermen and canoers will enjoy the river. On the way, you will pass the Keelan House, an antiques-filled 1820 Federal home on the river, a perfect B & B choice when you are looking for more moderate rates.

Continue on scenic River Road to West Arlington and you'll come to an inn with a special history. The Inn on Covered Bridge Green, a 200-year-old Colonial home, was Norman Rockwell's home for part of his stay in Arlington; his former studio can be rented as a two-bedroom cottage. When you see the New England views from the master bedroom of the little white church on the green and the covered bridge, you'll understand why this location would have appealed to the artist.

When you come into Bennington, turn right on Route 7 to historic Old Bennington, a stately beauty of a village with a host of magnificent eighteenth- and nineteenth-century homes. On the way you'll pass the stately Bennington Museum, which offers a delightful gallery devoted to one of the region's better-known painters, former resident Grandma Moses, who captured the surrounding Vermont landscape with so much naive charm. There are some 30 of her works on display, and if perchance you've never seen an original Grandma Moses, you have a treat in store.

The museum also offers a military gallery; a comprehensive collection of American pressed glass, including pieces by Louis Comfort Tiffany; and the largest collection of the well-known brown-glazed early Bennington pottery. Outside is the Grandma Moses Schoolhouse, the 1834 one-room school that the artist attended as a child, which features a photo story of her life.

Continuing west on Route 9, turn right on the main street of Old Bennington and drive up the hill to the impressive 360-foot stone obelisk commemorating the famous Battle of Bennington, a major turning point in the Revolutionary War. It was here that General John Stark turned back the British, saying, "There are the Redcoats and they are ours, or this night Molly Stark sleeps a widow." Route 9 has been named the Molly Stark Highway in her honor. The tall monument on the hill can be seen for miles around, and the elevator ride to the top affords an unforgettable view of the countryside. There is also a diorama, created by Vermont artist Paul Winters, in the monument depicting the battle. Take a walk down the hill from the Monument to really appreciate the details of the gracious houses on both sides of the road.

Another Bennington attraction is found at the Potter's Yard, where Bennington Pottery was founded some 50 years ago on the site of a former gristmill. Follow Route 7 two lights north of Route 9, then turn right on County Street to get there. The building now incorporates half a dozen art potteries under one roof. There is a tremendous collection of pottery for sale, priced at discounts from retail, in an attractive shop. The shop also sells woven goods and baskets from around the world, and adjoining shops have more attractive accessories for the home. Time your visit for lunch to sample the gourmet fare at the Brasserie, an outstanding restaurant adjoining the shops. For a more lavish dinner, the choice is the Four Chimneys Inn, a restored mansion in Old Bennington.

From Bennington, proceed east on Molly Stark's Route 9, a heavily wooded, very scenic road along a river that will bring you to Wilmington. Once a sleepy village, Wilmington has had an infusion of energy from all the skiers who come to town for Haystack Mountain or nearby

Mount Snow, and is now pleasantly alive with a variety of shops, including several galleries along Main Street. Quaigh Design Centre is a good place to look for works by New England artists; antiquers might try Left Bank Antiques, housed in a former 1850s bank building. There's another shot at a country store here, too, this one dating to 1836.

Music lovers may want to stay a while and drive farther east on Route 9 to Marlboro, where the New England Bach Festival holds some of its concerts in mid-October.

Otherwise, turn left onto Route 100 north and then make another left at Coldbrook, the road to Haystack Mountain, for the Hermitage, a gracious old inn above the mountain set on 24 acres of woods and fields that make for prime ski touring in winter and provide a view that goes on forever. Prize game and fowl, raised by the owner, are a specialty of the inn's dining room, along with trout from a pond on the property. The rooms here are big and handsome, each with a fireplace.

Come back to Route 100, continue north a few miles to West Dover, and cross the bridge to the Inn at Sawmill Farm. This onetime barn and stable now make up a luxurious antiques-filled inn that makes the best possible use of the soaring heights and beams of the old barn. The rustic setting is softened with warm brick and fieldstone, and comfortable upholstered pieces. It's elegant yet country in feel, the rooms are posh and enormous (ten of them have fireplaces), and the fare in the dining room is exceptional. The tab is hefty, but the inn is special, a member of the prestigious Relais & Châteaux group.

If you've timed your visit right, you can take in the annual Mount Snow Craft Show, usually held in the base lodge over the Columbus Day weekend.

When you get back to Route 30, a right turn to West Townshend and a left up the hill will bring you to Windham Hill, an inn that is the best of all worlds—totally private with wonderful mountain views, elegant yet still warm and comfortable. The meals I sampled were delicious. Rooms in the 1823 brick home are cozy, those in an addition are larger and more lavish. Best of all are the newest rooms in the renovated barn, some with private balconies and with views. A pool and a tennis court provide activity on the grounds, but you may be content to just settle in an Adirondack chair on the lawn and gaze at the mountains.

To end your tour with the arts, turn west again on Route 30 to the mammoth show at Stratton Mountain. The Stratton Arts Festival, a nonprofit event that began in 1963 as a Columbus Day art show with 30 participants, has grown into one of the largest displays of Vermont talent. The highly selective, juried show feature more than 200 exhibitors showing oils and watercolors, metal and stone sculpture, prints and photographs, and handcrafted clay, metal, ceramic, and fiber pieces. All of the work is for sale.

Exhibitors are present on weekends to demonstrate their work and talk about their craft, and each Saturday afternoon features free musical performances, from jazz to rock to classical. You can also take time out for a gondola ride to the top of Stratton Mountain for a tip-top perspective on the Vermont foliage.

It might be possible to take in all of this in a day, but it's not probable—or advisable. You'd do better to head back to your inn when your energy flags and save half the route for a second day, allowing plenty of time to enjoy the views, the outdoors, and your own discoveries along the way.

In fact, you could spend many happy weekends exploring the varied pleasures of this rich section of southern Vermont. When you've returned home, stored the apples and cheese and maple syrup, settled on spots for your newly purchased finds, and taken the film to be developed, you can begin figuring out which of those wonderful inns to try when you come back for a repeat performance.

Area Code: 802

DRIVING DIRECTIONS   Manchester Center is on Route 7A at the intersection of Routes 11 and 30. It is 160 miles from Boston, 248 miles from New York, and 138 miles from Hartford.

PUBLIC TRANSPORTATION   Vermont Transit provides bus service to Manchester and Bennington. Closest air service is Albany, New York, 90 minutes away.

ACCOMMODATIONS   *First choices, in alphabetical order:* **The Barrows House,** Dorset 05251, 867-4455, E–EE, MAP • **Cornucopia of Dorset,** PO Box 307, Route 30, Dorset 05251, 867-5751, M–E, CP; cottage suite, EE • **1811 House,** Route 7A, Manchester Village 05254, 362-1811, M–EE, CP • **Equinox Hotel,** Route 7A, Manchester Village 05254, 362-4700 or (800) 362-4747, many special packages, E–EE • **The Hermitage,** Coldbrook Road (off Route 100), Wilmington 05363, 464-3711, EE, MAP • **Inn at Ormsby Hill,** Route 7A, Manchester Center 05255, 362-1163 or (800) 670-2841, M–EE, CP • **Inn on Covered Bridge Green,** River Road, Arlington 05250, 375-9489 or (800) 726-9480, M–E, CP • **The Inn at Sawmill Farm,** Box 367, Mount Snow Valley, West Dover 05356, 464-8131, EE, MAP • **The Keelan House,** Route 313, Arlington 05250, 375-9029, good budget choice, M, CP • **Manchester Highlands Inn,** Highland Avenue, Manchester 05255, 362-4565 or (800) 743-4565, excellent value for this area, M, CP • **Reluctant Panther Inn,** West Road (off Route 7A), Manchester Village 05254, 362-2568, E–EE, CP • **West Mountain Inn,** Route 313, Arlington 05250, 375-6516, relaxed country charm, E–EE, MAP • **Wilburton Inn,** River Road, Manchester Village 05254, 362-2500 or (800) 648-4944, M–E, CP • **Windham Hill Inn,** Windham Hill Road, West Townshend 05359, 874-4080 or (800) 944-4080, E–EE, MAP.

More good choices: **The Dorset Inn,** Church and Main Streets, Dorset 05251, 867-5500, E–EE, MAP • **Dovetail Inn,** Route 30, Dorset 05251, 867-5747, M–E, CP • **The Inn at Manchester,** Box 41, Route 7A, Manchester 05254, 362-1793 or (800) 273-1793, a charming inn, wood-burning fireplaces, a nice pool, but right on the very busy road, E, CP • **Village Country Inn,** Route 7A, Manchester Village 05254, 362-1792 or (800) 370-0300, lavishly decorated, lovely gardens and pool, but again, right on the road, E–EE, MAP • **South Shire Inn,** 124 Elm Street, Bennington 05201, 447-3839, Queen Anne mansion in a residential neighborhood, M–E, CP. For motels and ski lodges, try the Manchester Chamber of Commerce Lodging Service, 824-6915, or Stratton Mountain Reservation Service, (800) 843-6867.

DINING   **Arlington Inn** (see above), M • **The Barrows House** (see above), varied menu, I–E • **The Black Swan,** Route 7A, Manchester, 362-3807, continental fare in an old farmhouse, M • **Bistro Henry,** Route 30, Manchester, 362-4982, French accent, M–E • **Chanticleer,** Route 7, East Dorset, 362-1616, Swiss and Provençal specialties, fine dining, E–EE • **Dorset Inn** (see above), longtime favorite, I–M • **Four Chimneys Inn,** 21 West Road (Route 9), Old Bennington, 447-3500, prix fixe, EE • **The Hermitage** (see above), known for game, but excellent varied menu also, M–E • **Inn at Sawmill Farm** (see above), EE • **Inn at Willow Pond,** Route 7A North, Manchester, 362-4733, northern Italian in a 1770 farmhouse, M–E • **Mistral's,** Toll Gate Road, Manchester Center, 362-1779, classic French menu, country decor, M–EE • **Reluctant Panther Inn** (see above), M–EE • **West Mountain Inn** (see above), prix fixe, EE • **Wilburton Inn** (see above), M–E • **Windham Hill Inn** (see above), prix fixe, EE. *Informal dining:* **East Arlington Café,** Old Mill Road, East Arlington, 375-6412, I–M • **Laney's,** Routes 11 and 30, Manchester Center, 362-4456, lively, open kitchen, ribs, chicken, brick-oven pizza, I–M • **The Brasserie,** 324 County Street, Bennington, 447-7922, lunch and light dinners until 8 P.M., I • **Garlic John's,** Routes 11 and 30, Manchester Center, 362-9843, cheerful spot for pasta, or regular menu, I–M • **River Café,** Route 30, Bondville, 297-1010, sandwiches, salads, pasta, deck with river view, I–M • **Artist's Palate Café,** Southern Vermont Art Center, Manchester, 362-4220, wonderful spot for lunch, I. For breakfast, the place is **Up for Breakfast,** 710 Main Street, Manchester Center, 362-4204, great muffins, scones, and more, I.

SIGHTSEEING   **Stratton Mountain Arts Festival,** Stratton Mountain Base Lodge, Route 30, Bondville, 297-3265. Hours: mid-September to mid-October, daily, 10 A.M. to 5 P.M. $$$; under 16, free. *Other fall arts events:* Phone for current dates, fee. **Mount Snow Harvest Craft Show,** Mount Snow Resort, 464-3333 or (800) 245-SNOW, usually on Columbus Day Weekend • **New England Bach Festival,** Marlboro, 257-

4523, usually mid-October • **Historic Hildene,** Route 7A, Manchester Village, 362-1788. Hours: mid-May through October, daily, tours beginning at 9:30 A.M.; last tour, 4 P.M. $$$ • **Hildene Foliage Antiques Festival,** late September • **Foliage Craft Festival,** first weekend in October, 362-1788 • **Southern Vermont Art Center,** West Road (off Route 7A), Manchester, 362-1405. Hours: late May to late October, Tuesday to Saturday and Monday holidays, 10 A.M. to 5 P.M., Sunday from noon; December to March, Monday to Saturday, 10 A.M. to 5 P.M. $$; under 13, free • **American Museum of Fly Fishing,** Route 7A, Manchester Village, 362-3300. Hours: May through October, daily, 10 A.M. to 4 P.M., rest of year, closed weekends. $$ • **Norman Rockwell Exhibition,** Route 7A, Arlington, 375-6423. Hours: May through October, daily, 9 A.M. to 5 P.M., $; November to April, 10 A.M. to 4 P.M., free • **Bennington Museum,** West Main Street, 447-1571. Hours: daily, 9 A.M. to 5 P.M.; June through October, to 6 P.M. $$; under 12, free.

INFORMATION   Manchester and the Mountains Chamber of Commerce, Box 928, Manchester Center, VT 05255, 362-2100; Bennington Chamber of Commerce, Veterans Memorial Drive, Bennington, VT 05201, 447-3311; Stratton Mountain, Stratton Mountain, VT 05155, (800) 843-6867.

Back to Nature on Cape Cod

For beach and nature lovers, the real Cape Cod begins at the "elbow," the bend that marks the break from the calm waters of Nantucket Sound to the rough surf of the Atlantic.

The wide, dune-backed ocean shores of the Outer Cape, stretching for 40 unbroken miles from Chatham and Orleans to the tip of Provincetown, are as fine as any beach area in the country. Thanks to the National Park Service, which took over when most of the area was declared a National Seashore in 1961, not only the beach but 27,000 acres of marshes, meadows, and ponds around it have been protected to provide recreation and beauty for swimmers, surfers, hikers, bikers, horseback riders—or anyone who just wants to sit on an uncrowded beach and contemplate the hypnotic rhythms of the sea.

This extraordinary seashore is at its most glorious in autumn, just when most of the tourists leave. The days are generally bright and sunny, but not too hot for outdoor activity; the evenings are cool and breezy, the better to enjoy the indoor pleasures of dining in good restaurants now relieved of their summer crowds.

You'll find the pick of the inns in and around Orleans, at the start of the Outer Cape. A personal favorite is the Nauset House Inn, an antiques-filled renovated farmhouse with a big inviting living room where guests congregate, and a wicker and plant-filled conservatory that is cheerful on even the gloomiest day. The warmth of the owners makes everyone feel at home here.

Nauset House Inn is within walking distance of Nauset Beach, a glorious unending stretch of sand, but even closer is the Ship's Knees Inn, a snug nautical haven with a pool and tennis court. Heading back toward town on the same road, the Parsonage Inn is a winning small inn with a pianist hostess who often delights guests with her classical recitals.

Hillbourne House, set on spacious lawns facing Pleasant Bay, is another choice stop, with rooms in a cozy pine-paneled 1798 home as well as a small adjacent motel and cottage units. Follow the road into Chatham to find the Captain's House, a lovely inn with exquisite Williamsburg decor, handsome canopy beds, and even a few fireplace rooms to warm a chilly night. For those who may prefer resort amenities, Chatham has two prime choices, the classic, century-old Chatham Bars Inn and the pleasant Wequassett Inn, a charming complex of historic houses and newer lodges. Both resorts offer shuttle boats to the National Seashore beaches.

South of Orleans, there's peace and privacy at the stylish Whalewalk Inn, just across the Orleans town line in Eastham. This 1830 whaling master's home is furnished with a mix of antiques and comfortable contemporary, and offers lodgings in the main house, in the renovated barn, or in cottages on the grounds.

Chatham is a town filled with strollers taking advantage of the many quaint shops in the village center. As the shopping hub for the Lower Cape, Orleans has been invaded by discount stores and fast-food outlets, but outside the commercial center it remains a placid and attractive town with some of the best restaurants in the area. The sections toward Rock Harbor and Cape Cod Bay, where early packet boats landed from Boston, are filled with gray-shingled cottages and white picket fences. Fishing boats are still a presence in the pretty harbor, and Skaket Beach, on the bay, is recommended for families who prefer warmer, calmer swimming than the ocean beaches provide. The lanes of East Orleans, near the ocean, are equally old New England in feel.

Orleans also provides necessary shops and diversions in the unhappy event of rain. The Artful Hand, Trees, and the Addison Gallery are the pick of the galleries.

Farther down the coast are more lodging choices in Wellfleet, Truro, and Provincetown. This is prime country for using the area bed-and-breakfast services, since private home accommodations allow you to stay in wooded settings in towns such as Truro that offer few inns. Staying in these towns will give you access to their beautiful private beaches.

Once you've settled in, begin your exploration with a stop at the Salt Pond Visitors' Center at Eastham or the Province Lands center near Provincetown, each right off the main highway (Route 6) and clearly marked. Both lead to excellent hiking, biking, and riding trails and beaches, and both have schedules of many ranger-guided walks and talks at the National Seashore.

The trails of the National Seashore are designed to show the variety of the terrain as well as the ever-changing effects of wind and water on this fragile land. The power of erosion is clearly seen at the Marconi Wireless Station, at Wellfleet, where the Cape is only a mile wide. Much of the cliff has disappeared, along with the towers that Guglielmo Marconi built here to transmit the first wireless communication from America to Europe in 1903—victims of the relentless tides that take away an average of three feet of coastline each year.

The Marconi site leads into the Atlantic White Cedar Swamp Trail, where lush green vegetation surrounds walkers as they thread their way through the swamp on an elevated boardwalk. There are many other trails for taking in the salt ponds, forests, and dunes. On any of the paths, you are also liable to find yourself suddenly in a clearing with pond or ocean views, a scenic bonus.

There are still more nature trails to be found at the Massachusetts Audubon Society headquarters in Wellfleet, which sponsors many guided activities. And when you've had enough nature for one day, there are two more worldly visitors' paths away from the seashore for a pleasant change of pace. One afternoon will do nicely for the galleries in Wellfleet and the historic narrow streets of Provincetown, and either is a good choice for dinner.

Wellfleet, a small, no-longer-sleepy town of church spires and Colonial homes, has developed into an art center. The local guide, available in any of the shops, lists a dozen galleries and shops offering paintings, crafts, and sculpture. The shops are easy to find, since most are right on Main Street or around the bend on Commercial Street. The Blue Heron, representing more than 30 artists, and Kendall Art Gallery, with a sculpture garden in back, are special stops.

A ten-minute drive to the tip of the Cape will bring you to Provincetown. With its spectacular dunes and open beach, this is the most beautiful area of the seashore, and the view from the deck of the Visitors' Center should not be missed.

It was at Provincetown, not Plymouth, that the Pilgrims first landed in 1620. The Mayflower Compact, drawn up during their five-week stay before heading for more sheltered waters, is considered the root of democratic government in America. A bronze plaque set into a boulder at the west end of Commercial Street on the present-day harbor marks their landing place. The tallest granite structure in the United States, the

255-foot Pilgrim Monument, was added in 1910 as a memorial and a landmark for fishermen, sailors, and tourists alike. Climb to the top for a view of the entire Cape and across the bay to Plymouth. On a clear day you can see Boston.

Provincetown itself has several distinct personalities. The Provincetown Heritage Museum, a national landmark, houses both reminders of the nineteenth-century whaling and fishing village and works that reflect the town's later emergence as an art colony. Local luminaries include Hans Hofmann and Edward Hopper.

The Provincetown Art Association and Museum, established in 1914, has an outstanding permanent collection of 500 works and features emerging artists as well. Its membership is a "who's who" of the American art world.

Writers and poets have also been inspired by the beauty of Provincetown. The list is an eminent one, boasting Eugene O'Neill, John Dos Passos, Tennessee Williams, and Sinclair Lewis. Many famous actors also appeared at the Provincetown Playhouse early in their careers.

Present-day Provincetown retains some of the flavor of the past. Artists and writers are still present, and fishermen can still be seen at work at MacMillan Wharf, their presence adding the bonus of good Portuguese food in town. And the waterfront along Commercial Street remains as beautiful as ever, despite the crowds that clog the sidewalks. Walk all the way east to find quiet lanes, some of the best of the galleries, and some very nice lodgings, many with harbor views.

The Dolphin Fleet, at the wharf, is the best known of the groups offering a taste of the past on whale-watching cruises, a popular Provincetown diversion.

The center of Commercial Street has become a kind of outdoor theater for the arty and the showy, and for strolling couples of the same as well as the opposite sex. Some find it fascinating; others consider it a turnoff. Whatever your reaction, you'll find things considerably calmer off-season—and if you have dinner at one of the town's host of fine restaurants on the waterfront, rest assured that you'll have no quibble about the view.

Area Code: 508

DRIVING DIRECTIONS   Cape Cod is reached via Route 3 south from Boston, or via I-95 or I-495 from the west. The Mid-Cape Highway, Route 6, goes directly to Orleans and is the only main road that continues from there to the tip at Provincetown. Orleans is 86 miles from Boston, 296 miles from New York, and 186 miles from Hartford.

PUBLIC TRANSPORTATION   Several airlines and Amtrak service to Hyannis. Bus service to Cape Cod is available via Peter Pan,

Bonanza, and Plymouth and Brockton, (508) 746-0370; several buses connect with Boston's Logan Airport. Finally, there is service from Boston to Provincetown via Bay State Cruise Company, (617) 723-7800. Carriers change, so it's best to contact the Cape Cod Chamber of Commerce for current information.

ACCOMMODATIONS **Nauset House Inn,** Beach Road, PO Box 774, East Orleans 02643, 255-2195, M–E, CP • **Parsonage Inn,** 202 Main Street, East Orleans 02643, 255-8217, M, CP • **Ship's Knees Inn,** Beach Road, PO Box 756, East Orleans 02643, 255-1312, tennis, pool, CP (don't stay at their Cove House Annex—it's in town) • **Hill-bourne House,** Route 28, PO Box 190, South Orleans 02662, 255-0780, I–M, CP • **The Captain's House Inn of Chatham,** 369 Old Harbor Road, Chatham 02633, 945-0127, exceptional decor, M–EE, CP • **Whalewalk Inn,** 220 Bridge Road, Eastham 02642, 255-0617, M –E, CP • **The Inn at Duck Creeke,** East Main Street, Wellfleet 02667, 349-9333, modest, comfortable, I–M, CP • **Cohoon Hollow Bed & Breakfast,** Wellfleet 02667, 349-6372, small, cozy 1842 sea captain's house, secluded, bicycles available for guests, M, CP • **Watermark Inn,** 603 Commercial Street, Provincetown 02657, 487-0165, attractive modern suites with kitchens, on the water, M–EE • **Hargood House,** 493 Commercial Street, Provincetown 02657, spacious waterfront studios and apartments, usually by the week but available for weekends out of season, M–E • A motel worth noting is **Nauset Knoll Motor Lodge,** PO Box 642, East Orleans 02643, 255-2364, directly across from Nauset Beach, M; there are dozens of additional motels all along busy Route 6, and one pleasant Victorian inn, **The Over Look Inn,** Route 6, PO Box 771, Eastham 02642, 255-1886, M, CP. *Resorts:* **Chatham Bars Inn,** 297 Shore Road, Chatham, 01633, 945-0096 or (800) 527-4884, overlooking the harbor, turn-of-the-century charm, pool, private beach, tennis, E–EE • **Wequassett Inn,** Pleasant Bay, Chatham, 01633, 432-5400 or (800) 225-7125, pool, tennis, sailing, private beach, EE.

DINING **Captain Linnell House,** Skaket Road, Orleans, 255-3400, 1840s mansion, formal dining, continental, M–E • **Nauset Beach Club,** 222 East Main Street, East Orleans, 255-8547, gourmet seafood and Italian specialties, excellent, M • **The Arbor,** Route 28, Orleans, 255-4847, continental menu, good value, M • **Binnacle Tavern,** part of the Arbor, gourmet pizza, outdoor seating, I • **Off the Bay Café,** 28 Main Street, Orleans, 255-5505, chic decor, good seafood, and excel-lent Sunday brunch, always packed though some say overpriced, M–E • **Barley Neck Inn,** Beach Road, East Orleans, 255-0212, old tavern has new owners, a lively bar and a highly regarded dining room, I–M • **Land Ho,** Route 6A and Cove Road, Orleans, 255-5165, for pub fare and fun, I • **Cap'n Cass,** on Rock Harbor, Orleans, no phone, a tiny place with the best lobster roll to be found, I • **Christian's,** and **Upstairs at Christians,** 443 Main Street, Chatham, 945-3362, excellent formal dining downstairs, lively atmosphere and light menu upstairs, I–M • **The Impudent Oyster,** 15 Chatham Bars Avenue, Chatham, 945-3545, a favorite for seafood, I–M • **Aesop's Table,** 508 Main Street, Wellfleet, 349-6450, creative cooking in an 1805 home, jazz in the upstairs bar in season, M–E • **Sweet Seasons,** the Inn at Duck Creeke, Wellfleet (see above), seafood specialties, M; lighter fare at the Tavern Room, I–M • **Flying Fish Café,** Briar Lane, Wellfleet, 349-3100, great café for breakfast and lunch, I • **Terra Luna,** 104 Shore Road (Route 6A), North Truro, 487-1019, Italian and Pacific Rim dishes, highly recommended locally, I–M • **Adrian's,** in the Outer Reach Motel, Route 6, North Truro, 487-4360, creative pasta and pizza, great breakfasts, I–M • **The Blacksmith Shop,** Truro Center, 349-6554, try the cioppino, a delicious Portuguese seafood stew, I–M • **Napi's,** 7 Freeman Street, Provincetown, 487-1145, delightful decor, eclectic menu, I–E • **The Mews,** 429 Commercial Street, Provincetown, 487-1500, charm and water views, M–E • **Café Mews,** lighter fare, I–M • **Front Street,** 230 Commercial Street, 487-9715, popular bistro, varied menu including moderately priced Italian, I–E • **Ciros' & Sal's,** 4 Kiley Court, Provincetown, 487-0049, excellent northern Italian, I–E • **The Red Inn,** 15 Commercial Street, 487-0050, restored Colonial building, great water views, M–E • **The Moors,** Beach Road and Bradford Street, Provincetown, 487-0840, the place to sample Portuguese cooking, lively piano bar, lunch, dinner, I–M. *For lobster and informal seafood, all I–M:* **The Lobster Claw,** Route 6A, Orleans, 255-1800 • **Kadee's Lobster and Clam Bar,** Main Street, East Orleans, 255-9706 • **The Eastham Lobster Pool,** Route 6, Eastham, 487-0842 • **The Lobster Pot,** 321 Commercial Street, Provincetown, 487-0842 • **Bayside Lobster Hutt,** Commercial Street, Wellfleet, 349-6333, where you order at the window, eat family-style, and get good food at good prices.

SIGHTSEEING **Cape Cod National Seashore,** five public beaches, ten guided nature trails, three bicycle trails, riding trails, ranger lectures, and walks • **Salt Pond Visitor Center,** Route 6, Eastham, 255-3421. Hours: open year-round, 9 A.M. to 4:30 P.M. in fall, extended hours in summer. Ten-minute orientation film, much free literature • **Province Lands Visitor Center,** off Race Point Road, Provincetown, 487-1256. Hours: open late mid-April through Thanksgiving weekend. June to Labor Day, daily, 9 A.M. to 6 P.M.; spring and fall to 4:30 P.M. Twenty-minute orientation film, free literature, great view from the deck • **Provincetown Heritage Museum,** Commercial and Center Streets, 487-7098. Hours: June to mid-October, daily, 10 A.M. to 6 P.M. $$$, under 12, free • **Provincetown Art Association and Museum,** 460 Commercial Street, 487-1750. Hours: Memorial Day to Labor

Day, daily, noon to 5 P.M. and 7 P.M. to 9 P.M.; October, daily, noon to 5 P.M., Friday and Saturday also 7 P.M. to 9 P.M.; rest of year, Tuesday to Saturday, noon to 4 P.M. $$ • **Pilgrim Monument and Provincetown Museum,** High Pole Hill (off Route 6), 487-1310. Hours: June through November, daily, 9 A.M. to 5 P.M.; July and August, to 7 P.M. $$. *Whale watching:* Cruises are available mid-April through October from Provincetown; phone for schedules and current rates. **Dolphin Fleet,** MacMillan Wharf, (800) 826-9300 • **Provincetown Whale Watch Inc.,** MacMillan Wharf, 487-3322 or (800) 992-9333, naturalists on board • **Portuguese Princess Whale Watch,** 487-2651 or (800) 442-3188. *Beaches:* The best beaches open to the public (all have parking fees in season; town beach fees are often steep). *Town beaches:* **Nauset Beach,** Orleans • **Cahoon Hollow,** Wellfleet • **Ballston,** Truro. *National Park Service beaches:* **Head of the Meadow,** Truro • **Race Point,** Provincetown (the last is the best for watching sunsets).

INFORMATION   Orleans Chamber of Commerce, PO Box 153, Orleans, MA 02653, 255-1386; Wellfleet Chamber of Commerce, PO Box 571, Wellfleet, MA 02687, 349-2510; Provincetown Chamber of Commerce, 307 Commercial Street at MacMillan Wharf, PO Box 1017, Provincetown, MA 02657, 487-3424; Cape Cod Chamber of Commerce, Routes 6 and 132, PO Box 16, Hyannis, MA 02601, 362-3225.

Fair Weather at Fryeburg

When's the last time you saw an oxen-pull competition? How about a pig scramble, or a sheep judging show, or an old-time fiddlers' contest? For that matter, when did you last watch someone milking a cow?

From July to October country fairs are in high gear all over the New England states, a harvest ritual that gives farmers a showcase for their crops and livestock, homemakers a place to exhibit their prize baking and canning, and city folks the opportunity to enjoy some old-fashioned down-on-the-farm fun.

Maine saves her best for last, early October in Fryeburg, a town in the western part of the state near New Hampshire's White Mountains. This affair dates back to 1850. It's the biggest fair in Maine, in what just might be the prettiest fairground setting in New England, with a mountain peak as a backdrop.

And to make it even better, Fryeburg is an easy drive from the heart of lake country as well as from Maine's share of the White Mountain National Forest, so you can have your pick of scenery at the height of foliage season.

At Fryeburg you'll see the traditional "pull" competitions—oxen, horses, and tractors all hauling heavy loads that make moving, much less racing, almost impossible. There's a sheepdog demonstration, pig races, and all the livestock and agricultural judging you'd expect at a major event of this kind.

Some things you might not expect have included a wreath maker's demonstration, a flower show, a shuffleboard tournament, and a skillet-throwing competition. The exact schedule of events might change, but fun is always assured. Of course, there is a midway with plenty of rides and games for kids big and small, plus country music shows and harness racing to keep things lively at night. Friday night's fun is usually capped with fireworks.

Assuming you are working your way west to Fryeburg from Portland on Route 302, you'll pass through Naples, the place to board for boat rides on the lakes, and Bridgton, a shopping center of the lakes area.

From the top of Pleasant Mountain, in Bridgton, you can get the lay of the land, or rather the lakes, for some 50 bodies of water can be seen here. The Sebago–Long Lake chain, made up of Sebago, the state's second largest lake, plus Little Sebago, the Songo River, Long Lake, and numerous lesser lakes and streams, covers hundreds of square miles. The 1,300-acre Sebago Lake State Park makes a fine place for a picnic with a water view.

Deciding where to stay is something of a dilemma. Migis Lodge, on Lake Sebago, is an escapist's dream, with cottages in the pines on 90 acres bordering the deep blue lake. Though autumn nights can be cool in lake country, you won't mind them here with your own fireplace in your own cozy cottage. And since late-September days are often warm and sunny, the location is ideal for hiking the many woodland trails on the grounds or enjoying the lodge's fleets of boats.

Through September you can also enjoy a ride on the *Songo River Queen II,* a 90-foot paddle wheeler out of Naples that offers one-hour cruises on Long Lake and longer trips through the narrow Songo River Lock into the expanse of Sebago Lake. The pier is headquarters as well for pleasure boats, windsurfers, and parasailers. Conveniently situated just up the hill is the Inn at Long Lake, a small hotel furnished with taste and country charm.

For those who prefer to paddle their own canoe, the Saco River is a popular waterway, especially the broad, flat portion from the New Hampshire state line to Hiram. There are many places to rent canoes, including Saco River Canoe & Kayak, on Route 5 north of Fryeburg, and Saco Bound, in Conway, just across the New Hampshire line.

The Noble House, a pleasant and welcoming bed-and-breakfast inn in Bridgton, offers swimming privileges and boating on Highland Lake. The knowledgeable owners help guests make the most of the area.

Golfers should note that the Bridgton Highlands Country Club is a first-class layout in a very picturesque setting.

North of Bridgton there are two other possibilities for lodging, both quaint, picture-perfect New England villages that are lovelier than ever when their white clapboard homes and church steeples stand out against the bright autumn foliage.

In the first of these towns, Bethel, the gracious Bethel Inn & Country Club faces an entire village common that has been declared a National Historic District. Golfers will enjoy the course here with its splendid views. There are many bed-and-breakfast inns in town as well. Rockhounds, too, might enjoy being in Bethel, an area rich in minerals. Stop at the Mt. Mann shop, in Bethel, or at Perham's, in West Paris, to see some of the local finds. The shops can tell you where to go for your own finds.

The second town, Waterford, is best described by its most celebrated resident, Charles Farrar Browne, better known as Artemus Ward, one of America's most famous early humorists. Ward said: "The village . . . is small. It does not contain over 40 houses, all told; but they are milk white with the greenest of blinds and for the most part are shaded with beautiful elms and willows. To the right of us is a mountain—to the left a lake. The village nestles between." There are three inns in this gem of a village, all recommended. If you stay in Waterford, you'll find Mt. Tir'em a relatively easy climb that is rewarded with a view of five lakes.

Finally, there are two excellent choices right in Fryeburg. The Oxford House Inn has Victorian charm and a highly regarded dining room, and the Admiral Peary House is a tastefully furnished bed-and-breakfast with spacious rooms, a big back lawn, and a clay tennis court. If you've forgotten your racket, the owners will provide a "loaner."

Wherever you stay, a loop taking in these towns will provide peak foliage vistas. From Fryeburg, take Route 302 east to Bridgton, Routes 37 and 35 north to Waterford, then Route 118 west to Route 5 south through Lovell and back to Fryeburg. While you are in Fryeburg, take a short drive to see one of Maine's picturesque covered bridges, the 1857 Hemlock Bridge, located off Route 302 three miles northwest of East Fryeburg, spanning an old channel of the Saco River.

What with time at the inn, the Fryeburg Fair, the lakes, some scenic drives, and a few country walks, you've almost filled a weekend. But be sure to block out some time for the nearby White Mountain foothills—spectacular scenery that shouldn't be missed, especially during foliage season. For a rewarding day, pack a picnic, lace up the walking shoes, and head north from Fryeburg on Route 113 to the White Mountain National Forest and Evans Notch. This scenic pass through the peaks offers any number of memorable views, including the Roost, a suspension bridge high above the Wild River that is a favorite of photographers. An easy half-mile trek will get you to the top of the Roost. There's good hiking territory for all capabilities, with some difficult and rewarding climbs to rocky ledges overlooking the river valley. Stop in Bethel at the Evans Notch Ranger District on Bridge Street for advice and maps.

Save the picnic, however, until the views get even better farther north. Take Route 2 west to Bethel, then go north on Route 26 to Grafton Notch State Park. Screw Auger Falls, the best-known spot in the park, fits its name; it cascades down the mountain in a series of spirals through the rocks. If you're up for a steep hike from the falls, you can reach the scenic overlook at Table Rock.

When you can't wait another minute for lunch, head for Cascade Falls and its prize picnic area nearby. Other sights to see are Mother Walker Falls and Moose Cave, a fascinating cavern in the rocks that is just a quarter of a mile from the main road. The trails are clearly marked off the road as you drive through. For serious hikers, there are trailheads for the Appalachian Trail and a loop trail up Old Speck, the third highest mountain in the state.

If luck is against you and it rains, you can still while away a pleasant afternoon in this area. The Jones Museum of Glass and Ceramics, off Route 107 in Sebago, is a rarity, displaying over 6,000 pieces of exquisite glass and ceramics from ancient Egypt to the present day; an adjacent shop sells ceramics and glassware. In Bethel, Philbrook Place, at 162 Main Street, is a complex of interesting shops, and Bonnema Potters, 146 Main, is a showroom for stoneware and porcelain in rich multicolors.

The Maine Theme, in Bridgton, offers handcrafts by state artisans and by artists from all over New England, the Bridgton Arts and Crafts Society displays local art and handmade crafts, and the Wales & Hamblen Antique Center has a wide selection of collectibles. The Cry of the Loon, on Route 302 in Casco, has seven rooms of gifts and crafts.

For sightseeing, a drive to Newfield, off Route 11, will bring you to Willowbrook, a restored nineteenth-century village. Another worthwhile drive of about half an hour will take you to the Sabbathday Lake Shaker Community and a fascinating tour of the last settlement where Shakers are still living and working. The village includes a library, a museum, an herb distributor, and a sheep farm. A wealth of Shaker furniture, tin and woodenware, folk and decorative arts, textiles, and early tools and farm implements is displayed in the Meeting House, Ministry's Shop, Sisters' Shop, and Boys' Shop. The Fryeburg Library has an unexpected attraction, a room devoted to Clarence Mulford, creator of Hopalong Cassidy.

You can pick up pumpkins, apples, and other produce of the season at roadside stands beside the farms on almost any back road; just watch for signs on village main streets pointing the way.

In an area where unspoiled villages, lakes, mountains, and forest wilderness come together within one superb backcountry area, fall in western Maine forecasts a fair weekend indeed.

Area Code: 207

DRIVING DIRECTIONS Fryeburg is on the western border of Maine, about 60 miles from Portland and about 6 miles from Conway and the White Mountains of New Hampshire. Take Route 302 west from Portland or Route 113 to Route 302 east from Conway, New Hampshire. Fryeburg is 180 miles from Boston, 380 miles from New York, and 270 miles from Hartford.

PUBLIC TRANSPORTATION Air service to Portland. Fryeburg is an easy drive by rental car from the Portland airport. Vermont Transit and Concord Trailways offer bus service to nearby North Conway, New Hampshire.

ACCOMMODATIONS **Oxford House Inn,** Route 302, Fryeburg 04037, 935-3442, M, CP • **Admiral Peary House,** 9 Elm Street, Fryeburg 04037, 935-3365, charm, tennis, hot tub, M, CP • **The Noble House,** Box 180, Bridgton 04009, 647-3733, on Highland Lake, casual, private beach, perfect for families, open June through October, M, CP • **Inn at Long Lake,** Lake House Road, Naples 04055, 693-6226 or (800) 437-0328, 1906 Victorian hotel, nicely renovated, M, CP • **Lake House,** Routes 35 and 37, Waterford 04088, 583-6078, simple country charmer, M, CP; E, MAP • **Kedarburn Inn,** Route 35, Box A-1, Waterford 04088, 583-6182, 1858 house on a brook, I–M, CP • **Waterford Inn,** PO Box 49 (off Route 37), East Waterford 04088, 583-4037, serene location with a gorgeous view, I–M, CP • **Center Lovell Inn,** Route 5, Center Lovell 04016, 925-1575 or (800) 777-2698, old-fashioned country inn across from Kezar Lake. *Resorts:* **Migis Lodge,** off Route 302, South Casco 04077, 655-4524, EE, AP • **Bethel Inn & Country Club,** on the common, Bethel 04217, 824-2175, ask about weekend packages, E–EE, MAP. For other Bethel lodgings, see pages 282–283.

DINING **Oxford House** (see above) Fryeburg, excellent, E • **Center Lovell Inn** (see above), highly regarded dining room, M–E • **Lake House** (see above), top reviews, prix fixe, EE • **Kedarburn Inn** (see above), American and continental, I–M • **Waterford Inn** (see above), advance reservations essential, prix fixe, EE • **Venezia,** Routes 302 and 93, 647-5333, Italian, well-recommended locally, I–M • **The Olde House Restaurant,** Route 85, Raymond, 655-7841, European/American in historic home, M–E • **Maurice,** 113 Main Street, South Paris, 743-2532, French menu, I–M • **Olde Mill Tavern,** Main Street, Harrison, 583-4992, restored gristmill, I–M • **Barnhouse Tavern,** Maine Route 35 at Route 302, North Windham, 892-2221, American menu, restored barn, I–M • **Black Horse Tavern,** Route 302, Bridgton, 647-

5300, informal dining in a converted barn, I–M • **The Colonial,** Route 301, Bridgton, 647-2547, casual, seafood and sirloins, I–M • **Naples Lobster Pound,** Route 302, Naples, 693-6580, no frills, I–M. Also see Bethel dining, page 283.

SIGHTSEEING   Fryeburg Fair, Route 5, Fryeburg, ME 04037. Runs for one week beginning the first Sunday in October; admission and parking charge. Write for current dates and fees • **Songo River Queen II,** Route 302, Naples, 693-6861. Hours: daily, July to Labor Day; weekends in June and September. Two half-hour Songo River cruise, $$$$; 1-hour Long Lake cruise, $$$; phone for current schedules • **Willowbrook at Newfield,** off Route 11, Newfield, 793-2784. Hours: daily, May 15 to September 30, 10 A.M. to 5 P.M. $$$ • **Jones Museum of Glass & Ceramics,** Douglas Hill (off Route 107), Sebago, 787-3370. Hours: May to mid-November, Monday to Saturday, 10 A.M. to 5 P.M., Sunday, 1 P.M. to 5 P.M. $$ • **The Shaker Museum,** Sabbathday Lake, Route 26, Poland Spring, 926-4597. Hours: Memorial Day to Columbus Day, Monday to Saturday, 10 A.M. to 4:30 P.M. Introductory tour, adults, $$; extended tour, $$$.

INFORMATION   Bridgton-Lakes Region Information Center, Route 302, PO Box 236, Bridgton, ME 04009, 647-3472.

Leafing Through the Northeast Kingdom

Anyone who despairs of making a fortune in this world can take heart from the story of Thaddeus Fairbanks.

Thaddeus is the man who invented the platform scale, which registers weight at eye level when an object or person is on the platform. Not such a remarkable notion, you say? Well, that simple invention made the Fairbanks family one of the ten wealthiest in the world back in the 1800s. And since members of the Fairbanks clan were generous with their fortune, their hometown of St. Johnsbury, Vermont, was transformed.

Thanks to the Fairbanks family, when you visit St. Johnsbury today you discover not just a center of the state's maple sugar industry but a town boasting one of the handsomest small-town public libraries and art galleries to be found, not to mention one of the most elaborate small museums. They are a surprise, way up here in rural northern Vermont—and only the first of the happy surprises waiting in this beautiful and relatively unexplored area known as the Northeast Kingdom.

Not the least of the reasons to plan your trip here during foliage season is the very fact that not too many people have discovered the mountains and lakes and exceptional inns in this quiet corner of the state. So while the roads are clogged farther south, you can drive the scenic routes and walk the wooded trails here without ever feeling jostled by the rest of the foliage watchers of the world.

A Northeast Kingdom weekend itinerary ideally includes half a day in St. Johnsbury, with the rest of the time allotted to the scenic back roads, country walks, oohs and ahs, and photos.

Don't expect traditional rural motifs when you step inside the Fairbanks Museum and Planetarium, in St. Johnsbury. Franklin Fairbanks, a nephew of Thaddeus, founded the museum in 1891, donating his own "Cabinet of Curiosities," a natural science collection that had outgrown his home. Franklin wanted nothing but the best and hired Lambert Packard, one of the great Victorian architects, to design the building. Packard did them proud, with soaring 30-foot barrel-vaulted ceilings, stained-glass windows (some by Tiffany), and lavish use of wood.

The exhibits are a mélange of history, archaeology, and science, with collections of dolls and Japanese netsuke carvings; "tapestries" of George Washington made of moths, beetles and bugs; tools of nineteenth-century life in northeastern Vermont; and enough stuffed animals and birds to gladden a taxidermist's heart. The wacky variety adds to the fun of a visit. The building also features northern Vermont's official weather station and its only public planetarium. And downstairs you can see some of the scales that made the Fairbanks fortune—and the museum—possible.

Visiting the St. Johnsbury Athenaeum means reentering the gracious world of the nineteenth century. It was built as a public library and was presented to the town in 1871 by Horace Fairbanks, a nephew of the inventor, who became president of the scale-manufacturing company and eventually governor of the state of Vermont. The cathedral ceilings, tall windows, spiral staircases, and elaborate woodwork and floors with alternating strips of oak and walnut make for a truly elegant structure.

In 1873 an art gallery was added to the main building to hold some of Horace Fairbanks's growing art collection. It is now the oldest unaltered art gallery in the country. The unusual design of the gallery was determined by the need to house Fairbanks's prize canvas, *The Domes of Yosemite,* an enormous 10-by-15-foot painting by Albert Bierstadt. The exceptional landscape, placed opposite the entrance to the gallery, benefits from natural light provided by an arched skyway, which enhances the feeling of looking down into the valley.

St. Johnsbury's additional claim to fame has nothing to do with its illustrious benefactors. This is the heart of Vermont maple sugar country, which in a typical year produces about two thirds of the nation's supply. Maple Grove, the world's largest maple candy factory, has been operating since 1915 and creates more than 200 kinds of delectable maple sweets. On weekdays you are invited to tour the Maple Grove factory for a close-up view of the vats of boiling sap being poured into different kinds of candy molds, to emerge in familiar Vermont shapes from maple leaves to pine trees.

Visitors are welcome anytime to visit the Maple Cabin here to see a 15-minute film on the maple sugar process. Actual kettles of sap are boiling year-round in the adjacent small Maple Museum, which features exhibitions of sugar-making equipment, both ancient and modern. After the tour you can taste free samples of the final result and stock up for the future at the gift shop.

Before you leave St. Johnsbury, have a look at the fine houses to be seen along Main Street. Then leave "city" business behind and strike out for the country roads waiting to show off their autumn colors. One prime route for scenery is to drive north from St. Johnsbury on Routes 5 and 114 to East Burke and Burke Mountain. On the way you'll pass through Lyndonville, whose claims to fame are the five covered bridges nearby. Stop at the delightful Bailey's Country Store in East Burke, where you'll find country gifts upstairs and nice things like yarn spun by hand on a local farm, and you can sample the all-natural beer being made out back at the Trout River Brewing Company. Near Bailey's, detour at the sign to West Burke and go up to the top of Darling Hill for a fantastic view of Burke Mountain. Then take the auto road to Burke's 3,267-foot summit for even more sweeping views of the countryside.

From here, head for Vermont lake country by connecting again with Route 5, then turning onto Route 5A north to Lake Willoughby. Two cliffs, Mt. Pisgah and Mt. Hor, rise from opposite sides of this lake, making a majestic vista. To get an even more spectacular view, take one of the well-maintained hiking trails in the 7,000-acre state forest surrounding the lake. The view from the cliffs is worth the climb.

There are some 15 lakes in this general area, providing recreation for boaters and fishermen and scenery for all. Almost all the lakes are surrounded by hills, and Crystal Lake, back on Route 5, is another beauty set against a dramatic cliff. If you detour off Route 5 a few miles north to Brownington Center, you'll come to the Old Stone House, run by the Orleans County Historical Society. This handsome granite-block building was designed and built as a school dormitory in the 1830s by the Reverend Alexander Twilight, the man believed to be America's first black college graduate and first black legislator. Twilight taught the region's children here for two decades. The 30-room building now serves as a showcase for furnishings, tools, needlework, art, and crafts of the region's past.

Turn south again on Route 16 and detour on Route 122 just past Glover for the most curious sight in the region, the Bread and Puppet Museum. This is a weathered old barn filled with over 1,000 puppets used by the avant-garde company for its productions protesting tyranny of all kinds. The puppets are not pretty, but some are enormous and skillfully made, and will be of interest to anyone interested in puppetry.

Continuing south, turn off to Greensboro for a pair of interesting shops, the Old Forge with woolens from Scotland, England, Ireland, and Wales, and the Miller's Thumb, offering a beautiful selection of fine Italian and Portuguese ceramics. Follow the road east past Caspian Lake and you'll come to Craftsbury and a string of villages so minute you can easily pass through them before you know you have arrived. The prettiest is Craftsbury Common, with its picture-book green surrounded by dazzling white clapboard buildings and a church. The Inn on the Common comprises three of the lovely white houses. The rooms here are spacious, the gardens glorious, and there are a tennis court and a pool for guests. Dinner is served family-style in a gracious dining room. The inn offers many special weekends, some including walking and biking.

If the tab at the Inn on the Common is too high, the Craftsbury Inn, a handsomely furnished 1850 country home, is also appealing, with an owner who is an excellent chef. For a real bargain, seek out the Craftsbury Bed & Breakfast, on Wylie Hill, a comfortable home where guests share baths and regal views.

The Craftsbury Center is another asset in this area, offering biking, sculling, and running camps plus cross-country skiing and snowshoeing in winter. Special family fun weekends and photography workshops are offered in summer and fall. The center has its own dorm and apartment lodgings and a dining room, as well as packages in cooperation with local inns. The center is much like a summer camp, set on the blue waters of Great Hosmer Pond. Guests have use of canoes and can rent mountain bikes on the site.

Craftsbury is one of four choice areas that can serve as an excellent home base for Northeast Kingdom exploring. Another prime candidate is Lower Waterford, about ten miles east of St. Johnsbury, a picture-book hamlet with wonderful views across the Connecticut River to the New Hampshire mountains. Rabbit Hill Inn, a lovely, columned, antiques-filled inn in town, is a romantic hideaway long known for its fine cuisine. Some of the suites offer fireplaces, skylights, and private balconies.

Farther north, heading toward Burke Mountain, is the Wildflower Inn, a country charmer set on a ridge with views that go on forever and with lots of windows to make the most of them. The inn has a tennis court and welcomes children with their own game room, a summer activity program, and a children's menu.

Atop Darling Hill in East Burke is the loveliest setting in the area, the Mountain View Creamery, an 1883 farm on 440 ridgetop acres with its historic red barns still intact. New owners have restored the handsome old red-brick creamery building as a gracious inn and have planted exquisite flower and vegetable gardens on the grounds. Farm animals, hiking trails, and a dining room in the space where butter and cheese were once produced are among this inn's many attractions—if you can tear yourself away from gazing at the view.

Another East Burke inn, the rustic little Old Cutter Inn, on the Burke Mountain Access Road, is well known locally for its Swiss fare.

Finally, for lake views, there is the attractive Willoughvale Inn. Especially appealing are the inn's fresh, pretty housekeeping cottages, right on the shore of Lake Willoughby, with sunrooms, screened porches, and decks. Across the lake is Fox Hall, a modest, homey, bed-and-breakfast inn that offers guests a private waterfront with boats, canoes, and windsurfers, and cross-country ski trails in winter.

As you drive around, watch for maple sugar houses such as Laplant's Sugarhouse, in Sutton, where horse-drawn hayrides into the country-side are offered in summer and fall, sleigh rides in winter, and maple sugaring in the spring. The Sugarmill Farm, in Barton, also stays open all year and offers a film on sugar making and tractor-drawn wagon tours through a covered bridge and into a maple orchard that is resplendent with color in autumn.

In late September each year, several of the tiny towns in the area join in the Northeast Kingdom's annual Foliage Festival, taking turns holding church lunches and suppers, crafts shows, backcountry tours, and special events. These are small affairs, nothing to write home or drive miles out of the way for, but if you plan your driving itinerary to pass through any of the towns on the day of the festivities, it may add a down-home touch and a home-cooked meal to your memories, served up on photogenic village greens or in white-spired churches.

If you head for Cabot, you can add a visit to the Cabot Farmers' Cooperative, watch the making of Vermont's best-known cheddar cheese, and enjoy tasting at the sample table. Most of the activity takes place before 1:00 P.M. In pretty Peacham, founded in 1776, the town that boasts it is the most photographed in the state, don't miss a stop at the Peacham Store, where the hostess turns out delicious hot gourmet lunches to go. Other towns on the tour are Plainfield, Barnet, Groton, Marshfield, Walden, and St. Johnsbury. An advance schedule of events is available from the Chamber of Commerce.

It was former U.S. Senator George Aiken who dubbed this area the Northeast Kingdom when he saw its untouched beauty during one brilliant fall foliage season some years ago. When you view the peaceful mosaic of the mountains and lakes, unspoiled villages, and placid farms, you may well agree that this corner of Vermont is, indeed, a world of its own.

Area Code: 802

DRIVING DIRECTIONS St. Johnsbury is off I-91 at exit 20. It is 150 miles from Boston, 300 miles from New York City, and 190 miles from Hartford.

PUBLIC TRANSPORTATION Vermont Transit has bus service to St. Johnsbury; Amtrak service to Montpelier. Closest air service is Burlington, Vermont, or Lebanon, New Hampshire.

ACCOMMODATIONS **Rabbit Hill Inn,** Route 18, Lower Waterford 05848, 748-5168 or (800) 76-BUNNY, E–EE, MAP • **Mountain View Creamery,** Darling Hill Road, East Burke 05832, 626-9924, M, CP • **The Wildflower Inn,** Star Route, Lyndonville 05851, 626-8310 or (800) 627-8310, M, CP; suites, E–EE, CP • **The Old Cutter Inn,** Burke Mountain Access Road, East Burke 05832, 826-5152, I or M, MAP • **The Inn on the Common,** Craftsbury Common 05827, 586-9619 or (800) 521-2233, EE, MAP • **Craftsbury Inn,** Craftsbury 05826, 586-2848 or (800) 336-2848, M, CP or E, MAP • **Craftsbury Bed & Breakfast on Wylie Hill,** Craftsbury Common 05827, 586-2206, I, CP • **Craftsbury Center,** Box 31, Craftsbury Center 05827, 586-7767, dormitory rooms to apartments, M–E, MAP • **Willoughvale Inn,** E, Route 5A, Westmore 05860, 525-4123 or (800) 594-9102, M, CP; cottages • **Fox Hall Inn,** Willoughby Lake Road, Westmore 05822, 525-6930, I–M, CP. For more area small inns, write to the Chamber of Commerce for "Vermont's Bed & Breakfasts of the Northeast Kingdom" brochure.

DINING **Rabbit Hill** (see above), prix fixe, by reservation only, EE • **Wildflower Inn** (see above), M • **The Old Cutter Inn** (see above), M; lighter menu, I–M • **Mountain View Creamery** (see above), M • **The River Garden Café,** Route 114, East Burke, 626-3514, light fare to full dinners, I–M • **Willoughvale Inn** (see above), M • **Craftsbury Inn** (see above), M • **The Creamery,** Hill Street, Danville (near St. Johnsbury), 684-3616, seafood and home-baked pies in a converted 1891 creamery, M • **Northern Lights Bookshop & Café,** 79 Railroad Avenue, St. Johnsbury, 748-4463, best place in town for lunch, I • **Rainbow Sweets,** Route 2, Marshfield, 426-3531, bakery-café for lunch and/or dessert, I • **Miss Vermont Diner,** Route 5, St. Johnsbury, 748-9751, or its sister, **Miss Lyndonville Diner,** Route 5, Lyndonville, 626-9890; both with good, plain country cooking, and lots of it, I.

SIGHTSEEING **Fairbanks Museum and Planetarium,** Main and Prospect Streets, St. Johnsbury, 748-2372. Hours: Monday to Saturday, 10 A.M. to 4 P.M., to 6 P.M. in July and August; Sunday, 1 P.M. to 5 P.M. $$ • **St. Johnsbury Athenaeum,** 30 Main Street, 748-8291. Library and art gallery hours: Monday and Wednesday, 10 A.M. to 8 P.M.; Tuesday, Thursday, Friday, 10 A.M. to 5:30 P.M.; Saturday, 9:30 A.M. to 4 P.M. Donation • **Maple Grove Museum,** Route 2 (on eastern edge of St. Johnsbury), 748-5141. Hours: Memorial Day to late October, daily, 8 A.M. to 4:45 P.M., factory tours weekdays. Admission $; under 12, free • **The Old Stone House,** Brownington, 754-2022. Hours: July and August, daily, 11 A.M. to 5 P.M.; May 15 to June 30 and September 1 to

October 15, Friday through Tuesday only, 11 A.M. to 5 P.M. $$ • **Cabot Farmers' Cooperative Creamery,** Main Street, Cabot, 563-2231. Hours: June through October, daily, 9 A.M. to 5 P.M.; rest of year, Monday to Saturday, 9 A.M. to 4 P.M., closed Sunday. $; under 12, free • **Bread & Puppet Museum,** Route 122, Glover. Hours: mid-May through October, daily, 10 A.M. to 5 P.M. Free. *Sugarhouses:* **Laplant's Sugarhouse,** Route 5, Sutton (three miles north of West Burke), 467-3900, hayrides and sleigh rides • **Sugarmill Farm,** off I-91, exit 25, Barton, 525-3701, sugarhouse tours, museum, wagon rides • **Northeast Kingdom Fall Foliage Festival,** PO Box 38, West Danville, VT 05873. Write for current year's schedule of events. *Outdoor recreation:* **Craftsbury Center,** Craftsbury Common, 586-7767, mountain bike rentals, cross-country skiing • **Burke Mountain,** East Burke, 626-3305 or (800) 541-5480, downhill and cross-country skiing.

INFORMATION   Northeast Kingdom Chamber of Commerce, 30 Western Avenue, St. Johnsbury, VT 05819, 748-3678.

Making a Pilgrimage to Plymouth

When the cranberries ripen to ruby red, that's the time to plan your pilgrimage to Plymouth, Massachusetts.

In case you didn't know, cranberries became part of our traditional Thanksgiving feast because the Mayflower Pilgrims happened to come to rest in the heart of America's cranberry-growing center.

The Pilgrims used this wild native fruit as a dye, to make poultices, and in a dried cake called pemmican, a mixture of berries, venison, and grains learned from Native Americans, who called the berry *"sassamanash."* There are more than 13,000 acres of cranberry bogs in southeastern Massachusetts today, continuing a tradition of formal cultivation begun in 1816.

Come late September, when the berries are ready for harvest, the countryside around Plymouth is transformed into a remarkable landscape of glowing red. Federal Furnace Road, between Plymouth and South Carver, is lined with bogs. Columbus Day weekend marks the annual Massachusetts Cranberry Harvest Festival in South Carver. It's an extra splash of color for a trip that ought to be made anyway by anyone who is interested in how our country began.

Don't expect a dull history lesson. Plymouth Rock and a reproduction of the *Mayflower* are here, of course, but the real story of the Pilgrims who landed at Plymouth is told best at Plimoth Plantation, an amazingly realistic re-creation of New England's first settlement. This authentic replica of the 1627 Pilgrim village is peopled with "residents" who have been intensely trained to re-create the atmosphere of the first surviving colony in New England.

You'll be entering a farming community where everyone is at work at typical seasonal tasks, and you can see firsthand what it was like to settle in a new land where almost everything had to be grown or made on the spot. The crafts of the 1620s are demonstrated at the Carriage House Crafts Center. The Pilgrim residents are so authentic they even have differing dialects to match the regions they left in England.

You may meet Myles Standish or John Alden and lots of other people who may tell you in the most believable way how it felt to make a home in the wilderness. They'll describe life in the old country as well as the new, talk about the *Mayflower* voyage—in fact, they'll answer any question you ask as long as it doesn't involve knowledge of anything past the year 1627.

The village is so well done that you'll almost forget it isn't real, just like the visiting kids eagerly approaching one after another of the residents to find out who is married to whom and which child belongs to which parent. Make Plimoth Plantation your first stop while you're fresh on Saturday morning, and count on staying for at least three hours to really make the most of this experience.

Check also for special activities at the plantation. These include herb walks, an annual communal house-raising, a Colonial Muster, lessons in herbal wreath making, and many children's activities, from storytelling to Pilgrim games to learning to talk like a Pilgrim.

Back in Plymouth, you can get some notion of how it felt for 102 passengers to cross the ocean on a 106-foot boat by boarding the reproduction of the *Mayflower,* the second part of the plantation's "living museum."

Mayflower II is docked at the harbor in town, next to what is probably the best-known boulder in the country, Plymouth Rock. An elaborate columned monument has been built over the rock to protect it and provide a viewing platform, and the waterfront area around it has been turned into a grassy promenade that is now a state park.

Across the street is Coles Hill, where you can get a panoramic view of Plymouth Harbor. The Pilgrims buried their dead in unmarked graves here during their first terrible winter. Also on Coles Hill is the statue of Massasoit, chief of the Wampanoag Indians, who befriended the newcomers and helped them to survive that winter. The 81-foot Pilgrim Monument, on Allerton Street, was built between 1859 and 1899, at the then-enormous cost of $155,000, to commemorate the bravery of these early settlers. Don't overlook the statue dedicated to the Pilgrim women; 25 made the crossing but only four survived.

Follow the signs inland a block or two for a visit to America's oldest public museum, Pilgrim Hall, which has preserved the possessions the Pilgrims used over 350 years ago. You'll see John Alden's Bible, William Bradford's chair, William Brewster's books, Myles Standish's sword, and many other possessions and furniture of the early settlers, as well as paintings by Gilbert Stuart and the only painting of a Mayflower Pilgrim, Edward Winslow.

There are several historic houses to be seen in Plymouth, the most impressive being the Mayflower Society House, headquarters of the General Society of Mayflower Descendants. The oldest house of all, the 1640 Richard Sparrow House, is now a pottery-making center and shop. The Harlow Old Fort House offers hands-on experience with such Colonial arts as spinning, weaving, and candle dipping. The house was built with timbers from the original fort.

A particularly pleasant walk will take you through Brewster Gardens with its placid duck pond to see Jenney Grist Mill, a working twentieth-century reconstruction of a seventeenth-century mill. The meal at the mill is for sale, and there are several other shops around.

All these shops are a sign that the waterfront in Plymouth is packed with tourists in season. The town has gone slightly commercial to take advantage of that fact, but so far things are not out of hand. The most extensive town shopping is in a complex called Village Landing, a group of clapboard and shingle shops built to resemble a nineteenth-century village. These shops offer everything from jewelry to hand-stenciled plaques to quality brassware and antiques. There's also a shop with homemade ice cream and a candy store, when you need a break.

Serious shoppers will want to drive another mile and a half west on Main Street to Cordage Park, a cluster of outlet stores and shops in a former rope factory.

When it comes to dining, the best choice in the area is the Crane Brook Restaurant, in South Carver, a restored foundry overlooking a pond. Besides gourmet dinners, they serve a nice afternoon tea. However, many Plymouth visitors are happy to just join the crowds at the informal restaurants around the waterfront offering traditional New England seafood, such as lobster, fried clams, and chowder. Modestly priced take-out stands where you can have your seafood at picnic tables with a water view are a real boon for families.

Save time for a walk along the long rock jetty into the harbor for a close-up look at the many sailboats and yachts that fill Plymouth Harbor today. If you want to get out on the water, several boat outings are available through the early fall, both harbor cruises and whale-watching excursions.

A pleasant way to see Plymouth's historic district and to hear some fascinating tales of early life is on the guided Colonial Lantern Tours, offered in the evening.

If you spend Saturday seeing the sights, you can devote Sunday to those cranberries. Visit the Ocean Spray Cranberry World Visitor Center, on Water Street, for a tour that traces how the berries have been grown and harvested throughout history. You'll learn how the quality of a berry is judged by its bounce, see a scale-model cranberry farm, and be able to inspect the tools for both dry and wet harvesting. At the demonstration kitchen downstairs, you can watch cranberry dishes being prepared and taste some of the goodies. There is the chance to sample a variety of cranberry juice products as well.

Free samples are also offered at the Plymouth Colony Winery, just outside town, where cranberry wine is made. Here you can take a stroll around the cranberry bogs.

But a more spectacular show is found if you drive west on Route 44 toward Carver, where the roadside is lined with bogs and you can watch harvesting in action. Many growers flood their bogs, then gently stir the water with a contraption like a giant eggbeater to bring the berries to the surface, where they are corralled and loaded on trucks via conveyers. Some growers have taken to using helicopters to hoist the bins away, a colorful sight.

On Columbus Day weekend, the Massachusetts Cranberry Harvest Festival takes place on Rochester Road, off Route 58, in South Carver, near one of the oldest of the bogs. Activities include guided tours of the bogs, cooking demonstrations and contests, art, photography and crafts displays, a farmers' market, live music, and lots of food.

October also brings celebrations of seventeenth-century foods and lifestyles at Plimoth Plantation and Harvest Feasts, a re-creation of the feasts and games that marked the end of the colony's successful growing season. Feasts continue into November, culminating with a New England Thanksgiving Buffet.

Come back in November, if you can, but early October is the ideal time to visit Plymouth. You'll leave with a lot more knowledge about your country and with a rosy cranberry glow as well.

Area Code: 508

DRIVING DIRECTIONS Plymouth is off Route 3 on Route 3A, 40 miles south of Boston, 245 miles from New York, and 135 miles from Hartford.

PUBLIC TRANSPORTATION Plymouth and Brockton bus lines run from Boston and Hyannis, 746-0378—or, in MA, (800) 328-9997. Nearest air service is Boston.

ACCOMMODATIONS All Plymouth zip codes are 02360. • **Plymouth Bay Manor,** 259 Court Street, Plymouth, 830-0426 or (800)

492-1828, turn-of-the-century mansion, airy rooms, views of Plymouth Bay from guest rooms and breakfast sunroom, M, CP • **Foxglove Cottage,** 101 Sandwich Road, 747-6576, restored 1820 cape in a country setting five minutes from town, Victorian decor, floral prints, canopy beds, fireplaces, no children under 12, M, CP • **Jackson-Russell-Whitfield House,** 26 North Street, 746-5289, charmingly restored small 1782 home just steps from the waterfront, antiques, no children under 12, M, CP • **Sheraton Inn,** 180 Water Street at Village Landing, 747-4900, best hotel/motel in town, indoor pool, M • **John Carver Motor Inn,** 25 Summer Street, 746-7100, walking distance to town, I–M • **Governor Bradford Motor Inn,** Water Street, 746-6200, across from the water in the middle of town, M • **Pilgrim Sands,** 150 Warren Avenue, 747-0900, waterfront location, three miles south of town near Plimoth Plantation, M.

DINING   **Mama Mia,** 122 Water Street, 747-4670, casual Italian dining across from the waterfront, I • **Café Nanina,** 14 Union Street, 747-4503, on the waterfront but away from the crowd, formal dining, I–M • **McGrath's,** 746-9751; **Lobster Hut,** 746-2270; and **Wood's,** 746-0261; all on the Town Pier, Water Street, are busy waterfront spots for sit-down and take-out seafood and water views, I–M • **1620 House,** Water Street, 746-9565, seafood, across the street from the harbor, not quite so frantic, I–M • **Cranberries,** 601 State Road (Route 3A), 224-5100, cranberry decor, standard American fare, I–M • **Iguana's,** 170 Water Street, Village Landing, 747-4000, change-of-pace Mexican fare, I • **Ernie's,** 330 Court Street, 746-3444, informal old-timer, seafood and Italian dishes, pizza, good for families, I • **Crane Brook Restaurant,** Tremont Street, South Carver, 866-3235, excellent innovative American fare in scenic surroundings, M–EE.

SIGHTSEEING   **Massachusetts Cranberry Harvest Festival,** Edaville Cranberry Bog, Rochester Road (off Route 58), South Carver. Held for three days on Columbus Day weekend, 10 A.M. to 4 P.M. Free. For information, phone Cranberry World, 747-2350 • **Plimoth Plantation,** Route 3A three miles south of Plymouth, 746-1622. Hours: April through November, daily, 9 A.M. to 5 P.M. $$$$$. Combination tickets available for Pilgrim Village and *Mayflower II*. Admission good for two days. Write for schedule of special events, harvest feasts, and children's activities. • **Cranberry World Visitors' Center,** Water Street, Plymouth, 747-2350. Hours: May to November, daily, 9:30 A.M. to 5 P.M. Free • **Pilgrim Hall Museum,** 75 Court Street (Route 3A), 746-1620. Hours: February through December, daily, 9:30 A.M. to 4:30 P.M. $$ • **Harlow Old Fort House Museum,** 119 Sandwich Street, 746-3017. Hours: June through mid-October, Friday and Saturday, 10 A.M. to 4 P.M. $$ • **Mayflower Society House,** 4 Winslow Street, 746-2590. Hours:

July and August, daily, 10 A.M. to 5 P.M.; June and September to mid-October, Friday to Sunday, 10 A.M. to 4:15 P.M. $$ • **Richard Sparrow House,** 42 Summer Street, 747-1240. Hours: Thursday through Tuesday, 10 A.M. to 5 P.M. $ • **Colonial Lantern Light Walking Tours,** PO Box 3541, 747-4161. Hours: June through October, nightly, 7:30 P.M. and 9 P.M. 90-minute tours from the lobby of the John Carver Inn. April, May, November, weekends only. $$$$. *Cruises:* A variety of options, from harbor cruises to foliage tour to whale-watching; check current offerings. **Cape Cod Cruises,** *Mayflower II* Pier, 747-2400 • **Capt. John Boats,** 117 Standish Avenue, 746-2643 • **Andy Lynn Boats,** Town Wharf, 746-7776 • **Splashdown Amphibious Tours,** (800) 225-4000, "duck" tours on land and into the harbor.

INFORMATION   Destination Plymouth, 225 Water Street, Suite 202, Plymouth, MA 02360 (800) USA-1620.

Fall Foliage in Franconia

Men hang out signs indicative of their respective trades; shoemakers hang out a giant shoe; jewelers a monster watch; and a dentist hangs out a gold tooth; but up in the mountains of New Hampshire God Almighty has hung out a sign to show that there He makes men.

It was Daniel Webster who wrote these words upon viewing the Old Man of the Mountain, an unmistakable craggy profile in stone carved on a mountainside by some celestial sculptor.

The rugged visage of the Old Man is now the official symbol of New Hampshire, the Granite State. It can be seen clearly, high on a rock cliff at the end of the eight-mile mountain pass called Franconia Notch, where it presides over a panorama of peaks and valleys, awesome gorges, tumbling waterfalls, and ice-blue mountain lakes, a vista that has few peers in New England.

Add the region's most scenic highway, aflame in fall foliage, and a chance to view it all from a cable car that travels 4,200 feet into the sky and you have the makings for an unforgettable fall outing.

Since this is a deservedly popular destination in the fall and inns are small, it's well to begin by reserving a place early. Some of the favorites are above Franconia in the little town of Sugar Hill, named for its many maple trees. The local guide aptly describes this region as an area of small villages and big mountains, and Sugar Hill is the quaintest of the villages. The one main road, Route 117, climbs up, up the hill with views all around. Along the way is the Sugar Hill Inn, a tasteful 1748

Colonial with charming rooms done in traditional Laura Ashley, warm hosts, and a fine dining room. Farther up the hill is the Hilltop Inn, a cozy Victorian, circa 1895, decorated with stenciling, local crafts, and quilts, and with lovely gardens. On the same road is Foxglove, an elegant, small, antiques-filled, designer-decorated, turn-of-the-century home, where breakfast is served on fine china and crystal and bedrooms are adorned with antique lace. The caring host and hostess provide their own special maps and guides for day tours in the area and will whip up delicious dinners for guests on request.

The Franconia Inn, set on 107 acres, off on quiet Route 116 south of Franconia in the Easton Valley, is a longtime mainstay. It was rebuilt after a 1934 fire to resemble the original Colonial inn of the 1860s and has been refurbished once again to provide modern baths and a few Jacuzzi tubs. Here you have your pick of views, meadow, or mountain, and there are horses for riding, tennis courts, a pool, a fishing stream, and a hot tub for guests. In winter, the inn offers ice skating and its own cross-country skiing center.

Continue farther on Route 116, Easton Valley Road, for the Bungay Jar, a delightful eighteenth-century barn turned bed-and-breakfast, full of folk art, whimsy, and charm. There are heavenly views from the inn's many decks, a sauna for relaxing, and room to wander wooded paths through the lush garden to a hidden river out back. On the same road is the more modest Blanche's B&B, a good bet for budget watchers, with an artist-hostess who has filled the rooms with hand-painted surprises—stars on the ceiling or fish swimming across the bathroom wall. Her original floor mats, found in fine shops, are also for sale here.

Tucked away on a side road to the north is the Inn at Forest Hills, a turn-of-the-century English Tudor home with an eventful history. Another possibility north of Franconia, in Bethlehem, is Adair, a former lavish country estate on 200 acres, with a pool and tennis courts.

Near the start of the Kancamagus Highway to the south in Lincoln, the Mill House Inn is another kind of option, a pleasant modern hotel that is part of a restored mill complex, offering tennis, indoor and outdoor pools, exercise equipment, and shopping.

Once you've made your choice and settled in, you're in for two days of spectacular sights. If you want to enjoy the area to the fullest, you can easily spend an entire day driving, walking, and picnicking in the fantastic beauty of Franconia Notch State Park. Route 93, a limited-access parkway, takes you directly through, with exits at major points. A nine-mile bike path separate from the road is a treat for pedalers.

You might as well drive right to that famous profile at Franconia Notch. Profile Lake has been dubbed the "Old Man's Washbowl" for its location 1,200 feet below the outline of the Old Man himself. A parking area along the lake gives a magnificent view of mountains reflected in the dark water and is also the best vantage point for seeing the distinct face above, which is actually composed of five separate granite ledges.

The forehead alone is made of a 20-foot-long granite block weighing about 30 tons. The profile is 25 feet wide and measures about 40 feet from chin to forehead.

Continuing on the main road, you'll come to a waterfall cascading into a granite pool called the Basin. It is believed that the granite was eroded by a melting glacier 25,000 years ago. Below is a water-eroded rock formation, then comes the rushing water of the Baby Flume, a forerunner of what lies ahead.

The Flume is a natural gorge whose 70- to 90-foot granite walls extend for 800 feet along the southern flank of Mount Liberty. A bus takes you to within 500 yards of the gorge, then it's an easy two-mile round-trip hike along the paths and wooden walkways crisscrossing the stream to reach the actual Flume and the crescendo of sound that announces Avalanche Falls, a torrent of water crashing 23 feet down the canyon into a pool. A short trail leads you to the Cascades, another rush of mountain streams tumbling into a narrow valley known as Liberty Gorge. On the way back you'll pass a deep basin called simply the Pool, fed by a cascading river. In 1938 a giant pine uprooted by a hurricane fell across the river and now forms a base for the Sentinel Pine Bridge, which offers the best viewing point for the Pool.

By now you've surely worked up an appetite for lunch. There is a cafeteria at the Flume Visitor Center, but with all that scenery around, it's better to bring a picnic. The closest picnic grounds are right across from the Flume; the most scenic are back in the other direction at Echo Lake, a pool in a setting of granite cliffs.

There's boating and fishing at Echo Lake, and a sandy beach near the picnic area. If you're up for a $1\frac{1}{2}$-mile walk, Artist's Bluff, up above, is a rocky palisade with fine views of the Franconia and Kinsman Ranges. The name comes from yet another profile carved in the mountain, this one known as the Artist.

Now it's time for the view that beats them all, the thrilling cable car ascent via the Cannon Mountain Aerial Tramway to the 4,200-foot peak of Cannon Mountain. This was the first such lift in America, and it is still one of the most spectacular. The present tram, completed in 1980, goes a mile straight up, a five-minute ride that affords amazing views of all the White Mountain ranges in their best fall dress. There are trails at the summit up to an observation tower for a longer view.

At the base of the tramway is the New England Ski Museum, which claims the most extensive collection of historical ski equipment, clothing, art, and photography in the Northeast.

If you still have energy, another area attraction worth a visit is Frost Place, the simple frame house where poet Robert Frost lived and worked. You can stand at his desk or on the front porch, sharing the mountain views that inspired him.

After a hearty breakfast at the inn, start Sunday by exploring one of the less heralded but no less intriguing natural attractions of the area, the strange formations known as Lost River. The river here flows through a narrow, steep-walled glacial gorge and disappears beneath immense blocks of granite that tumbled into the gorge eons ago. You can follow the river's course on a wooden walkway as the water moves through the gorge and canyons and down Paradise Falls. There are bridges and ladders all along the way that let you wander into caves and through hidden passages in the boulders. Kids absolutely love it—but then, so do the grown-ups. The walk takes about an hour.

In Lincoln you can get another bird's-eye view of the colorful mountains from the Loon Mountain Gondola, which bills itself as the state's longest aerial ride. At the top, the Summit Cave Walk explores the area's unique glacial caves, or you can climb the four-story Sky Tower for an even loftier view.

But the major attraction for this day is down to earth, a drive that gets my vote as the most beautiful in New England. The Kancamagus Highway (Route 112) runs for 32 miles through the heart of the White Mountain National Forest between the villages of Lincoln and Conway. It was designed by the U.S. Forest Service to make the most of the views and to give access to the magnificent wilderness on either side with picnic areas and hiking trails. The road was designated a National Scenic Byway in 1989.

The drive alone is extraordinary, especially with the added glow of autumn color, but to make the most of the highway you really should get out and investigate the scenic areas on the way. A special one is the Rocky Gorge area, where the Swift River has worn a cleft in the rock now known as Rocky Gorge. Within this area is Falls Pond, a five-minute walk over the gorge via a rustic footbridge.

Some other easy walks are to Boulder Loop, which gives a spectacular view of Mt. Chocorua and the Swift River Valley from the ledges, and Sabbaday Falls, a picturesque series of cascades in a narrow flume. You can spend an hour here—or a day.

At the end of the road in Conway, you're very much back in civilization, with many shops to choose from—and lots of good restaurants as well. But somehow it seems a shame to lose the glow of all that pristine beauty. A better move may be to take the return trip on the Kancamagus, seeing it all from a different perspective this time, and heading home with the glorious New Hampshire autumn recorded in your mind's eye to sustain you through the winter ahead.

Area Code: 603

DRIVING DIRECTIONS   Franconia is on the west side of the White Mountains in upper New Hampshire and can be reached via I-93. It is 115 miles from Boston, 325 miles from New York, and 215 miles from Hartford.

PUBLIC TRANSPORTATION   Air service to Manchester or Lebanon, New Hampshire; Concord Trailways bus service from Boston to Franconia.

ACCOMMODATIONS   Sugar Hill Inn, Route 117, Franconia 03580, 823-5621 or (800) 548-4748, M–E, CP; EE, MAP • **Foxglove,** Route 117, Sugar Hill 03585, 823-8840, M–E, CP • **Hilltop Inn,** Main Street (Route 117), Sugar Hill 03585, 823-5695 or (800) 770-5695, M–E, CP • **Franconia Inn,** Easton Road (Route 116), Franconia 03580, 823-5542, M, CP; E, MAP • **Bungay Jar,** PO Box 15, Easton Valley Road (Route 116), Franconia 03580, 823-7775, I–M, CP; suites, M–E, CP • **Inn at Forest Hills,** PO Box 783, Franconia 03580, 823-9550 or (800) 280-9550, grand Tudor home, M, CP; in foliage season, M–E, CP • **Blanche's B&B,** Easton Valley Road, Franconia 03580, 823-7061, I–M, CP • **Adair Country Inn,** 80 Guilder Lane, PO Box 850, Bethlehem 03574, 444-2600, ten minutes north of Franconia, E, CP; suites, E–EE, CP • **Mill House Inn,** Route 112, Box 696, Lincoln 03251, 745-6261 or (800) 654-6183, I–M.

DINING   Franconia Inn (see above), continental menu, highly recommended, M • **Hunt Room at the Horse & Hound,** 205 Wells Road (off Route 18), 823-5501, another old-time favorite, M • **Sugar Hill Inn** (see above), by reservation only, M–E, or prix fixe, EE • **Rosa Flamingo,** Route 302, Bethlehem, 869-3111, Italian-American, I–M • **Adair Country Inn** (see above), dining room open seasonally—check availability, M • **Clement Room,** Woodstock Inn, Route 3, North Woodstock, 745-3951, formal and informal dining rooms in a Victorian home, M–E; also known for its breakfasts, I • **Common Man,** Route 112 and Pollard Road, Lincoln, 745-3463, old-timer in area, rustic farmhouse setting, basic menu, I–M • **Polly's Pancake Parlor,** Route 117, Sugar Hill, 823-5525, a local legend for home-ground cornmeal and whole-wheat pancakes and waffles with luscious fillings and home-made sausages, I. Take-out picnic sandwiches are available at the **Cannonball Pizza & Deli,** Main Street (Route 18), Franconia, 823-7478.

SIGHTSEEING   Franconia Notch State Park, Routes 3 and 93, Franconia, 823-5563. Hours: free admission to park; attractions open daily, mid-May through mid-October, 9 A.M. to 4:30 P.M., July 4 to Labor Day to 7 P.M. Major attractions include the **Flume,** 745-8391, $$$; **Cannon Mountain Aerial Tramway,** $$$; **New England Ski Museum,** next to Cannon Mountain Tram, PO Box 267, Franconia, 823-7177. Hours: late May to mid-October, daily, noon to 5 P.M.; December to March, Thursday to Tuesday, noon to 5 P.M. Free • **The Frost Place,** off Route 116, Franconia, 823-5510. Hours: July to Columbus Day, daily except Tuesday, 1 P.M. to 5 P.M.; June, weekends only. $$ • **Lost River Reservation,** Route 112, Kinsman Notch, North Woodstock, 745-8031. Hours: May through October, daily, 9 A.M. to 5 P.M.; July and August to 6 P.M. $$$ • **Loon Mountain Gondola Skyride,** Lincoln, 745-8111. Hours: daily 9 A.M. to 5 P.M. $$$$.

INFORMATION   Franconia/Easton/Sugar Hill Chamber of Commerce, P.O. Box 780, Franconia, NH 03580, 823-5661 or (800) 237-9007; White Mountains Visitors Bureau, PO Box 10, North Woodstock, NH 03262, 745-8720 or (800) 346-3687.

Meandering the Mohawk Trail

It was the Pocumtuck Indians who first blazed the trail, invading the lands of the Mohawks in 1663 by creating a footpath from their home in Deerfield, Massachusetts, through the Berkshire Mountains to Mohawk territory in Troy, New York. Later pioneers made this strategic route the first toll-free interstate road, opening the Berkshires to tourists.

Eventually the 63-mile route, still known as the Mohawk Trail, became the first official scenic drive in New England, opened to the public in 1914. It stretches from the Massachusetts–New York border to the Connecticut River Valley just east of Greenfield, an up-and-down route of twists and turns and amazing mountain views. With a couple of slight detours, one 42-mile segment can connect two beautiful New England towns, Deerfield and Williamstown, as well as provide access to Greylock Mountain, the state's highest peak, with soaring views of fall foliage. There are few more rewarding autumn journeys.

Deerfield, with one of America's most magnificent main streets aglow in autumn color, is a beautiful beginning to the weekend.

Known simply as the Street, Old Deerfield's main avenue is a mile-long row of more than 50 fine Colonial and Federal houses, each one carefully maintained in its original condition. In the dozen buildings open to the public, visitors can see more than 100 rooms filled with china, glassware, silver, pewter, fabrics, and furniture—all testaments to the good taste of our early settlers.

But this is by no means a museum town. The houses on the Street have been continuously occupied over the years, and even the museum homes have apartments in the rear for the faculty of Deerfield Academy, the noted school that has stood on the Street since 1797, giving Deerfield a rare living continuity with the past that is evident the moment you arrive. It is heightened by the fact that no modern intrusions such as telephone wires have been allowed; they are carefully buried to preserve the Street's untouched beauty.

It's hard to believe that this peaceful, elm-shaded village was once a frontier outpost, twice besieged by Indian attacks. The stubborn survivors rebuilt their town, worked their farms, and began to prosper, replacing their primitive homes with gracious, weathered clapboard houses in the Connecticut Valley tradition, marked by distinctively carved doorways. Though these houses are rustic compared to houses in Boston or Philadelphia, their very simplicity makes them all the lovelier.

Deerfield's farmers used their new wealth to commission the finest furnishings they could find, particularly from the excellent craftsmen and cabinetmakers of their own valley. Fortunately, this era of good taste has been preserved, thanks largely to the generosity of Mr. and Mrs. Henry Flynt, who came to Deerfield in the 1930s, when their son was enrolled at the academy. The Flynts first bought and restored the white-columned inn at the center of town, which remains a gracious Colonial lodging, and then acquired one of the old houses for themselves. One house led to another until, in 1952, they founded Historic Deerfield, Inc., to care for the properties.

Though Deerfield is only a village, it deserves a full day of touring if you want to savor all it has to offer. A visit to Historic Deerfield includes a walking tour of the village, but you might prefer to start on your own by strolling the Street, with time to savor the town's setting among wooded hills and observing the exteriors of the saltbox houses, with their steep-pitched gambrel roofs, weathered clapboard siding, and carved doorways. Note the Academy buildings, the old brick church, and the post office, a replica of a 1696 meetinghouse.

You may want to take a detour onto the Channing Blake Meadow Walk, a half-mile footpath leading from the village into the nearly 1,000 acres of beautiful meadows that surround the western and northern edges of the community. It gives a close-up view of the fields that have been farmed continuously for more than three centuries and brings into focus the critical roles of agriculture in past and present-day rural New England. Then head for the Hall Tavern Information Center, where color photos will help you make the difficult choice of which houses to visit during a limited stay. Each house tour takes 30 minutes.

You can begin with Hall Tavern itself, once a hostelry for travelers. One of its seven rooms is an unusual ballroom with gaily stenciled walls. A must on any tour is Ashley House (circa 1730), the home of Deerfield's Tory minister during the American Revolution. Many may have quarreled with the Reverend Jonathan Ashley's politics, but no one could fault his taste. The north parlor, with blue walls setting off red shell-crowned cupboards, a gold satin settee, and rich oriental rugs, has been called one of the most beautiful rooms in America.

Each of the other houses has its own special attractions and a knowledgeable guide to point them out. The Sheldon-Hawks House (1743), home of the town's historian, contains fine paneling, a display of sewing equipment, and a memorable bedroom with brilliant flame-stitch bed hangings and red moreen curtains and chairs. Behind the austere Colonial facade of the Wells-Thorn House (1717/1751) is a series of rooms furnished to depict changing periods in Deerfield's history. The Dwight House (1725) has an elegant parlor and a doctor's office behind its weathered exterior.

The Asa Stebbins House (1799), the town's first brick edifice, was built by the wealthiest landowner and decorated with French wallpapers and freehand wall drawings. Like many of Deerfield's homes, this one has an excellent collection of early export china.

Mr. Stebbins built the town's other brick house for his son, Asa Junior, in 1824. Now called Wright House, it is distinguished for its exquisite collection of Federal furniture.

Frary House (1720/1768), a home with a double history, is another highly recommended stop. Its location on the town common made it a refuge for the Frary family in pioneer days and a profitable tavern for the Barnards later on. The house contains a ballroom, many examples of country furniture, and a variety of cooking, spinning, and weaving equipment. There is also a "touch it" room where children and adults may handle some of the tools that are off-limits elsewhere.

The newest home on the tour is the Hinsdale and Anna Williams House, opened to the public in 1993 after 12 years of painstaking restoration and research. The furnishings are based on the personal inventory of household property owned by Hinsdale Williams at his death on June 1, 1838.

For a change of pace, step into some of the specialized buildings such as the Henry N. Flynt Silver and Metalware Collection, a farmhouse containing a smith's workshop, a pewter collection, and an outstanding display of American and English silver. The house dates from around 1810. Inside a Victorian barn is the Helen Geier Flynt Textile Collection, a remarkable assemblage of American, English, and European needlework, textiles, quilts, bed hangings, and costumes.

In the fall of 1998, the Textile Collection will be moved into its own climate-controlled gallery in a new Collections Study Center, which will also feature changing exhibition galleries and study galleries with a sampling of Historic Deerfield's renowned decorative arts collections. The center will greatly increase public access to the collections and the curatorial staff.

Historic Deerfield holds special events year-round, including open-hearth cooking demonstrations, an antique auto show, wreath-making workshops, special holiday exhibits, and seminars on various early decorative arts, architecture, and furnishings

Annual Old Deerfield Crafts Fairs are held by Deerfield's Memorial Hall Museum in June and late September. The museum also hosts a

Living History weekend in October with a military encampment and historical reenactments. The building itself is something of a town attic, with memorabilia that includes doors still bearing gashes from the 1704 massacre.

The Deerfield Inn, on the Street, is a wonderful haven in the proper Colonial mood. Its monthly wine-tasting dinners are a special treat. Another highly praised restaurant nearby is Siena, in South Deerfield, and many good choices are found in Northampton, about 10 miles to the south on Route 5.

If the Deerfield Inn is full, a happy alternative is the Brandt House, an airy bed-and-breakfast home in Greenfield overlooking three acres of lawns and woodland, including a clay tennis court. There's good reason for a stop in Greenfield if only to visit the Lunt Design Center and Marketplace, a handsome contemporary showcase for the finest in silver, crystal, and contemporary crafts, adjoining the Lunt silver factory. Visitors can watch at work in the factory, and also see artisans such as silversmiths and glassblowers practicing their craft. The center also includes a restaurant featuring many special events, from jazz concerts to cooking demonstrations, with special celebrations planned during the fall harvest season.

If you've given Saturday to Deerfield and Greenfield, plan an early start Sunday to allow for the scenery and sights awaiting along the Mohawk Trail, Route 2, and its many vistas heading west. Allow at least two hours for the 42-mile trip because of the dips and twists and stunning scenery along the way.

There are several interesting little detours along the way. A turn north from Route 2 on the Colrain-Shelburne Road leads into the steep hills toward tiny Colrain and allows for a stop at the West County Winery for a tasting of hard cider, the house specialty, and a look into the Green Emporium, a funky café in an old church on the Colrain common.

Shelburne Falls, south of Route 2, is a funky little village divided by the Deerfield River into areas known as Shelburne and Buckland. Shelburne Falls is best known for the Bridge of Flowers, an old trolley bridge across the river that's now covered with a profusion of shrubs and blossoms, and for Salmon Falls, the site of many ancient glacial potholes that can be viewed from the riverbanks. Both sides of the river are lined with small shops and galleries. Two special places of interest on the Shelburne side are the Salmon Falls Artisans Showroom, in an old grain building up the hill from the Bridge of Flowers that houses, a collection of works by over 150 artisans, and North River Glass, near the overlook for the potholes, where you can watch glassblowers in action.

The rural village of Charlemont is the site for Mohawk Trail concerts, held from May to October in the old, acoustically perfect Charlemont Federated Church. Across the Indian Bridge in Charlemont is a monument to the memory of the five Indian nations of the Mohawk Trail, *Hail to the Sunrise,* a 900-pound bronze casting set on a nine-ton boulder. Facing east, the Mohawk Indian looks across the Deerfield River with uplifted arms in supplication to the Great Spirit. The memorial includes a pool with 100 inscribed stones from various tribes and councils from all over the country.

Scenery takes the spotlight for the rest of the drive. You can't miss the best views because, sad to say, they've been marked by signs at local souvenir shops and restaurants adjoining scenic lookouts. Whitcomb Summit, at the top of the trail past the hamlet of Florida, has an elevation of over 2,000 feet with views of mountains as far away as Vermont and New Hampshire. Not far beyond is the most famous of the lookouts, the Hairpin Turn, opening to another soaring mountain vista. Other than these well-visited spots, much of the trail remains wooded and unblemished, allowing you to enjoy this state's premier autumn panoramas.

By the time you get to North Adams, the Mohawk Trail has leveled off and scenery has given way to commercial establishments. North Adams itself is an old industrial little town on the way up. This is where you can see New England's only "natural bridge"—a white marble span over Hudson Brook, located in Natural Bridge State Park, a half mile north of downtown on State Route 8. The bridge was formed when waters from melting glaciers cut through the natural marble.

The interesting history of this region is told at the Visitors' Center, in a former freight house at Western Gateway Heritage State Park. In an exhibit housed in a tunnellike setting, you learn about the building of the Hoosac Mountain Tunnel, the longest railway tunnel of its time, which connected Boston to the west. It was considered a marvel back in the 1850s, created by digging 1,000 feet straight down through rock. There are also films of steam train days. Some of the old freight houses now house the Marketplace, a complex with a few shops and a café. All the wooden railroad buildings here are on the National Register of Historic Places.

Some of the industrial past is being transformed in other ways. The old historic Beaver Mill is now the Contemporary Artists Center and Gallery, with working space for artists and changing exhibitions.

Progress has been slow, but an enormous mill complex that once employed 4,000 people is taking shape as the Massachusetts Museum of Contemporary Art, an ambitiously planned cultural arts center that will feature the visual arts as well as theater, dance, history, and music. The official opening is tentatively planned for sometime in 1998, but meanwhile art exhibits are already being held, and well-established Berkshires groups such as the Williamstown Theater and the Jacob's Pillow Dance Company have begun scheduling a few performances here in summer.

If you are ready for refreshments, a highly recommended detour is the Miss Adams Diner, an old-fashioned diner that is a longtime institution.

If you watch for the signs on Route 2 in North Adams and make a left turn onto Notch Road, you'll be on the road to the 3,491-foot summit of Mt. Greylock, the state's highest peak, and the most stunning view of all. The road may seem bumpy at the start, but it gets better as you ascend.

At the summit, in Bascom Lodge, you'll find an information center manned by the Appalachian Mountain Club (AMC), with maps covering the 35 miles of hiking trails available here for hikers of all abilities. A favorite hiking destination is the Hopper, a wildlife preserve of giant conifers and lush growth where the natural scene is untouched by any human development. By car, follow the signs to Stony Ledge for an outlook over this heavily wooded, brook-coursed canyon.

The famous hiking route, the Appalachian Trail, also passes through Mt. Greylock Reservation, a 10,000-acre preserve around the mountain maintained by the Massachusetts Department of Environmental Management. The state agency and the Appalachian Mountain Club combine to offer many guided tours and talks on the mountain. The Ramble, a hike to the summit, sponsored by the Adams Chamber of Commerce each year on Columbus Day, attracts some 2,000 hikers. Hard-core hikers may want to consider the spartan but clean accommodations at Bascom Lodge, on the mountain. The rooms are real bargains.

You can return to the bottom on Notch Road or on the road that takes you to the Route 7 Information Center in Lanesboro. Either way, your last stop on the Mohawk Trail is Williamstown, a classic New England town with a college dating back to 1793 as its center. Williamstown has many places for an overnight stay, but its attractions really deserve a weekend on their own, so you may want to save it for a longer visit. For more about the town, see page 253.

Whether you make a return scenic trip on the Mohawk Trail or find another route home, you'll be bringing back memories of the New England autumn at its best.

Area Code: 413

DRIVING DIRECTIONS   Deerfield can be reached via I-91, exit 24 northbound or exit 25 southbound to Route 5, which leads six miles north into town. The Mohawk Trail is reached directly via I-91, exit 26. Though the portion designated as the Mohawk Trail stops at Millers Falls, Route 2 continues east to Boston. Deerfield is about 100 miles from Boston, 187 miles from New York, and 77 miles from Hartford.

PUBLIC TRANSPORTATION   Peter Pan bus service to Deerfield. You'll need a car to travel on the Mohawk Trail.

ACCOMMODATIONS   Deerfield Inn, the Street, Deerfield 01342, 774-5587, E • **Brandt House,** 29 Highland Avenue, Greenfield 01301, 774-3329 or (800) 235-3329, M–E, CP • **AMC Bascom Lodge,** Mt. Greylock, PO Box 686, Lanesboro 02137, 743-1591, I.

DINING   Deerfield Inn (see above), M–E • **Sienna,** 6 Elm Street, South Deerfield, 665-0215, creative chef is widely praised, M • **Artisans,** Lunt Design Center, 298 Federal Street, Greenfield, 772-0767; dinner Wednesday to Sunday, I–M; lunch, I • **Miss Adams Diner,** 53 Park Street, Adams, 743-5300, they don't make them like this anymore, home cooking, breakfast all day, I • **Copper Angel,** State Street, Shelburne Falls (Buckland side), 625-2727, good lunch spot overlooking the river, I.

INFORMATION   The Mohawk Trail Association, PO Box J, Charlemont, MA 01339, 664-6256. See also listings for Williamstown, pages 257–258, and Northampton, pages 66–67.

SIGHTSEEING   Historic Deerfield, PO Box 321, Deerfield 01342, 774-5581. Hours: daily, 9:30 A.M. to 4:30 P.M. $$$$ • **Memorial Hall Museum,** Memorial Street, Deerfield, 774-7476. Hours: May through November, daily, 10 A.M. to 4:30 P.M. $$ • **Lunt Design Center & Marketplace,** 312 Federal Street, Greenfield, 774-4680 or (800) 344-LUNT. Hours: Monday to Thursday 10 A.M. to 6 P.M.; Friday, Saturday, Sunday, 10 A.M. to 8 P.M. Free • **West County Winery,** Colrain-Shelburne Road, Colrain, 624-3481. Hours: Tastings available June 1 to December 31, Thursday to Sunday, 11 A.M. to 5 P.M., January to March, phone for hours; April and May, Friday to Sunday, 11 A.M. to 5 P.M. Free.

Breezing Through the Past in Essex

Standing on the docks at Essex, Connecticut, enjoying the sea breeze and admiring the panorama of sleek sailboats in the harbor, you'll find it hard to believe that this placid spot was once the most bustling landing on the Connecticut River.

With its pleasure boats, lanes of picket fences, and handsome white clapboard Colonial and Federal homes, today's Essex is the picture of early American serenity, a mecca for sailors and strollers.

But for more than 300 eventful years of history, this town has been a major port on the 410-mile river that has served as a main artery for much of New England. There's rich history to be explored—as well as some special pleasures of the present, including a cruise on the majestic river, some unusual shops, and several exceptional inns.

Just up the river is a Victorian jewel box of a theater offering classic American musical comedies. Here, too, is Connecticut's answer to those romantic castles on the Rhine, not to mention the chance nearby to ride a puffing, chugging turn-of-the-century steam train, all adding even more incentive to make the trip.

Start your get-acquainted tour of Essex at its most significant site, Steamboat Dock, at the foot of Main Street on the riverfront. Situated in lush countryside just five miles above the spot where the Connecticut River feeds into the sea, Essex has been inextricably tied to its river from 1648, when settlers from the shore colony of Old Saybrook decided to form a farming community a bit inland. The first wharf at the site of the present Steamboat Dock was in operation as early as 1656, and trade with the West Indies had begun by the 1660s.

Shipbuilding was soon a major activity as well, and Connecticut's first warship, the *Oliver Cromwell,* was built at the Hayden Yard here in 1776. The British raided and burned the 28 ships in the harbor during the War of 1812. That event is commemorated with a marker at the foot of the harbor, as well as by the Essex Fife and Drum Corps, known as the Sailing Masters of 1812, who parade down Main Street in period dress to mark most national holidays.

Things revived after the war, however, and Essex's ships and sailors were known to nineteenth-century commerce throughout the world. A new era of prominence came with the arrival of steamboat service on the river in 1823; the original Steamboat Dock was built in 1845 to accommodate the growing traffic. It was enlarged and the dockhouse was built in the 1860s. The three-story clapboard structure with its graceful cupola became a well-known landmark for river passengers.

The Connecticut River Foundation has restored the exterior of the historic dockhouse and a portion of the interior as it was in its warehouse days. The building also houses a small museum with exhibits telling the story of the waterway and Essex-built ships with tools, navigational instruments, paintings, and scale-model steamboats.

An unusual display is a full-size reproduction of the *Turtle,* America's first submarine, designed in 1776 in nearby Old Sayville. Though the sub fared better in its river trials than it did once it went to war, it is still a fascinating exhibit.

From here, it's on to the rest of the town's sights. You'll certainly want to check out some of the many shops on Main Street and in a little shopping complex just behind it for antiques, handicrafts, gifts, and gewgaws, many with a nautical bent.

For those who want a closer look at the river itself, there are several excursion trips offered nearby, including lunch and dinner cruises.

Bushnell Park, off Bushnell Street above the boatyards, and the town park, off Main Street, are ideal spots for a picnic lunch on land with water views.

The town tour leads past the gracious homes that once belonged to schooner captains and shipbuilders, and past the churches and other historic buildings that tell more about the Essex of yesterday. As you follow along Main to Essex Square and up Methodist Hill to Prospect Street and West Avenue, watch for some of the distinctive fanlights, the handsome doorknobs and knockers, and the unusual brick patterns and chimneys that mark many of the homes in town.

The Pratt House, at 20 West Avenue, restored and furnished by the Essex Historical Society, gives a glimpse of life in Essex in the mid-1800s. Inside you'll see fine oak and chestnut beams, burnished paneling, and many rare antiques originally owned by the Pratts, an important early family in town. The Essex Garden Club has planted a fragrant Colonial herb garden around the house.

The 1845 Baptist Church is hard to miss, with its white steeple and gold dome. It is one of only two examples of Egyptian Revival architecture in the country.

Walk to the end of Prospect and turn left on North Main and you'll be at the Riverview Cemetery, resting place of the Pratts, the Haydens, and other of Essex's first families. This is a cemetery with a river view —a lovely panorama across the Connecticut River to the Lyme hills.

The Griswold Inn, in Essex, should be part of any tour. Even the British troops who invaded in 1814 made a point of staying at "the Gris," which has been open for business on the same spot on Main Street since 1776 and has hardly changed on the outside over the years.

You'll have to call early to get one of the much-in-demand rooms here, but a stop is a must, at least for a meal and a visit. The Sunday Hunt Breakfast, a local tradition, includes the inn's 1776 sausages, made from a recipe handed down for eight generations.

If the inn is filled, there are other fine possibilities in the neighborhood. The Copper Beech Inn, in Ivoryton, has elegant rooms and a restaurant to match, and the Inn at Chester is a country hotel with an excellent dining room. The Riverwind Inn, in Deep River, is a true country charmer, and Bishopsgate Inn, in East Haddam, is an attractive small inn with a special advantage—it is within walking distance of one of the area's best attractions, the Goodspeed Opera House.

Reserve well ahead for all the choice small inns in this popular region as well as for performances at the Goodspeed Opera House, a highlight of your Connecticut River Valley visit. Musicals of the 1920s and 1930s are served up here in a restored Victorian theater on the river, a playhouse full of froufrous and charm. There is a newer branch of the Goodspeed in Chester that is dedicated to new musicals.

If you've spent Saturday on foot in Essex, you might want to begin Sunday's sightseeing with a drive along River Road, with glimpses of water and many fine houses along the way. Then it's on to a different kind of ride—or two of them, to be exact, by land and by sea. The Valley Railroad, just a couple of miles from the center of town, offers a double dose of nostalgia, a ten-mile excursion into the countryside aboard the same kind of steam train that Grandpa might have ridden when he was a boy, then an optional connection to a riverboat for a half-hour cruise up the Connecticut River.

If you haven't taken a ride on the river, don't miss the opportunity. The pristine and beautiful woodland banks are a pleasure to behold anytime and a blaze of color in autumn foliage season. And there are enough diversions to whip photographers into action—hilltop mansions, the gingerbread facade of the Goodspeed Opera House, and the stone turrets of Gillette Castle.

When you get back to shore, take the three-minute ride across the river from Chester to Hadlyme aboard one of the region's oldest and smallest ferryboats, and head on to East Haddam for a close-up view of Gillette Castle, a one-of-a-kind curiosity.

It was built by William Gillette, a somewhat eccentric gentleman who gained fame and fortune by portraying Sherlock Holmes on the stage. The castle cost over a million dollars, quite a sum when it was built in the early 1900s. Complete with turrets and balconies, it was meant to re-create the feel of the castles on the Rhine that Gillette had admired in Europe.

Among Mr. Gillette's eccentricities was a dislike for metal. All the doors are fitted with wooden locks operated by hidden springs, and even the light switches are made of wood. The walls are made of wood also, hand-carved oak. There are some 47 different kinds of latching doors and cabinets. To protect all that wood, Gillette had fire hoses and a sprinkler system installed, safety features that were many years ahead of their time. Trick locks and trapdoors fascinate, and children are intrigued by Gillette's love for cats and frogs, evident throughout the house in the form of bookends, salt shakers, and even a wishing well where his frogs used to live.

Whatever you think of the castle, you'll certainly admire the clifftop river view. The grounds are now a state park and the perfect place for a picnic with a last sweeping perspective on the Connecticut River as it winds its way downstream to Essex and on to the sea.

After the castle, there are plenty of diversions in either direction. A short drive north, in Higganum, is the Sundial Gardens, with formal herb gardens for touring and a shop selling herbs and tasteful gifts. Teas and tours are offered on many Sunday afternoons.

Downriver a bit, pretty little Chester is a perfect town for browsing. The shops include the Connecticut River Artisans Cooperative, showing the work of local artists. Farther east, the Great American Trading Company, in Deep River, is a treasure of toy nostalgia filled with old-time favorites such as wooden pick-up sticks, marbles, and Chinese checkers.

Heading on toward Old Saybrook, the Essex-Saybrook Antiques Village has a little bit of everything, with 80 dealers under one roof.

In Old Saybrook, where the Connecticut River meets Long Island Sound, you can wind up the weekend with a fine seafood dinner. Whether you pick plain or fancy surroundings, the water view is grand.

Area Code: 860

DRIVING DIRECTIONS   Essex is reached via I-95 or I-91. From either direction, take Route 9 to exit 3, then Route 153, which becomes Main Street. It is about 133 miles from Boston, 118 miles from New York, and 35 miles from Hartford.

PUBLIC TRANSPORTATION   Amtrak to Old Saybrook; Greyhound to Middletown. Both are just a short drive from Essex, but a car is needed to get around the area.

ACCOMMODATIONS   **Griswold Inn,** Main Street, Essex 06426, 767-1776, M, CP; suites, M–E, CP • **Copper Beech Inn,** 46 Main Street, Ivoryton 06442, 767-0330, M–E, CP • **Bishopsgate Inn,** Goodspeed Landing, East Haddam 06423, 873-1677, M, CP • **The Inn at Chester,** 318 West Main Street (Route 148), Chester 06412, 526-9541, M–E, CP; suites, E–EE • **Riverwind Inn,** 209 Main Street, Deep River 06147, 526-2014, wonderful country decor, M–E, CP.

DINING   **Griswold Inn** (see above), dinner, M–E; Sunday Hunt Breakfast, M • **Copper Beech Inn** (see above), fine dining, E–EE • **Oliver's Taverne,** Route 152, Essex, 767-2633, informal, popular, I–M • **The Post and Beam,** the Inn at Chester (see above), E • **Restaurant du Village,** 59 Main Street, Chester, 526-5301, country French bistro, E • **Fiddler's Seafood Restaurant,** 4 Water Street, Chester, 526-3210, country decor, good food, M • **Gelston House Restaurant,** Goodspeed Landing, East Haddam, 873-1411, M–E • **Steve's Centerbrook Café,** Main Street, Centerbrook, 767-1277, attractive café decorated with paintings, wide-ranging menu from a top area chef, M • **Dock and Dine,** Saybrook Point, Old Saybrook, 388-4665, M–E • **Saybrook Fish House,** 99 Essex Road, Old Saybrook, 388-4836, M • **Saybrook Point Inn,** 2 Bridge Street, Old Saybrook, 395-2000, M–E.

SIGHTSEEING   **Valley Railroad,** exit 3 off Route 9, Essex, 767-0103. Open May through October and December; hours vary with seasons. Call for current schedule and rates • **Connecticut River Museum,** Steamboat Dock, foot of Main Street, Essex, 767-8269. Hours: Tuesday to Sunday, 10 A.M. to 5 P.M. $$ • **Pratt House,** West Avenue, Essex, 767-0681. Hours: June to Labor Day, Saturday and Sunday, 1 P.M. to 4 P.M. $; under age 12, free • **Goodspeed Opera**

House, East Haddam, 873-8668. Performances April to November. Phone for current offerings • **Gillette Castle,** Gillette Castle State Park, 67 River Road (off Route 82), East Haddam, 526-2336. Hours: Memorial Day to Columbus Day, daily, 10 A.M. to 5 P.M.; October to mid-December, weekends only, 10 A.M. to 4 P.M. $$. Park open all year; no fee for visiting the park • **Camelot Cruises,** 1 Marine Park, Haddam, 345-8591, phone for current schedules and rates for lunch and dinner cruises • **Deep River Navigation Company,** River Street, Deep River, 526-4954. Phone for information about cruises connecting with the steam train and out of Middletown.

INFORMATION   Connecticut River and Shoreline Visitors Council, 393 Main Street, Middletown, CT 06457, 347-0028 or (800) 486-3346.

Mountains and Sea in Camden

Captain John Smith (of Pocahontas fame) said it well: "Camden lies under the high mountains of the Penobscot against whose feet the sea doth beat."

In less poetic terms, Camden, Maine, is a town where the mountains meet the sea. The deep blue natural harbor fed by rushing falls reflects the wooded slopes of Mt. Battie and Mt. Megunticook in a scenic juxtaposition that has won the admiration of visitors ever since the days of Samuel de Champlain and other early explorers.

It is a winning summer destination that becomes doubly appealing in early fall when the crowds recede and the harbor begins to mirror the myriad autumn colors of the mountains. Middle to late September, before the Camden windjammer fleet calls it a season, is an ideal time for a visit.

At the turn of the century, Camden's favored location attracted the wealthy, who built elaborate summer homes here and traveled up the coast by steamer to vacation. The homes still grace the town, but today Camden is a tourist magnet for everyone. The well-kept village, festooned with hanging flowerpots on every available lamppost, has good reason for its boast of being "the prettiest town in Maine." The harbor scene has been made even more picturesque by the presence of New England's largest fleet of windjammers, the many-masted sailing ships patterned after clipper ships of old.

The resulting influx of visitors has transformed quiet Camden into an attractive browser's town filled with shops, galleries, and restaurants, and has led to a bumper crop of lodgings that can't be beat anywhere on the Maine coast.

The queen is Norumbega, a virtual castle, with many porches and balconies overlooking the ocean. The elaborate carving, golden oak paneling, and other touches that make this residence so distinctive have been restored to mint condition. The furnishings in the public rooms and seven bedrooms do justice to their formal setting.

Camden also has a number of attractive small bed-and-breakfast inns, most of them on High Street, which is U.S. Route 1 up the hill just north of town. One of the nicest is the Edgecombe-Coles House, right across the street from Norumbega. Set well back from the road, it is one of the early summer homes, furnished with antiques and with a warm country feel. Though many of the inns are first-rate, Route 1 can be quite busy, and the Nathaniel Hosmer Inn has special appeal because of its location, on a quiet block in town away from traffic but with easy walking distance of shops and the harbor. The white clapboard inn is done in authentic early American decor.

The rambling Whitehall Inn, circa 1834, is the dowager resort in town, the place where Edna St. Vincent Millay was discovered by a wealthy patron when she read her poem "Renascence" in the parlor now named for her. Two other options are the High Tide Inn, an unpretentious lodge-and-cottage arrangement right on the water, and the Samoset Resort, not far away in Rockport, which provides tennis, golf, and many other amenities in a setting hugging the sea.

Wherever you stay, it's Camden's public landing that most people head for first of all, to admire the sleek boats in the harbor and to take in the extraordinary view—Camden's hills rising on one side, Penobscot Bay opening on the other.

The tall-masted windjammers in the harbor can be sailed for two hours, overnight, or on three-to-six-day cruises, returning in a regal display of furling sails. Although some of these "tall ships" were built exclusively for the tourist trade, others had intriguing histories as Grand Banks fishing schooners or as pilot ships before they were converted to passenger vessels.

The local tourist office is behind the parking lot at the landing and is well stocked with information and maps. You can't miss all the shops on Bayview Street, Bayview Landing, and Main Street. A town tour proceeds from the landing left past the shops to the Yacht Club, a fixture on the docks since 1906, and along the water to the Camden Harbour Inn, which has an especially nice harbor view from the front porch.

Turn right on Limerock past the inn, then right again on Chestnut to see some of the town's finest homes. Number 77 is Thayercroft, a distinguished 1821 house that was a setting for the movie *Peyton Place*. This entire block is lined with historic homes from the late 1700s and early 1800s, including the Hathaway-Cushing-Millay House, at number 31, which belonged to members of the family of Edna St. Vincent Millay.

Past the Baptist church, you'll be back at the village green, where you can bear left to Elm and Wood and Pleasant to see more homes, or take a stroll down Main Street to see some more interesting nineteenth-century town architecture while you check out the shops. You'll no doubt want to return to the many other shops around the landing as well.

Like many Maine towns that attract tourists, Camden has become a showcase for talented state artisans, and you'll be able to find anything from hand-thrown pottery to handmade fisherman's sweaters. The Patchwork Barn offers the work of many Maine craftspeople, and Once A Tree displays fine woodworking. Among the many shops on Bayview, Unique 1 specializes in Maine woolen sweaters plus ceramics, and Ducktrap Bay Trading Company, near the public landing, has decoys and other nautical carvings. Back on Main, you'll be offered complimentary coffee or tea on a balcony overlooking the harbor at the Smiling Cow, a crafts and gift store that has been run by the same family on the same spot since 1940. The Admiral's Buttons is one of many clothing stores in town that sell chic and practical boating attire.

If you're ready for a lunch break, two good choices are Cappy's Chowder House, on Main, or the Waterfront, with a deck on the harbor. Or you might choose to pick up a lunch and picnic on the grassy slopes of the Camden Amphitheater, behind the library, a pleasant place from which to gaze at the harbor view. Another possibility is the shoreside picnic area at Camden Hills State Park, on Route 1 just north of town.

Lunch or not, take the park toll road to the top of Mt. Battie for an exceptional view of the town and the harbor below. A short, steep hiking trail from Megunticook Street in Camden will also bring you to the top.

In fact, some of Maine's most scenic hiking is in this park. The top of Mt. Megunticook, the second highest point on the Atlantic seaboard, can be reached from park headquarters on Route 1 in a one-hour hike that includes a stop at a natural grotto. Megunticook Lake and Megunticook River separate the several peaks in the park's 5,000 acres from the Camden hills, making for views on all sides. In winter, Mt. Battie and Camden Snow Bowl are among the rare places where you can see the sea as you ski.

If you prefer your water views from the side of a boat, you'll find several going out on excursions from the landing into Penobscot Bay. The season ends in late fall, but year-round you can drive north to Lincolnville and board the ferry for the 25-minute crossing to Isleboro or go south to Rockland for the ferry rides to Vinalhaven or North Ferry Islands, an hour and a half and an hour and ten minutes away, respectively. Boats to Monhegan Island leave from Port Clyde.

Vinalhaven is the biggest of the islands, with shops and an art gallery, and Monhegan is by far the most scenic, with dramatic clifftop vistas of the sea. Isleboro offers a state park, a Sailor's Memorial Museum, a gallery, beaches, and the Dark Harbor House, if you want to get away from it all. These are pleasant outings on a fine fall day. There's also a good chance of spotting seals cavorting in the water along the way—and even dolphins and whales, if you are lucky. Some of the ferries do not operate on Sunday, so check current schedules before you plan a trip. Excursions and windjammers go out of Rockland Harbor as well; inquire at the public landing.

Rockland, a working fishermen's town, is coming into its own with a most attractive inn and some excellent dining. The big draw here is the Farnsworth Art Museum, a superior regional museum of paintings and sculpture. Among the Maine collections are works by all three generations of Wyeths, who will soon have their own gallery in a converted church near the museum. The handsome Farnsworth Homestead, the home of the museum's benefactress, adjoins the museum. Museum goers have attracted a few excellent art galleries to town.

Another highly recommended excursion is the six-mile drive to Rockport Village, a tiny and totally charming fishing and shipbuilding village dating back to the early 1770s. The entire village was made a Historic District in the mid-1970s, and there are some 127 buildings listed in the inventory.

In Marine Park, overlooking the harbor, you'll find a statue of Andre the Seal, a late local hero who used to swim up from Boston to spend the summer every year. Smart seal.

Rockport has become very much an artists' town; it is the home of the Maine Coast Artists Gallery, in a strikingly renovated old livery station-cum-firehouse, and is also host to the campus of the respected Maine Photography Workshops. The restored Town Hall–Opera House is known for its acoustics and is home to summer Bay Chamber Concerts, theater, and other cultural events.

What to do in Rockport? Visit the Artists Gallery, check for a last exhibition at the Photography Workshop Gallery, and wander through the handful of galleries and shops on Main Street. Then admire the many fine historic homes on almost any village street and drive out to Vesper Hill, known as the Children's Chapel, a gift to the community from a former resident, for a quiet and beautiful spot overlooking the sea. You'll understand why this is a favorite locale for marriages. The Sail Loft is the place if you want to have Sunday brunch or dinner overlooking the harbor. If you fall in love with the town, as many visitors do, you may be able to arrange for rooms in the Rockport Harbor Inn, with smashing views of the harbor.

Area Code: 207

DRIVING DIRECTIONS   Camden is about halfway between Portland and Bar Harbor on U.S. Route 1 on the Maine coast. From the

Maine Turnpike, take Route 17 east to Route 90 to Route 1. It is about 200 miles from Boston, 400 miles from New York, and 290 miles from Hartford.

PUBLIC TRANSPORTATION   Concord Trailways bus service to Camden. Air service to Bangor, 50 miles away; Portland, 85 miles away; or Rockland, 8 miles away. You can manage easily without a car if you stay in town; get to the park by hike or bike, or use the Camden shuttle, which runs from mid-June through October.

ACCOMMODATIONS   All Camden addresses are zip code 04843. *Top picks:* **Norumbega,** 61 High Street, 236-4646, exceptional, EE, CP • **Edgecombe-Coles House,** 64 High Street, 236-2336, M–E, CP • **Nathaniel Hosmer Inn,** 4 Pleasant Street, 236-4012 or (800) 423-4012, M, CP. *More good choices:* **Whitehall Inn,** 52 High Street, Camden, 236-3391, full-service inn with tennis, boating, golf privileges for guests, M–E, CP; E, MAP • **Camden Harbour Inn,** 83 Bayview Street, Camden, 236-4200, M–EE, CP • **Swan House,** 49 Mountain Street, Camden, 236-8275 or (800) 207-8275, cozy, nice location off the main highway, very special rooms are in the Cygnet Annex, I–M, CP • **Maine Stay,** 22 High Street, Camden, 236-9636, 1802 home with a grand old-fashioned kitchen complete with cast-iron stove, M, CP • **Windward House,** 6 High Street, 236-9656, Greek Revival home circa 1854, canopy beds, comfortable decor, M–E, CP • **Hawthorn Inn,** 9 High Street, 236-8842, 1894 Victorian, carriage house rooms have Jacuzzis, TV-VCRs, fireplaces, M–E, CP • **Highland Mill Inn,** Mechanic and Washington Streets, Camden, 236-1057 or (800) 841-5590, refurbished mill on the river, some decks, M–E, CP • **Rockport Harbor House,** 11 Mechanic Street, Rockport 04856, 236-2422, just two rooms, but a stunning home with balconies on the harbor, M–E, CP • **The High Tide Inn,** Route 1 North, Camden, 236-3724, motel directly on the water north of town, inn rooms, M; cottages, I–E; oceanview motel, I–M; oceanfront motel, M–E • **Samoset Resort,** Rockport 04856, 594-2511 or (800) 341-1650, tennis, golf, indoor and outdoor pools, gym, E–EE • **Captain Lindsey House Inn,** 5 Lindsey Street, Rockland 04841, 596-7950, stylishly furnished rooms, hotel amenities, M–E, CP • **Inn at Sunrise Point,** Lincolnville (north of Camden), 236-7716 or (800) 435-6278, private hideaway on the water, light and airy rooms, very private cottages, E–EE, CP; cottages, EE, CP.

DINING   **Belmont,** 6 Belmont Avenue, 236-8053, long considered one of the best in town, M–E • **The Waterfront,** Bayview Street, Harbor Square, 236-3747, outdoor deck on the harbor, good for lunch, or dinner, I–M • **Frogwater Café,** 31 Elm Street, Camden, 236-8998, healthy, innovative menus, many vegetarian dishes, I–M • **Peter Ott's,**

16 Bayview Street, 236-4032, reliable old-timer, varied menu, salad bar, I–E • **O'Neil's,** 21 Bayview Street, 236-3272, casual, brick oven pizza, I–M • **Whitehall Dining Room** (see above), New England fare, M • **Marcel's,** Samoset Resort (see above), continental, recommended both for cuisine and setting, M–E • **Chez Michel,** Route 1, Lincolnville Beach, 789-5600, country French, M • **The Sail Loft,** Public Landing, Rockport, 236-2330, seafood and harbor views, I–E • **Jessica's Bistro,** 2 South Main Street, Rockland, 596-0770, M • **Café Miranda,** 15 Oak Street, Rockland, 594-2034, pasta, brick oven pizza, seafood, and grill dishes, I–M. *Informal fare:* **Cappy's Chowder House,** 1 Main Street, Camden, 236-2254, open 7:30 A.M. to midnight, try the chowder, I–M • **Sea Dog Brewing Company,** 43 Mechanic Street, 236-6863, brew-pub, tavern menu; brewery tours daily June through October at 11 A.M., rest of year on Saturday at 3 P.M., I–M • **The Waterworks,** Lindsey Street, Rockland, 596-7950, I–M. *For lobster:* **Lobster Pound Restaurant,** Route 1, Lincolnville Beach (next town north of Camden), 789-5550, open 11:30 A.M. to 9 P.M. in summer, after Labor Day best to check hours; closes Columbus Day • **Young's Lobster Pound,** Mitchell Avenue (follow signs from Route 1), Belfast, 469-3963, classic by-the-sea setting for those who are driving farther north from Camden.

SIGHTSEEING **Camden Hills State Park,** Route 1 North, Camden, 236-3109. Free except toll road to top of Mt. Battie. Shore area open May to November, small fee. Hiking trail maps available at Information Center on Route 1 • **Maine Coast Artists Gallery,** Russell Avenue, Rockport, 236-2875. Hours: April through mid-October, daily, 10 A.M. to 5 P.M. Donation • **Farnsworth Museum,** 352 Main Street (Route 1), Rockland, 596-6457. Hours: June to mid-October, Monday to Saturday, 10 A.M. to 5 P.M., Sunday from noon. Closed Mondays from October. $$; under 8, free. Admission includes Farnsworth Homestead, open June to September. *Cruises:* Public landing, June to September, many options; inquire at Camden Chamber of Commerce for current schedules and rates • **Maine State Ferry Service,** Route 1, Lincolnville Beach, 780-5611, and 517A Main Street, Rockland, 596-2202; inquire for current schedules. *Windjammer Cruise Information:* Maine Windjammer Association, PO Box 1144, Blue Hill, ME, 04614, (800) 807-WIND.

INFORMATION Rockport-Camden-Lincolnville Chamber of Commerce, PO Box 919, Camden, ME 04843, 236-4404. Information booth at public landing parking lot.

A Bewitching Halloween in Salem

It stands to reason. Since Salem, Massachusetts, is known for the long-ago days when witch fever swept the town, it seems only natural that Halloween is a cause for celebration here.

Not that Salem today bears much resemblance to the town that was notorious for its witch hunting. These days visitors will see a pleasant New England maritime center dating back to 1626, with a nicely spruced up historic waterfront and center. It is as much a literary shrine for its "House of Seven Gables" complex as a reminder of witch-trial terror. For a relatively small town, Salem has a large share of sights, including an exceptional museum and some handsome old sea captains' mansions.

But there's no question that Salem is a great place to be at Halloween, since the whole town gets into the spirit of the holiday for a full three weeks before the big day, with almost all of the many attractions in town turning eerie for the occasion. There are haunted houses for touring, ghost-story tellings, spooky tours on foot and by trolley, costume contests, and a costume parade on the common—even a Psychic Fair and Witchcraft Expo with lots of psychics on hand, ready to read your fortune. You can join a spooky candlelit tour of the House of Seven Gables or take in Eerie Events at the Peabody Essex Museum, where professional actors in historical costumes present legends in the museum's historic houses and gardens. If you really want to get into the spirit of things, you can take a class on mediumship and attend a séance. Latter-day witches wearing "Ask a Witch" buttons are posted throughout town to give factual answers about Halloween customs and practices, Salem history, and the state of witchcraft today.

The events change slightly from year to year as more activities are continually added to the roster. Contact the Office of Tourism in advance for the printed program so you can plan your time.

A highlight for most people is the Salem Witch Museum, a stone building on Washington Square, across from the Salem Common. It is crowded during Halloween weekends, so an early or late visit is a good idea. On weekends before and on Halloween night, the museum usually stays open until midnight. The excellent presentation here puts you in the center of a darkened room and uses spotlights to showcase the life-size reenactments of the shameful 1692 hysteria.

Salem's was not the only witchcraft trial in New England, but it was by far the worst. The only thing to be said for the debacle was that the revulsion it caused finally put an end to sentencing so-called witches to death. To mark the 300th anniversary of the trials in 1992, the town erected a simple stone memorial as a reminder of the need for tolerance.

If you want more witching entertainment, there's no shortage in town. The Salem Witch Village goes into facts and fictions associated with witchcraft, and the Witch Dungeon Museum presents a re-creation of the 1692 events with live actors, purportedly taking their scripts from historical transcripts.

The Witch House, in Salem, turns out to be the restored home of Jonathan Corwin, judge of the original witchcraft court. Preliminary examinations of the accused were held here, but the residence is actually of far more interest as one of the oldest dwellings in the United States. Built in the early seventeenth century, it is filled with a fine collection of furniture and household items from that period.

A number of other handsome historic houses in Salem have been preserved with period furnishings and been opened to the public. One standout is the Stephen Phillips Memorial Trust House, a Federal-style mansion filled with early English and American furnishings, rare Chinese porcelains, and memorabilia from the era of sailing ships.

Several fine homes are maintained and operated by the Peabody Essex Museum. The oldest of these houses, the John Ward House, dates to 1684, with furnishings reflecting the spare ambience of the seventeenth century. The Crowninshield-Bentley House, circa 1727, is a handsome example of Salem's eighteenth-century architecture with furnishings befitting the home of a prominent merchant during Salem's heyday as a shipping port.

The Peabody Essex Museum was created in 1992 by merging two institutions, one of the oldest historical societies in the country and the oldest continuously operating museum. It is now one of New England's largest museums, and its expansion has transformed the center of Salem. On display are nearly half a million objects, including important art and artifacts from Japan, China, the Pacific Islands, Southeast Asia, and Africa. One of the superb research libraries, the Phillips Library, contains the original court documents of the 1692 witch trials, along with original manuscripts by Nathaniel Hawthorne and rare ships' logs from early voyages to China.

The Essex Street portion of the two-building complex contains the art and artifacts of Salem's Essex County since its beginnings, including displays of furniture, clocks, china, silver, paintings, and military memorabilia. It is attractively laid out on two floors around a Federal-period garden.

The Liberty Street building, across the square, holds treasures brought back by Salem mariners who navigated the seas near or beyond the Cape of Good Hope or Cape Horn. In those days, Salem was one of the busiest seaports on the East Coast, and her ships were found in all the world's waters. The "curiosities" garnered by the ships' captains formed the basis of the original Peabody Museum. The holdings were augmented when the Peabody merged with the China Trade Museum of Milton, Massachusetts, in 1984. A whole wing was added to house the permanent collection of some 12,000 pieces of Asian export art, paintings, and decorative works. It also holds some fascinating nautical exhibits of scrimshaw, figureheads, old fishing implements, and navigational instruments. There's even a full-size reconstruction of the master's saloon on the *Cleopatra's Barge,* built in 1816 as America's first oceangoing vessel.

It's probably best to schedule one museum per day to get the most of each—but even then you won't have exhausted the most important sights of Salem. The Salem Maritime National Historic Site, overseen by the National Park Service, is playing a growing role, as is evidenced by the information center that opened in 1994 near the Peabody Essex Museum in the heart of the town's central pedestrians-only mall.

The Park Service has recently completed restoring Salem's three historic wharves: Derby Wharf, Hatch's Wharf, and Central Wharf. All were originally built in the 1760s and are the only remaining earthen wharfs in North America. At the height of Salem's boom seaport years, there were 50 such wharves in the harbor.

A 171-foot full-size replica of the three-masted East India sailing merchant ship *Friendship,* launched in 1797, is docked at Derby Wharf.

On land, the 9.4-acre Salem Maritime National Historic Site includes the original 1819 U.S. Customs House, where Nathaniel Hawthorne worked as a surveyor of the port of Salem in the late 1840s. Other buildings include the historic Derby, Narbonne, and Hawkes Houses, and the West India Goods Store, believed to have been established about 1800 by Captain Henry Prince to sell cargoes he brought back from Africa. It is now a combination history exhibit and gift shop.

Across the street is the House of Seven Gables, made immortal by Nathaniel Hawthorne's novel. It was actually the 1668 home of ship captain John Turner. The house, with its secret stairway, is a charmer, and it is easy to see why it captured Hawthorne's imagination when he came to visit his cousin, Susan Ingersoll, whose family lived in the house. The Turner house is part of a small historic complex of early homes, including Hawthorne's own birthplace, an antiques-filled, gambrel-roofed, seventeenth-century residence that was moved to this appropriate site in 1958. An outdoor café here is set amid lovely perennial gardens.

A more modern addition to the waterfront is nearby Pickering Wharf, a replica of a commercial wharf lined with shops and restaurants.

Also of interest, especially if you've brought children along, is the Salem 1630: Pioneer Village, a living history museum re-creating the earlest Salem settlement, with thatched cottages, workshops, wigwams, gardens, and animals of the period. Guides in period costumes tell about the people, conditions, and politics of the era, and demonstrate period skills and chores.

As if it weren't difficult enough to fit all of Salem's sights into a weekend, there's the lure of Marblehead, one of the shore's most picturesque seaside communities, beckoning just four miles away. When George Washington visited here, he noted that Marblehead certainly had "the look of antiquity." Some 200 years later you can walk the same twisting streets and see the same mix of merchants' mansions and steep-gabled fishermen's cottages that mark this village's 350-year existence as a seaport. The harbor is a veritable forest of sailboat masts; the tiny village is lined with intriguing shops.

A ride along the steep shoreline past the homes crowded pell-mell along the winding lanes is exceptional and shouldn't be missed. The area's loveliest inns are here, including Spraycliff, right on the water with spectacular views. If you can't stay a while, at least stop for fried clams and chowder at the Barnacle, the best place in town for boat-watching, and give yourself time for a drive. The biggest houses are across the causeway at Marblehead Neck, the hilly peninsula that shelters the harbor from the open sea. You can actually stay here at the Seagull Inn, where there are more water vistas.

Better yet, enjoy the spooky high jinks of Halloween and then think about a return visit to Marblehead in the spring. After the goblins have gone, you can concentrate on the rest of the sights of these two intriguing neighbors by the sea.

Area Codes: Salem, 978; Marblehead, 617

DRIVING DIRECTIONS Salem is located on the Massachusetts shore 16 miles north of Boston at exit 25E off Route 128. Parking is difficult; entering the city, follow information signs for downtown parking. Salem is 238 miles from New York and 128 miles from Hartford.

PUBLIC TRANSPORTATION MBTA bus and North Station train service from Boston; call (800) 392-6100 for bus or train information. All lodgings listed in Salem are in the center of town, within easy walking distance to all sights.

ACCOMMODATIONS All Salem zip codes are 01970. • **Hawthorne Hotel,** 18 Washington Square West, Salem, 744-4080, Federal-style, renovated 1920s landmark in the town center, M–E • **Salem Inn,** 7 Summer Street, Salem, 741-0680 or (800) 446-2995, two brick 1800s sea captains' homes, pleasant rooms, a top choice, M–E, CP • **Amelia Payson Guest House,** 16 Winter Street, Salem, 744-8304, 1845 Greek Revival home, small, nicely decorated, M, CP • **The Stepping Stone Inn,** 19 Washington Square North, 745-2156, bed-and-breakfast home on the green, M, CP • **Suzannah Flint House,** 98 Essex Street, Salem, 744-5281 or (800) 752-5281, modest bed-and-breakfast inn, central location, M, CP • **The Inn at 7 Winter Street,** 7 Winter Street, Salem,

745-9520, Victorian bed-and-breakfast inn, M–E, CP • **Spray Cliff,** 25 Spray Avenue, Marblehead 01945, 744-8924 or (800) 626-1530, English Tudor with airy, attractive decor, grand ocean views, E, CP • **Harbor Light Inn,** 58 Washington Street, Marblehead 01945, 631-2186, elegant, special, beams and four-posters, pool, in the center of town, M –EE, CP • **Seagull Inn B&B,** 106 Harbor Avenue, Marblehead 01945, 631-6789 or (800) 626-1530, spacious quarters, TV-VCRs with big film library, distant water views, one great suite/apartment with deck, M–EE, CP.

DINING   Lyceum Bar and Grill, 43 Church Street, Salem, 745-7665, historic building, longtime local favorite, M • **Nathaniel's,** Hawthorne Hotel, Salem (see above), elegant dining room, American menu, M–E • **Museum Café,** Peabody Essex Museum, East India Square, Salem, 745-1876, fine dining overlooking oriental garden; lunch and Sunday brunch, I; Friday evening prix fixe dinner, EE • **Roosevelt's,** 300 Derby Street, Salem, 745-9608, fun Teddy Roosevelt decor, I–M • **Stromberg's,** 2 Bridge Street, Salem, 744-1863, informal, good chowder, seafood, outdoor deck with harbor view, I–M • **The Barnacle,** 141 Front Street, Marblehead, 631-4236, basic seafood and the best view in town, I–M • **The Landing,** 81 Front Street, Marblehead, 631-1878, pub/restaurant, deck directly on the harbor, I–M • **Pellino's Fine Italian Dining,** 261 Washington Street, Marblehead, 631-3344, the name says it, M.

SIGHTSEEING   Salem Halloween Happenings, three weeks in October, ending on Halloween. Write to Office of Tourism for complete current schedule • **Salem Witch Museum,** 19 Washington Square North, 744-1692. Hours: daily, 10 A.M. to 5 P.M.; July and August to 7 P.M.; later during Halloween weekends. $$ • **Peabody Essex Museum,** East India Square, 745-9500. Hours: June through October, Monday to Saturday, 10 A.M. to 5 P.M., Friday to 8 P.M., Sunday noon to 5 P.M.; November through Memorial Day, closed Mondays. Admission, including historic houses, $$ • **Salem Maritime National Historic Site,** 174 Derby Street, 740-1680. Hours: daily, 9 A.M. to 4:30 P.M. Guided tours available. Free • **House of Seven Gables,** 54 Turner Street, 744-0991. Guided tours, July to Labor Day, daily, 9 A.M. to 6 P.M.; rest of year, daily, 10 A.M. to 4:30 P.M. $$$ • **The Witch House,** 310 Essex Street, 744-0180. Hours: July 1 to Labor Day, 10 A.M. to 6 P.M., May 15 to July 30 and Labor Day to December 1, 10 A.M. to 4:30 P.M. $$ • **Salem Witch Village,** 282 Rear Derby Street, 740-9229. Hours: May through October, daily, 9 A.M. to 6 P.M.; rest of year to 5 P.M. $$ • **Witch Dungeon Museum,** 16 Lynde Street, 741-3570. Hours: April through November, daily, 10 A.M. to 5 P.M. $$ • **Salem 1630: Pioneer Village,** Forest River Park (off West Avenue), Salem, 745-0525. Hours: Memorial Day to October 31, Monday to Saturday,

10 A.M. to 5 P.M., Sunday and holidays, noon to 5 P.M. $$ • **National Park Service Visitor Center,** 2 Liberty Street, 740-1650. Area information, film on historic Essex County. Hours: Summer, daily, 9 A.M. to 6 P.M.; winter, weekdays only, 10 A.M. to 5 P.M.

INFORMATION Salem Office of Tourism and Cultural Affairs, Old Town Hall, 93 Washington Street, Salem, MA 01970, 745-9595.

A Peak Experience at Killington

Back in 1739, Reverend Samuel Peters stood atop the 4,241-foot peak of Killington Mountain, surveyed the land around him, and christened the land "Verd-Mont," the name that stuck ever after, eventually causing Vermont to be known as the Green Mountain State.

It's probably fortunate that the good reverend made the climb in the "verd" of summer, for had he come to the top of Killington in autumn, Vermont might have gone nameless. The five-state panorama of mountains and valleys cloaked in crimson, gold, and orange has left more than one viewer at a total loss for words.

The good news is that nowadays you don't even have to climb for the view. The Killington gondola and Skyeship are in service in the fall; the new gondola brings leaf watchers to the highest point reached by aerial lift in Vermont.

The rides alone are good reason to plan an early October weekend near Killington, but the area has more than its share of lures all year long. In addition to being the largest ski complex in the East, with six mountains to choose from, this is prime hiking territory, offering both the Appalachian and Long Trails, which converge on Route 4 at a point near Pico, Killington's smaller ski mountain neighbor. Tennis and golf facilities are plentiful, and you'll search far to find more scenic backroading via bike, horseback, or car. Mountain-biking enthusiasts take their bikes up on the Killington gondola and enjoy panoramic views coming down on 37 miles of trails. The interesting sights to be seen nearby make a visit all the more rewarding.

The same rugged terrain that makes the area so attractive also prevents it from having a central village. Rutland is 16 miles to the west on Route 4, and Woodstock is 19 miles to the east on the same road. But other than the ski-lodge motels on the access road, accommodations near Killington are scattered. They run the gamut from motel to condominium to cozy inn to full-scale resort, and where you stay may well depend on just how much activity you have in mind, as well as on your budget.

One major advantage to a popular ski area with over 100 lodgings in the vicinity is that even at the height of the foliage season, when all the country inns have been booked up for months, some of those motels on the access road or Route 4 may still have vacancy signs. And the Lodging Bureau of the Killington & Pico Areas Association is available to help you find a place with just one phone call.

If you plan ahead, two of the prime inn candidates are in Chittenden, a small village with an attractive reservoir, tucked away from it all in the woods on a back road about six miles from Route 4. For a secluded, homey country inn where meals are served family-style and guests get a chance to know one another, Tulip Tree Inn is the place. This is just what many people imagine a country inn should be—tastefully done but simple, comfortable, and warm. The newest addition here is fireplaces in the guest rooms.

Not far away is Mountain Top Inn, an unpretentious small resort with a spectacular 500-acre site high above a lake surrounded by mountains. The views from the inn terrace and dining rooms are unbeatable. There's everything to do here, and if the tab is within your budget, you won't go wrong.

Red Clover Inn, on 13 acres with mountain views, offers a gracious stay out in the country in Mendon and some lovely new accommodations with fireplaces and double whirlpool tubs. Vermont Inn, just off Route 4, is homey and more reasonably priced, and though it has a motel layout, the Cortina Inn is quite elegant; both have resort facilities.

The Inn of the Six Mountains, located on the Killington access road, is a somewhat citified hotel but has nicely furnished rooms, indoor and outdoor pools, and exercise and game rooms. The Villages at Killington will suit those who like spacious condominium accommodations. It is a mountainside community with tennis, golf, lakes, and ponds.

One last luxurious possibility is Hawk Inn and Mountain Resort, not far from Killington on Route 100 in Plymouth. There's a well-appointed small modern inn, but for views and privacy, opt for the fieldstone-and-wood condos and homes high on the mountainside, where you'll have picture windows to bring in the view and big stone fireplaces to warm those cool Vermont evenings.

If you choose more modest accommodations, take note that you can still have access to the stables at Mountain Top and Hawk, and tennis courts can be rented at Cortina Inn or at the Killington Resorts. Bikes can be rented at the Peak Performance Sport Shop, on the Killington Road, or at the Mountain Bike Shop, at the Killington Base Lodge. You can also take advantage of the many health spas offering whirlpool, massage, and other nice things. These include the Pico Sports Center, the Spa at the Woods, and the Mountain Green Health Spa.

Having settled in, you can plan your activities. If hiking is on the agenda, a popular short trek is the Deer Leap Trail at Sherburne Pass, which takes about half an hour to go up a steep winding path ending on a cliff with a panoramic view from 2,390 feet up. All the skiing trails on Killington and Pico become hiking trails off-season. The Merrell Hiking Center, located at the Killington base lodge, can provide both guided hikes and an educational trail map for self-guided tours in the area. A combination tour includes a three-hour guided hike and a gondola ride to the summit.

Vermont's well-known Long Trail runs from Killington Mountain to Pico and then down to Sherburne Pass on Route 4. If you start at the top by taking the gondola to the summit, average time down is about three hours.

Hike or not, that gondola ride is quite something, with the Green, White, Berkshire, and Adirondack Mountains spread out around you. On the right day, you can see all the way to Canada. The Skyeship offers almost equally thrilling views.

There is a more adventurous scenic ride in store if you take the chairlift up to the Alpine Slide at Pico and come down the trails traveling some 3,410 feet on a sled. The sled has a control stick, so you needn't worry about descending at breakneck speed; you set your own pace. Pico's attractions also include a trampoline and mini-golf.

Most people choose a more earthbound kind of ride, doing the back roads by car. It's usually most pleasant to plan a route with sightseeing stops along the way, and that's easy to do in this area.

Heading north, you might want to begin by following Route 4 through Rutland and then north on Route 3 to Proctor, a town where everything is made of marble, from the schools and churches to the sidewalks and the bridge spanning Otter Creek.

Proctor is the heart of the Vermont marble industry and the largest marble production center in the country. A film at the Vermont Marble Exhibit briefly explains how the marble quarried from the Green Mountains is processed into the handsome polished slabs that mark many of the nation's best-known buildings. From the visitor's gallery you can watch huge slabs weighing up to ten tons swing through the air to the diamond-blade coping saws that slice them right before your eyes.

A sculptor is in residence to show how marble can be polished and carved into works of art, and the hall of presidents displays the heads of 40 former chief executives, carved from purest white marble, a 20-year project for one of Vermont's finest sculptors. Slabs and seconds are for sale at the marble market outside, in case you want to take home a tabletop as a souvenir, and many smaller marble items are available inside at the gift shop.

The little town of Proctor is also home to Wilson Castle, a nineteenth-century mansion on a 115-acre estate. It is quite a place, with 84 stained-glass windows, hand-painted ceilings, and priceless oriental and European antiques, as well as fine art and sculpture.

Having had your fill of finery, head north from Proctor to Route 7 and Pittsford, where you can learn about another backbone Vermont industry, maple sugaring, at the New England Maple Museum. This small museum doesn't look too promising at first glance, but it turns out to be quite interesting. Watch the slide show to find out how sap is turned to syrup, then inspect the tools involved—in this case, one of the largest collections of antique sugaring equipment ever assembled. The history of maple sugaring is shown in over 100 feet of murals painted by artist Grace Brigham. There's also a simulation of modern techniques, complete with sap dripping from a tree into a bucket, with the wonderful smell of boiling syrup at the end of the process permeating everything. Needless to say, there is a gift shop waiting, filled with you-know-what, and you get the chance to sample different grades of maple syrup.

A little farther north is Brandon, a pleasant village with some 200 historic buildings around two village greens. Among these buildings is the Stephen Douglas Homestead, the home of the famous orator who debated Abraham Lincoln. The Brandon Antiques Center, on Route 7, is a recommended stop for treasure hunters.

For views, the best bets are the roads that cut across the mountains. Brandon Gap, running from Route 7 to Route 100, is unexcelled. If you want to do a giant scenic loop back, follow Route 100 five miles north to Hancock, with a detour there to Route 125 to see the cascades at the Texas Falls Recreation Area.

Then make the drive from Route 100 back to Route 7 across the Middlebury Gap, also known as the Robert Frost Memorial Drive. Frost's home was in Ripton, a town along the gap road. You'll come out in East Middlebury, just four miles from the attractive college town with its excellent Vermont State Crafts Center at Frog Hollow. Middlebury also has many shops that make for pleasant browsing. (Read more about the town's sights on pages 130–131.)

An alternative return route is to go back to Brandon and then south on Route 30 to Lake Bomoseen in Castleton or Lake St. Catherine in Poultney, both in attractive state parks and ideal for picnicking.

You can easily fill a weekend admiring nature via gondola, slide, hiking boots, or automobile, but if you want indoor diversions, Rutland offers the Chaffee Art Gallery, with continuous exhibits, and the Norman Rockwell Museum, on Route 4 east of town, which has more than 1,000 pictures, including his famous Four Freedoms and Boy Scouts series, Rockwell memorabilia, and all 326 of his *Saturday Evening Post* covers.

For attractive shops, drive farther east on Route 4 to the lovely town of Woodstock. Or, for a final dose of both scenery and history, make the 11-mile drive south on Route 100 to the Plymouth Notch Historic District, and enjoy the view that made Calvin Coolidge decide he'd rather be in Vermont than be president.

<u>Area Code: 802</u>

DRIVING DIRECTIONS   Killington Mountain is on U.S. Route 4 near the junction with Route 100. Killington is 158 miles from Boston, 250 miles from New York, and 166 miles from Hartford.

PUBLIC TRANSPORTATION   Closest air service is Colgan Air to Rutland, (800) 272-5488, or major airline service to Burlington, VT; Albany, NY; or Lebanon, NH. Amtrak's Ethan Allen Express runs from New York's Penn Station to Rutland, a five-hour ride, with transfer service available to the mountain. Vermont Transit buses go to Sherburne (Killington), Rutland, and Woodstock.

ACCOMMODATIONS   Lower rates usually apply on weekdays and off-season; expect highest rates in autumn. *Resorts and resort motel/hotels:* **Mountain Top Inn,** Mountain Top Road, Chittenden 05737, 483-2311 or (800) 445-2100, pool, tennis, golf, driving range, boating, fly-fishing, horseback riding, claybird shooting, indoor exercise and recreation rooms, sauna, whirlpool, E–EE; EE, MAP • **Killington Resort Villages,** 715 Killington Road, Killington 05751, 422-3101 or (800) 789-6676, access to tennis, golf, pool, hiking, condominium units M–EE, Villager Motor Inn, pool, access to all facilities, M–E, CP • **Hawk Inn and Mountain Resort,** Route 100, Plymouth 05056, 672-3811 or (800) 451-4109, boating, fishing, horseback riding, hiking, and cycling trails, swimming pond with beach, indoor pool, health spa. Inn rooms, E–EE; town houses and homes, expensive but worth it, EE • **Cortina Inn,** Route 4, Killington 05751, 773-3331 or (800) 451-6108, upscale motel ambience, tennis, hiking, indoor pool, fitness center, CP • **Vermont Inn,** U.S. Route 4, Killington 05751, 775-0708 or (800) 541-7795, upscale motel with some inn ambience, outdoor pool, tennis, whirlpool, M–E, MAP • **The Inn of the Six Mountains,** Killington Road, Killington 05751, 422-4302 or (800) 225-0888, mountainside hotel, tennis, sauna, whirlpools, M–EE CP. *Inns:* **Tulip Tree Inn,** Chittenden Dam Road, Chittenden 05737, 483-6213 or (800) 707-0017, M–EE, MAP • **Red Clover Inn,** Woodward Road, Mendon 05701, 775-2290 or (800) 752-0571, M–EE, MAP • **Mountain Meadows Lodge,** Thundering Brook Road, Killington 05751, 775-1010 or (800) 370-4567, family-style lodge, comfortable, no frills, reasonable, M, MAP. For information on last-minute vacancies and free area reservations, contact Killington Lodging Service, (800) 621-6867.

DINING   **Hemingway's,** Route 4 (east of Route 100), 422-3886, continental, the area's best, prix fixe, EE • **Panache,** The Woods Resort, Killington Road, 422-8622, game specialties, M–EE • **Red Clover Inn** (see above), pleasant ambience in restored farmhouse, recommended, M –E • **Zola's Grille,** Cortina Inn (see above), M • **Claude's,** Killington

Road, Killington, 422-4030, elegant continental menu, M–E; or casual dining at **Choices,** I–M • **Mountain Top Inn** (see above), unbeatable view, go when it's light, M–E • **Vermont Inn** (see above), American menu, fireplace, M–E • **Santa Fe Steak House,** Killington Road, 422-2124, Southwestern plus standard menu, recommended locally, M–E • **Countryman's Pleasure,** Townline Road (off Route 4), Mendon, 773-7141, fine dining in a country home, German-Austrian menu, M–E • **Royal's 121 Hearthside,** 37 North Main Street, Rutland, 775-0856, New England specialties, I–M. *Casual dining on Killington Road, all I–M:* **Peppers,** 422-3177; **Powderhounds,** 422-4141; **Casey's Caboose,** 422-3795; **Mother Shapiro's,** 422-9933 (entertainment on weekends); and **Wobbly Barn,** 422-3392. Also see listings for Woodstock, page 7.

SIGHTSEEING **Killington Gondola,** Killington Road (five miles from junction of Routes 4 and 100), 422-6200. Hours: daily, mid-June to mid-October, 10 A.M. to 4 P.M., 9 A.M. on fall weekends, $$$$$; one-way (hike down) $$$$ • **Killington Skyeship,** Route 4 (east of Route 100), 422-6200. Same hours and similar rates to above • **Pico Alpine Slide,** Route 4, Pico, 775-4346. Hours: Memorial Day through Columbus Day, daily (weather permitting), 10 A.M. to 6 P.M., shorter hours vary after Labor Day—best to check. $$ • **Vermont Marble Exhibit,** 62 Main Street, Proctor, 459-3311. Hours: mid-May through October, daily, 9 A.M. to 5:30 P.M.; rest of year, Monday to Saturday, 9 A.M. to 4 P.M. $$ • **Wilson Castle,** West Proctor Road (off Route 4), Proctor, 773-3284. Hours: late May to mid-October, daily, 9 A.M. to 5:30 P.M. $$$ • **New England Maple Museum and Gift Shop,** U.S. Route 7, Pittsford, 483-9414. Hours: late May through October, daily, 8:30 A.M. to 5:30 P.M.; rest of year, 10 A.M. to 4 P.M.; closed January and February. $ • **Chaffee Art Center,** 16 S. Main Street (U.S. Route 7), Rutland, 775-0356. Hours: June to October, daily except Tuesday, 10 A.M. to 5 P.M.; November to May, 11 A.M. to 4 P.M. Free • **Norman Rockwell Museum,** Route 4 East, Rutland, 773-6095. Hours: daily, 9 A.M. to 6 P.M. $$ • **Plymouth Notch Historic District,** Route 100, Plymouth, 672-3773. Hours: late May to mid-October, daily, 9:30 A.M. to 5:30 P.M. $$; under age 14, free.

INFORMATION Killington and Pico Areas Association, PO Box 114, Killington, VT, 773-4181 or (800) 337-1928; Rutland Region Chamber of Commerce, 256 N. Main Street, Rutland, VT 05701, 773-2747.

Bringing the Kids to Boston

Guthrie the sea lion isn't what you would call bashful. When young volunteers help to put him through his paces—showing off his prowess at balancing balls on his nose, leaping into the air, and otherwise showing off in the water for the delighted audience at the New England Aquarium—Guthrie rewards them with a big, wet kiss, making the audience cheer even louder.

Guthrie and his equally flamboyant flippered friends are perennial favorites, but their antics are just one of many things children can cheer about in Boston. From the playful sea lions at the Aquarium to wonderfully creative museums to the Boston Tea Party ship, where visitors take a turn at tossing chests of tea overboard, this is a town filled with family activities that are as much fun for grown-ups as for the youngsters. It's hard to imagine a better joint outing for either generation. The fact that much of the fun is also educational is just icing on the cake.

Making things even nicer is a welcome from city hotels who have joined to offer "family friendly" packages. They run the gamut from video games and fun packs at Howard Johnson to miniature bath-robes, teddy bears, a reasonable children's menu, and nightly milk and cookies at the Four Seasons. The Visitors Bureau has published a special children's guide to the city. It features a sculpture tour that includes grasshoppers, dolphins, lions, horses, and a giant 12-foot bronze teddy bear outside the local FAO Schwarz on Boylston Street. And lots of other kooky pleasures are listed under the heading "Cool for Kids," including Alexander Graham Bell's Garret, the Boston Marathon Finish Line, the city's narrowest house (at 44 Hull Street in the North End), and a steaming kettle that has been boiling since 1872!

The New England Aquarium is literally guaranteed to start things off with a splash. The exhibits of more than 10,000 exotic fish and aquatic animals from around the world are exceptional, particularly the 24-foot-deep, 187,000-gallon central tank simulating a Caribbean coral reef in all its dazzling colors and shapes. A spiraling ramp lets you see huge sea turtles, inquisitive sharks, Technicolor fish, and sleek moray eels from every angle. Everyone is entranced when deep-sea divers plunge into the giant tank to feed its residents. Other exhibits guaranteed to please are the colony of penguins on the ground level, the sea otter exhibit in a naturalistic California rocky coast environment, and the "Edge of the Sea" exhibit, a replica of a Maine tidal pool that allows visitors to actually touch tidepool creatures such as sea urchins and starfish. In the show held in a boat theater next door, the performing sea lions not only entertain the kids but teach them a lot about sea mammals, ecology, and conservation.

The striking $20 million West Wing, opened in 1998, adds a two-level changing exhibit gallery, a larger free outdoor harbor seal exhibit with views above and below the water line, an enlarged book and gift shop, and a new restaurant. Exhibits here are enhanced with computer stations for more detailed information, and a television theater.

Another new attraction is the Aquarium's Medical Center, an actual working animal hospital where you can see the veterinary staff caring for sick animals and stranded animals rescued from local beaches. There's more aquatic education in store for families who sign up for the Aquarium's harbor and whale-watching cruises.

Countless groups of schoolchildren have gotten a lively lesson in American history by following the three-mile, red-brick line of Boston's Freedom Trail. It's a good idea to make the trail your introduction to the city first thing Saturday, while everyone is still fresh. It takes from two to three hours if you do the whole thing, strolling three centuries of American history. You can begin anywhere along the clearly marked lines, and any city information booth has brochures to tell you about the sights. But the best place to start is at the National Park Service Information Center, across from the Old State House. The Park Service officially maintains the major structures as Boston National Historical Park. It has guides to both the Freedom Trail and a Harbor Walk—and it also offers free guided tours.

Boston by Foot, an organization that sponsors walking tours of the city, also has a special tour, "Boston by Little Feet," designed for six- to twelve-year-olds (accompanied by adults).

If you don't think little ones can make it all on foot, there are trolleys with narration that allow you to get on and off as often as you like all day.

From the information center, the Freedom Trail runs roughly in a figure eight with a tail leading into the North End. In one loop are Boston Common, the land set aside for common use in 1634 that was a training ground for Revolutionary soldiers and is now the nation's oldest public park; the golden-domed State House, designed by Charles Bulfinch for the newly independent Commonwealth of Massachusetts; Park Street Church, where the song "America" was first sung publicly; and the Granary Burying Ground, where Paul Revere, Samuel Adams, John Hancock, James Otis, and other patriots are buried.

While you are at Boston Common, you may want to stroll over to the more formal Public Garden next door and take a ride on the famous Swan Boats, which have been a fixture here since 1877. A statue honors Mrs. Mallard and her brood, who were immortalized in Robert McCloskey's classic children's tale set in the Public Garden, *Make Way for Ducklings*.

Sights on the second loop include the 1749 Kings Chapel, the first Anglican church in the United States and later the first for the Unitarian faith; the Kings Chapel Burying Ground, established in 1630; the Old State House, where James Otis roused his countrymen in 1761 when he proclaimed, "Taxation without representation is tyranny"; and the Old Corner Book Store, a 1712 home that later became a meeting place for such authors as Longfellow, Hawthorne, Emerson, Holmes, Stowe, and Whittier.

Ahead is Faneuil Hall, nicknamed "The Cradle of Liberty" by John Adams for its fiery and eloquent town meetings of Colonial patriots. Beyond, just as the younger tour members may be getting restless, is the perfect place to take a pause from history for some good food and fun—the historic world of food at Quincy Market. There's pizza, barbecue, Chinese food, shish kebab, gyros, Polish sausage, and just about everything in between in the market stalls. Deciding which of the luscious displays to patronize is half the fun. Unless you choose to pass up the stalls to dine at one of the cafés around the market, you'll take your selection to benches outside, where there is often entertainment by street musicians to go with your meal.

After lunch, continue along the trail to the North End to see Paul Revere's home and the Old North Church, where Revere got the signal to begin his fateful ride to warn the Colonists at Lexington and Concord: "The British are coming."

The Freedom Trail ends beyond the North End in Charlestown, with two historic sites that are usually favorites of young people. In Charlestown, you can board the USS *Constitution,* the oldest commissioned ship afloat in the U.S. Navy, nicknamed "Old Ironsides" for its strong oak planking. A film, *Whites of Their Eyes,* is shown at the nearby Bunker Hill Pavilion and tells the story of the historic battle. And you can climb Bunker Hill, with its 330-foot obelisk commemorating the famous battle of June 17, 1775. A trip up the spiral stairway to the top of the monument is rewarded with a fabulous view of the city.

If you've spent the afternoon in this part of town, dinner in one of the many North End Italian restaurants is a perfect way to end the day. At the least, stop for a cannoli.

At night, one of the exciting things to do in Boston is to get a skyscraper-high view of the glimmering city from the fiftieth floor of the Prudential Tower or from the top of the John Hancock Tower.

On Sunday, head for the Children's Museum and the Computer Museum, two outstanding institutions sharing a restored warehouse on the waterfront at Museum Wharf.

The participatory displays at the Children's Museum are designed to exercise mind and muscles, teach about other cultures, introduce a bit of science—and much more. Kids in this four-story educational playland may visit a life-size Japanese home or sit in a wigwam, experiment with gravity by playing with balls on a series of giant ramps or by blowing five-foot bubbles, scale a two-story puzzle maze, or clamber through a castle. The "Grandparents' House" may bring nostalgia to parents, since it is furnished with appliances of the 1950s that many will remember. Exhibits may have changed by the time you visit, but you can depend on imagination and fun, along with a variety of activities, from crafts workshops to games from other countries.

The one-of-a-kind Computer Museum is found on the top two floors of the building. It is guaranteed to intrigue. Take a walk through the world's only two-story model of a personal computer and learn what really makes these machines tick. Kids love climbing on a giant mouse and rolling the trackball or standing on a larger-than-life keyboard, then walking inside to watch lights flash, drives spin, and information flow.

You can walk through time tunnels tracing today's personal computers back to their giant ancestors of the 1940s and 1950s, or take a turn at over 25 interactive stations that invite you to explore all the amazing things you can do with a personal computer, from experiencing virtual reality to starring in a video commercial. Equally exciting changing exhibits allow visitors to experience the latest computer developments.

The Computer Museum takes you to the future; at the other end of the street is a bit of the past, the Boston Tea Party Ship and Museum, which includes the full-scale replica tea ship, the *Brig Beaver II.* The small museum located beside the ship features exhibits and video presentations explaining what the famous tea party of Revolutionary days was all about. The big attraction is the reenactment, where you can join the Colonial guides, tossing your own case of tea overboard into the harbor, just like the protesting patriots of 1773.

The historic Harbor Walk, marked out in blue lines along the rejuvenated Boston waterfront, traces the maritime history of the city and takes you to the handsome waterfront park beyond the Marriott Hotel at Long Wharf.

If you haven't already been, you can end your day with the aquarium; it's right in front of the Marriott. If time allows, there are also harbor cruises from the Long Wharf, a treat for young seafarers.

For older children, Boston's Museum of Science is a fascinating place, with everything from dinosaur bones to an explanation of how a telephone works. This museum also has many sophisticated participatory exhibits, as well as an OMNI theater and its own fine planetarium shows. Since it is open late on Friday night, this museum can be a good warm-up for the weekend.

Nor will you find a better introduction to art than the Museum of Fine Arts, one of the country's premier art museums. It is even more spectacular since the addition of the skylighted West Wing designed by I. M. Pei.

You can also introduce your youngsters to first-class ballet in Boston, or attend the symphony—or show them how American cities looked almost 200 years ago on Beacon Hill—or step back to the re-created world of the Kennedy presidency at the museum at the John F. Kennedy Library. Or just forget about history and culture and go down to the Esplanade by the Charles River to watch the skaters and joggers in action on land and the sailboats on the water. There are several play areas to channel youthful energy with swings, slides, animal climb-ons, and jungle gyms, or you can rent a sailboat or Windsurfer at Community Boating and join the boats on the river.

Boston is a city loaded with pleasures of all kinds for all ages. It's almost guaranteed that if you come once with your family, everyone will want a second helping.

Area Code: 617

DIRECTIONS AND TRANSPORTATION   See page 80.

ACCOMMODATIONS   Most hotels, including luxury options such as the Four Seasons and Boston Harbor Hotel, have family packages; ask the Visitors Bureau for a copy of the current family-friendly hotel package brochure. Also see pages 80–81.

DINING   *A few inexpensive family recommendations:* **Bristol,** Four Seasons Hotel, 200 Boylston Street, 338-4400, featuring kids' favorites for pint-size prices, well-behaved youngsters get a menu coloring book, I; adults, M • **California Pizza Kitchen,** Prudential Center, 800 Boylston Street, 247-2352, children's menu, I • **Hard Rock Café,** 131 Clarendon Street, 424-7625, kids love it, M • **Durgin Park,** North Market (Street/Level), 227-2038, for older kids, shared tables, an only-in-Boston experience, I–M • **Faneuil Hall,** pick any of the informal cafés or patronize the stands and eat outside watching the street performers, I–M • **The Old Spaghetti Factory,** 44 Pittsburgh Street, 737-8757, near the Children's Museum, I–M • **Fuddruckers,** 8 Park Place, 723-3833, good hamburgers, children's menu, I • **Jimbo's Fish Shanty,** 245 Northern Avenue, 542-5600, on the pier, seafood in an informal setting, I–M • **Bennigan's,** 191 Stuart Street, 227-3754, predictable chain menu, reasonable, I–M • **Dick's Last Resort,** 55 Huntington Avenue, 267-8080, theme restaurant has kids' menu, balloons, colorable tablecloths, and waiters who make creative hats, I–M. For additional family dining, see lower-priced choices on pages 81–82.

SIGHTSEEING   **New England Aquarium,** Central Wharf, 973-5200. Hours: early September to June 30, Monday to Friday, 9 A.M. to 5 P.M., Saturday, Sunday, and holidays, 9 A.M. to 6 P.M.; July 1 to Labor Day, Monday, Tuesday, and Friday, 9 A.M. to 6 P.M., Wednesday and Thursday, 9 A.M. to 8 P.M., Saturday, Sunday, and holidays, 9 A.M. to 7 P.M. $$$$ • **Aquarium Harbor Tours,** April through November, check current schedules, $$$$; combination discount tickets available for aquarium and cruise • **Children's Museum of Boston,** Museum Wharf, 300 Congress Street, 426-8855. Hours: July 1 to Labor Day, daily, 10 A.M. to 5 P.M., Friday to 9 P.M.; rest of year, closed Monday except holidays. $$$; Fridays, 5 P.M. to 9 P.M., $ • **Computer Museum,** Museum Wharf, 300 Congress Street, 426-2800. Hours: Tuesday to Sunday, 10 A.M. to 5 P.M., mid-June through Labor Day to 6 P.M. $$; half price on Sunday 3 P.M. to 5 P.M. • **Boston Tea Party Ship and Museum,** Congress Street Bridge (near Museum Wharf), 338-1773. Hours: daily, March through December, 9 A.M. to 5 P.M. $$$ • **Museum of Science,** Science Park, 723-2500. Hours: daily, 9 A.M. to 5 P.M., Friday to 9 P.M. $$$$. Planetarium show, $$$; Mugar theater, $$$; discount combinations available for admission and shows • **Swan Boat Rides,** Public Garden, 522-1966. Hours: late June to Labor Day, daily, 10 A.M. to 5 P.M., weather permitting; April to June and Labor Day to mid-September, weekdays, noon to 4 P.M., weekends, 10 A.M. to 4 P.M. $. *Harbor cruises:* See pages 83–84. *Walking tours:* "Boston by Little Feet," for ages 6 to 12 (accompanied by a parent); phone Boston by Foot, 367-2345, for current information. For all other city attractions, see pages 83–84.

INFORMATION Boston Common Visitor Information Booth, Tremont Street; and Prudential Center Visitor Center, 9 A.M. to 5 P.M. daily. National Park Service Visitor Center, 15 State Street, Monday to Friday, 8 A.M. to 5 P.M., Saturday and Sunday, 9 A.M. to 5 P.M., June through August to 6 P.M. For written information, Greater Boston Convention and Visitors Bureau, Prudential Plaza, Box 490, Boston, MA 02199, 536-4100 or (800) 888-5515. Send $3.25 for a copy of the city guide for children, "Kids Love Boston."

Winter

Overleaf: *Old Sturbridge Village, Massachusetts.*

Merry Days at Mystic

Seaman John Blood was puzzled. Here it was, Christmas Eve, 1876. His boat had overcome rough seas to dock in the evening, barely in time to get him home for Christmas. And just as he was hurrying home, he was being asked to take time out to show a group of strangers through the town. An unlikely lot they were at that, wearing odd clothes like none he had ever seen before.

But it was, after all, the holiday season, so Blood decided not to leave the strangers stranded. He took up his lantern and led the way, lighting the paths of town for his charges as they wended their way to see how Christmas was celebrated a century ago in seaside towns like Mystic, Connecticut.

Lantern Light Tours at Mystic Seaport have become a treasured tradition in southeastern Connecticut, the way many families choose to mark the official start of the holiday season.

The seaport staff and local volunteers love the custom, too, and they enjoy getting into the spirit of Christmas past, taking the parts of characters who might have lived in Mystic a century ago. The hour-long tours, usually held nightly for about three weeks before Christmas, are a little different every year but take you into a variety of homes and places such as the local tavern, store, and chapel, as well as aboard a tall ship such as the *Charles W. Morgan,* where the occupants are in the midst of celebrating the season. There's plenty of merriment down at the tavern, as well, and visitors are cordially invited to join in dancing to the tune of the fiddle.

By the mid-1850s, families such as the Burrowses decorated and baked for the holidays almost the way we do today. But this Christmas Eve, Mrs. Burrows is far from happy. Her seafaring son is overdue, and she is fearful. Blood and his group have arrived just in time to see him slip in the back door to surprise his overjoyed mother.

At a stop aboard ship, the captain reminisces about Christmases spent at sea, and in the village store the shopkeeper shows the kinds of toys children will be finding under their trees on Christmas morning.

Then, as everyone pauses at the window to admire the tree in the Edmondsons' house, who should appear in the living room but St. Nicholas himself, filling stockings with toys for the little ones who are sleeping upstairs. At the final stop, the Thomas Greenman home, a prosperous Victorian family is celebrating the holiday.

Lantern Light Tours at Mystic Seaport are a little bit educational and a lot sentimental, and when followed by a glass of hot cider or a roast goose dinner at the Seamen's Inne, next door to the seaport, they lend a cheerful start to a family holiday excursion.

Though Mystic Seaport is usually thought of as a warm-weather destination, it has a special charm in the winter chill, especially if a dusting of snow has covered the village green. Christmas trees are tied atop the masts of the tall ships to herald the season, oyster shells glitter on silver-ribbon wreaths, and greens adorn the village buildings.

This museum of America and the sea boasts the largest collection of boats and maritime photography in the world. But Mystic Seaport is more than just a collection of ships. It is a complete 17-acre re-creation of a nineteenth-century waterfront village. All the exhibit buildings— as well as the ships themselves—remain open for winter visitors.

Mystic's history as a nautical center dates back to the 1600s. The real Thomas Greenman headed a major shipbuilding company on this same site in the 1800s, a yard that produced some of the fastest clipper ships on the seas. In 1929, three local residents got together to form a marine historical association to preserve some of this maritime heritage, and the project steadily gained support from sea-minded friends all over the country. To date, the museum has grown to encompass 60 historic buildings, four major vessels, and more than 400 smaller boats, important collections of maritime artifacts and paintings, and a planetarium to teach the secrets of celestial navigation. The Christmas show focuses on the skies in winter. Visitors can attend before or after the Lantern Light Tours, as well as during the day.

There are additional special programs for children and for adults, before and after Christmas. Like the Lantern Light Tours, those requiring reservations are filled quickly, so it's best to get in touch with the Mystic Seaport office well in advance to get the schedule.

Boarding the ships remains the best part of Mystic Seaport for most people, and December or no, you're still able to walk the decks, examine the intricate rigging and enormous masts, and go below to see the cramped quarters where the captains and crews lived.

In winter you're likely to spend more time at the indoor exhibits that sometimes get short shrift on warmer days. In the village shops the warmth of coal stoves and wood fires welcomes guests, and the ship carver, shipsmith, chandler, and all the local craftspeople find time for an extra chat.

There are several fine galleries on the grounds displaying maritime art, ship models, and scrimshaw, and tracing the development of the maritime and fishing industries from the seventeenth to the nineteenth centuries. One of the most delightful exhibits is the collection of ships' figureheads and wood carvings in the Wendell Building.

Younger visitors love the Children's Museum, designed for those age seven and under, where they can swab the deck, move cargo, cook in the galley, dress in sailors' garb, and climb into sailors' bunks.

And don't think the sights of Mystic are finished when you leave the seaport. The rapidly expanding Mystic Marinelife Aquarium, with its dolphins, seals, and penguin pavilion, is almost as popular with youngsters as the Mystic Seaport itself. The aquarium's 40 exhibits include

3,500 specimens from around the world, from New England sharks to Pacific octopus to Australian lion fish.

The town of Mystic is also appealing, with many fine old homes lining its streets and plenty of shops to explore. Olde Mystick Village, a pseudo-Colonial shopping mall, has dozens of stores; there are discount outlets nearby, and shops in town sell just about everything, including antiques. Don't overlook the Mystic Seaport stores, where there is a tremendous selection to choose from, everything from stick candy and fresh-baked goods to Christmas ornaments, books, paintings, and many tasteful gift ideas with a nautical theme.

While this is a wonderful family outing, Mystic and nearby towns such as Ledyard, Noank, and North Stonington also boast some of Connecticut's loveliest inns, making for a romantic holiday getaway.

You can shop. You can sightsee. You can relive the old-fashioned holiday traditions of yesterday. A Mystic weekend is a special way to bring back Christmas past—and to get everyone into the spirit of Christmas present.

Area Code: 860

DRIVING DIRECTIONS   Mystic Seaport is located on Route 27, one mile south of I-95 at exit 90. Mystic is about 95 miles from Boston, 127 miles from New York, and 55 miles from Hartford.

PUBLIC TRANSPORTATION   Mystic is served by Greyhound buses and Amtrak.

ACCOMMODATIONS   Steamboat Inn, 73 Steamboat Wharf, Mystic 06355, 536-8300, romantic quarters in town on the river, M–EE, CP • **Red Brook Inn,** 2750 Gold Star Highway, Box 237, Old Mystic 06372, 572-0349, bed-and-breakfast in two authentically furnished early American houses, hostess sometimes does fireplace cooking, M–E, CP • **House of 1833,** 72 North Stonington Road, Mystic 06355, 536-6325 or (800) FOR-1833, Greek Revival mansion furnished with elegance and charm, tennis and pool in season, M–EE, CP • **The Old Mystic Inn,** 58 Main Street, Old Mystic 06372, 572-9422, cozy Colonial, more spacious quarters in the carriage house, E, CP • **Stonecroft,** 515 Pumpkin Hill Road, Ledyard 06339, 572-0771, country elegance, a Georgian Colonial with spacious rooms, tasteful furnishings, delightful murals, a romantic retreat, M–E, CP • **Applewood Farms Inn,** 528 Colonel Ledyard Highway, Ledyard 06339, 536-2022, old-fashioned country farmhouse, ten minutes from Mystic, I–M, CP • **Antiques & Accommodations,** 32 Main Street, North Stonington, 06359, 535-1736, 1861 Victorian home formally furnished with exquisite antiques; adjoining early American 1820 home has good spaces for families, M–EE, CP • **Whaler's Inn,** 20 East Main Street, Mystic

06355, 536-1506, three small hotels with early American decor, convenient in-town location, M • **Palmer Inn,** 25 Church Street, Noank, 06340, 572-9000, shipbuilder's Southern-style pillared mansion, grand spaces, filled with Victoriana, collectibles, and memorabilia M–EE, CP • **The Inn at Mystic** (motel and a real inn), Route 1 at Route 27, Mystic 06355, 536-9604 or (800) 237-2415, tennis in season, I–EE • **Mystic Hilton,** 20 Coogan Boulevard, Mystic 06355, 572-0731, hotel with convenient location, indoor pool, M–EE. *Family choices:* Higher rates are for summer; all are less in winter. **Comfort Inn of Mystic,** 48 Whitehall Avenue (Route 27 off I-95), Mystic 06355, 572-8531, under 17 free in parents' room, I–E, CP • **Days Inn of Mystic,** 55 Whitehall Avenue (Route 27 off I-95), Mystic 06355, 572-0574, under 18 free in parents' room, I–E • **Best Western Sovereign Hotel** (motel), 9 Whitehall Avenue (Route 27 off I-95), Mystic 06355, 536-4281, I–M.

DINING   **Seamen's Inne,** Greenmanville Avenue, 536-9649, seafood specialties, I, lunch; dinner, M–E • **Flood Tide,** The Inn at Mystic (see above), 536-8140, continental, highly regarded, E • **The Mooring,** Mystic Hilton (see above), nautical decor, regional specialties, children's menu, I–E • **J. P. Daniels,** Route 184, 572-9564, top choice, converted barn, standard menu, good food at affordable prices, lighter portions available, I–M • **Bravo, Bravo,** Whaler's Inn (see above), Italian bistro, one of the town's best, M–E • **Captain Daniel Packer Inne,** 32 Water Street, Mystic, 536-3555, 1754 inn with period decor, fireplaces, M • **Mystic Pizza,** 56 West Main Street, 536-3737, pizza parlor featured in the movie, I • **Randall's Ordinary,** Route 2, North Stonington, 599-4540, authentic Colonial open-hearth cooking in an eighteenth-century farmhouse; reserve ahead, there is only one seating nightly, prix fixe, EE. In summer, visit **Abbott's Lobster in the Rough,** 117 Pearl Street, Noank, 536-7719, for outdoor service with a water view, I–M.

SIGHTSEEING   **Mystic Seaport,** 75 Greenmanville Avenue (Route 27), Mystic, 572-5315. Hours: daily except Christmas Day; winter hours, 10 A.M. to 4 P.M.; spring and fall, 9 A.M. to 5 P.M.; summer season, 9 A.M. to 6 P.M. $$$$; under 5, free • **Lantern Light Tours,** Hours: daily, 5 P.M. to 9 P.M., about three weeks in December. Check for current dates and fees • **Mystic Marinelife Aquarium,** 55 Coogan Boulevard, Mystic, 536-3323. Hours: daily, 9 A.M. to 5 P.M., to 7 P.M. in summer. $$$$$.

INFORMATION   Southeastern Connecticut Tourism District, PO Box 89, 27 Masonic Street, New London, CT 06320, 444-2206.

Christmas Card Country in Hanover

No doubt about it. This is Christmas card country.

Cradled in the beautiful upper Connecticut River Valley between the White Mountains of New Hampshire and the Green Mountains across the state line in Vermont, Hanover and its heart, the picture-perfect Dartmouth College campus, make an idyllic scene any time of year. Sprinkle a cover of snow on the combination campus green and town center; add a tall, twinkling Christmas tree; and you'll have to look far to find a more magical holiday setting.

With that kind of inspiration, it's no wonder the season is celebrated in a big way here. December brings the "Dickens" holiday celebration with the shops and their proprietors decked in Victorian garb and an annual ice show. Add the annual Christmas Revels entertainment that literally has folks dancing in the aisles, and Christmas festivities at the Hanover Inn that rival home for their warmth and tradition, and Hanover is just the place to spend a memorable December weekend.

It's impossible to talk about Hanover without talking about Dartmouth because, even more than most college towns, this little community of 6,800 was shaped from the start by the school. The town was founded in 1761 by a venturesome band of Connecticut families ready to carve a new frontier in what was then wilderness. Just eight years later Dartmouth was established beside the new settlement, a dream that many thought would be impossible to achieve.

Eleazar Wheelock, a Connecticut missionary with a vision of civilizing the wilderness, chose this unlikely site for his "grand design" precisely because it was on the frontier of the northern colonies and near the Indians, in whose education he had a special interest. Against all odds, Dartmouth survived to become one of the nation's great names in higher education, with an unbroken succession of graduating classes since the first class enrolled in 1771.

A walking tour of the campus with its original Colonial buildings and many handsome later additions is a first order of business on a Hanover visit. Student-guided tours leave from the Admissions Office in McNutt Hall, off North Main Street—check for current schedules—or you can stroll on your own. Ask at the Hanover Inn for a walking guide.

Especially notable are the four classic Federal and Georgian buildings around the green known as Dartmouth Row, the oldest dating to 1784. Be sure to go into the Baker Memorial Library, the imposing spired building on the green, to see the 3,000-square-foot fresco by the great Mexican muralist Jose Clemente Orozco; the mural can be found downstairs on the basement level.

When you see this lovely school, you may better understand Daniel Webster's sentiments 150 years ago when he defended the independence of his young alma mater in a famed case in front of the U.S. Supreme Court: "It is, as I have said, sir, a small college, but there are those who love it."

The history of the Hanover Inn, just across the green from the college, parallels that of the school. Eleven years after Dartmouth's founding, one General Ebenezer Brewster arrived in Hanover to accept a position as college steward and redesigned his home on the present inn site to serve as a tavern, no doubt to supplement his academic earnings. One historian noted that the new enterprise was "not altogether, it would seem, to the gratification of the College authorities," but still the business flourished—so much so that Brewster's son had the tavern moved to another site and put up a much larger building in its place, naming it the Dartmouth Hotel.

When that structure burned in 1887, a new hotel, the Wheelock, was built, and in 1901 the college undertook extensive remodeling and renamed the building the Hanover Inn. With many additions and modernizations, that building still stands, and it is as gracious a Colonial hostelry as you could wish for. The furnishings are on the traditional side—wing chairs, Queen Anne tables, canopied beds—as is the handsome dining room with its fireplaces and chandeliers. But the perennial presence of young Dartmouth men and women keeps things from becoming stuffy. Guests here may use the athletic facilties at Dartmouth, including the Dartmouth Skiway.

At Christmastime the inn is at its best. Two giant trees go up, covered with luscious, brightly decorated cookies, one in the dining room and the other right in the front window. Since the decorations are all but irresistible, the trees bear a sign pleading "Please don't eat the cookies."

The Hanover Inn is definitely the place to stay in the heart of Hanover, but for those who prefer cozier surroundings there are two very attractive bed-and-breakfast inns not far away. Stonecrest Farm, in Wilder, Vermont, a quick three-and-a-half-mile drive, is a tastefuly decorated 1810 home on two very private acres. It is a favorite with Dartmouth visitors who enjoy being a guest in a gracious antiques-filled home; a red barn outside serves as a picturesque reminder of the many years when this was a working dairy farm.

On the outskirts of Hanover in a wooded country setting is another charmer, the Trumbull House, a sunny and spacious Colonial-style home built in 1919 as a private residence. The fresh, livable decor may inspire many guests with decorating ideas.

Another option is the old-fashioned Norwich Inn, which has redecorated its modest rooms and offers reasonable rates. It is one mile from the campus, just across the river in Norwich, Vermont. Two additional appealing choices within a 20-minute drive, the Chase House and Home Hill, are listed below.

If children are along, you'll definitely want to pay a visit to Norwich for the Montshire Museum of Science. This wonderfully creative $4 million science museum was created for young children and is filled with lively hands-on exhibits that fascinate while they educate. Displays include aquariums and live animals. It makes for a great family outing. Norwich also boasts one of the best restaurants in the region, a charming little French café called La Poule a Dents.

For location, however, you can't beat the Hanover Inn. It is connected by a covered walkway to the Hood Museum and the Hopkins Center, both sources of culture and entertainment for the region as well as the campus. The Hood Museum's rotating art exhibits are always worth a look, and the Hopkins Center has an ongoing roster of concerts, theater, and films that many a larger city might envy.

Hanover's most treasured local holiday tradition, the Christmas Revels, takes place at Hopkins Center, usually on the second weekend of December each year. The revels are a combination hometown musicale and salute to the season. Though the look and the direction are professional, the actors are locals and the costumes are made by volunteers. Each year the cast salutes the customs of another culture. The production is unusual, lively, and full of color and music, with a minimum of the expected caroling. Just about everybody in town turns out for one of the performances, which are perennial sellouts. So faithfully do audiences come that they seem to know in unison exactly when the moment has arrived to join the cast in song and dance. If you're not prepared, you may be shocked when your neighbor all but leaps over you to get to the merriment in the aisles. The revels are guaranteed to lift your spirits.

You'll search far for a pleasanter place to do a bit of Christmas shopping than Hanover. Shops are on the traditional side, but the Dartmouth Co-op has a wide range of merchandise, the Dartmouth Book Store is one of the best in northern New England, and you may be able to pick up some one-of-a-kind treasures from the League of New Hampshire Craftsmen's store, at 13 Lebanon Street. The league has showcased the best crafts of the state's artisans for more than 50 years. Just down the block, at 3 Lebanon, is Hanover Park, a pleasant small shopping complex where you'll find attractive country furniture and accessories at Pompanoosuc Mills, homemade candies at the Chocolate Shop, and quality toys from British toy soldiers to miniature trains at Nostalgia Toy Company.

There's more shopping to be found about 20 minutes away in the many shops of Woodstock, Vermont. On the way, make a detour off Route 4 into Quechee to see glassblower Simon Pearce's studio in a restored mill. Pottery, Irish sweaters and woolens, and antiques are for sale here, along with Pearce's exquisite handblown glassware. The restaurant overlooking the waterfall that powers the glassblowing operation is an excellent choice for lunch or dinner.

If you'd rather enjoy the outdoors than browse the shops, there's every opportunity around Hanover. You can set off cross-country skiing within a few blocks of Main Street. There's downhill skiing at the Dartmouth Skiway, 13 miles away, or at the smaller Oak Hill area on the edge of town, and ice skating is excellent at Occum Pond, adjacent to the Dartmouth Outing Club. The pond is cleared and lighted for night skating. There's also indoor skating at Thompson Arena and Davis Rink, in case you don't want to brave the winter weather. Both offer rental skates.

The final special holiday observance each year takes place at the Hanover Inn, a celebration so special it may change your mind about spending the holiday at home.

Events many change slightly from year to year, but you can expect things to start off on December 23 with a wassail party followed by a multicourse "groaning board" buffet, served up in the cheerily decorated Daniel Webster Room. Christmas carols and more libations may follow in the Ivy Grill.

Christmas Eve begins with storytelling in the lounge, followed by a baking demonstration and hands-on workshop with the inn's chef, who reveals the secets for his stained-glass cookies. In the afternoon, horse-drawn carraiges are waiting to tour you around the Dartmouth Green, followed by high tea at the Dartmouth Outing Club, with blazing fires in the clubhouse to warm the frosty noses and fingers of those who've been out skating or skiing.

The Christmas Eve candlelight dinner is an elegant affair with live entertainment, followed by cordials and carols around the piano. You'll wake on Christmas morning to find that Santa has left a little something outside your door.

Christmas dinner is the traditional turkey plus lots of trimmings, and there's a "second-time-round" buffet starting at 6:00 P.M., when the turkeys and other goodies reappear so you can make sandwiches and nibble on the stuffing, just like home.

Whether you come to celebrate Christmas or to get into the spirit of things in advance, you may well agree that there's no place like Hanover for the holidays.

Area Code: 603

DRIVING DIRECTIONS Hanover can be reached off I-89 at exit 18, Lebanon, or from I-91 at exit 13, Norwich, Vermont. It is 135 miles from Boston, 270 miles from New York, and 150 miles from Hartford.

PUBLIC TRANSPORTATION Vermont Transit bus service to Hanover and Amtrak service to White River Junction, Vermont. Air service to Lebanon, New Hampshire, ten miles away. Airport shuttle service to Hanover from Manchester, New Hampshire, and Boston airports.

ACCOMMODATIONS **Hanover Inn,** Dartmouth College Green, Hanover 03755, 643-4300 or (800) 443-7024, EE; write for special Christmas brochure and prices • **Trumbull House,** 40 Etna Road, Hanover 03755, 643-2370 or (800) 651-5141, M–E, CP • **Stonecrest Farm,** 119 Christian Street, Wilder, VT 05088, (802) 296-2425 or (800) 730-2425, M, CP • **Norwich Inn,** Main Street, Norwich, VT 05055, (802) 649-1143, I–M • **The Chase House,** Route 12A, Cornish 03745, 675-5391, eighteenth-century inn with spacious modern addition, wonderful Colonial ambience, 130 acres, cross-country skiing, about 20 minutes south of Hanover, M, CP • **Home Hill,** River Road, Plainfield 03781, 675-6165, secluded estate about 15 minutes from Hanover, cross-country skiing, ice skating, M–E, CP.

DINING **Hanover Inn** (see above), **Daniel Webster Room,** formal dining room, four-star rating, M–E; **Ivy Grill,** innovative bistro menu, burgers to duckling, I–M • **La Poule a Dents,** Main Street, Norwich, VT, (802) 649-2922, pleasant setting, French menu, extensive wine cellar, M–E • **Café Buon Gustaio,** 72 South Main Steet, Hanover, 643-5711, Italian, good reviews, M • **Molly's Balloon,** 45 South Main Street, Hanover, 643-2570, casual, cheerful, wide menu, I–M • **Old Pete's Tavern,** 39 Main Street, Hanover, 643-2345, informal, good for families, I–M • **Lou's Restaurant and Main Street Bakery,** 30 South Main Street, Hanover, 643-3321, a longtime standby for breakfast and lunch, I • **Itas'ca,** 2 North Main Street, White River Junction, VT, (802) 295-1025, residents say take the drive for exceptional dining, American menu, M–E • **Sweet Tomatoes Trattoria,** 23 Church Street, Lebanon, NH, (603) 448-1711, everyone's favorite Italian in the area, I • **Home Hill** (see above), take the drive for highly regarded French cuisine, prix fixe, $$. Also see listings for Quechee, page 89, and Woodstock, page 7.

SIGHTSEEING **Hopkins Center,** 6041 Lower Level, Wilson Hall, Hanover 03755, 646-2422. Write for current dates and prices of the Christmas Revels and a full program of December events • **Hood Museum of Art,** south side of the green, Hanover, 646-2900. Hours: Tuesday to Saturday, 11 A.M. to 5 P.M.; Sunday, noon to 5 P.M. Free • **Dartmouth College information:** 646-2900 • **Montshire Museum of Science,** Montshire Road (just west of Hanover, right off I-91 at exit 13, Norwich, VT, (802) 649-2200. Hours: daily, 10 A.M. to 5 P.M. $$.

INFORMATION Hanover Chamber of Commerce, PO Box 5105, 216 Nugget Building, Main Street, Hanover, NH 03755, 643-3115.

Shopping by the Sea
in Portsmouth

"Have yourself a merry little Christmas," caroled the speaker in one of
the shops in Portsmouth, New Hampshire. We were doing just that.

Portsmouth is a lovely old seafaring town with a wide harbor, handsome sea captains' homes, and a long, proud history. In summer it is
filled with tourists—and therefore it is a town filled with shops.

Come December, the crowds are gone but the many shops remain,
offering choice selections for shoppers in picturesque surroundings.
There's a bonus, too, since New Hampshire has no sales tax.

Things are made even more inviting with gala decorations and
music. Little Prescott Park sets the waterfront aglow with tiny twinkling lights on every tree, and the town tree is lit in Market Square.
Portsmouth also offers an event that is absolutely guaranteed to imbue
even Ebenezer Scrooge with Christmas spirit—the annual Candlelight
Stroll at Strawbery Banke.

When the first settlers arrived in Portsmouth, they found the area
covered with luscious wild strawberries, inspiring them to name their
new home "Strawbery Banke." It became the third settlement in the
New World, preceded only by Plymouth and Jamestown.

Though the town name changed in 1653, Strawbery Banke lives on
today in the form of 40 original buildings in various stages of restoration, a village representing 350 years of the town's history. Many of the
homes were continuously occupied until the 1950s. Preservationists
stepped in when there was a proposal to raze the decaying neighborhood. Rather than following other restorations that re-create only the
early settlement, they chose to portray life as it has changed over the
years, a fascinating approach. For more about seeing the village in season when the houses are open for daytime touring, see page 253.

On the first and second weekends of December, Strawbery Banke
becomes a haven of holiday cheer. The streets are lit by candleglow and
music fills the air with a melodious salute to the season. For the annual
Candlelight Stroll, a tradition for more than a decade, each home is
bedecked with period holiday decorations. When you enter, each one
holds its own delightful musical surprise—professional musicians playing early Christmas airs. A harpsichord and early winds consort may
greet you in one, a flutist in another, perhaps a chorus in yet a third.

The village uses some of its historic houses as places for local artisans to work, displaying their skills and selling their wares. A potter
and a cooper are usually present for the evening festivities, offering you
a chance to pick up handmade one-of-a-kind gifts for special names on
your Christmas list as you stroll.

More gifts are to be found at the old-fashioned Dunaway Store, on the grounds, and at a second gift shop, both good bets for tasteful presents. The Dunaway Store has a wonderful selection of books.

It's an unbeatable evening in a town that makes gift shopping a true pleasure. Market Square is the center of town. Market Street, which runs out from the square paralleling the Piscataqua River, and curving Bow Street, which intersects Market, offer just about anything you could ask for—woodenware, art glass, Southwestern jewelry, candles, mugs, clothing, you name it. Handmade crafts are plentiful, from leather goods to hand-forged iron pieces to jewelry.

There are plenty of antiques shops if you want to splurge for someone special—including yourself. Carter's, at number 175, near the foot of Market, is one of the nicest of the antiquers' stops, packed with furniture, folk art, hooked rugs, antique decoys, and antique Christmas lights. Old Port Artisans, across the street at number 206, will delight fans of folk art. Among the offerings are charming hand-painted pieces by owner-artist Lisa Carpenter. State Street has more antiques and other shops with a funkier feel.

For bargains, drive just across the bridge to Kittery, Maine, and you'll find discount shopping galore, including outlet stores for Dansk, Mikasa, Lenox, Waterford, Wedgwood, Hathaway, Bass, Timberland, and just about any brand label you can name, all in a series of outlet centers along Route 1.

Remember, too, that prices at the state-run liquor stores in New Hampshire are excellent. The nearest one, at the Portsmouth Traffic Circle on I-95, is the biggest in the state.

Portsmouth has an increasingly varied selection of good restaurants, and though winter is technically off-season, the fact that many young professionals are moving to town permanently means that there are places to go at night year-round for jazz or other live music. Ask your innkeeper who is playing where.

Though the Candlelight Stroll and special Christmas tour hours enable December visitors to get inside Strawbery Banke's homes, you'll have to return in summer to do full justice to the complex and its beautiful gardens and to go into the historic showplace mansions on "the Portsmouth Trail." But you can have a look at some of them, and at many other fine homes as well, by making your own compact driving tour. Be sure to see the Wentworth-Gardner House, at 141 Mechanic Street; the Moffatt-Ladd House, at 154 Market; the Rundlet-May House, at 364 Middle Street; the Warner House, at the corner of Daniel and Chapel; the Governor John Langdon House, at 143 Pleasant Street; and finally, the most historic of all, the John Paul Jones House, at Middle and State. This is the place where the admiral oversaw fittings for his new command, the *Ranger,* which sailed out of Portsmouth Harbor on November 1, 1777, bearing the first American flag to be flown at sea.

The Portsmouth Tourist Information Office may not be open on winter weekends, but you can write in advance for material to guide you on your tour.

Portsmouth has much to offer in the summer—when the houses are open, the gardens are in bloom at Strawbery Banke and Prescott Park, and the sightseeing cruise boats are out in the harbor or heading for the Shoals Islands. But there's magic on a frosty December night, when Strawbery Banke is aglow with candlelight and music and the Christmas tree stands guard in Market Square. And when it comes to Christmas shopping, you won't find a snugger port anywhere.

Area Code: 603

DRIVING DIRECTIONS Portsmouth is on I-95, 60 miles north of Boston, 268 miles from New York, and 158 miles from Hartford.

PUBLIC TRANSPORTATION Air service and Greyhound bus service.

ACCOMMODATIONS All Portsmouth zip codes are 03801. • **Sise Inn,** 40 Court Street, Portsmouth, 433-1200, handsome Victorian ambience, hotel services, M, CP • **Martin Hill Inn,** 404 Islington, Portsmouth, 436-2287, cozy, lovely decor, hearty breakfasts, M, CP • **Oracle House Inn,** 38 Marcy Street, Portsmouth, 433-8827, small inn in a 1700s Colonial home near Strawbery Banke, E, CP • **Inn at Strawbery Banke,** 314 Court Street, Portsmouth, 436-7242 or (800) 428-3933, modest inn in early 1800s home, M, CP • **Gundalow Inn,** 6 Water Street, Kittery, ME 03904, (207) 439-4040, snug Victorian just across the river on Portsmouth Harbor, fabulous four-course breakfasts, M, CP. Also see listings for York, page 110.

DINING **Lindbergh's Crossing,** 29 Ceres Street, 431-0887, cozy candlelit bistro, sophisticated international menu, excellent reviews, M • **The Oar House,** 55 Ceres Street, 436-4205, restored waterfront warehouse with great atmosphere and seafood specialties, perennial favorite, M–E • **The Dolphin Striker,** 15 Bow Street, 431-5222, another atmospheric restored warehouse, equally popular, M–E • **Porto Bello,** 67 Bow Street (upstairs), 431-2989, much-praised Italian, I–M • **Café Meditteraneo,** 152 Fleet Street, 431-0407, another popular Italian choice, I–M • **Café Mirabelle,** 64 Bridge Street, 430-9301, attractive French café, M; **La Creperie,** downstairs, serves crepes and salads, I • **The Metro,** 20 High Street, 436-0521, brasserie, stained glass, gaslights, varied American menu, known for chowder, M • **The Library,** 401 State Street, 431-5202, book-lined walls and a varied menu, M • **Blue Mermaid World Grill,** the Hill, 427-2583, Southwestern and Caribbean, wood-burning grill, young crowd, entertainment on weekends, I–M • **Stockpot,** 53 Bow Street, 431-1851, informal dining, on the water, I–M • **Karen's,** 105 Daniel Street, 431-1948, great spot for breakfast, lunch, and light dinners, Thursday to Saturday, I • **Portsmouth Brewery,** 56 Market Street, 431-1115, brew-pub, lively, I–M • **Dunfey's Aboard the John Wanamaker,** Harbour Place Marina (foot of State Street), 433-3111, continental menu served aboard a restored tugboat moored at the waterfront, M.

SIGHTSEEING **Strawbery Banke,** Hancock and Marcy Streets, 436-1100. Candlelight Stroll, first and second weekends in December, Friday and Saturday evenings, 3:30 P.M. to 8:30 P.M. Adults, $10; children, $7; under 6, free. Regular hours: late April to early November, Thanksgiving weekend, daily, 10 A.M. to 5 P.M. $$$$ • **Children's Museum of Portsmouth,** 280 Marcy Street, 436-3853. Hours: Tuesday to Saturday, 10 A.M. to 5 P.M., Sunday 1 P.M. to 5 P.M. Open Mondays during summer and school vacations. $$.

INFORMATION Greater Portsmouth Chamber of Commerce, 500 Market Street, PO Box 239, Portsmouth, NH 03801, 436-1118.

An Artful Weekend in Williamstown

So the winter doldrums have set in, you don't ski, and you can't think of anything else to do? Head for Williamstown, in the Berkshire hills of Massachusetts. Yes, lots of people do come here for the excellent skiing nearby, but there is also a rich bounty of indoor diversions in winter, from antiquing and boutiquing to world-class art museums and a rich schedule of music. As for the snow-covered scenery in the town that's often called "the Village Beautiful," it will surely tempt you to whip out your camera—and maybe a paintbrush, as well.

The most notable attraction here is one of the most inviting and impressive small museums to be found anywhere, the Sterling and Francine Clark Art Institute. Sterling Clark had the good fortune to be heir to the fortune his grandfather amassed as a partner to Isaac Singer, the sewing machine king. Clark began using his inheritance to collect fine art around 1912, beginning with works of the Old Masters. But with the encouragement of his French-born wife, he shifted emphasis in the 1920s and 1930s to concentrate on nineteenth-century French painters, especially the Impressionists, with some attention also to American artists such as Sargent, Remington, and Winslow Homer, who is represented by seven choice oils.

Clark's grandfather attended Williams College, and he was also friendly with Karl Weston, a Williams art history professor who helped to garner important alumni collections for the Williams Museum of Art. So in the 1950s, when the Clarks decided to build a structure to house their collection, they chose Williamstown for the beauty of its pastoral setting and had a building designed to make the most of it. Tall windows in the corridors look out on natural scenes that are works of art in themselves and that add to the pleasure of visiting the museum. The fact that the original galleries are done to drawing room scale and are furnished in many cases with fine antiques also makes the museum more rewarding.

You'll see excellent examples of some of the world's greatest painters here, dating from the Renaissance and later, including Van Ruisdael, Hals, Gainsborough, Tiepolo, Goya, Turner, and Mary Cassatt. The French works include these of Géricault, Courbet, Daumier, Corot, and Millet, but the real heart of the museum, the paintings that may remain in your mind's eye long after you've left the galleries, are the exceptional works by Pisarro, Monet, Degas, and Renoir. There are more than 30 Renoirs in the collection. Among the most memorable pieces are Monet's *Tulip Fields at Sassenheim* and one of his Rouen Cathedral series, and Renoir's *At the Concert* and *Sleeping Girl with Cat.*

The silver collection is also remarkable, comprising five centuries of the most exquisite pieces of the silversmith's art.

An expansive new wing opened in 1996 allows for changing exhibitions as well as for permanent installations—and adds a convenient café to the building. There may be grander and more famous museums than the Clark Art Institute, but few offer a more satisfying visual experience.

All of Williamstown, in fact, is a visual delight. It is a beautiful old New England town with a college dating to 1793 at its center. The town was settled in 1753 as West Hoosuck. The name changed in 1765 when Colonel Ephriam Williams, commander of a pioneer fort, left a bequest to found a free school, provided the town was named after him.

The school, which became Williams College, is so much a part of its hometown that it is hard to distinguish where the campus ends and the town begins. College buildings occupy much of Main Street, and most of the landmarks on the town's printed historical walking tour belong to the school. The architecture runs the gamut from Georgian to Greek Revival to mansard-roofed Victorian Gothic. There are many buildings worth a visit.

The Hopkins Observatory, built between 1836 and 1838, is the oldest astronomical observatory in the United States; it is open to the public. The Chapin Library, on the second floor of Stetson Hall, has an extensive collection of rare books—roughly 17,000 of them—and changing exhibits on English and American literature. This is the only place where you can see originals of all four founding documents of the United States together: the Declaration of Independence, the Bill of

Rights, the Constitution, and the Articles of Confederation. But you'll have to do it on a weekday; the library, unfortunately, is closed on weekends.

The Williams College Museum of Art is exceptional, with a notable collection of sculpture and paintings dating from ancient Assyrian stone reliefs to the last self-portrait by Andy Warhol. There are prints by Dürer and Rembrandt; oils and watercolors by Homer, Inness, Rivers, and Hopper; and contemporary sculptures by George Segal and Anthony Caro. Highlights include a whole room devoted to Spanish art, a section of early American paintings and furnishings, and the Bloedel Collection of Twentieth Century American Art. The Prendergast Archives and Study Center is a resource for research on the American modernists Maurice and Charles Prendergast and their contemporaries.

The addition to the museum, built in 1983, is a work of art in itself. The architecture repeats the octagonal design of the original 1846 neoclassical rotunda in soaring new skylit galleries.

If you've absorbed your artistic limit for the day, walk over to Water Street (Route 43) and poke through half a dozen shops that include custom leather goods, gold and silver jewelry, and gift shops with a mix of wares. Water Street Books has a good selection of books on the Berkshires and New England, and is also the official Williams College bookstore. Another recommended stop on the town's main shopping street is Library Antiques, 70 Spring Street, with a wide range of antiques and collectibles, everything from furniture to porcelain to pillows, Victoriana to Asian decorative arts.

For outdoor diversion, take a turn on the ice at Williams College's Chapman Rink or at the Vietnam Veterans Memorial Skating Rink, in neighborhing North Adams.

The most elaborate lodging in Williamstown is The Orchards, which is not Colonial from the outside, but most definitely is Colonial within, decorated in handsome period decor. The Williams Inn is actually a hotel but manages to maintain the feeling of New England warmth, and has the bonus of an indoor pool. Field Farm, the striking modern home of the late art collector Lawrence Bloedel, is now operated as a bed-and-breakfast under the auspices of the Trustees of Reservations, and offers exceptional surroundings and views and cross-country skiing on the expansive property. There are some pleasant small bed-and-breakfast inns in town, as well.

The Wild Amber Grill, Mezze, and Robin's are among the recommended dining places in town. After dinner, the Images Cinema, in Williamstown, offers first-rate art films, and the Williams College Music Department has a full schedule of events, from the college choral society to the Berkshire Symphony to jazz. The Clark Art Institute also shows films and hosts chamber concerts throughout the year.

For a delicious light lunch, stop south of town at the Store at Five Corners, at the intersection of Routes 7 and 43, where you can also buy many types of culinary equipment, gourmet foods, and cookbooks. The building was originally the Sloan Tavern, circa 1770. This is one of several historic South Williamstown structures within a short walk of the store. If the weather is conducive, ask at the store for the historic walking tour pamphlet.

When you are ready for more sightseeing, you can take your pick of directions. To the north about 20 minutes, in Bennington, Vermont, is the Bennington Museum, with a delightful gallery devoted to Grandma Moses, who captured the surrounding Vermont landscapes with so much naive charm. There are some 30 of her works on display. Outside is the Grandma Moses Schoolhouse, the 1834 one-room school that she attended as a child and that offers a photo story of her life. The museum also offers a military gallery; a comprehensive collection of American pressed glass, including pieces by Louis Comfort Tiffany; and a collection of the well-known brown-glazed early Bennington pottery.

Or you can head south about 10 minutes to Pittsfield and the Berkshire Museum, a museum of art, history, and natural science, with something to interest almost everyone. History exhibits range from tools to dolls to a woodland Indian collection. Six galleries of natural science feature extensive displays of rocks, minerals, and shells; miniature dioramas of dinosaurs; and an aquarium with over 100 live animals and fish. The heart of the art collection is nineteenth-century work by masters such as Inness, Church, Bierstadt, Copley, and Peale. The twentieth century is also well represented, with many paintings by artists with ties to the Berkshires. This museum also hosts an excellent film series, along with special lecture and music programs.

If you are a lover of Herman Melville, phone ahead for an appointment to visit Arrowhead, in Pittsfield, where Melville lived from 1850 to 1863 and where he wrote his epic *Moby Dick*. The 1780s farmstead has been partially restored to the Melville era under the auspices of the Berkshire County Historical Society.

A drive of about half an hour farther south to Stockbridge will bring you to another treasure, the Norman Rockwell Museum, dedicated to the artist who spent the last 25 years of his life in Stockbridge and immortalized the town in his drawings. The world's largest collection of his work can be seen in this stunning museum on a 36-acre former estate in the countryside. The museum inspires a new appreciation for Rockwell's talents at mirroring changes in American society. His studio has also been moved to this site.

On the first weekend in December, Rockwell's well-known painting *Stockbridge Main Street at Christmas* is re-created along Main Street, complete with antique cars as he drew them, a bit of nostalgia that is great fun to see. Modern cars are banned, and Santa and Mrs. Claus lead the crowd in singing carols as they walk along the street. Sleigh or hay rides add to the fun.

The festive holiday spirit has spread throughout the Berkshires for this weekend. Williamstown and Lenox stage their own holiday strolls, the Berkshire Botanical Garden puts on special holiday displays, and the Hancock Shaker Village holds an annual holiday weekend.

In the southern Berkshires, you can also take in the many shops in Stockbridge, West Stockbridge, and Lenox; check out the growing number of art galleries in old mills in Housatonic; browse the dozens of antiques shops in Sheffield; and sample the hot new restaurants in Great Barrington.

With Williamstown as a picture-perfect home base, the Berkshires in all directions are guaranteed to warm away the winter blues.

Area Code: 413

DRIVING DIRECTIONS From the Mass Pike (I-90) exit 2, follow U.S. Route 20 past Lenox and Pittsfield to Route 7 and Williamstown. Williamstown is 135 miles from Boston, 155 miles from New York, 105 miles from Hartford.

PUBLIC TRANSPORTATION Bonanza and Peter Pan bus lines serve Williamstown; Amtrak stops in Pittsfield. Closest airports are Albany, New York, 45 miles; or Springfield, Massachusetts, 70 miles.

ACCOMMODATIONS **The Orchards,** 222 Adams Road, Williamstown 01267, 458-9611, spacious, gracious, M–EE, (ask about weekend packages) • **Williams Inn,** on the green, Williamstown 01267, 458-9371, M–E • **Field Farm Guest House,** 554 Sloan Road, Williamstown 01267, 458-3135, exceptional, art-filled modern home on 254 scenic acres, M, CP • **The House on Main Street,** 1120 Main Street, Williamstown 01267, 458-3031, pleasant home, walking distance to town, I–M, CP • **Goldberry's,** 39 Cold Spring Road (Route 7), Williamstown 01267, 458-3935, attractive 1830s home, also within a walk of town, M, CP • **River Bend Farm,** 643 Simonds Road, Williamstown 01267, 458-3121, charming authentically restored 1770 Georgian Colonial on the National Register, closed in winter but worth knowing about for other visits, M, CP • **1896 House,** Cold Spring Road (Route 7), Williamstown 01267, 458-8125, particularly pleasant motel outside town, I–M, CP. For southern Berkshires accommodations, see page 145.

DINING **Wild Amber Grill,** 101 North Street, Williamstown, 458-4000, contemporary American, one of the best in town, M–E • **Robin's Restaurant,** foot of Spring Street, 458-4489, interesting variety of cuisines, M–E • **Le Jardin Inn,** Route 7 and Cold Spring Road, Williamstown, 458-8032, converted estate, continental menu, M–E •

The Orchards (see above), formal dining, M–EE • **Mezze,** 84 Water Street, Williamstown, 458-0123, Mediterranean dishes, I–M • **Hobson's Choice,** 159 Water Street, 458-9101, cozy, informal, I–M • **Water Street Grill,** 123 Water Street, 458-2175, varied menu, popular, I–M • **Cobble Café,** 27 Spring Street, Williamstown, 458-5930, small and pleasant, good bet for all three meals, dinners, M • **The Store at Five Corners,** Routes 7 and 43, Williamstown, 458-3176, great spot for lunch and snacks, I. For southern Berkshires dining, see pages 145–146.

SIGHTSEEING **Sterling and Francine Clark Art Institute,** South Street, Williamstown, 458-9545. Hours: Tuesday to Sunday, 10 A.M. to 5 P.M. Free • **Williams College Museum of Art,** 1846 Lawrence Hall, 597-2429. Hours: Tuesday to Saturday, 10 A.M. to 5 P.M.; Sunday, 1 P.M. to 5 P.M. Free • **Chapin Library,** Stetson Hall, 597-2462. Hours: Monday to Friday, 10 A.M. to noon, and 1:30 P.M. to 4:30 P.M.; closed on weekends. Free • **Berkshire Museum,** 39 South Street (Route 7), Pittsfield, 443-7171. Hours: Tuesday to Saturday, 10 A.M. to 5 P.M.; Sunday 1 P.M. to 5 P.M.; open Monday in July and August. $$. Free admission all day Wednesday and Saturday, 10 A.M. to noon • **Arrowhead,** 780 Holmes Road, Pittsfield, 442-1793. Phone for appointment in winter. Seasonal hours: Memorial Day to Labor Day, daily, 10 A.M. to 5 P.M.; Labor Day to October 31, Friday to Monday, 10 A.M. to 5 P.M. $$. See Bennington Museum hours, page 177; southern Berkshires attractions, pages 146–147.

ICE SKATING **Chapman Rink,** Williams College, 597-2433; **Vietnam Veterans Memorial Skating Rink,** Route 8A, North Adams, 664-9474.

SKIING Phone for current rates and information. **Jiminy Peak,** Corey Road, Hancock, 738-5500, daily and night skiing • **Brodie,** Route 7, New Ashford, 443-4752, daily and night skiing • **Bousquet Ski Area,** Tamarack Road, Pittsfield, 442-8316, daily and night skiing. For winter brochure with details on vertical drops, number of trails, lift ticket prices, and special ski packages available at local lodgings, write to Berkshire Visitors' Bureau.

INFORMATION Berkshire Visitors' Bureau, Berkshire Common, Pittsfield, MA 01201, 443-9186 or (800) BERKSHR; Williamstown Board of Trade, c/o Northern Berkshire Chamber of Commerce, 40 Main Street, North Adams, MA 01247, 663-3735.

Winter Carnival at Stowe

"Stowe Is King," proclaimed the ice sculptures at a recent Winter Carnival in Stowe, Vermont. Three generations of skiers would agree. But you don't have to be a skier to love the hometown of Mt. Mansfield, Vermont's highest mountain peak.

Stowe blends the charm of a New England village in a stunning mountain setting with sophisticated food and lodgings that few ski resorts can match. Come Winter Carnival, with fanciful ice carvings, parades, ski racing, and other gala events added to the agenda, it's a stellar winter destination for all.

The mountain scenery has been attracting visitors since the 1840s, when the first inn was built under the mountain and another, Mansfield House, arose in Stowe Village to house 600 guests. The Dartmouth College team was skiing the Toll Road as early as 1914, but it was in 1933, just as agriculture was declining as a source of revenue, that the Civilian Conservation Corps cut a four-mile trail down the mountain and serious skiing began. The next year the Mt. Mansfield Ski Club was formed, setting up lodging in a former logging camp at the bottom of the trail, and by 1937 the first rope tow was in place. Those who are used to paying $50 a day to ski might like to know that use of that first lift cost 50 cents a day, $5 for the season.

Winter recreation saved the town of Stowe from the hard times that the demise of small farming brought to many other Vermont communities. Mt. Mansfield emerged as the eastern skier's supreme test, with the steep trails known as the "Front Four," including "Starr" and "Goat," becoming legendary for their challenge. And although it has competition from emerging giants such as Killington, now Vermont's biggest mountain, Stowe's special cachet remains unmatched. The proliferation of fine facilities that grew up around skiing now makes Stowe a prime year-round resort destination.

The first Winter Carnival, held in 1921, consisted of ski jumping and tobogganing on a hill in the village. The tradition was abandoned for a time but was reborn in 1974 as an antidote to the late January doldrums common to ski areas. Today Stowe hosts a multiday "king of carnivals," offering something for everyone, sports enthusiast and spectator alike.

Each year's theme is spelled out in an ice sculpture contest, with the fanciful carvings appearing in front of almost every inn and restaurant. It's a feast for photographers. Popeye, King Kong, and the *Star Wars* crew are just a few of the elaborate sculptures seen in recent years.

Festivities include everything from ski races, snow-golf, and snow board and snowshoe competitions to theme nights such as a toga party, a bartender's ball, or Las Vegas Night. Everyone turns out for Village Night, a block party along Main Street that includes clowns, magicians, jugglers, and a parade of locals in storybook costumes, traditionally followed by fireworks. Whatever is slated during your visit, you can count on a spirited schedule.

When it comes to choosing a place to stay at Stowe, the possibilities are enormous. At the top of the scale, Topnotch is just that. You can skate here, go sledding or sleigh riding, use the on-premises Cross-Country Ski Center, take advantage of the extensive indoor tennis facilities, swim at an indoor pool with a waterfall, or luxuriate at a multimillion-dollar spa. Equally pleasant is sitting in front of the giant fireplace and looking out the 12-foot windows at snow-covered Mt. Mansfield from a living room that is a tasteful blend of rustic fieldstone and country antiques.

Skiers may appreciate the convenience of the Stowe Mountain Resort. Decor is basic; the big advantage is direct access to the mountain from their own double chairlift. There's a choice of hotel or condo accommodations.

Ten Acres Lodge is the definite choice for those who enjoy a more traditional antiques-filled Colonial-style New England inn. The Alpine-style Trapp Family Lodge is big and busy but may appeal to cross-country skiers for its excellent Ski Touring Center and its extensive trails. Edson Hill Manor, with a secluded location and a pleasant rustic feel, also offers ski touring as well as a riding center on its 500 acres.

There are a number of more modest accommodations as well: the Siebeness Inn is a delightful, sunny, and welcoming small inn decorated with country charm and with a hot tub for sore muscles; the congenial, old-fashioned Gables welcomes you home each afternoon with hot soup and hors d'oeuvres on the house; the Brass Lantern is a pleasant B&B just north of town; and Timberholm Inn is tucked away on a quiet wooded hillside away from traffic but just one block from the mountain road. A family resort, Golden Eagle, has more moderate rates than most resorts and includes an indoor pool and health club, sleigh rides, ice skating, and children's programs.

The Wood Chip Inn is a best bet for those on a budget, along with the Inn at Blush Hill, ten miles away in Woodbury, perched on a high ridge with fabulous mountain views.

There are dozens of other lodgings—over 60 at last count. Contact the Stowe Area Association for further information and free reservation service.

When it comes to food, Stowe offers some of the best dining in ski country, with dozens of restaurants to choose from. Top recommendations include fine dining at Edson Hill Manor and Ten Acres Lodge, Italian at Trattoria La Festa, and creative American menus at the Blue Moon, a small café that wins raves in town. Isle de France, a fine classic French restaurant, offers terrific value at its bar-café, known as Claudine's Bistro.

Popular for après-ski are the Shed and, for a change of pace, Mr. Pickwick's Pub for a pub menu accompanied by British folk songs and a pint of ale. The prize breakfast in town is at the Gables Inn, where you can choose from the extensive menu until noon.

Even without the Winter Carnival, you can stay busy at Stowe with a dozen different activities, beginning but not ending with the 350 miles of alpine skiing terrain and over 100 miles of cross-country trails. Besides the tough stuff for the experts, the 6,400-foot Toll House Chairlift opens many trails for novices. The original Toll Road is now a four-mile run from top to bottom, and one of the most scenic novice trails to be found. In recent years, Stowe has added one of the world's fastest eight-passenger gondola lifts and night skiing on the longest lighted trail in northern New England. And there's now a resturant on the top of the mountain.

If you don't ski, you can choose from ice skating at the indoor Jackson Arena in the village or outdoor and indoor fun open to the public at some of the area resorts; a sleigh ride for two at Stowehof Inn or in a wagon for 20 at the Trapp Family Lodge; indoor tennis lessons from the pros at Topnotch; horseback riding at Edson Hill Manor; or exercise at the Golden Eagle Resort Spa. Guided outings on snowshoes are offered by Umiak outfitters. Several inns offer their indoor pools to non-guests for a fee.

If your favorite sport is shopping, you've still come to the right place. There are scores of possibilities in town and all along Route 108, the road to the mountain. A recommended stop at the beginning of the mountain road is the Stowe Crafts Gallery, a converted old red mill with excellent woodenware, including handcrafted ski and tennis racks, as well as attractive pottery, glass, and jewelry. In town, the old Depot Building features handsome reproduction country furniture, crafts, and a big bookstore; and Prints and Patches, across the street, has everything quilted, from king-size spreads to bibs and eyeglass cases, as well as hand-hooked rugs. Quilts can be ordered in your own color scheme. Harrington's is known for cob-smoked hams and Vermont cheese—and don't overlook Everything Cows, a "bovine boutique" featuring that famous Vermont black-and-white-cow motif on anything you can think of. Try the Stowe Antique Center for collectibles, and Shaw's General Store for almost anything.

If you want a tour of the Ben and Jerry's Ice Cream Factory, from whence comes Vermont's best-known sweet treat, you'll find it on Route 100 in Waterbury. On the way, you'll pass the Cold Hollow Cider Mill, where you can see cider making year-round—and get free samples, to boot. Waterbury's Ziemke Glass Blowing Studio offers glassblowing demonstrations as well as a showrooom of colorful wares.

In fact, there's not much of anything you can't find in and around Stowe, a town that richly deserves its title as king—carnival or not.

Area Code: 802

DRIVING DIRECTIONS   Stowe is in northern Vermont on Route 100, ten minutes north of exit 10 on I-89. It is about 185 miles from Boston, 325 miles from New York, and 200 miles from Hartford.

PUBLIC TRANSPORTATION   Air service connects to Burlington, 45 minutes away; shuttle service is available to Stowe from the airport, as are many car rentals offering special ski packages. Vermont Transit, Greyhound bus service, and Amtrak rail provide service to Waterbury, which is ten miles away, and taxis are available for the rest of the route. The Stowe Area Association offers discounted air/car rental packages. Regular shuttle bus service from the village to the slopes makes it easy to get around without a car during the day, and many restaurants are within walking distance of lodgings.

ACCOMMODATIONS   All Stowe zip codes are 05672. All lodgings are less on weekdays; also ask about weekend or ski packages. **Topnotch at Stowe,** Mountain Road, Stowe, 253-8585 or (800) 451-8686, E–EE, CP • **Stowehof Inn,** Edson Hill Road, Stowe, 253-9722 or (800) 422-9922, luxury accommodations, M–EE, CP • **Stowe Mountain Resort,** Mountain Road, Stowe, 253-8610 or (800) 253-4SKI, Inn at the Mountain, EE, MAP; condominiums, EE • **Ten Acres Lodge,** Luce Hill, Stowe, 253-7638, M–E, CP • **Trapp Family Lodge,** Luce Hill Road, Stowe, 253-8511 or (800) 826-7000, M–EE, CP • **Edson Hill Manor,** Edson Hill Road, Stowe, 253-7371, M–E, CP; E–EE, MAP • **Green Mountain Inn,** Main Street, Stowe, 253-7301, village landmark, M–E • **The Gables Inn,** Stowe, 253-7730 or (800) GABLES-1, M–E, CP • **Golden Eagle Resort,** Mountain Road, Stowe, 253-2561 or (800) 626-1010, M–E, CP. *Bed-and-breakfast inns:* **The Siebeness Inn,** 3681 Mountain Road, Stowe, 253-8942 or (800) 426-9001, M, CP; rooms with fireplace, M–E, CP; mountain-view suites, Jacuzzi, fireplace, M–E, CP • **Timberholm Inn,** Cottage Club Road, Stowe, 253-7603, M, CP • **Brass Lantern,** Route 100 North, Stowe, 253-2229, M, CP; fireplace and/or whirlpool, M–E, CP • **Wood Chip Inn,** Mountain Road, Stowe, 253-9080 or (800) 676-9181, I–M, CP • **Inn at Blush Hill,** Blush Hill Road, Waterbury 05676, 244-7529 or (800) 736-7522, I–M, CP.

DINING   **Blue Moon Café,** 35 School Street, 253-7006, modest quarters, innovative chef, M • **Ten Acres Lodge** (see above), excellent, eclectic menu, M–E • **Isle de France,** 253-7751, elegant French, E–EE; **Claudine's Bistro,** same fine chef, much lower prices, deservedly crowded, I–M • **Edson Hill Manor** (see above), highly regarded locally, M–E • **Trattoria La Festa,** Mountain Road, 253-8480, Italian favorite, I–M • **Partridge Inn,** Mountain Road, 253-8000, seafood specialties, M • **Whiskers,** Mountain Road, 253-8996, casual, prime ribs, steak, salad bar, M • **Restaurant Swisspot,** Main Street, 253-4622, a tiny charmer noted for fondue and quiche, I–M • **Cliff House,** atop Mt. Mansfield, 253-3665, ride the gondola up for elegant meals and a great view; skiers can take the lighted trail down, prix fixe, EE. *Less formal fare and lunch:* **The Shed,** Mountain Road, 253-4364, I–M • **Gracie's,** Main Street, 253-8741, I–M • **Depot Street Malt Shop,** Depot Street, 253-4269, burgers and sandwiches as well as sweets, I. *For breakfast, all I:* **The Gables Inn** (above); the **Siebeness Inn** (above); or **Green Mountain Inn,** Main Street, 253-7301. *Après-ski:* **Mr. Pickwick's Pub Ye Olde New England Inn,** Mountain Road, 253-7558; and **The Shed** (see above).

SIGHTSEEING **Stowe Winter Carnival,** several days in late January and early February; dates and schedule of events available from Stowe Area Association (see below). *Ski information:* Mt. Mansfield, 253-3000; Snowphone, 253-3600. *Sleigh rides:* **Pristine Meadows,** 253-9901 • **Charley Horse,** 253-2215; **Stowehof Inn,** 253-9722; **Edson Hill Manor,** 253-7371 • **Trapp Family Lodge,** 253-8511. *Ice skating:* **Jackson Arena,** 253-6148. *Cross-country skiing:* **Edson Hill Manor,** 253-8954 • **Stowe Mountain Resort,** 253-7311 • **Topnotch,** 253-8585 • **Trapp Family Lodge,** 253-8511. *Snowshoeing:* **Umiak,** 253-2317 • **Ben & Jerry's Ice Cream Factory Tours,** Route 100, Waterbury. Hours: year-round, Monday to Saturday, 9 A.M. to 4 P.M. Admission donation goes to charity; under 12, free.

INFORMATION Stowe Area Association, Box 1320, Stowe, VT 05672, 253-7321 or (800) 24-STOWE, for lodging, general Stowe information, and free reservation service.

Stirring Things Up at Sturbridge

The soup kettle was simmering and the spit was being turned, searing the joint of beef to a crispy brown and sending heavenly smells through the kitchen. Several guests were busy preparing potatoes, carrots, and onions to be browned in the drippings, the men as involved with the chores as the women.

Another group was filling a pottery dish with whole-wheat pie crust, ready to receive chicken and gravy and vegetables, then be baked into a savory pie in the cast-iron Dutch oven heating in the hot coals. Meanwhile, some were busy forming wafers fresh from the wafer iron into cone shapes that would hold sweet fillings for dessert.

It's one thing to visit the Colonial kitchen of a restored New England home. It's a lot more fun to roll up your sleeves and pitch in preparing dinner on the open hearth, just the way it was done 150 years ago. That's just what you can do if you sign up for "Dinner in a Country Village," a cooking-and-dining program held Saturday nights during the winter months at Old Sturbridge Village in Massachusetts.

New England's largest historical restoration, Old Sturbridge Village is a lively re-creation of a rural New England village of the early nineteenth century, with "villagers" in authentic dress demonstrating what work and daily life were like in early America. The 200-acre property includes more than 40 New England homes, mills, meetinghouses, craft shops, and a fully operating period farm.

But for the lucky 14 who snag a place at Saturday dinner, the real fun begins when the gates close and everyone else heads home. That's when the kitchen of the white saltbox Parsonage on the Village Common swings into action.

Dinner guests are escorted into the 1748 home, restored to reflect the fashions and furnishings of a clergyman's family in the 1830s, and are greeted by members of the village staff who are well versed in the art of fireplace cooking. Everyone helps in the preparation of a full-course meal that might have been served in a home like this one, using historical kitchen utensils reproduced from the Sturbridge Village collections.

With the group limited in number, everyone really gets a chance to participate, and while dinner cooks there is time to socialize and learn to play some early nineteenth-century parlor games.

Dinners are limited to those age 14 and older, but families with younger children can also get in on the cooking fun during the "Breakfast on a Farm" programs, which are offered on Saturday mornings and are open to children age 8 and up. Morning participants help with the morning chores and prepare a hearty hearth-cooked breakfast at the Freeman Farm.

It's a delicious way to relive a bit of the past, something you can do all day at Old Sturbridge Village. In this quieter time of year, Old Sturbridge is a perfect destination for families, providing a chance for all ages to step back in time, watching some of the skills that were necessary long ago.

Visiting the village in winter is also a special treat. A coat of winter white only makes the village more beautiful—and it gives you a chance to ride in a horse-drawn sleigh. A cold weather visit also allows you to see the special activities of the peaceful winter season. Outdoors, you might find farmers hauling logs with a team of oxen to make repairs in the split-rail fences or provide material for the sawmill. Indoors, you can join country artisans in front of a cheery fireplace or cast-iron stove, a mighty welcome invention in early America.

The usual crafts demonstrations—weaving, printing, tinsmithing, and the like—still take place in the winter, and the artisans have more time to chat and answer questions. The schoolteacher will give you a colorful introduction to education as it was in the 1830s, guaranteed to fascinate all ages. Special activities at Old Sturbridge mark winter holidays, including Christmas, New Year's, and George Washington's birthday, and there's old-fashioned, mystifying fun for all the family at Saturday evening performances by actors portraying a rowdy magician from eighteenth-century London and Richard Potter, America's first magician.

And you finally may have time to take a look at some of the indoor exhibits that tend to be forgotten in the summer. There are seven galleries to be seen, filled with firearms, lighting devices, folk art, textiles, blown and molded glass, mirrors, scientific instruments, hand-sewn and knitted garments, weaving, quilts, and much more. The Cheney Wells Clock Gallery, adjoining the Visitor Center, is a standout.

There's a real village of Sturbridge to be explored as well, an authentic New England town with its original green and many historic buildings intact. A host of enticing shops beckons. Sadie Green's Curiosity Shop has a name that does not do justice to the enormous selection of original design jewelry made with luminous antique glass. There are two locations, one on the common, another on Route 20 near Basketville, a shop known for its hundreds of wicker items.

The Seraph has fine reproductions of early American furniture, and the Shaker Shop features Shaker furniture designs. The Marketplace, a restored mill, offers a little of everything, including a whole top floor of handcrafts. Antiquers will find many lures. Some of the larger selections are available at collectives with a number of dealers under one roof, such as the Antique Center of Sturbridge and Sturbridge Antiques.

When it comes to choosing lodging for the night, the most attractive Sturbridge inn is the 1771 Publick House, a longtime New England standby that is full of Colonial charm, and its equally attractive, cozier, and quieter adjunct, the Colonial Ebenezer Crafts Inn. The Publick House runs a series of very pleasant "Yankee Winter Weekends," featuring lots of hearty fare and visits to Old Sturbridge. However, the package includes dinner, something of a waste if you plan to take part in cooking at the village. Old Sturbridge Village has a motor lodge adjoining the grounds, as well as the Oliver Wight House, a handsome, restored early American home that is a very fitting lodging for the weekend. Another inn alternative is the Wildwood Inn in Ware, about 20 miles away, a Victorian charmer with very reasonable prices.

On Sunday you have a choice of destinations, depending on whether you want indoor or outdoor activity. For starters, you might follow

Route 20 a few miles east to Auburn for the year-round antiques fair and flea market, held on Route 12. Clock fanciers should take the Mass Pike east a few miles to Grafton for the Willard House and Clock Museum, the birthplace of the famous Willard clock makers. Featured are many fine early clocks, including some prize tall clocks, as well as eighteenth-century furnishings.

Worcester, Massachusetts's second largest city, is just 20 miles from Sturbridge via Routes 90 and 290. Worcester is still thought of by many as primarily a factory town, but it is actually much more. In addition to a Colonial heritage dating back to 1673, an attractively hilly terrain, and lovely residential areas, Worcester is the home of 12 college campuses and three interesting small museums.

The Higgins Armory Museum, unique and worth a visit, is a showcase for over 70 suits of shining armor and a multitude of weapons and artifacts from medieval and Renaissance Europe, ancient Greece and Rome, and feudal Japan. They are displayed in a splendidly appropriate setting—a Great Hall with soaring arches, stained glass, and tapestries.

The New England Science Center complex, a museum and wildlife center on 60 acres, offers participatory science exhibits, a solar/lunar observatory and planetarium, and an indoor/outdoor zoo. In winter, the stars of the outdoor show are the polar bears. A special window lets you watch them swimming under water.

The Worcester Art Museum, a handsome traditional stone building, may surprise you as well, with a collection of paintings that tell the story of art through 50 centuries of development. Rembrandts, Gainsboroughs, Goyas, Monets, Matisses, and Picassos are among the treasures here, along with a fine Asian collection. One particularly fine exhibit is a thirteenth-century French chapel rebuilt here stone by stone.

The museums are easy to find, as signs are posted pointing the way no matter where you enter the city. And when you're done with gallery hopping, you'll find that some of those dull factories in the city have been converted into very lively places for food and drink. Maxwell Silverman's Tool House, on Union, is a prime example. Bargain hunters may want to check out the Worcester Common Outlets, an indoor mall with over 100 shops, including a Saks Fifth Avenue outlet, located on Front Street across from the Centrum, the city's civic center.

If you prefer ski slopes to city, follow Route 20 east to Route 31 north and turn off on Route 62 in Princeton for Wachusett Mountain, a small, friendly ski area with good snow-making facilities and a most attractive lodge.

Wherever you've spent the day, you may want to consider a drive to West Brookfield, northwest of Sturbridge, for dinner at the Salem Cross Inn, a fine restaurant in a beamed and beautiful Colonial home that is listed in the National Register of Historic Places. Meats are roasted here in a giant 42-foot fireplace, and now that you're an amateur expert, you can test their mettle.

Area Code: 508

DRIVING DIRECTIONS   Sturbridge is located on Route 20 in south-central Massachusetts, exit 9 on I-90, the Massachusetts Turnpike, or exit 2 off I-84. It is 55 miles from Boston, 160 miles from New York, and 40 miles from Hartford.

PUBLIC TRANSPORTATION   Sturbridge can be reached by Amtrak to Worcester, Springfield, or Boston; or by Peter Pan bus lines from Boston, New York, or Hartford. Airport transport service is available from Boston, Worcester, and Hartford-Springfield's Bradley International Airport.

ACCOMMODATIONS   The lower rates listed are generally available in winter. **The Publick House,** Main Street, Sturbridge 01566, 347-3313, I–E, many reasonable packages including breakfast and dinner; under same management: **Country Motor Lodge,** I–M; **Colonel Ebenezer Crafts Inn,** Fiske Hill (off Route 20), Sturbridge 01566, 347-3313, Colonial bed-and-breakfast, I–E, CP • **Old Sturbridge Village Motor Lodge,** Route 20, Sturbridge 01566, 347-3327, pool and playground, I–M; under same management: **Oliver Wight House,** M • **Sturbridge Host Hotel and Conference Center,** Route 20, Sturbridge 01566, 347-7393, resort-motel with indoor pool, tennis, and mini-golf in season, M–E • **Wildwood Inn,** 121 Church Street, Ware 01082, 967-7798, tops for value, I, CP • **Commonwealth Cottage,** 11 Summit Avenue, Sturbridge 01566, 347-7708, Queen Anne Victorian bed-and-breakfast home, M–E, CP.

DINING   **The Publick House** (see above), main dining room, M–EE; **Ebenezer's Tavern,** I–M • **The Whistling Swan,** 502 Main Street (Route 20), 347-2321, attractive 1855 home and barn, continental, excellent, M–E; **Ugly Duckling,** loft for casual dining, I–M • **Le Bearn Restaurant Française,** 12 Cedar Street, Sturbridge, 347-5800, good French food in a Cape Cod home, M–E • **Charlie Brown's Steakhouse,** Haynes Street, Sturbridge, 347-5559, informal, good for families, I–E • **Piccadilly Pub,** 362 Main Street, Sturbridge, 347-8189, pub fare, popular lounge, I • **Salem Cross Inn,** Route 9, West Brookfield, 867-2345, M–E • **Maxwell Silverman's Tool House,** 25 Union Street, Worcester, 755-1200, M.

SIGHTSEEING   **Old Sturbridge Village,** Route 20, Sturbridge, MA 01566, 347-3362 or (800) SEE-1830. "Dinner in a Country Village," Saturday nights at 5 P.M., December through March, limited to 14 people, minimum age 14, reservations required, approximately $60 per person. "Breakfast on a Farm," Saturday mornings at 8:30 A.M., same dates as above, $30 per person. General admission to the restoration,

$$$$$. Hours: April to October, 9 A.M. to 4 P.M.; November to January 1 and late February to March, 10 A.M. to 4 P.M.; January 2 to President's Day, weekends only, 10 A.M. to 4 P.M. • **Willard House and Clock Museum, Inc.,** 11 Willard Street, Grafton, 839-3500. Hours: Tuesday to Saturday, 10 A.M. to 4 P.M.; Sunday, 1 P.M. to 5 P.M. $$ • **Higgins Armory Museum,** 100 Barber Avenue, Worcester, 853-6015. Hours: Tuesday to Saturday, 10 A.M. to 4 P.M., Sunday noon to 4 P.M. $$ • **Worcester Art Museum,** 55 Salisbury Street, 799-4406. Hours: mid-February to December 31, Wednesday to Friday, 11 A.M. to 3 P.M.; on Saturday, 10 A.M. to 5 P.M.; Sunday, 11 A.M. to 5 P.M. $$; 12 and under, free; free to all Saturday 10 A.M. to noon • **New England Science Center,** 222 Harrington Way, Worcester, 791-9211. Hours: Monday to Saturday, 10 A.M. to 5 P.M.; Sunday from 12 noon. $$$ • **Wachusett Mountain State Reservation,** Princeton, 464-2712, ski area with one triple and two double chairlifts, beginner's area and teaching facilities.

INFORMATION Sturbridge Area Tourist Association, PO Box 66, Route 20, Sturbridge, MA 01566, 347-7594; Worcester County Convention and Visitors Bureau, 33 Waldo Street, Worcester, MA 01608, 753-2920.

Happy Landings in Salisbury

They fly through the air with the greatest of ease, those graceful ski jumpers in Salisbury, Connecticut.

Ever since 1926 the best of these daring young people, including many of our top Olympic contenders, have shown off their style each year in early February at the United States Eastern Ski Jump Championships, held at Salisbury's Satre Hill.

Even the most sedentary spectator will appreciate the extraordinary coordination and skill required to make a 55-meter jump with a happy landing. Sports enthusiasts and firesiders alike will also appreciate the many cozy inns and other attractions of this particularly charming corner of the state.

Northwest Connecticut is Currier and Ives country, set in the rolling foothills of the Berkshire Mountains and blessed with a string of picture-pretty Colonial towns. It has long attracted writers and artists, but though the area now has also been well discovered by wealthy New Yorkers looking for vacation homes, it has escaped any obvious kind of commercialization. Except for inflated real estate prices and the appearance of such items as gourmet pasta and cheese in local grocery stores, villages such as Salisbury, Sharon, and Lakeville retain the unspoiled air that attracted the newcomers in the first place.

This is also ideal country for anyone who wants to learn to ski, either downhill or cross-country, with low-key Mohawk Mountain, a few miles south in Cornwall, offering excellent facilities without the hassles found at the bigger areas farther north. This area is so civilized that the ski lodge even hangs up potted plants and provides a library of books for nonskiers. There are extensive snowmaking facilities to help ensure the necessary white stuff on the slopes, as well as miles of cross-country trails in the adjacent state forest.

The Ski Jump Championship, a one-of-a-kind event in the East, is held both Saturday and Sunday from 11 A.M. Saturday's jump is the annual Salisbury Invitational, Sunday is the official eastern competition. The old 217-foot record may already have been bettered by this time.

In their slick, skintight jumpsuits, with special light boots, bindings, and skis, the jumpers are a thrilling sight as they leap off into space. All it takes is some watching to begin to understand the standards that go into making a champion. In addition to the length of the jump, the bend of the body, the position of the skis, the spring of the takeoff, and the grace of the landing are all calculated by the judges before each competitor is given a score.

Even with the coffee or hot chocolate served at a convenient stand, a couple of hours in the cold is enough for most viewers, so there is plenty of time to explore Salisbury and some of the surrounding towns. The lack of touristy attractions is one of this area's chief delights, but there are enough unique shops to keep you occupied for a pleasant hour in town and to give you an excuse to tour some of the nearby territory.

Right in the village, you'll find the Salisbury Antiques Center on Library Street, just off Route 44, with an interesting and eclectic selection. Serious antiquers should proceed north on Route 7 across the Massachusetts state line to Sheffield, where every other house on the main street seems to have blossomed into an antiques shop.

Other stops in Salisbury are Garlande Limited, on Main Street, with a selection of interesting gifts and accessories in a restored 1832 home; and Amandari, tucked away on Academy Street, with a unique collection of designer home accessories and jewelry, mostly from Bali. Lauray, a plant shop on Undermountain Road, is a top source for cacti and succulent plants, which can be bought in person or by mail. Chaiwalla is the place to sample exotic teas, then buy your own to take home. You can also have a delicious light lunch in the tearoom.

Go back on Route 41 and take Route 44 west to Lakeville, home of the prestigious Hotchkiss School, where you'll find a few upscale shops and Harney & Sons, which supplies fine teas to some of the country's leading restaurants, including Ritz Carlton hotels nationwide. A tasting room allows you to sample some of the blends before you buy.

Or you can follow Route 44 east into East Canaan for the Connecticut Woodcarvers' Gallery, a shop featuring hand-carved birds, animals, clocks, frames, and other objects done by some 14 professional woodcarvers. If you don't see what you want, they'll carve it to order for you.

Romantics should drive farther east on Route 44 into Norfolk to discover one of the prettiest towns around, complete with village green, church steeples, shuttered Colonial houses, and a mansion in the middle of town that serves as summer quarters for the Yale School of Music. Norfolk boasts three of the most charming inns in Connecticut, as well as the chance for a sleigh ride through the snow at Loon Farms, complete with jingle bells and hot mulled cider. They switch to carriage rides if the weather is uncooperative.

When snow is on the ground, there are cross-country ski trails at Dennis Hill State Park, where you can ski through a pine forest to a gazebo with a view.

Check out the current art exhibit in the handsome 1889 library building here, and admire the fine French eighteenth- and nineteenth-century antiques at L. Joseph Stannard, in the historic Arcanum Building in the center of town. Just down the block are the Norfolk Artisans' Guild, with a nice selection of handcrafts, and the Pub and Restaurant, which boasts of having "the widest selection of the finest beers in the world." When you see the long list, you won't doubt them.

Continue east to Winsted if you want to visit Folkcraft Instruments, which features handcrafted harps, dulcimers, and psalteries. The owners claim they'll teach you to play the dulcimer in ten minutes—15 for slow learners. There are interesting records and books here also in this folk music center.

Then take Route 20 north and you'll arrive in Riverton, once known as Hitchcockville for the factory that opened here in 1826 where Lambert Hitchcock produced the famous painted and stenciled chairs that bear his name. A collection of the originals can be seen in the Hitchcock Museum, in an old church in the center of town. Chairs are still made in the factory using many of the original hand procedures, and new models of the old patterns are for sale at the showroom and shop adjoining the factory.

Riverton offers a few interesting shops as well, such as Gifts of Distinction, with Victorian silverplate, jewelry and decorative accents, and an exceptional array of garden ornaments and sculptures. Stop at the Catnip Mouse Tearoom for a homemade lunch and top it with chocolates or rich ice cream at the Village Sweet Shop.

The Old Riverton Inn is one of Connecticut's oldest inns, a good bet for a meal or an overnight stay. The inn often offers special packages for skiers at Sundown, a ski area in New Hartford that offers night skiing. Other traditional inn lodgings are to be found in Salisbury and Norfolk, and Lakeville's Interlaken Inn is a mini-resort, often with attractive ski packages at Mohawk Mountain and at the Catamount ski area, just across the state line. If your idea of a winter weekend means cuddling by the fire, most of the inns can oblige you with the proper setting.

If you have more touring time after the ski-jump competitions on Sunday, drive south about 25 miles from Salisbury on Route 7 and then Route 63 to Litchfield, a town that is invariably high on the list of most beautiful Main Streets in New England. You'll probably recognize the Congregational Church on the green, since it shows up in countless magazine photos of New England scenes. Next door is the 1787 parsonage where Harriet Beecher Stowe was born. The extraordinarily fine homes here are still occupied, some by descendants of the original occupants. Take a walk or a slow drive on North and South Streets to see the handsome early architecture, and make special note of the little house on South where Tapping Reeve opened the nation's first law school in 1773 with his brother-in-law, Aaron Burr, as his first pupil. The fine collections of the Litchfield Historical Society are closed in winter, but there are many art galleries and some shops that make for pleasant browsing. The Workshop, opposite the town green, has a choice selection of clothing and home accesssories, and at Susan Wakeen, on Route 202, you can buy limited editions by a noted doll artist or create your own doll. The West Street Grill, on the green, is one of the best in the state, highly recommended for a lunch or dinner stop.

Litchfield's White Memorial Foundation offers 35 miles of cross-country skiing trails for those who want to make the most of the wintry weather. Ski rentals are available at the Wilderness Shop, on Route 202, about a mile from the foundation property.

Or follow Route 202 west out of Litchfield to Bantam Lake to end your winter outing by watching yet another speedy sport, for this is the home course for the Connecticut Ice Yachting Club. Up to 30 boats gather here every weekend for this unusual activity, which requires just the kind of winter conditions most of us try to avoid—high winds and frigid temperatures. The hardy competitors seem to find the thrills and speed ample compensation, however, and when conditions are right, it's not unusual to see a DN-60 or Skeeter-class boat skimming along at up to 100 miles an hour. It's great fun to watch—just be sure to dress for the weather.

Area Code: 860

DRIVING DIRECTIONS Salisbury is on Route 44, reached via Route 7 from the east and Route 22 from the west. Salisbury is about 150 miles from Boston, 103 miles from New York, and 65 miles from Hartford.

PUBLIC TRANSPORTATION Bonanza bus service to Canaan, Connecticut, a few miles from Salisbury.

ACCOMMODATIONS   Ask about weekend and ski packages. **Under Mountain Inn,** Undermountain Road (Route 41), Salisbury 06068, 435-0242, attractive 1700s home, country ambience, warm British hosts, English breakfasts, British-inspired video collection in the lounge, E–EE, MAP • **The White Hart,** Village Green, Salisbury 06968, 435-0030, longtime local landmark and gathering place, Colonial ambience, nicely refurbished, M–E • **Interlaken Inn,** Route 122, Lakeville 06039, 435-9878, modern resort building or Victorian-style inn on grounds, indoor sauna and Jacuzzi, ice skating nearby, M–E • **Wake Robin Inn,** Route 41, Lakeville 06039, 435-2515, former private school turned inn, nicely furnished but some rooms are quite small, ask for a larger room, M–EE, CP • **Manor House,** PO Box 701, Maple Avenue, Norfolk 06058, 542-5690, showplace 1898 Victorian, spacious rooms, fine wood paneling, stained glass, fireplaces, breakfast in bed on request, M–E, CP • **Angel Hill,** 54 Greenwoods Road East, Norfolk 06058, 542-5920, haven for romantics, canopies, fireplaces, Jacuzzis, candlelight breakfasts, a guardian angel in every room, M–E, CP • **Greenwoods Gate,** Greenwoods Road East, Norfolk 06058, 542-5439, stylishly furnished Federal-era inn, all suites, one with oversized spa bath, E–EE, CP • **Mountain View Inn,** Route 272, Norfolk 06058, 542-6991, homey Victorian, I–M, CP • **Old Riverton Inn,** Route 20, Riverton 06065, 379-8678 or (800) EST-1796, atmospheric classic 1796 Colonial inn, I–M, CP • **Tollgate Hill,** Route 202, Litchfield 06759, 482-6116, best known as a restaurant, but rooms have pleasant period decor in 1700s Colonial building, M–E. Two exceptional bed-and-breakfast homes deserve mention though they have limited space: **Cathedral Pines Farm,** Cornwall, 672-6747, offers one bedroom with private bath in a Colonial-style farmhouse that has been featured in *House Beautiful;* llamas are at play in the pasture, as the hosts raise llamas, and guests have use of a hot tub under the stars, M, CP; **Armstrong Bed and Breakfast,** Ethan Allen Street, Lakeville 06039, 435-9964, is across the hedges from the town's beautiful, big lake; the second floor with a private entrance offers two bedrooms, one bath, an eat-in kitchen, and a large living room, M, CP.

DINING   **The American Grill,** The White Hart (see above), M–E; Garden Room and Tap Room, informal meals, M • **Under Mountain Inn** (see above), British specialties, on weekends only by advance reservation, M • **The Pub and Restaurant,** Station Place, Norfolk, 542-5716, informal, I–M • **Woodland,** Route 41, Lakeville, 435-0578, casual, popular locally, good bet for Sunday brunch, M • **The Cannery,** 85 Main Street, Route 44, Canaan, 824-7333, decorated with canning jars, Cajun and other good things on the menu, M • **Mountain View Inn** (see above), varied menu, M • **Old Riverton Inn** (see above), M • **West Street Grill,** 43 West Street, Litchfield, 567-3885, M–E • **Grappa Restaurant and Trattoria,** the Litchfield Commons, 26 Commons Drive (off Route 202), Litchfield, 567-1616, I–M • **Tollgate Hill** (see above), Colonial ambience, traditional menu, M–E.

SIGHTSEEING   U.S. Eastern Ski Jumping Championships, two days, usually first weekend in February, single tickets or combination for both days. Write to Salisbury Winter Sports Association, Salisbury, CT 06068, for current dates and ticket prices, or contact Chamber of Commerce. *Skiing:* **Mohawk Mountain Ski Area,** Great Hollow Road (off Route 4), Cornwall, 672-6464 • **Ski Sundown,** Ratlun Road, Route 219, New Hartford, 379-9851.

INFORMATION   Litchfield Hills Travel Council, PO Box 968, Litchfield, CT 06759, 567-4506.

Wintering in the White Mountains

Winter is the magic season in the White Mountains of New Hampshire.

Well-paved roads lead through mountain passes beneath imposing peaks that are all the more beautiful under winter coats of white. The snow adds its crowning softness to the tall pines and maples in the national forests that surround the mountains, and to the rooftops and village greens. In tiny roadside villages, skaters on the ponds make living Grandma Moses scenes.

The stupendous scenery, unmatched in the East, plus the great variety of activities and facilities available in the White Mountains, make New England's highest peaks the peak choice for couples or families who have differing abilities or enthusiasm for the ski slopes.

Whatever your winter pleasure, you'll find it here. Skiers can take their turns at more than half a dozen nearby slopes for all abilities; ski tourers have miles and miles of exquisite cross-country trails from which to choose. There's also ample opportunity for such pastimes as sledding, tobogganing, snowshoeing, and ice skating. And for indoor challenge, the North Conway bargains await—a whopping total of some 150 discount outlets in the general area.

The unsurpassed setting makes many people content to spend a weekend just driving the scenic highways, riding the mountain cable cars for the views, or simply settling in front of a fireplace at a cozy inn and enjoying the view from a picture window.

For those who do come to ski, White Mountain loyalists claim that many ski areas here still have an old-fashioned flavor that is missing in the slicker, newer resorts. Tradition is strong, after all, and northeastern skiing was born in these mountains. Norwegian immigrants were skiing here as early as the 1870s, and the first American Alpine ski school, started in the 1920s by Austrian champion Sig Buchmayr, made Franconia the Northeast's first great winter resort.

The boom continued when the first aerial tramway was built at Cannon Mountain in 1938, and prospered even further when Austrian Hannes Schneider came to North Conway in 1939 and built the first skimobile at Mt. Cranmore. Families who are into a third generation of skiing at Mt. Cranmore now enjoy modern amenities such as night skiing and a triple chair to the summit. Cranmore has 100 percent snowmaking coverage and is within walking distance of North Conway, all good reasons why it still appeals to families.

There are many other ski areas in the White Mountains, with something for just about everyone. In the North Conway–Jackson area, Wildcat, located near Mt. Washington and legendary for its howling winds, is a challenging mountain, even more so with the addition of new gladed trails, reputed to be some of the steepest in the state. Best known for its long trails and views, it also has a separate beginner area with its own triple chairlift and bargain rates. The base lodge offers sit-down dining and spectacular views of Tuckerman Ravine and the Presidential Range.

Bretton Woods is small but growing, gentler than Wildcat, and also prides itself on spectacular views and on wide-open, top-to-bottom cruising terrain that is ideal for beginners and intermediates. A "super chair" high-speed quad lift was recently installed, and there is a restaurant at the top with spectacular vistas. Black Mountain, another family area, has its own bit of history—the first overhead cable tow in America, built in 1935 and is billed as "sunny, friendly, and affordable." Half of the mountain is teaching or novice terrain. Snow tubing is a popular addition here.

Attitash Bear Peak, owned by the big American Ski Company, is expanding rapidly. The area now boasts two mountain peaks, two base lodges, 48 trails, and a new grand hotel at the slopes. One of the state's largest snowmaking operations has helped make it number one in New Hampshire for skier visits.

Across the mountains in Franconia is Cannon Mountain, owned by the state, the largest ski resort in the area with 35 trails, nine of them for experts but plenty left for everyone else, and 50 miles of nearby ski-touring trails past scenery that may tempt you to trade in your ski poles for a paintbrush. The mountain boasts New Hampshire's only aerial tramway. Cannon remains an unspoiled world of white—no condos or commercial development in sight.

The New England Ski Museum at Cannon features audiovisual exhibits showing some early skiers in action and displays of the wooden skis belonging to Sig Buchmayr and other adventurers such as

Lowell Thomas. Other displays include the progression of skis and ski clothing from the nineteenth century to today, plus ski art and photos.

To the south are two other newer complexes that don't quite fit the old-fashioned mold. The Mountain Club on Loon has the distinction of being the only ski resort with an operating steam train; it shuttles skiers between two base complexes. Loon also boasts a high-speed gondola, good intermediate slopes, and a resort complex with its own lodge. The newest innovation here is snow tubing, which is available by night as well as by day.

Waterville Valley, with two mountains and trails for all abilities, is a chic resort that is a village in itself, with hundreds of condominiums, a sports center, restaurants, and some very choice inns. Waterville is a convenient choice for families, since a bus makes the rounds from village accommodations to the slopes regularly, allowing parents to sleep in while their kids get to be first on the trails. Sleigh rides and ice skating add to the fun. Waterville recently added snowmaking to a cross-country loop, guaranteeing good conditions.

For cross-country skiing, the White Mountains are hard to beat. Cannon and Bretton Woods take the prize for mountain scenery, but Jackson, one of the prettiest of the White Mountain villages, offers the largest ski-touring complex in the East, run by the Jackson Ski Touring Foundation and offering lessons and 150 kilometers of trails for all abilities. Experts can try their mettle on the Wildcat Valley Trail, which begins at the top of Wildcat Mountain and then swoops down 3,400 feet to meet the rest of the trail system. At Bretton Woods, cross-country skiers can take the quad chairlift for lunch at the Top O'Quad restaurant and a five-mile intermediate descent on the Mountain Road trail.

The Mt. Washington Valley Ski Touring Foundation, in Intervale, north of North Conway, also offers 60 kilometers of trails that link nine small inns to Mt. Cranmore. Many ski areas act as hosts in the Ski NH "Tour du Jour," a program of guided tours from 5 to 15 kilometers traversing a variety of scenic parts of the mountains.

Great Glen Trails at Pinkham Notch, in the shadow of Mt. Washington, is a great addition to the region, with a handsome contemporary timber frame base lodge and 40 kilometers of well-groomed cross-country trails. The Sno-Cat Shuttle takes passengers halfway up Mt. Washington to ski or snowshoe down. Guided wildlife tours are among the many special events at this excellent facility, which has extensive snowmaking to ensure good conditions. Ski-touring by the light of the moon is a special thrill at Great Glen, and is also offered on certain dates at the Mt. Washington Valley Ski Touring Association, at Bretton Woods, and at the Bear Notch Ski Touring Center in Bartlett. Great Glen also has an ice skating rink, as does the Franconia Village Cross-Country Center.

Snowshoeing has caught on big among those who want outdoor exercise without skis, and rentals are available at all resorts. Great Glen and Attitash Bear Peak offer guided tours. The Appalachian Mountain Club at Pinkham Notch also offers many weekend activities, from snowshoe adventures to dog sledding.

Chocolate lovers will want to check on this year's date for the annual Chocolate Festival, usually in late February, which allows participants to ski, snowshoe, or (for the lazy) drive from business to business and inn to inn, sampling chocolate delicacies along the way. Hand-dipped chocolate strawberries, chocolate truffle cheesecake, and Bailey's Irish Cream brownies are among the treats you might expect, along with real hot cocoa. Call the Mt. Washington Valley Chamber of Commerce for this year's details.

The accommodations in the White Mountains are as extensive as the skiing choices, ranging from lodges on the slopes to resorts to secluded country inns.

When you're settled in and the skiers are happily challenging the slopes, nonskiers will want to take the "scenic tour." From North Conway, the recommended route is the drive down to Conway on Route 16 and west on the magnificent 32-mile Kancamagus Highway, through the White Mountain National Forest from Cannon to Lincoln. At Lincoln, take Routes 3/93 north to Franconia Notch State Park.

The road travels through Franconia Notch, a natural mountain pass between the towering peaks of the Kinsman and Franconia Ranges, with some of the most spectacular scenery in the White Mountains. Here's where you'll meet the symbol of New Hampshire, the Old Man of the Mountain, that famous face carved in granite on the mountainside by some celestial sculptor.

The views and picture-book villages continue north if you detour on Route 18 to Sugar Hill, then continue west on Route 3 to connect with Route 302 at Twin Mountain for the drive back to North Conway, past Bretton Woods and Crawford Notch and turning south again on Route 16 at Glen.

Shopping is the thing in North Conway. If you need ski equipment or outdoor clothing, you won't do better than the Jack Frost, Eastern Mountain Sports, and International Mountain Equipment and Ragged Mountain Equipment stores here, plus well-stocked shops at each ski area.

Check the Scottish Lion for a fine selection of wares and choice sweaters from Scotland, Ireland, England, and Wales. You'll also find casual clothing, country collectibles, and a few art galleries and antiques shops to explore on Main Street (Route 16). Among the larger antiques shops are the Antiques & Collectibles Barn and North Conway Antiques & Collectibles, both group shops featuring a variety of dealers. The League of New Hampshire Craftsmen shop in North Conway is always worth a look for its fine selection of work by state artisans; the Hand Crafter's Barn, across the way, has folksier collectibles.

For bargains, there are outlet stores galore in North Conway, including Anne Klein, Calvin Klein, Barbizon, Cole Hahn, Corning,

Danskin, Donna Karan, L. L. Bean, Levi's, London Fog, Oshkosh, Gorham, J. Crew, Liz Claiborne, Polo/Ralph Lauren, Seiko, and Timberland. And just a few miles farther in Conway, Hathaway, Bass, Cannon Mills, and other outlet stores await.

With all that skiing, scenery, and shopping, the days fly by. Come dinner hour, there are more fine choices than can ever be fit into one weekend.

For après-ski, try the Wildcat Tavern, in Jackson Village; the Red Parka Pub, in Glen; or, in North Conway, the Up Country Saloon, Horsefeathers, or Barnaby's.

Day or night, about the only thing you may find lacking in the White Mountains is time to do justice to the cornucopia of winter pleasures.

Area Code: 603

DRIVING DIRECTIONS North Conway and Jackson, in the Mt. Washington Valley, are reached via Route 16 or Route 302, connecting from I-95. Franconia is on I-93 and Route 3; Waterville Valley is reached via I-93 to exit 28, then 11 miles to Route 49 to the valley. North Conway is 145 miles from Boston, 335 miles from New York, and 245 miles from Hartford; Franconia and Waterville are roughly 15 miles closer.

PUBLIC TRANSPORTATION Concord Trailways has bus service to Conway and Jackson; air service to Portsmouth (1½ hours) or Manchester (2 hours), New Hampshire, or to Portland, Maine (1½ hours).

ACCOMMODATIONS In addition to inns listed for Mt. Washington Valley on pages 103–104, and for Franconia on page 203, the following are convenient for ski areas. All post their highest rates in winter; ask about weekend and ski week packages. **Bretton Woods Area,** Bretton Woods 03575, 278-1000 or (800) 258-0330, includes: **The Bretton Woods Motor Inn,** indoor pool, racquetball courts, exercise room, sauna, Jacuzzi, M; **Bretton Woods Townhomes,** condos, M–EE; and **Bretton Arms,** a bed-and-breakfast inn, M–E, CP. Ask about ski packages • **Grand Summit Hotel at Attitash Bear Peak,** Route 302, Bartlett 03812, 374-1900 or (800) 223-7669, new ski-in/out facility, health club, year-round outdoor pool with Jacuzzi, M–E • **Attitash Mountain Village,** Bartlett 03812, 374-6501, indoor pool, hot tub, game room, ice skating, snowmobiling, slopeside motel, I–M; condos, M–EE • **Whitney's Inn at Black Mountain,** Jackson 03846, 383-8916, at the base of the mountain, ice skating, ME, CP • **The Mill House Inn,** Route 112, Lincoln 03251, 745-6261 or (800) 654-6183, attractive hotel, indoor pool, exercise room, free shuttle to the mountain, rooms I–M, suites, M–E; also part of the Mill development, with similar rates and free ski shuttles, are: **Rivergreen Resort Hotel,** with in-room

Jacuzzis and suites with kitchens, 745-2450 or (800) 654-6183; and the **Lodge at Lincoln Station,** 745-3441 or (800) 654-6188, with an indoor pool; both with the same rate range • **The Mountain Club on Loon,** Kancamagus Highway, Lincoln 03251, 745-8111 or (800) 229-STAY, whirlpool, exercise equipment, squash, racquetball, M–E; suites and condos on the mountain, E • **Waterville Valley Lodging Bureau,** Waterville Valley 03215, 236-8311 or (800) GO-VALLEY, upscale condos or modern inns with indoor pools, saunas, Jacuzzis, etc.; ice skating, sleigh rides, sports club; excellent package rates, kids free; condos, M–EE; **Snowy Owl Inn,** M–EE; **Black Bear Lodge,** M–EE, suites; **Golden Eagle Lodge,** M–EE; and **Valley Inn,** M–EE • The homey **Cranmore Mountain Lodge,** Kearsarge Road, North Conway 03860, 356-2044, M, CP; the classic New England **Franconia Inn,** Easton Road (Route 116), Franconia 03580, 823-5542 or (800) 473-5299, M–E, CP; and the elegant Victorian **Nestlenook Inn,** PO Box Q, Dinsmore Road, Jackson 03846, 383-8071, E–EE, CP, have their own ski-touring trails as well as ice skating. Franconia Inn and Nestlenook offer sleigh rides as well. Free reservation service for the Mt. Washington Valley, (800) 367-3364.

DINING   See listings for Mt. Washington Valley, pages 104–105; and Franconia, page 203.

SIGHTSEEING   **New England Ski Museum,** next to Cannon Mountain Tram, PO Box 267, Franconia, 823-7177. Hours: December through March, Thursday to Tuesday, noon to 5 P.M.; Memorial Day to Columbus Day, daily, noon to 5 P.M. Free. *Ski areas (write for trail maps and current rates):* **Attitash Bear Peak,** Route 302, Bartlett 03812, 374-2368 or (800) 223-SNOW for lodging; **Black Mountain,** Jackson 03846, 383-4490 or (800) 475-4669; **Mt. Cranmore,** off Routes 302 and 16, North Conway 03860, 356-5544 or (800) SUN-N-SKI; **Wildcat,** Route 16, Jackson 03846, 466-3326 or (800) 255-6439; **Bretton Woods,** Route 302, Bretton Woods 03575, 278-5000 or (800) 232-2972; **Loon Mountain,** Lincoln 03251, 745-8111 or (800) 229-STAY; **Cannon Mountain,** Route 3, Franconia 03580, 823-7771 or (800) 227-4191; **Waterville Valley,** Waterville Valley 03215, 236-8371 or (800) 468-2553. *Cross-country skiing:* **Great Glen Trails,** Route 16, Pinkham Notch, Gorham 03581, 466-2333; **Jackson Ski Touring Foundation,** Jackson 03846, 383-9355 or (800) XC-SNOWS; **Mt. Washington Valley Ski Touring Foundation,** Routes 16 and 302, Intervale 03845, 356-9920; **Appalachian Mountain Club,** Pinkham Notch Visitor Center, Route 16, Pinkham Notch (10 miles north of Jackson), 03581, 466-2727.

INFORMATION   White Mountains Visitors Bureau, PO Box 10, North Woodstock, NH 03262, 745-8720 or (800) 346-3687; Mt. Washington Valley Chamber of Commerce, Route 16, PO Box 2300, North

Conway, NH 03860, 356-31711 or (800) 367-3364; Franconia–Sugar Hill Chamber of Commerce, Franconia, NH 03580, 823-5661 or (800) 237-9007. For New Hampshire ski information and a free regional guide: Ski New Hampshire, PO Box 10, North Woodstock, NH 03262, 745-9396 or (800) 88-SKI-NH.

Back to Nature in Bethel

When a noted Cleveland surgeon, Dr. John Gehring, suffered a nervous breakdown in 1887, he came to the peaceful New England village of Bethel, Maine, to recover.

The cure worked so well that Gehring opened a pioneering clinic in Bethel, and it soon became famous. Many prominent people came to regain their health and good spirits with a program that combined outdoor activities such as planting crops and cutting wood with contemplating the beauty of the surrounding forests and mountains.

The formula still works. Visitors these days are more likely to get their exercise hiking or skiing, but for a restorative weekend close to nature, it's hard to beat this quiet and beautiful corner of western Maine. Bethel has become a mecca for skiers, both downhill and cross-country, and offers many other winter diversions, as well.

The history of this handsome Colonial town of 2,500 goes back much further than Dr. Gehring's day, and much of it can be revisited on a walk through town. Bethel was founded in 1774 as Sudbury, Canada, after the original grantees from Sudbury, Massachusetts, all of whom had fought in the campaign to conquer Canada. The early sawmills and farms along the Androscoggin River prospered after the Revolutionary War, and in 1796 the town was incorporated as Bethel, a biblical name meaning "House of God."

With the arrival of the railway, wood products became (and remain) an important factor in the town's economy. The trains also brought the first summer visitors to enjoy the town's extraordinary setting in the White Mountains foothills.

The 1836 founding of Gould Academy, one of Maine's oldest prep schools, brought notice to the town. Later, the residency of William Rogers Chapman, an outstanding musician who attracted many of the nation's music greats to visit, and the 1947 arrival of the National Training Laboratories with their experimental human relations and leadership programs, further helped give Bethel a prominence beyond its size.

Much of the center of Bethel is now a National Historic District marking the early landmarks. Stroll down to the end of the aptly named

Broad Street and you can see Dr. Gehring's original clinic, an 1896 Queen Anne home that is presently the headquarters of the National Training Laboratories.

It was Dr. Gehring and one of his patients, William Bingham II, who in 1913 built the Bethel Inn on the choice spot facing the long town common. The inn presently consists of the old main building and a series of surrounding 1800s residences bought up over the years for additional lodging space. It isn't quite as formal or as elegant as it once was, but it is still attractive, with big warming fireplaces and picture windows in the dining room and main lounges that look out on an evergreen-rimmed golf course and the White Mountains beyond. In winter, the course is a perfect place for cross-country skiers. The inn offers 36 kilometers of trails connecting to some of the many other touring trails in the area, plus a sauna to ease aching muscles when tired skiers come home. It also operates a touring center with rentals and instruction open to all. And if you stay at the inn, you can splash around in an outdoor pool heated to 91 degrees, a treat when the world around you is covered with snow.

Cross-country ski enthusiasts will find another center on the Sunday River access road with 40 kilometers of trails. The Telemark Inn and Philbrook Farm, both in the countryside outside town, provide their own cross-country trails for guests.

Everyone is invited to enjoy ice skating on the community pond, just off the town common. Skate rentals are available at the Bethel Inn.

Around the common are some classic clapboard mansions such as the 1848 Greek Revival Major Gideon Hastings House, built by the founder of one of western Maine's timberland and lumbering dynasties, and the Moses Mason House, the circa-1813 Federal-style home of one of the town's leading early residents. The Mason House is now a museum of eight period rooms restored by the Bethel Historical Society. Though it is generally open in winter only by appointment, during the annual February Heritage Day celebration the house hosts special tours and demonstrations of old-time crafts.

One of the attractive homes on the common is now the Red Geranium, a sunny and appealing bed-and-breakfast inn.

The handsome Gould Academy campus, at the other end of town, includes the Owen Art Gallery and offers a variety of performances in Bingham Hall; check to see what is on while you are in town.

The white-spired West Parish Congregational Church, near the school, housed the congregation led by the Reverend Daniel Gould, a teacher and pastor, for whom the academy was named.

Having seen the sights of Bethel, skiers will want to make haste north on Route 26 to Newry and Sunday River, New England's fastest-growing ski areas. From its beginnings as a community ski area, Sunday River has grown to include eight peaks, 121 trails, 17 lifts (including five triple and eight quad chairs), and more than 645 acres of skiing with 92 percent snowmaking coverage. These days, you need never leave the mountain for lodging or dining variety. Among many recent additions are two slopeside condominium hotels, more condos, and the North Peak Lodge with food service at the summit. Après-ski fun and food ranges from Bumps!, a sports pub, to a variety of fine dining.

Après-ski at Sunday River on weekends and holidays includes the kids, who can enjoy sledding, games, ski movies, and more. Teens have their own supervised club. Getting around the complex is easy, with trolley service that covers the parking areas, base lodges, and most condo complexes.

South of Bethel are Mt. Abram, five miles from town on Route 26, and Shawnee Peak, a bit farther away in Bridgton, both low-key family areas with very reasonable rates and both with night skiing. Mt. Abram also offers a snow-tubing facility and ice skating.

If you want a more unique winter experience, the Mahoosuc Guide Service, in Newry, and Winter Journeys, in East Stoneham, offer a variety of dog sled tours.

Bethel isn't loaded with touristy shopping, but there are some interesting stops around town. For products made in the Pine Tree State, stop at Maine Line Products, on Main Street, with everything from birdhouses to pine furniture to weather sticks made by Maine artisans. Mountain Side Country Crafts, on the Sunday River access road, specializes in Maine-made handcrafts.

If you drop in at Mt. Mann Jewelers, 57 Main Street, gemologist Jim Mann will show off some of the treasures from nearby quarries that make the Bethel area a summer favorite with rockhounds. Mann has a "crystal cave" where you can collect buckets of gems and identify each type for a small fee, a favorite activity for families. He is planning to install a gem museum with hundreds of exhibits.

Philbrook Place, at 162 Main Street, is a shopping complex in a restored period home, with a variety of shops selling clothing, books, toys, wine, gourmet foods, outdoor apparel, and travel gear, and a surprise—Asian furniture and gifts at Far East Antiques.

Bonnema Potters, 146 Main, is a showroom for stoneware and porcelain in rich multicolors.

Keep going down Main Street, across the railroad tracks, and turn left onto Cross Street to see the newest development in town, Bethel Station, where you'll find a four-screen movie theater, an arcade, the visitor information office, and the Iron Horse, a restaurant housed in railroad cars right on the tracks.

A tour of other towns in the area will bring you to more shops and some lovely winter scenery. On Route 26 in West Paris, you'll find both the Mollyocket Marketplace Antique Center, a big group shop, and a dazzling gem display at Perham's, with quarries nearby that can be visited. A little further afield, Bridgton, Harrison, and Naples also offer stops for antiquers, and Mt. Mica Rarities, in Locke Mills, has antiques and more prize hand-crafted gem jewelry.

Be sure to include the perfect little Colonial hamlet of Waterford in your travels, another good prospect for lodging with three exceptional small inns to choose from—and fine dining as well. On the way south from Bethel to Waterford on Route 35, you'll pass through Lynchville, where you can photograph the famous road sign pointing in all directions to such faraway places as Norway, Paris, Denmark, Naples, Poland, Peru, and China—all of them nearby villages in Maine.

Area Code: 207

DRIVING DIRECTIONS   Bethel is about 70 miles northwest of Portland and its airport. It can be reached via Route 26 from the Gray exit of the Maine Turnpike or from the west via Route 2, which connects to I-91 at St. Johnsbury, Vermont. It is 175 miles from Boston, 385 miles from New York, and 275 miles from Hartford.

PUBLIC TRANSPORTATION   Closest air service is Portland, 70 miles away. Shuttle service from Portland is available by reservation; phone (207) 824-4646.

ACCOMMODATIONS   Bethel Area Reservation Service for all lodgings: (800) 442-5826. **Bethel Inn & Country Club,** Bethel 04217, 824-2175, M–EE, MAP; ask about weekend packages • **Red Geranium,** Broad Street, PO Box 16, Bethel 04217, 824-3170, sunny, spacious 1859 home on the common, I–M, CP • **L'Auberge,** PO Box 21, Bethel 04217, 824-2774 or (800) 760-2774, simple secluded village inn, M, CP • **Sudbury Inn,** Main Street, PO Box 521, Bethel 04217, 824-2174 or (800) 395-7837, unpretentious village inn with a good dining room, I–M, CP • **Holidae House,** Main Street, Bethel 04217, 824-3400, antiques-filled Victorian, I–M, CP • **Chapman Inn,** Bethel 04217, 824-2657, 1865 home, informal, M, CP; dorm for skiers, I, CP, on the common • **Sunday River Ski Resort,** Newry 04217, 824-3000 or (800) 543-2SKI, includes: **Summit Hotel,** luxury slopeside condohotel, heated outdoor pool, rooms and studios, M–EE; **Jordan Grand Hotel,** newest slopeside luxury condo-hotel, health club and outdoor pool, M–EE; **Sunday River Condominiums,** Sunday River 04217, family-pleasing units offering heated indoor pools, game rooms, and laundry facilities, one-bedroom units sleeping four, E–EE; **Snow Cap Ski Dorm,** budget-priced five- and eight-person bunkrooms with private baths, I • **Sunday River Inn,** RFD 2, Box 1688, Newry 04217, 824-2410, ski lodge and dorm at cross-country ski center, dorms, I; lodge packages with meals and skiing, M–E, MAP • **Telemark Inn,** RFD 2, Box 800, Bethel 04217, 836-2703, rustic retreat with 20 kilometers of groomed cross-country trails, ice skating, snowshoeing, and horse-drawn sleigh rides, E–EE, AP (includes skiing) • **Philbrook Farm Inn,** off Route 2, Shelburne, NH 03581, (603) 466-3831, cozy country farmhouse not far from Bethel, on 100 acres with its own cross-country and snowshoeing trails, M–E, MAP. Also see Waterford accommodations, page 187.

DINING **Bethel Inn & Country Club** (see above), M • **Mother's,** Upper Main Street, Bethel, 824-2589, cozy ambience and good food in a village home, I–M • **Sudbury Inn** (see above), restaurant, M; and Suds Pub, I • **L'Auberge** (see above), sophisticated menu for this area, M–E • **Iron Horse,** Bethel Station, 824-0960, American fare served aboard vintage rail cars, M • **Matterhorn,** Main and Cross Streets, 824-OVEN, gourmet pizza from a wood-burning oven, I • **Center Lovell Inn,** Route 5, Center Lovell, 925-1575, fine country dining, M • **Maurice,** 113 Main Street (Route 26), South Paris, 743-2532, French menu, M • **Sunday River Brewing Company,** Route 2 and Sunday River Road, 824-4ALE, brew-pub and restaurant serving steak to pizza, I–M. Also see listings for Waterford and Bridgton dining, page 187.

SKI AREAS **Sunday River Ski Resort,** Route 26, Newry (six miles north of Bethel), 824-3000 or (800) 543-2SKI • **Mt. Abram Ski Slopes,** Route 26, Locke Mills (five miles south of Bethel), 875-5003 • **Shawnee Peak Ski Area,** at Pleasant Mountain, Mountain Road (off Route 302), Bridgton, 647-8444 • **Sunday River Cross-Country Ski Center,** Sunday River Access Road, RFD 2, Box 1688, Newry, 824-2410 • **Telemark Inn,** RFD 2, Box 800, Bethel (phone for directions), 836-2703.

DOG SLEDDING Phone for current offerings. **Winter Journeys,** East Stoneham, 928-2026; **Mahoosuc Guide Service,** Newry, 824-2073.

INFORMATION Bethel Area Chamber of Commerce, PO Box 439, Bethel, ME 04217, 824-2346.

Beyond the Mansions in Newport

Newport, Rhode Island, is a town with multiple personalities.

There's the opulent Newport, summer bastion of the superwealthy, evidenced by some of the grandest mansions in the country.

There's the nautical Newport, easy to discern in summer by the dozens of yachts in the harbor and enough visitors clad in Top-Siders to sink a ship. The old wharfs have bloomed anew with restaurants and shops to accommodate all the sailors plus the army of landlubbers who join them on warm-weather weekends, giving rise to the touristy Newport.

And then there is the Newport that tends to get lost in all the tourist activity—a town of rare scenic beauty. The beauty is seen best on the spectacular ten-mile Ocean Drive, along a clifftop overlooking the sea, and on the Cliff Walk, along the bluffs.

And don't forget Colonial Newport, a town of enormous charm whose narrow old streets have undergone one of the most impressive restorations in the country.

In the quiet off-season, when the harbor is still and the hordes of tourists are gone, it is these last and sometimes neglected aspects of Newport that shine through. And with the mansions and many other attractions still open for sightseeing and the shops and restaurants still very much in business, there's plenty of activity when you want it. Add the drama of wintry winds that send waves dashing against the cliffs and you have a winning winter getaway. To make things even nicer, lodging rates go way down.

The town has made things livelier in its slow season with a February Winter Festival that grows larger by the year. Horse-drawn hayrides, snow sculptures, an ice-carving competition, and a scavenger hunt through town are among over 100 events. Magicians, clowns, and fireworks are part of the fun. And when the weather is right, a favorite feature is the Cliffwalk Society Winter Stroll, a guided walk along Newport's scenic path above the sea.

One of the tastiest sides of this festival is food. A festival ticket entitles you to visit restaurants all around town and sample their specialties, Southwestern ribs to New England clam chowder. Restaurants also feature dinner specials during festival week, including progressive dinners, moving to different locations for each course. Come evening, jazz concerts and candlelight tours of historic homes are on the agenda.

If Newport today seems to have more than its share of personalities, it may be because of the town's unusual past. It was founded in 1639 by settlers seeking religious freedom but soon prospered as a major seaport of the infamous "Triangle Trade"—actually an extension of the slave trade—using African slaves to obtain West Indian sugar and molasses to be made into Newport rum. The pineapple, Newport's hospitality symbol, was first brought to town by sea captains returning from the West Indies who placed the exotic fruit in front of the house to tell neighbors they were home safely and welcoming visitors.

Newport's era of prominence as a port ended when the British burned the harbor, once during the Revolutionary War and again during the War of 1812. Later it became a haunt of artists and writers taken with its natural beauty. They were followed in the late 1800s by the wealthy, who put up the opulent palaces by the sea, which they called "cottages," to be used for a feverish six-week season that became the nation's most elaborate social scene.

Though many wealthy summer people remain, Newport's Gilded Age died out with changing times. The mansions survive as tourist attractions. The seven homes operated by the Newport Preservation Society currently draw a million visitors a year.

The building of a bridge connecting Newport to Jamestown in 1969 made it far more accessible for travelers; and in 1973, when the navy moved out of the base that had helped support the town economy, the city fathers began to encourage the trend further. The waterfront was restored, and shops and restaurants opened, attracting a seasonal flood of tourists.

During all this activity, a part-time resident, the late Doris Duke, had begun to take interest in the many fine early eighteenth-century buildings that had been allowed to decay. She set up a foundation that renovated some six dozen of the houses, renting them at reasonable rates to residents who would appreciate and protect their heritage. Others soon followed suit, spreading the restoration area.

A good overview of the city's diverse past can be found at the Museum of Newport History, a project of the Newport Historical Society, housed in the restored 1762 Brick Market Building. The exhibits progress from the earliest inhabitants, the Native Americans who settled the area over 12,000 years ago, to fine ship models and exquisite Colonial silver to a ball gown worn by a member of summer society. Paintings and hundreds of historic photographs help bring the story to life.

But there's nothing like seeing the real thing. If you want to start your Newport tour chronologically, a stroll up the cobbled streets leading uphill from the town center and along the waterfront on Washington Street—the area known as the Point—will show you early Newport in a series of some 400 pastel-hued town houses that are perhaps the nation's most extensive collection of authentic Colonial dwellings. Washington Street has some particularly fine homes. You can rent a taped driving or walking tour at the Chamber of Commerce if you want to know more about the history of this area, as well as about the rest of the town.

Next, a tour on the well-marked Ocean Drive past the mansions and out on the bluffs will show you the views that attracted all those millionaires to Newport. If the weather is kind, stop off along Bellevue Avenue, bundle up, and follow some of the Cliff Walk, a 3½-mile path along the top that gives you a rare perspective of lawns and mansions on one side and an eagle's-eye ocean view on the other.

By now you'll probably be dying to see the insides of the houses. If you think we had no royalty in America, you may well change your mind when you see the massive scale, the marble floors and chandeliers, and the priceless brocades of the summer palaces of America's upper crust.

Three of the finest of the houses remain open for touring on weekends all year: Marble House, designed by Richard Morris Hunt for William K. Vanderbilt and named for the many colors of marble used in its construction and decorations; the Elms, a summer residence of Philadelphia coal magnate Edward Berwind, modeled after the Château d'Asnieres, near Paris; and Château-sur-Mer, one of the most lavish examples of Victorian architecture and the site of Newport's first ballroom.

There are other mansions to be toured as well. Mrs. Astor's Beechwood takes you back to 1891, when Caroline Astor ruled as queen of American society. The Gilded Age is brought to life with lavish theatrical performances. Belcourt Castle, built by Oliver Hazard Perry Belmont, heir to the American Rothschild fortune, cost $3 million, an unbelievable amount a century ago. Still a private residence, the house boasts fine woodwork and stained glass, and is furnished with art treasures and furniture collected from 40 Newport mansions of its era, as well as from European and Oriental palaces.

Back in town, everything centers on the harbor, where the first American navy was established in 1775 to provide protection against the British fleet. Along the restored wooden wharves, in old warehouses, and in new structures with Colonial-modern lines, is the touristy Newport with the usual assortment of shops to be found wherever visitors congregate.

At Bowen and Bannister Wharves, right on the waterfront, there are clothes from the Greek Isles or Ireland, original gold and silver jewelry designs, handcrafted leather, children's clothing and toys, and a candy store noted for its homemade fudge. Across the street at the Brick Market Place, a cobbled maze of condominiums and shops, there is even more variety.

If antiquing is your goal, you'll find shops on lower Thames and on parallel Spring Street, as well as on the side streets in between, particularly Franklin Street. Newport shop hours are irregular in the winter, so check the times for the stores that interest you or call for an appointment.

When it comes to lodgings, the town is now chock-a-block with choices. The coziest accommodations are the inns. Top choice for a romantic outlook is the Inn at Castle Hill, on Ocean Drive. The rambling Victorian mansion, recently handsomely refurbished, has spacious rooms, an unmatched view of the rocky coast, and a crackling fire downstairs to ward off winter chills.

The Francis Malbone House, on Thames Street, is one of the most elegant lodgings, a 1760 mansion beautifully furnished in Federal style and with a lovely garden out back, a rarity in crowded Newport. A delightful choice closer to the beach is Elm Tree Cottage, with spacious rooms done in elegant country style by artistic young innkeepers. Cliffside, also near the beach, is a flamboyant Victorian with some of the most elaborate decor in Newport, including lots of fireplaces, Jacuzzis, and showers for two. The Inn at Old Beach, a more modest Victorian, is an 1879 home with seven guest rooms furnished with taste and charm.

There are many appealing smaller guest houses in the Historic District. Longtime favorites are the three "Admirals." My favorite is the modest Admiral Farragut Inn on Clarke Street, a quiet block that is just a stroll from all the action in town. The inn is filled with handmade Shaker-style furniture, painted chests, hand-glazed walls, and whimsical original folk art murals. The Admiral Benbow, now an old-timer in rapidly changing Newport, still has loyal fans for its pretty rooms. The Admiral Fitzroy also has lots of hand-painted touches, this time in a Victorian mood.

In the Point, the oldest section of town, near the waterfront, the Sanford-Covell Villa Marina is an ornate 1870s Victorian with elaborate trim right on the water with dazzling views and a pool, a rare find in summer.

Excellent restaurants are plentiful. Some of the better ones are a bit on the formal side, so gentlemen should be prepared with jacket and tie.

If Saturday was filled with mansions and scenery, Sunday brings another set of Newport sights, mostly clustered around Touro Street and Bellevue Avenue. From the grand days, there is the Tennis Hall of Fame, located on Bellevue in the old Newport Casino Building, designed by Stanford White. Pass through the arch to see the fashionable resort that once was the epitome of recreation for the "cottage set," with lawn games, tennis and racket courts, and bowling alleys. You can try your hand at tennis here at the Casino Indoor Racquet Club or in summer on those gorgeous grass courts. The Hall of Fame museum was recently remodeled with lots of new audiovisual effects and will surely please tennis fans with its exciting look at the history of the game, from the first rackets and quaint costumes to today's champions.

Touro Synagogue, a National Historic Site, is the oldest Jewish house of worship in the country, a sign of the religious freedom of the early Rhode Island colony. The building, dedicated in 1763, is a beautiful edifice designed by Peter Harrison, the nation's first architect, in Colonial style that has been carefully preserved. It is worth a visit for anyone interested in early American architecture.

In Queen Anne Square, on Spring Street, you can see Trinity Church, the first Anglican parish in the state, with Tiffany windows, an organ tested by Handel, and the silver service and bell dating from its dedication in 1726. The Second Congregational Church, on Clarke Street, is another early building, commissioned in 1735 and attended by many prominent Colonial citizens. St. Mary's Church, on Spring Street, is of interest as the place where John Kennedy married Jacqueline Bouvier, who summered in Newport at her mother's home, Hammersmith Farm, which is now open to the public in the warmer months.

More? The Newport Historical Society, on Touro Street, has Colonial art, prize Newport silver and china, and early American glass and furniture. Changing exhibits are featured at the Newport Art Association, on Bellevue Avenue, a Beaux Arts building dating back to 1862; and the Museum of Yachting, on Ocean Drive, is open to fans in winter by appointment. Even the Redwood Library, on Bellevue, is historic; it is the oldest library building in the country in continuous use. Among those who used it were painter Gilbert Stuart and writers William and Henry James and Edith Wharton.

Mansion or not, almost every building in Newport seems to have a history worth noting, and this is a town where you could spend hours tracing the past. That is, unless you'd rather forget it all to head back to the Cliff Walk and gaze a little longer at that mesmerizing winter seascape. It's the side of Newport that many people like best of all.

Area Code: 401

DRIVING DIRECTIONS   From the south, I-95 leads to Route 138 and the Newport Bridge; from the north, follow I-95 to Route 114 south; from Boston take Route 128 south to Route 24 south via the Sakonnet River Bridge to Route 114 or Route 138 into town. Newport is about 75 miles from Boston, 185 miles from New York, and 75 miles from Hartford.

PUBLIC TRANSPORTATION   Bonanza Bus Line serves Newport. Amtrak, (800) 523-8720, runs from New York and Boston to Providence, with bus connections from the station to Newport. Major airlines serve T. F. Green Airport in Providence, with limo connections from the airport. Much of the town is walkable.

ACCOMMODATIONS   Rates listed are for high season; all are considerably lower in winter, some as much as 50 percent. Ask about special rates, and send for the hotel package brochure printed by the Convention and Visitors' Bureau. All zip codes are 02840. *Top picks (be sure inns provide parking space):* **The Inn at Castle Hill,** Ocean Drive, 849-3800, E–EE, CP • **Francis Malbone House,** 392 Thames Street, 846-0392, E–EE, CP • **Elm Tree Cottage,** 336 Gibbs Avenue, 849-1610, E–EE, CP • **Cliffside Inn,** 2 Seaview Avenue, 847-1811, E–EE, CP • **The Admirals** (reservations for all at 846-4256 or toll-free (800) 343-2863 outside Rhode Island): **Admiral Farragut Inn,** 31 Clarke Street, I–E, CP; **Admiral Fitzroy,** 398 Thames Street, M–EE, CP; **Admiral Benbow,** 93 Pelham Street, M–E, CP • **The Inn at Old Beach,** 19 Old Beach Road, 849-3479, M–E, CP. *More good choices:* **Sanford-Covell Villa Marina,** 72 Washington Avenue, the Point, 847-0206, for lovers of high Victoriana and water views, M–EE, CP • **The Inntowne,** 6 Mary Street, 846-9200, hotel amenities in an inn setting, E, CP • **The Victorian Ladies,** 63 Memorial Boulevard, 849-9960, nicely decorated small inn, M–E, CP • **Wayside,** Bellevue Avenue, 847-0302, imposing home on mansion row, M–E, CP • **The Clarkston,** 28 Clarke Street, 848-5300, M–E, CP • **Melville House,** 39 Clarke Street, 847-0640, small and cozy, I–E, CP • **Brinley Victorian,** 23 Brinley Street, 849-7645 or (800) 999-8523, modest, cheerful, I–E, CP. *Resorts and larger hotels:* **Vanderbilt Hall,** 41 Mary Street, 846-6200 or (888) 826-4255, the old YMCA transformed into a lavish 50-room luxury hotel, indoor pool, fitness center, billiards room, EE • **Doubletree Islander Resort,** Goat Island, 849-2600, on a private island, EE • **Newport Harbor Hotel and Marina,** America's Cup Avenue, 847-9000, on the harbor, EE • **Newport Marriott,** 25 America's Cup Avenue, 849-1000, also on the harbor, EE • **Inn on the Harbor,** 359 Thames Street, 849-6789 or (800) 225-3522, modern 58-suite hotel with mini-kitchens, M–EE.

DINING *Serious dining:* **La Petite Auberge,** 19 Charles Street, 849-6669, highly regarded chef, E–EE • **Le Bistro,** 250 Thames Street, 849-7778, French café, one flight up, I–E • **The Black Pearl,** Bannister's Wharf, 846-5264, converted wharf warehouse, elegant dining, E–EE • **Restaurant Bouchard,** 505 Thames Street, 846-0123, cozy ambience, classic French fare, M–EE • **The Place at Yesterday's,** 28 Washington Square, 847-0116, creative chef, widely praised contemporary dishes, M–E; more casual pub menu, M • **White Horse Tavern,** Marlborough and Farewell Streets, 849-3600, nation's oldest continuously operating tavern, nicely restored, E–EE; or go for a special lunch, I–M • **Inn at Castle Hill** (see above), E–EE; brunch with a smashing view, M. *Other good choices:* **The West Deck,** 1 Waite's Wharf, 847-3610, innovative chef, contemporary menu, M–EE • **Asterix & Obelix,** 599 Lower Thames Street, 841-8833, creative dining in a funky former garage, M–E • **Rhumbline,** 62 Bridge Street, the Point, 849-6950, snug Colonial home, M • **Puerini's,** 24 Memorial Boulevard, 847-5506, tiny, reasonable, always crowded Italian, BYOB, I–M • **The Pier,** W.

Howard Wharf (off lower Thames Street), 847-3645, overlooking the harbor, entertainment on weekends, busy, I–E • **Sea Fare's American Café,** Brick Market at Thames, 849-9188, pizza and burgers to full meals, regional American, I–M • **Scales and Shells,** 527 Thames Street, 846-3474, seafood any way you like it, including Italian style, recommended, I–M • **Anthony's Shore Dinner Hall,** Waites Wharf (off lower Thames Street), 848-5058, totally informal, counter service, I–M. *Informal fare:* **The Black Pearl** (see above), has a very good café adjunct; also try the **Brick Alley Pub,** 140 Thames, 849-6334; or **The Boathouse,** 636 Thames Street, 846-7700.

SIGHTSEEING **Newport Mansions,** Preservation Society of Newport County, 424 Bellevue Avenue, 847-1000. Hours: Marble House, the Elms, and Château-sur-Mer: November to March, Saturday, Sunday, and Monday holidays, 10 A.M. to 4 P.M.; except open daily early December until Christmas week and December 26 to 30. Other mansions have varying weekend and daily schedules from late March to April; all are open May to October, daily, 10 A.M. to 5 P.M., later hours in summer. Admission: $$$–$$$$$ at each house. Combination tickets for two or more houses save money • **International Tennis Hall of Fame and Tennis Museum,** Newport Casino, Bellevue Avenue, 846-3990. Hours: daily, 9:30 A.M. to 5 P.M. $$$$ • **Touro Synagogue,** 72 Touro Street, 847-4794. Hours: tours October to May, by appointment, Monday to Friday at 2 P.M., Sunday 1 P.M. to 3 P.M.; rest of year, Monday to Friday, 1 P.M. to 3 P.M., Sunday 11 A.M. to 3 P.M. Free • **Trinity Church,** Church and Spring Streets, 846-0660. Hours: mid-October to May, Monday to Friday, 10 A.M. to 1 P.M.; July to Labor Day, daily, 10 A.M. to 4 P.M.; September to Columbus Day, Monday to Friday, 10 A.M. to 4 P.m. Many afternoon concert and choral performances are held year-round; phone for the schedule • **Newport Art Museum,** 76 Bellevue Avenue, 848-8200. Hours: Labor Day to Memorial Day, Tuesday to Saturday, 10 A.M. to 4 P.M., Sunday, 1 P.M. to 4 P.M.; summer, daily, 10 A.M. to 5 P.M. $$ • **Belcourt Castle,** Bellevue Avenue, 846-0669. Hours: May to October 15, daily, 9 A.M. to 5 P.M.; mid-October through December and February vacation week, Monday to Saturday, from 10 A.M.; February through April, Saturday and Sunday, from 10 A.M.; off-season closing times vary, so best to check. Closed January. $$$ • **Astor's Beechwood,** Bellevue Avenue, 846-3772. Hours: May through October, daily, 10 A.M. to 5 P.M.; November through December, daily, to 4 P.M.; rest of year, Friday to Sunday, 10 A.M. to 4 P.M. Off-season hours may vary, so best to phone. $$$ • **The Musem of Newport History at the Brick Market,** 82 Touro Street (at Thames Street), 841-8770. Hours: Monday, Wednesday to Saturday, 10 A.M. to 5 P.M.; Sunday, 1 P.M. to 5 P.M. Closed Tuesday. $$ • **Hammersmith Farm,** Ocean Drive, 846-7346. Hours: April to November 15, daily,

10 A.M. to 5 P.M., special holiday tours in early December. $$$$ • **Newport Winter Festival,** usually first week of February; write to Visitors' Bureau for current schedule.

INFORMATION Newport Convention and Visitors' Bureau, 23 America's Cup Avenue, Newport, RI 02840, 849-8098 or (800) 326-6030.

Boning Up on Cambridge

Igor, the Russian puppeteer, is in his usual spot off Brattle Street, maneuvering his marionettes around a circle of admirers. Down the block, the crowd is cheering for Asa the juggler, whose quips are as quick as the balls he whirls in the air. And across the way a costumed band from the Andes is offering a serenade. It's just another typical evening in Cambridge, Massachusetts, where the pavements of Harvard Square are alive with a nonstop show.

Guidebooks and many visitors tend to lump this city with Boston, just across the Charles River, but that's a mistake. Two prominent residents, Harvard, the nation's oldest and proudest university, and MIT, considered by many to be the birthplace of modern technology, make this as rightful an attraction for U.S. visitors as Oxford or the original Cambridge University are for travelers to Britain. And our Cambridge is a lot more fun—a one-of-a-kind, perfect mix of culture and funk, well worth a weekend on its own to bone up on a fascinating community.

Among the main attractions in Cambridge are the bountiful resources and museums of Harvard, some 34 bookstores, the top-notch American Repertory Theatre, and several restaurants that are rated among the best in Boston. Prize 300-year-old architecture can be admired in neighborhoods where such people as Julia Child, John Irving, and John Kenneth Galbraith are in residence. Stores around Harvard Square still offer the most traditional Ivy League wear.

But then there is the other Cambridge: offbeat shops, ethnic dives, coffeehouses, and folksingers that manage to coexist happily with the establishment, adding spice to the scene. If you settle in near Harvard Square, most of this is close enough to explore on foot. But be forewarned—a weekend is hardly enough time to take it all in.

The nation's oldest university and its environs have been the heart of Cambridge from the start. The settlement of Newtowne, founded by the Puritans in 1630, was renamed for England's famed university town when the college came along six years later, created to train the Puritan clergy and political leaders needed in the New World. Two years later the school was named for local minister John Harvard, who died in 1638, leaving his fortune and library to the institution. As Harvard grew to greatness, Cambridge flowered as well.

Step off the busy sidewalks into the calm greenery of Harvard Yard and you'll feel tradition all around you. Self-guiding maps and free hour-long guided campus tours are offered by the Harvard Information Office, located on the plaza at Holyoke Center, 1350 Massachusetts Avenue, just off the square,

If you prefer to tour on your own, cross the street and enter Harvard Yard through the Quincy Gate to see the oldest part of the campus. Massachusetts Hall, where the university president has his office, has stood on this spot since 1720. Holden Chapel, dating from 1744, is a gem of Georgian architecture. Untold numbers of students and visitors to the campus have had their pictures taken with the seated statue of John Harvard that stands in front of University Hall, the gray stone building designed in 1815 by Charles Bulfinch. If you take the guided tour, you'll learn that this isn't actually Harvard at all. There were no portraits of the late patron when Daniel Chester French was commissioned to do the statue, so he recruited a handsome student from the class of 1882 as his model.

The quadrangle in back of University Hall is dominated by the bulk of Widener Library, the largest university library in the world. Behind Widener's Corinthian portico are ten stories holding the equivalent of 50 miles of books, some three million volumes. Walk inside to see panoramic scale models of Harvard and Cambridge, old and new.

Across the quadrangle are two more of Harvard's many architectural treasures, the steepled 1932 Memorial Chapel and Sever Hall, an 1880 classroom building designed by H. H. Richardson, the late-nineteenth-century master architect.

Walk straight on to Robinson Hall, then left past Emerson Hall and onto Quincy Street and you'll come to the Fogg Art Museum, whose collections include almost every significant period of Western art. The Wertheim Collection of Impressionist and post-Impressionist art is world-class, with paintings by Monet, van Gogh, Renoir, and Picasso. The Fogg is a training ground for curators the world over.

The second floor of the building connects to the adjoining Busch-Reisinger Museum, one of the few museums in this country specializing in the art of north and central Europe, with an extensive Bauhaus collection and paintings by Kandinsky, Klee, Kokoschka, and Munch.

Next door to the Fogg is the Carpenter Center for the Visual Arts, a sweep of glass and concrete that is the only Le Corbusier building in North America.

Exit the Fogg Museum on Quincy, turn right, and cross the street to Broadway and the Arthur M. Sackler Museum, the newest campus art repository. This small museum is a dazzler, a showcase for Islamic and Oriental art that includes the world's richest collection of Chinese bronzes. The Buddhist stone sculptures displayed on the fourth floor are standouts.

Continuing on Quincy, on the left is Memorial Hall, a massive cathedral-like brick building with a tiled roof. It houses the Sanders Theater, where many of the area's music and dance groups often perform.

Back on Kirkland, turn right on Oxford and you'll come to the Harvard University Museum, where four museums under one roof include everything from dinosaurs to rare jewels. The garden of Blaschka glass flowers in the Botanical Museum is world-renowned—bigger than life and absolutely true to nature.

In addition to the interesting museum displays of North, Central, and South American cultures, the gift shop in the Peabody Museum of Archaeology and Ethnology is worth a visit. It is filled with the finest in Indian baskets, Eskimo carvings, beadwork, and fine Navajo jewelry, among many other unique handcrafts.

The printed guide will lead you to more Harvard, Radcliffe, and Cambridge sights. In addition to the museums, you can see the fine residence houses of the campus between Harvard Square and the Charles River. Dunster, Lowell, and Elliot Houses are the three domes you see standing out. The huge modern complex off Massachusetts Avenue is the new Science Center. A campus map will show you where other schools are located.

Outside the campus, Cambridge history merges with that of the college. At the edge of Harvard Yard is the Wadsworth House, a 1726 frame house that was for 100 years the residence of Harvard presidents and was also the site of George Washington's militia offices in 1775. It now houses the Harvard alumni office.

Across the square from the Yard is the 1631 Ancient Burying Ground, where both Harvard presidents and important Revolutionary leaders are buried. It is beside the nineteenth-century wooden Gothic building of the First Parish Unitarian Church. Next to the Burying Ground on Garden Street, opposite the common, is Christ Church, the town's oldest, worth a look inside for its handsome Georgian interior. The church became a barracks during the American Revolution but was restored to its intended use by George Washington, who worshiped here in 1775 and 1776.

Historic Cambridge Common, the starting place for many events that led to our nation's freedom, is where the Massachusetts Bay Colony held its elections in the seventeenth century, where French militia trained for the French and Indian Wars, and where George Washington took command of the First Continental Army. Today it is crowded by twentieth-century buildings, including the Harvard Law School.

Having seen the sights, go back to Harvard Square to explore the funky mix of bookstores, cafés, and shops that is a hub not only for

Harvard but for the thousands of students at Boston's many colleges—you certainly needn't be a student to enjoy Harvard Square.

Harvard's red-brick architecture is extended here in new buildings, sidewalks, and crosswalks, but though it is as lively as ever, the square has lost a bit of its character in recent years with such stores as the Gap and Crate & Barrel replacing more eccentric emporiums. The enormous Harvard Co-op is all but overwhelming—a sort of intellectual department store occupying several buildings, selling clothing and almost everything else you can think of emblazoned with the college logo. It's disappointing to know that the big college bookstore is now operated by Barnes and Noble, but the selection is still enormous.

All of Cambridge, in fact, is an extraordinary place for book lovers, with more bookstores per capita than any city in America. The variety is truly amazing. Revolution Books, 1156 Massachusetts Avenue, has everything there is to know about Marxism and Maoism, and the Grolier Poetry Book Shop, 6 Plimpton Street, claims to carry all the poetry that is in print, some 14,000 titles. Mandrake, 8 Story Street, stresses psychotherapy; Savanna, 1132 Massachusetts Avenue, specializes in books about people of color; and Pandemonium Books & Games, 36 JFK Street, stocks stacks of science fiction, fantasy, and horror literature. Less esoteric are the bargain sections of the Harvard Book Store, 1256 Massachusetts Avenue (not to be confused with the Harvard Co-op), and the aptly named Buck A Book, 30 JFK Street. Words Worth, on Brattle Street, is a discount bookstore with a huge range of titles, and there are a host of used and rare bookstores packed with dusty treasures.

What else is around the square? Jeans and fine tailoring; stationery and wares from Greece; herbs and incense; Russian wooden dolls, fringed shawls, and exotic earrings; pricey women's clothing and inexpensive cottons from India; posters and housewares for the home; and traditional Ivy League dress. You'll see the shops as you walk Mt. Auburn, Dunster, Massachusetts, and the other narrow streets off Harvard Square and in small complexes such as the Garage, on Dunster.

A good street for browsing is Brattle, where the Brattle Street Theater has old film fare to delight buffs. Radcliffe Yard, another lovely academic complex, is on Brattle across from the Loeb Drama Center, the home of the excellent productions of the American Repertory Theater.

Brattle was once known as Tory Row, and you'll see why if you continue walking past the impressive homes on the street. The Longfellow House, at 105, is a National Historic Site, the place where the poet lived and wrote many of his poems while he taught at Harvard. Just beyond is the oldest home, the Hooper-Lee-Nichols House, circa 1685.

The Blacksmith House nearby is the present home of the Cambridge Center for Adult Education, where you'll find many interesting evening programs. It was at one time the home of the "village smithy" made famous by Longfellow's poem. At the end of Brattle is the Mt. Auburn

Cemetery, a virtual botanical garden that is the resting place of such notables as Longfellow, Amy Lowell, and Oliver Wendell Holmes. Within are ten miles of leafy paths and ponds.

Cambridge is still home to creative minds producing a prodigious number of books, poems, plays, theories, music, art, and ideas. The feeling of creativity is almost tangible, particularly in the coffeehouses and cafés, where Cambridge literati often seem to arrive with works in progress. The Algiers Coffee House and Au Bon Pain, the French bakery café, are popular spots. The outdoor café in front of the latter is a gathering spot for chatters and chess players on all but the most frigid days.

The restaurants in Cambridge reflect the community's cosmopolitan makeup. You'll find everything from haute cuisine to inexpensive ethnic, something for every taste and budget. A standout is Rialto, in the Charles Hotel, where chef Jody Adams wins universal praise for her original Mediterranean dishes. Also in the Charles is the informal Henrietta's Table, with home-style New England cooking and an indoor farmer's market. The romantic Upstairs at the Pudding (above the famous Hasty Pudding Club) is a longtime culinary star and a top choice for brunch, particularly in warmer weather, when the leafy terrace is open.

About ten blocks from Harvard Square is Inman Square, a lower-rent district that has become a culinary hot spot in more ways than one. East Coast Grill is renowned for its fire-breathing barbecue sauce. Next door is Jae's Cafe, a hip branch of a Boston favorite, where there's often a line for Asian cuisine from Korean to curry. More good restaurants are found in Central Square and Kendall Square, closer to MIT, and in Porter Square, down Massachusetts Avenue in the opposite direction.

There is a range of hotels as well, with the stylish Charles, near Harvard Square, at the top of the list. Rooms have Shaker-style furniture and handmade quilts, and the hotel is set in a modern red-brick square of its own, with an outdoor terrace and a walkway to the Charles River. There's a first-class spa and indoor pool here, and the Regatta Bar is a favorite gathering place to hear jazz.

Another convenient choice is the rather staid Inn at Harvard, on the eastern edge of the square. There are motels with lower rates, including the Harvard Square Hotel almost directly on the square, and a growing number of bed-and-breakfast inns, the most attractive being the Mary Prentice Inn, an 1843 home on a residential block about ten minutes from Harvard Square.

The Hyatt Regency affords the best view of the Charles and the Boston skyline from its revolving rooftop restaurant and has an indoor pool and health club, while the Royal Sonesta offers excellent weekend packages, but both are far from the action around Harvard Square.

Having devoted Saturday to Harvard and Harvard Square, fortify yourself with Sunday brunch and move on to the impressive campus of

MIT, on the Charles River. It's a five-minute drive straight down Massachusetts Avenue toward Boston, or two stops on the "T" from Harvard Square to Kendall Square. Instead of ivied red-brick halls, you'll find stately stone neoclassic buildings and stunning modern architecture. Many of the newer buildings are significant contributions by contemporary architectural greats such as Eero Saarinen, who designed the Kresge Auditorium and the MIT Chapel.

As you might expect, the MIT Museum concentrates on science and technology; it claims the largest collection of holograms in the world. Just to prove that scientists have a sense of humor, there is a Hackers Hall of Fame memorializing memorable campus pranks, such as hoisting a life-size model of a police car onto the dome of a major building. The car is preserved complete with mannequin police officers and empty doughnut cartons. The Hart Nautical Galleries concentrate on marine engineering.

Contemporary art may be seen at the List Visual Arts Center, and the entire MIT campus is a museum of outdoor sculpture by Calder, Moore, Picasso, and other masters.

From MIT you can drive directly across the Massachusetts Avenue Bridge over the Charles River and be in Boston in two minutes. An eight-minute ride on the "T" from Harvard Square will also put you in the heart of the city. Assuming that this is a winter weekend, it may be just the chance to catch up on some of the indoor Boston attractions you may have missed in warmer weather—the treasure-filled Museum of Fine Arts, perhaps, or the Isabella Stewart Gardener Museum, the Museum of Science, or the John F. Kennedy Library.

But though easy access to Boston has always been a plus for Cambridge, this exceptional small city really needs no added incentive to make it a prime destination. Wherever you go in Cambridge, whether sightseeing at Harvard and MIT, browsing for books, or sipping espresso in a café, you know that you are in the company of people and ideas that have shaped America's past and may well be molding its future.

Area Code: 617

DRIVING DIRECTIONS   Cambridge is on the northwest bank of the Charles River, four miles east of Boston and connected to the city by many bridges over the Charles as well as via the "T," the local subway system. See Boston directions on page 80.

ACCOMMODATIONS   Many hotels have weekend package rates much lower than the daily rates given here; ask for them. **Charles Hotel,** One Bennett Street (at Eliot Street), 02138, 864-1200, the top choice, ask about weekend bed-and-breakfast packages, EE • **Inn at**

Harvard, 1201 Massachusetts Avenue, 02138, 491-2222 or (800) 222-8733, E–EE • **Sheraton Commander,** 16 Garden Street (opposite the common), 02138, 547-4800, M–EE • **Harvard Square Hotel,** 110 Mt. Auburn Street, 02138, 864-5200 or (800) 458-5886, well-located motel, M–E, CP • **Hyatt Regency Cambridge,** 575 Memorial Drive, 02139, 492-1234, EE • **Royal Sonesta Hotel,** 5 Cambridge Parkway, 02142, 491-3600, E–EE • **Mary Prentiss Inn,** 6 Prentiss Street, 661-2929, delightful bed-and-breakfast home near Porter Square, a ten-minutes walk from Harvard Square, M–E, CP • **Irving House,** 24 Irving Street, 547-4600, small bed-and-breakfast inn, a budget choice, I–M, CP.

DINING   Rialto, Charles Hotel (see above), tops, M–E • **Henrietta's Table,** Charles Hotel (see above), good value, I–M • **Upstairs at the Pudding,** 10 Holyoke Street, 864-1933, elegant northern Italian, EE; also highly recommended for brunch, I • **Café Celador,** 5 Craigie Circle (near Harvard Square), 661-4073, cozy, continental, M • **8 Holyoke Grill,** 8 Holyoke Street (near Harvard Square), 497-5300, Mediterranean dishes, tapas, M–E • **Cambridge Common,** 1667 Massachusetts Avenue (between Harvard and Porter Squares), 547-1228, American home cooking, burgers, 24 kinds of beer on tap, I • **Mr. and Mrs. Bartley's Burger Cottage,** 1246 Massachusetts Avenue (near Harvard Square), 354-6559, virtual student landmark for huge hamburgers, I • **East Coast Grill,** 1271 Cambridge Street, Inman Square, 491-6568, barbecue, seafood, and more, M • **Jae's Café & Grill,** 1281 Cambridge Street, 497-8380, Asian cuisines, bigger version of a Boston favorite, I–M • **Daddy-O's Bohemian Café,** 134 Hampshire Street, 354-8371, funky, Mediterranean-Jewish, I • **Cottonwood Café,** 1815 Massachusetts Avenue (near Porter Square), 661-7440, excellent Southwestern fare, M • **Anago Bistro,** 798 Main, 876-8444, Central Square, interesting Mediterranean menu, M–E • **Salamander,** First and Atheneum Streets, 225-2121, out of the way but rave reviews for creative American with Asian accents, M–E • **Legal Sea Foods,** 5 Cambridge Center, Kendall Square, 864-3400, a local institution, don't miss the chowder, M–E. *Brew-pubs serving food:* **John Harvard's Brewhouse,** 33 Dunster Street, I; **Brew Moon,** 868-3585, 50 Church Street, 499-2739, I. *Inexpensive ethnic choices (all near Harvard Square):* **Cafe of India,** 52A Brattle Street, 661-0683, Indian, I–M • **Il Panino Express,** 1100 Massachusetts Avenue, 547-5818, pasta and great pizza, I • **Border Café,** 32 Church Street, 861-6100, Mexican, expect long lines to get in, I • **Skewers,** 92 Mt. Auburn Street, 491-3079, Middle Eastern, Greek, I • **Iruna,** 56 John F. Kennedy Street, 868-5633, Spanish, I • **Singha House,** 1105 Massachusetts Avenue, 864-5154, Thai, I • **Ha Long,** 35 Dunster Street, 354-4445, Vietnamese, I. Highly recommended is brunch at **House of Blues,** 96 Winthrop Street, 491-2583, a southern-style buffet accompanied by live gospel music, M. This is one of several good jazz clubs in Cambridge; others include **Regatta Bar,** in the Charles Hotel, and **Ryles,** 212 Hampshire Street, 547-4600.

SIGHTSEEING   Harvard University, Information Center, 1350 Massachusetts Avenue, 495-1573. Monday through Saturday, 9 A.M. to 4:45 P.M. Student-led free one-hour tours leave from this address during the academic year Monday through Friday, 10 A.M. and 2 P.M., Saturday 2 P.M.; June through August, Monday through Saturday, 10 A.M., 11:15 A.M., 2 P.M., 3:15 P.M.; Sunday, 1:30 P.M. and 3 P.M. Best to recheck current schedule • **Harvard Art Museums,** 495-9400. Hours for all: Monday to Saturday, 10 A.M. to 5 P.M., Sunday, 1 P.M. to 5 P.M. Admission includes all three museums: $$; under 18, free; free to all on Saturday, 10 A.M. to noon. **Fogg Art Museum,** 32 Quincy Street; **Arthur M. Sackler Museum,** 485 Broadway; **Busch-Reisinger Museum,** enter through Fogg Art Museum • **Harvard University Museums of Cultural and Natural History,** 26 Oxford Street, 495-1910. Hours: Monday to Saturday, 9 A.M. to 5 P.M.; Sunday, 1 P.M. to 5 P.M. $$; free Saturday 9 A.M. to noon • **Massachusetts Institute of Technology,** Information Center, 77 Massachusetts Avenue, 253-1000. Hours: weekdays only, 9 A.M. to 5 P.M.; free campus tours 10 A.M. and 2 P.M.; phone 253-4795 for tour information • **MIT Museum,** 265 Massachusetts Avenue, 253-4444. Hours: Tuesday to Friday, 9 A.M. to 5 P.M.; Saturday and Sunday, noon to 5 P.M. Adults, $3; children, $1 • **Hart Nautical Galleries,** 77 Massachusetts Avenue, 253-4444. Hours: daily, 9 A.M. to 8 P.M. Free • **List Visual Arts Center,** Wiesner Building, 20 Ames Street, 253-4680. Hours: Tuesday to Friday, noon to 6 P.M.; Saturday and Sunday, 1 P.M. to 5 P.M. Free • **Longfellow National Historic Site,** 105 Brattle Street, 876-4491. Hours: daily, 10 A.M. to 4:30 P.M. Adults, $2; under 17 with adult, free • **American Repertory Theater,** 64 Brattle Street, 547-8300. Check for current offerings.

INFORMATION   Cambridge Chamber of Commerce, 859 Massachusetts Avenue, Cambridge, MA 02139, 876-4100.

Sugaring Off in Grafton

Maples and Vermont are all but synonymous. So it is not surprising that maple sugaring—a major state industry and a livelihood for hundreds of Vermont farmers—is a cause for local celebration. After a long winter, the rising of the maple sap is the first sure sign of spring, despite the layers of snow that may still be on the ground.

Seeing how the sap is collected and made into syrup, and getting in on a traditional "sugar on snow" party—with fresh syrup hardened into candy in the snow—is good reason for a late-winter visit. Dozens of Vermont sugarmakers welcome visitors, though most appreciate a call for an appointment first. A list of sugarmaking farms is available free from the state Department of Agriculture.

It takes cold nights and warm days to make the sap rise, so the timing of the sugaring season is entirely in the hands of Mother Nature. Unusual weather can speed or slow the season, so be sure to phone and check before you set off on a trip. Usually, early to mid-March is the peak in the southern part of the state; it comes a little later up north.

The state's official Maple Festival is held in late April way up north in St. Albans, but since the most interesting visit for most people is to a farm, you needn't journey quite so far or wait so long. Farms all over the state carry on the traditional tapping of the trees and gathering of the buckets, a task that is often still accomplished best by horse and sled despite all the modern improvements in methods. But some sugarmakers have switched to more advanced techniques, using plastic piping, gravity-fed tanks, and reverse osmosis. It's fun to see both old and new methods—and to know that the syrup is equally delicious either way.

One excellent southern home base for viewing this century-old operation is Grafton, a town with a wonderful inn and a special ambience that will add much to your stay. Grafton's own Plummer's Sugar House is open for tours, and the town is located within easy reach of farms in Chester, Ludlow, Putney, and several other small towns. Plummer's, a modern operation, has some 4,500 taps on its pipeline but still uses the traditional wood-fired evaporator to cook down the sap.

You can enjoy a horse-drawn sleigh ride through the "sugar bush," the area where sap is running, at the Putney farm of Donald and Madeline Harlow. They offer homemade donuts and coffee as well as the traditional "sugar on snow" treat. The Harlows have assembled a small exhibit of old-time sugaring methods, with photos of the oxen-drawn sleds that were used to gather the buckets, and displays of old kettles and other utensils. A film about the Vermont maple sugaring industry is shown regularly in their little gift shop, where you can buy pure Vermont maple syrup and maple candy year-round.

If you've never seen how maple syrup is made, you may be surprised to learn that the sweet sap running from the trees is as thin and clear as water. When the syrup is transported to the sugarhouse, it is emptied into an evaporator to simmer slowly over the fire until it thickens into a golden, gooey, and delicious syrup. On hillsides all over Vermont, you can see the clouds of smoke day and night, marking a sugarhouse in action.

An average tree will produce 40 quarts of sap drip by drip, which must be hauled down day by day to the evaporator. You may understand better why the syrup is so costly when you learn that it takes 40 gallons of sap to produce a single gallon of syrup. To provide enough heat to boil down that much sap requires a log as big as a man, split, sawed, and dried.

The finished syrup comes in grades, fancy for the lightest and sweetest; medium-amber Grade A for general use on pancakes and French toast; dark Grade B, a robust caramel flavor used in cooking; and grade C, an even stronger flavor, also used for cooking. Some people find the richer flavor of the B and C grades more to their liking than the more costly A syrups.

The picture-perfect village of Grafton is an ideal destination for any season. The town still looks much the way it did in its 1800s prime, and that is no accident. It is a town that had the good fortune to be "adopted" by the Windham Foundation, which was founded by millionaire Dean Mathey, former chairman of the Bank of New York.

Mathey had no children, so most of his fortune went to the foundation after his death in 1962. The trustees looked for a project he would have approved and decided there was no more appropriate idea than the salvation of the tiny town of Grafton, a place that Mathey loved. He had his own summer home right on Main Street, and many of his family members were longtime residents as well.

Once a prosperous mill and agricultural center, Grafton, like many such towns, had declined by the early twentieth century. The population had dwindled to less than 500, and many of the old buildings had been left to deteriorate, though their original charm could still be seen.

In the 1960s, the Windham Foundation, named for Grafton's home county, set out to bring the town back to its former self. The first project was a practical one. The old grocery store was in sad shape, and the townspeople found themselves having to travel elsewhere for food and other daily necessities. So the derelict building was shored up, sagging floors were leveled, warped walls were straightened, and pretty soon the store was looking much the way it had when it was finished back in 1841, at least on the outside. Inside it became a complete modern market.

One by one the village houses were also purchased and refurbished. At the same time the Windham Foundation took on the renewal of the Old Tavern, once a noted stopping place when Grafton was a trading center. The old guest books list such notables as Rudyard Kipling, Ulysses S. Grant, Daniel Webster, Oliver Wendell Holmes, Theodore Roosevelt, and Ralph Waldo Emerson.

With the restoration the tavern became one of New England's most elegant little inns; early reservations are advised.

If the inn is filled, a delightful alternative is the Inn at Woodchuck Hill Farm, an antiques-filled 1790 farmhouse on 200 acres just outside town. The property is on a hilltop with soaring views. Rooms are in the main house or in larger spaces in the quaint restored barn.

What to do in Grafton? Very little, which is very much part of this town's charm. If there is snow, you can downhill-ski at Stratton Mountain nearby, or make tracks through the woods at the Grafton Ponds Cross-Country Ski Center, which is run by the Old Tavern. If the spring thaw has set in, or if you don't ski, paddle tennis is available at the inn, or you can simply stroll through Grafton's picturesque streets or take a bike ride or a hike on the walking trails that abound around town. The inn will give you a folder of trails that will show you the Grafton of old. If you hike the more wooded trails, be forewarned that spring is known as "mud season" in Vermont, so bring proper footgear.

Cheese is still made at the Grafton Village Cheese Company, a century-old tradition. After a fire destroyed the original factory, the Windham Foundation rebuilt the facility, and visitors are welcome to come by to witness the cheese-making process. Hidden Orchard Farms, just west of the village on Route 121, has pick-your-own apples and berries in season, maple syrup in the spring, and its own chunky preserves and fruit butters for sale all year. Grafton Goodjam, a bit farther west on the same road, offers jams and chutneys made with maple syrup and organically grown fruit.

There are a few interesting browsing stops in town. The Gallery North Star features artwork by Vermont artists, and Grafton Handmade is devoted to crafts by Vermont artisans. Grafton Gathering Place Antiques, a two-story barn filled with furniture and accessories such hooked rugs, is located on Sylvan Road, north of town off Route 35.

Come into Chester, just seven miles to the north via Route 35, to see another picturesque village with a Main Street built around a long, narrow village green. One of the old Victorian homes on the green is the Hugging Bear Inn, catering to families, and offering your choice of teddy bears to take to bed. The shop behind the inn is chock full of hundreds of stuffed bears and animals of every description. A variety of other shops can be found along the green, and the Raspberries & Tyme café is a convenient spot for a tasty lunch or afternoon tea.

More diversions can be found about 14 miles south of Grafton in Newfane. The Newfane Country Store is chock-a-block with New England quilts, and is a choice place to shop for handicrafts, homemade baked goods, and old-fashioned penny candy as well. There's an art gallery upstairs. If you come back from May to October, you can look for treasures at the big flea market held on weekends on Route 30, the oldest and largest open-air market in Vermont.

Newfane is another particularly lovely Vermont town; bring a camera to capture the columned buildings around its perfect village green. Plan to stay for dinner, too, for the local inns, the Four Columns Inn and the Old Newfane Inn, have renowned dining rooms. These are also happy alternatives for lodging as well; the Four Columns Inn is first choice.

For those who prefer a more rustic farmhouse setting and the chance to go horseback riding (a nice way to see the countryside this time of year), the West River Lodge provides homey and comfortable surroundings and very congenial hosts. Two lovely inns in the general vicinity are the Windham Hill Inn, a totally charming hideaway set on a secluded 160-acre hilltop in West Townshend with wonderful mountain views and fine dining, (and a pool and tennis in season), and Rowell's Inn, an 1820 stagecoach stop filled with atmosphere, antiques, and informal warmth.

One final possibility is the Governor's Inn, in Ludlow, north of Chester, a small inn that has gained renown for its lavish six-course dinners served by waitresses in Victorian costume.

This is a weekend that will take you back to the tranquillity of another time—a visit to the farm, a stroll through peaceful country towns and village shops. At day's end there's lots of time to savor a drink in front of a roaring fire and dinner in a cozy, beamed dining room. To make it even better, there's that delicious maple syrup to bring home as a sweet souvenir of the trip.

Area Code: 802

DRIVING DIRECTIONS From I-91, exit 5 (North Westminster and Bellows Falls), take Route 121 west to Grafton. Alternate route: From I-91, exit 2, Brattleboro, follow Route 30 west to Newfane, then Route 35 north to Grafton. Call each farm for specific driving directions. Grafton is 152 miles from Boston, 221 miles from New York, and 111 miles from Hartford.

PUBLIC TRANSPORTATION Vermont Transit has bus service to Bellows Falls, about 15 miles from Grafton.

ACCOMMODATIONS The Old Tavern at Grafton, Grafton 05146, 843-2231, main building and annex, M–E, CP • **The Inn at Woodchuck Hill Farm,** Middletown Road, Grafton 05146, 843-2398, delightful country hideaway, M–E, CP • **The Hugging Bear Inn,** Main Street, Chester, 05143, 875-2432, M, CP • **The Four Columns Inn,** Route 30, Newfane 05345, 365-7713, M–E, CP • **Old Newfane Inn,** Route 30, Newfane 05345, 365-4427, E, CP; suites, M, CP • **West**

River Lodge, Hill Road, PO Box 693, Newfane 05345, 365-7745, M, CP; MAP also available • **Windham Hill Inn,** Windham Hill Road, RR 1, Box 44, West Townshend 05359, 874-4080, E–EE, MAP • **Rowell's Inn,** RR 1, Box 269, Simonsville 05143, 875-3658, EE, MAP • **The Governor's Inn,** 86 Main Street, Ludlow 05149, 228-8830, E–EE, MAP.

DINING   The Old Tavern at Grafton (see above), M–E • **The Four Columns Inn** (see above), E–EE • **Old Newfane Inn** (see above), M–E • **Windham Hill Inn** (see above), prix fixe, EE • **The Governor's Inn** (see above), prix fixe, EE.

SIGHTSEEING   Farm visits to watch maple sugaring are free, but you must call ahead to make sure the weather is right and syrup is being made. Ask for driving directions as well. The Vermont Department of Agriculture prints a complete listing of farms in the state that invite visitors. Write to them at 116 State Street, Drawer 20, Montpelier, VT 05602, 828-2416. Farms mentioned here are: **Harlow's Sugar House,** Route 5, RD 1, Box 395, Putney, 387-5852 • **Plummer's Sugarhouse,** Townshend Road, PO Box 85, Grafton, 843-2207.

INFORMATION   Vermont Chamber of Commerce, Box 37, Montpelier, VT 05601, (802) 223-3443; Vermont Department of Tourism, 134 State Street, Montpelier, VT 05602, (802) 828-3237.

Maps

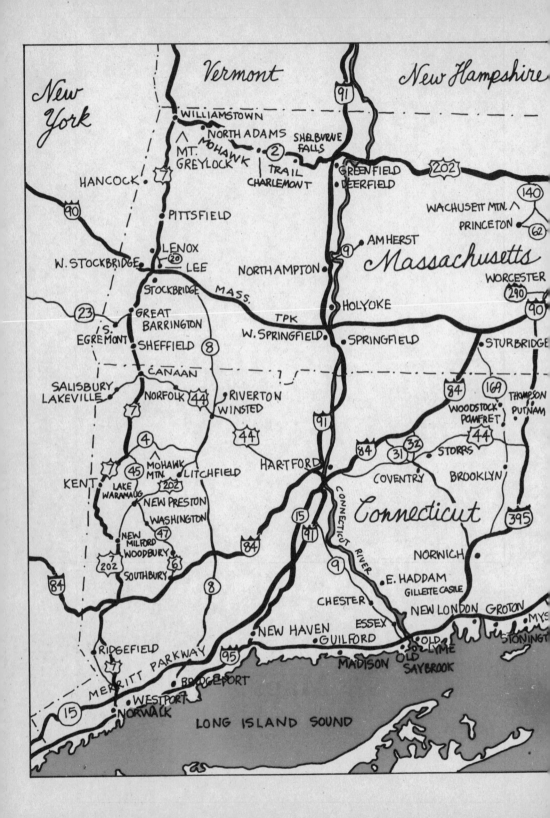

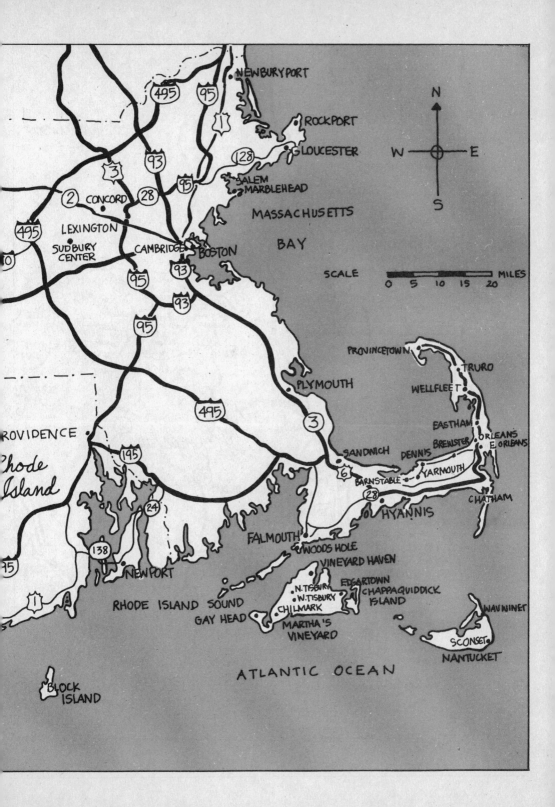

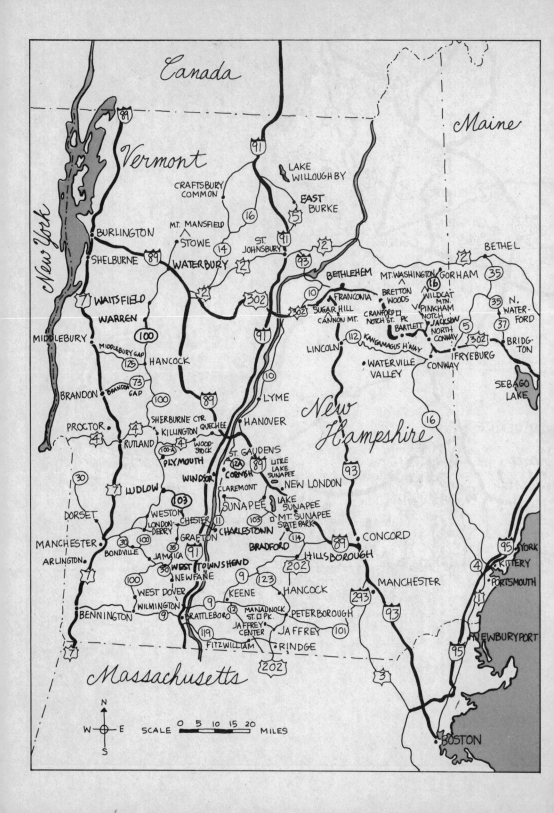

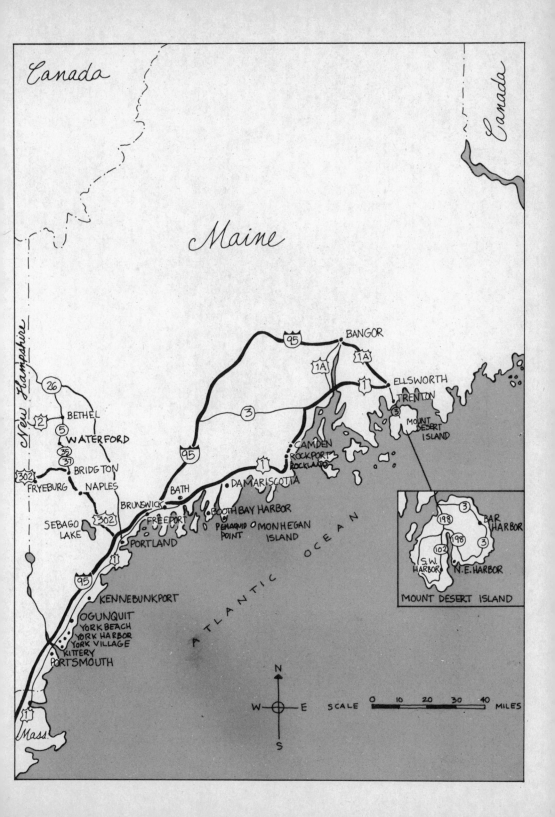

Canada

Maine

Canada

New Hampshire

95
BANGOR
1A
1A
1
ELLSWORTH
TRENTON
26
3
BETHEL
2
5
3
WATERFORD
MOUNT DESERT ISLAND
35
37
95
1
CAMDEN
ROCKPORT
ROCKLAND
302
BRIDGTON
FRYEBURG
NAPLES
BATH
DAMARISCOTTA
BRUNSWICK
SEBAGO LAKE
302
FREEPORT
BOOTHBAY HARBOR
PORTLAND
PEMAQUID POINT
MONHEGAN ISLAND

ATLANTIC OCEAN

1
95
KENNEBUNKPORT
OGUNQUIT
YORK BEACH
YORK HARBOR
YORK VILLAGE
KITTERY
PORTSMOUTH

1
Mass.

MOUNT DESERT ISLAND
3
198
BAR HARBOR
198
3
102
S.W. HARBOR
N.E. HARBOR

N
W — E
S
SCALE 0 10 20 30 40 MILES

GENERAL INDEX

Acadia National Park, 133–134
Acadia Repertory Theater, 136
Agamenticus Wilderness Reserve, 108
Albany Berkshire Ballet, 142, 147
Aldrich House, 29
American Crafts Council Craftfair, 62, 67
American Museum of Fly Fishing, 171, 177
American Precision Museum, 151, 153
American Repertory Theatre, 291
American Stage Festival, 116, 120
Amherst, Mass., 64
Amherst College, 64
Ancient Burying Ground, 293
Andover, N.H., 150
Andre the Seal, 218
Andy Lynn Boats, 199
Appalachian Mountain Club, 102, 105, 144, 209, 276, 278
Appalachian Trail, 144, 170, 186, 209, 226
Apple Hill Chamber Players, 116
Appledore, 158
Arlington, Vt., 172
Arrowhead, 144, 146, 257, 258
Arthur M. Sackler Museum, 292, 298
Artist's Bluff, 201
Arts Center at Brickyard Pond, 116
Arts Jubilee, 102
Asa Stebbins House, 206
Ashley Falls, Mass., 144
Ashley House, 205
Asticou Gardens, 135
Aston Magna Foundation, 142, 147
Astors' Beechwood, 286, 290
Atlantic White Cedar Swamp Trail, 179
Attitash Bear Peak Mountain, N.H., 101, 102, 103, 274, 276, 278
Attitash Bear Peak Alpine Slide 103, 105
Attitash Bear Peak Chair Lift, 101, 105
Auburn, Mass., 265–266
Author's Ridge, 11
Avalanche Falls, 201

Baby Flume, 201
Back Bay, 76–77
Baker Memorial Library, 245–46

Ballard Institute and Museum of Puppetry, 15,16
Ballston beach, 183
Balmy Days, 154, 155, 158
Bantam Lake, 48, 271
Baptist Church, (Essex) 212
Bar Harbor, Maine, 133, 136–137
Bar Harbor Festival of Chamber Music, 136
Bar Harbor Historical Society, 137, 139
Bar Harbor Music Festival, 136
Bar Harbor Oceanarium, 136–37
Barnet, Vt., 192
Barrett's farm, 9
Bartholomew's Cobble, 144, 147
Barton, Vt., 192
Bascom Lodge, 144, 209
Basin, The, 201
Basin Harbor Club, 127
Basketball Hall of Fame, 63, 67
Bass Harbor, 136
Bath, Maine, 41–42
Bath Iron Works, 41, 154
Battle of Bennington monument, 173
Battle Road Visitor's Center, 9, 13
Bay Chamber Concerts, 218
Bay Lady, 158
Beacon Hill, 76, 235
Bear Notch Ski Touring Center, 275
Bearskin Neck, 35
Beartown State Forest, 144
Beauport Museum, 35, 38
Becket, Mass., 141, 142,
Belcourt Castle, 286, 290
Ben and Jerry's Ice Cream Factory, 261
Benedict Pond, 144
Bennington, Vt., 173, 256
Bennington Museum, 173, 256
Bennington Pottery, 129, 173
Berkshire Botanical Garden, 144, 147, 257
Berkshire Center of Contemporary Glass, 143
Berkshire Choral Festival, 142, 147
Berkshire Community College Arts Center, 142
Berkshire Museum, 256, 258

Berkshire Opera Festival, 142, 147
Berkshire School, 142
Berkshire Theater Festival, 142, 147
Berkshires region, Mass, 140–147, 253–258
Berkshires skiing, 258
Bethel, Maine, 185, 186, 279–283
Billings Farm and Museum, 5, 8
Black Mountain, 274, 278
Blacksmith House, 294
Black Top path, 102
Block Island, RI, 69, 111–115
Blowing Cave, 165, 166
Blue Heron, 179
Bluenose Ferry, 136
Bonnema Pottery, 186
Bookport Building, 166
Boothbay Harbor, Maine, 153–58
Boothbay Harbor cruises, 158
Boothbay Railway Village, 155, 158
Boothbay Region Art Foundation Gallery,
     155, 158
Boston, Mass., 75–84, 223–237, 296
Boston by Little Feet, 233, 237
Boston City Hall, 78
Boston Common, 76, 233
Boston Harbor Cruises, 83, 237
Boston National Historical Park, 83, 233
Boston Pops Orchestra, 76
Boston Public Garden, 76
Boston Public Library, 77
Boston Symphony, 140, 141–42
Boston Tea Party Ship and Museum, 232,
     235, 237
Boston Trolley Tours, 83–84, 233
Boston University, 77
Boston Walking Tours, 83
Botanical Museum (Harvard), 293
Botany Trail, 171
Boulder Loop, 202
Bowdoin College, 40–41, 44
Bowdoin Museum of Art, 40, 44
Brandon, Vt., 229
Brandon Gap, 229
Brattle Street Theater, 294
Brayton Grist Mill, 16, 19
Bread and Puppet Museum, 190
Bretton Woods, 102, 274, 275, 276, 278
Brewster Gardens, 196
Brick Church, 205
Brick Store Museum, 167, 169
Brickyard Pond Arts Center, 116
Bridge of Flowers, 207
Bridgton, Maine, 184, 186, 281
Bromley Mountain, 170
Brooklyn, Conn, 17
Brownington Center, Vt., 190
Brown University, 28, 30
Brunswick, Maine, 40–41

Brunswick Naval Air Station, 41
Bullet Hole House, 9
Bunker Hill, 79, 234
Burke Mountain, 190, 191–192
Burlington, Vt., 127–133
Burlington Square Mall, 128, 129
Busch-Reisinger Museum, 292, 298
Bush residence, 166

Cabot, Vt., 192
Cabot Creamery (Burlington), 129
Cabot Farmers' Cooperative Creamery
     (Cabot), 192, 194
Cahoon Hollow beach, 183
Cambridge, Mass., 291–298
Cambridge Common, 293
Camden, Maine, 215–220
Camden Hills State Park, 217, 220
Camden Public Landing, 216
Camden Snow Bowl, 217
Camden Windjammer fleet, 216, 220
Camelot Cruises, 215
Candlelight Stroll, (Portsmouth) 250–251,
     253
Cannon Mountain, 201, 274, 275, 278
Cannon Mountain Aerial Tramway, 201,
     203, 274
Cannondale Village, CT, 93
Cape Ann, 33–38
Cape Ann Historical Museum, 35, 37
Cape Ann Whale Watch, 33, 37
Cape Arundel, 166
Cape Arundel Cruises, 169
Cape Cod, 51–56, 177–83
Cape Cod Cruises, 199
Cape Cod, Outer Cape beaches, 183
Cape Cod National Seashore, 177, 179, 182
Cape Cod National Seashore beaches, 183
Cape Cod Scenic Railroad, 53, 55–56
Cape Elizabeth, 59
Cape Neddick, 107–108
Cape Pogue Wildlife Refuge, 124
Cape Porpoise, 166–167
Cap'n Fish's Goodtimes Sightseeing Boat
     Trips, 158
Caprilands Herb Farm, 14–15, 17, 18
Capt. Bill & Son's Whale Watching, 37
Capt. John Boats, 199
Captain Francis Pease House, 123
Carousel Music Theater, 156
Carpenter Center for the Visual Arts, 292
Cascade Falls, (Maine)186
Cascades, (NH) 188
Casco Bay, 41, 56
Casco Bay Lines, 58, 61
Caspian Lake, 191
Castleton, Vt., 229
Cathedral Ledge, 102

Cathedral of the Pines, 118, 121
Cathedral Woods, 155
Cedar Tree Neck, 124
Central Wharf, 223
Chaffee Art Gallery, 229, 231
Champlain College, 129
Champlain Mill, 129
Channing Blake Meadow Walk, 205
Chapin Library, 254–255, 258
Chapman Rink, 255
Chappaquidick, Mass., 124
Charlemont, Mass, 207
Charles River, 76, 236, 291, 296
Charlestown, Mass., 79, 234
Charles W. Morgan, 241
Charlotte, VT, 131
Château-sur-Mer, 286
Chatham, Mass., 177, 178
Chester, Conn., 212, 213
Chester, Vt., 301
Chesterwood, 144, 146
Children's Chapel, 218
Children's Museum of Boston, 234–235, 237
Children's Museum of Maine, 59, 61
Children's Museum of Southeastern Connecticut, 70, 74
Chilmark, Mass., 124
Chittenden, Vt., 227
Chocolate festival, 276
Chocolate Church for the Arts, 42
Christ Church, 293
Christian Science Center, 79
Christmas Revels, 245, 247, 249
Church Street Marketplace, 129
City Park, (Bath), 42
Claire Murray, 151
Clark Art Institute, 141, 253–254
Cliff Walk, 284, 286
Colby-Sawyer College, 149
Cold Hollow Cider Mill, 261
Coles Hill, 195
College Hill Historic District, 27–28
College of the Atlantic Natural History Museum, 137, 139
Colonial Lantern Tours, (Plymouth) 196, 199
Colonial Pemaquid State Historic Site, 156
Colrain, Mass, 207
Computer Museum, 235, 237
Concord, Mass., 8–14
Concord Art Association, 11
Concord Library, 11, 13
Concord Museum, 11, 13
Concord River, 12
Congressional Church, 4
Connecticut College, 70
Connecticut College Aboretum, 70, 73

Connecticut Ice Yachting Club, 271
Connecticut Repertory Company, 16
Connecticut River cruises, 213, 215
Connecticut River Artisans Cooperative, 213
Connecticut River Foundation Museum, 211
Connecticut River Valley, 204, 245
Connecticut Valley Historical Museum, 63
Connecticut Woodcarvers' Gallery, 270
Constitution, USS, 79, 83, 234
Conway, N.H., 184, 202, 276
Coolidge home, 6
Copley Square, 77
Cornish, N.H., 150
Cornwall, Conn., 269
Court Square, 63
Coventry, Conn., 14–15
Craftsbury, Vt., 191
Craftsbury Center, the, 191
Craftsbury Common, Vt., 191
Cranbury Harvest Festival, 194, 197, 198
Cranberry World Visitors Center, 196–197, 198
Crawford Notch, 202, 276
Crescent Beach, 112
Crescent Neck Beach State Park, 59
Crystal Lake, 190
Custom House Wharf, 58
Customs House (New London), 69
Customs House (Salem), 223

Daffodil Festival, 20, 22, 25–26
Dale Huntington Library, 123
Damariscotta, Maine, 156
Dana House, 4, 7–8
Darling Hill, 190
Dartmouth College, 89, 245–46
Dartmouth Outing Club, 248
Dartmouth Players Repertory Company, 150
Dartmouth Skiway, 248
David Winton Bell Gallery, 28, 32
Davis Rink, 248
Deborah Ann cruises, 99
Deep River, Conn., 212
Deep River Navigation Company, 215
Deerfield, Mass., 65, 67–68, 204–207
Deerfield Academy, 204, 205
Deer Leap Trail, 228
Derby Wharf, 223
Deshon-Allyn House, 70
Dexter Grist Mill, 52
Diana's Bath, 102
Dickinson Homestead, 65, 68
Dock Square Market, 166
Dolphin Mini-Golf Course, 156
Dolphin Fleet, 180, 182

Dorset, Vt., 170–71
Dorset Field Club, 170
Dorset Playhouse, 170
Downtown Crossing, 78
Drisco House, 109
Drumlin Farm, 12, 14
Dublin, N.H., 118
Dwight House, 206

Eagle, 69, 73
East Arlington, Vt., 172
East Beach, 124
East Boothbay, Maine, 154
East Burke, Vt., 190
East Canaan, Conn., 270
Eastern Cemetery, 59
Eastern Point Sanctuary, 36
Eastern Promenade, 59
Eastern Ski Jumping Championships, 268,
    273
Eastern States Exposition Center, 62
East Haddam, Conn., 213
Eastham, Mass., 179
Easton Valley, N.H., 200
East Orleans, Mass., 178
Echo Lake, (Franconia) 201
Echo Lake State Park, (North Conway), 102
Edgartown, Mass., 122–123, 125–127
Edith Wharton Restoration, 142
Elizabeth Perkins House, 107
Elms, The, 286
Emerson House, 10, 13
Emerson-Wilcox House, 107
Esplanade, 75, 76, 236
Essex, Conn., 210–215
Essex, VT, 128, 129
Ethan Allen Homestead, 129, 132–33
Eugene O'Neill Theater Center, 69, 74
Evans Notch, 185, 186

Fairbanks Museum and Planetarium, 189,
    193
Fairbanks, Thaddeus, 188
Fair Street Museum, 26
Faneuil Hall, 79, 234
Faneuil Hall Marketplace, 79, 234
Farnsworth Art Museum, 218, 220
Farnsworth Homestead, 218
February Heritage Day, 280
February Winter Festival, 284
Federal Hill, 30
Federated Church, 122
Felix Neck, 124
Fells, the, 149, 153
Fenway Park, 77, 80
Ferry Beach, 59
Filene's Basement, 78
Finestkind cruises, 97, 99

First Baptist Meeting House, 29, 32
First Church of Christ, (Sandwich) 52
First Parish Church (Portland), 57
First Parish Meetinghouse (Sandwich), 52
First Parish Unitarian Church, (Kennebunk),
    167
First Parish Unitarian Church, (Cambridge)
    293
Fish Beach, 155
Fisher House, 122–123
Fishermen's Walk, 108
Fishers Island, 69
Fitzwilliam, N.H., 117, 118
Flanders Nature Center, 47, 50
Florence Griswold Museum, 71–72, 74
Flume, The, 201, 203
Flying Horses Carousel, 123
Fogg Art Museum, 292, 298
Fort Allen Park, 59
Fort McClary State Memorial, 109
Fort Griswold Battlefield State Park, 70, 74
Fort William Henry, 156
Fort Williams Park, 59
Foster Maritime Gallery, 123
Foxwoods Resort Casino, 71
Francestown, N.H., 118
Franconia, N.H., 199–204, 274, 275, 276
Franconia Notch, 199, 200
Franconia Notch State Park, 200, 203, 276
Franconia Village Cross Country Center,
    275
Franklin Pierce Homestead, 119
Frary House, 206
Fred Benson Beach, 112
Freedom Trail, 75, 78–79, 233–234
Freeport, Maine, 36–37, 38, 40
Frenchman's Bay Company, 136
Friendly Farm, 118, 121
Frost Place, 201, 203–204
Fryeburg, Maine, 183–188
Fryeburg Fair, 183, 184, 188
Fryeburg Library, 186

Gay Head, 124
Gaylordsville, Conn., 47
Gehring, Dr. John, 279, 280
Georges Mill, N.H., 150
George Walter Vincent Smith Art Museum,
    63
Gillette Castle, 213, 215
Gingerbread House, 144, 146
Gleason Fine Art, 155
Glebe House, 45, 50
Gloucester, Mass., 33–35
Gloucester Stage Company, 35
Glover, Vt., 190
Goodspeed Opera House, 212, 213,
    214–215

Goose Rocks Beach, 166
Gould Academy, 279, 280
Government Center, 78–79
Governor John Langdon House, 251
Governor Stephen Hopkins House, 29, 32
Grafton, Mass., 266
Grafton, Vt., 299–303
Grafton Notch State Park, Maine, 186
Grafton Ponds Cross-Country Ski-Center,
    Vt., 301
Grafton Village Cheese Company, 301
Granary Burying Ground, 233
Grandma Moses Schoolhouse, 173, 256
Grapevine Cottage, 11
Great American Trading Company, 213
Great Barrington, Mass., 141, 257
Great Glen Trails, 275, 278
Great Hosmer Pond, 191
Great Meadows National Wildlife Refuge,
    12, 14
Great Point, 161
Great State of Maine Air Show, 41
Greenfield, Mass., 207
Greenfield State Park, (NH), 117, 121
Greensboro, Vt., 191
Griswold Inn, 212
Groton, Conn., 70
Groton, Vt., 192
Groton Monument, 70
Gunn Historical Museum, 46, 50

Hadlyme, Conn., 213
Hadwen House, 22, 26
Hail to the Sunrise Monument, 208
Hairpin Turn, 208
Halibut Point State Park, 36, 38
Hall Tavern, 205
Hammersmith Farm, 2 88, 290
Hammond Castle Museum, 35, 38
Hampshire College, 64
Hancock, Vt., 229
Hancock, N.H., 118
Hancock Shaker Village, 140, 142–43, 257
Hanover Inn, 246, 248, 249
Hanover, N.H., 89, 150, 245–249
Harbor Walk, 235
Harkness Memorial Park Summer Music,
    69, 74
Harlow Old Fort House, 196, 198
Harney & Sons teas, 269
Harlow's Sugar House, 299, 303
Harpswells, the, Maine, 41
Harrison, Maine, 281
Harrisville, N.H., 118
Hart Nautical Galleries, 296, 298
Harvard Art Museums, 292–293, 298
Harvard Square, 291, 293–294
Harvard University, 291–293, 298

Harvard University Museum, 293, 298
Harvard Yard, 292
Hatch Memorial Shell, 76
Hatch's Wharf, 223
Hathaway-Cushing-Millay House, 216–217
Hayden Yard, 211
Haystack Mountain, 173, 174
Headlands, 35
Head of the Meadow beach, 183
Hemlock Bridge, 185
Hempsted House, 69, 73
Helen Geier Flynt Textile Collection, 206
Henry N. Flynt Silver and Metalware
    Collection, 206
Heritage New Hampshire, 103, 105
Heritage Plantation, 51, 53–55
Heron American Craft Gallery, 47
Higganum, Conn., 213
Higgins Armory Museum, 266, 268
Higgins Beach, 59
Highland Lake, 184
Hildene, 171, 177
Hildene Antique Festival, 171
Hildene Foliage Craft Festival, 171
Hillsborough, N.H., 118–119
Hinsdale and Anna Williams House, 206
Historic Deerfield, 205–206, 210
Historic Northampton, 64, 67
Historic Ship Nautilus Memorial, 70, 74
Historic York, 107, 110–111
Hitchcock Museum, 270
Holden Chapel, 292
Hood Museum, 247, 249
Hoosac Mountain Tunnel, 208
Hopkins Center, 89, 150, 247, 249
Hopper, the, 209
Housatonic, Mass, 143, 257
Hotchkiss School, 269
House of Seven Gables, 223, 225
Hoxie House, 52
Hudson Brook, 208
Hull's Cove, 134

Illumination Night, 123
Inman Square, 295
Institute for American Indian Studies,
    46–50
International Tennis Hall of Fame, 287, 290
Intervale, NH, 275
Isabella Stewart Gardner Museum, 77, 83
Isleboro, Maine, 218
Isle of Shoals, 109, 252
Ivoryton, Conn., 212

Jackson, NH, 275
Jackson Arena (Stowe), 261
Jackson, NH, Ski Touring Foundation, 275,
    278

Jacob's Pillow Dance Festival, 140, 142, 147
Jaffrey, N.H., 117
James B. Owen Art Gallery, 280
Jefferd's Tavern, 107
Jeffreys Ledge, 33
Jenney Grist Mill, 196
Jesup Memorial Library, 137
Jethro Coffin House, 21, 26
John Bray House, 109
John Brown House, 29, 32
John F. Kennedy Library Museum, 79–80, 83, 236, 296
John Hancock Observatory, 83
John Hancock Tower, 77, 83, 234
John Paul Jones House, 10 9, 251
Jonathan Trumbull House, 16, 19
Jones Museum of Glass and Ceramics, 186, 188
Jordan Pond House, 134, 138
Joshua L. Chamberlain Museum, 41, 44

Kancamagus Highway, 103, 202, 276
Katama Beach, 124
Kearsarge, 149
Kedron Valley Stables, 4
Keene, N.H., 118
Keene State College, 116, 118
Kendall Art Gallery, 179
Kenmore Square, 77
Kennebec River, 42
Kennebunk, Maine, 167
Kennebunkport, Maine, 165–69
Kent, Conn., 47–48, 49–50
Kent Art Association Gallery, 47
Kent Falls State Park, 47–48
Kent Station Square, 47
Kezar Lake, 149
Killington, Vt., 226–231
Killington Gondola, 226, 228, 231
Killington Skyeship, 226, 228, 231
Kings Chapel, 234
Kings Chapel Burying Ground, 234
Kittery, Maine, 109, 251
Kittery Naval Museum, 109

Lady Pepperell House, 109
Lake Bomoseen, 229
Lake Champlain, 127,128, 129
Lake Champlain ferry, 133
Lake Sebago, 184
Lake St. Catherine, 229
Lake Sunapee area, 148–53
Lake Sunapee Harbor, 148–49
Lakeville, Conn., 269
Lake Waramaug State Park, 47
Lake Waumgumbaug, 15
Lake Willoughby, 190, 192

Lanesboro, Mass., 209
Lantern Light Tours, (Mystic) 241, 242, 244
Laplant's Sugarhouse, 192, 194
Larry LiVolsi Gallery, 48, 51
League of New Hampshire Craftsmen Fair, 148, 152
League of New Hampshire Craftsmen's shops, 102, 247
Lee, Mass., 141
Lenox, Mass., 141, 142, 143, 257
Levitt Pavilion, 94, 96
Lincoln Bridge, 4
Lincoln, NH, 200, 202, 276
Lincolnville, Maine, 219
List Arts Center (Cambridge), 296, 298
Litchfield, Conn., 48–51, 271
Litchfield Congregational Church, 271
Litchfield Historical Society, 48, 50
Little Lake Sunapee, 150
Little Sebago Lake, 184
L.L. Bean, 38–39
Lobster Cove, 155
Lobster Hatchery, 137
Lockwood-Mathews Mansion, 92–93, 95
Loeb Drama Center, 294
Longfellow National Historic Site, 294, 298
Long Lake, 184
Long Point, 124
Long Trail Hiking Path, 170, 228
Long Wharf, 235
Loon Mountain, 201, 275, 278
Loon Mountain Gondola Skyride and Cave Walk, 202, 204
Lost River Reservation, 202, 204
Louisburg Square, 76
Lower Waterford, Vt., 191
Ludlow, Vt., 302
Lunt Design Center and Marketplace, 207, 210
Lyman Allen Museum, 70, 73
Lyman Plant House, 64
Lyme Historical Society, Conn, 72
Lynchville, Maine, 282
Lyndonville, Vt., 190

MacDowell Colony, 117
MacMillan Wharf, 180
Maine Coast Artists Gallery, 218, 220
Maine Festival, 41
Maine Highland Games, 41
Maine Maritime Museum, 41–42, 44
Maine Photography Workshops, 218
Maine Photography Workshop Gallery, 218
Maine State Ferry Service, 217, 220
Maine State Music Theater, 41
Maine Summer Music Festival, 41
Major Gideon Hastings House, 280
Manchester Center, Vt., 170

Manchester Commons, 170
Manchester Village, 171–172
Maple Grove Maple Candy Factory and
    Museum, 189–190, 193
Marblehead, Mass., 224
Marble House, 286
Marconi Wireless Station, 179
Marginal Way, 96
Maria Mitchell Science Center, 21, 26
Marine Park, 218
Marine Resources Aquarium, 158
Maritime Aquarium at Norwalk, 92, 95–96
Marlboro, Vt., 174
Marshfield, Vt., 192
Martha's Vineyard, 121–127
Martha's Vineyard Historical Society, 123
Mary Eliza, 158
Mashantucket Pequot Museum and
    Research Center, 71
Massachusetts Audubon Society, 12, 179
Massachusetts Cranberry Harvest Festival,
    194, 197, 198
Massachusetts Institute of Technology
    (MIT), 296, 298
Massachusetts Museum of Contemporary
    Art, 208
Mast Landing Sanctuary, 39, 44
Mayflower II, 195, 198
Mayflower Society House, 196, 198
Mead Art Gallery, 67
Megunticook Lake, 217
Megunticook River, 217
Mendon, Vt., 226
Memorial Hall (Harvard), 292
Memorial Hall Museum, 206–297
Menemsha, Mass., 124
Meriam's Corner, 9
Merrell Hiking Center, 228
Merrymeeting Bay, 42
Middlebury, Vt., 130–131, 229
Middlebury Gap, 229
Miller State Park, 117, 121
Minuteman National Historical Park, 9, 13
Miss Boothbay, 158
MIT Chapel, 296
MIT Museum, 296
Moffatt-Ladd House, 251
Mohawk Mountain, 269, 273
Mohawk Mountain Ski Area, 269, 273
Mohawk Trail, Mass, 204–210
Mohegan Bluffs, 113
Mohegan Sun Casino, 71
Monadnock region, NH, 116–121
Monadnock Music, 116, 120
Monhegan Island, 153, 154–155, 217
Monte Cristo Cottage, 69, 73–74
Montshire Museum of Science, 247, 249
Monument Mountain, 144

Monument Square, 9
Moose Cave, 186
Morse Mountain, 42
Moses Mason House, 280
Mother Walker Falls, 186
Mount, The, 142, 146
Mt. Abram Ski Slopes, 281, 283
Mt. Auburn Cemetery, 294–295
Mt. Battie, 215, 217
Mt. Cadillac, 134
Mt. Chocorua, 202
Mt. Cranmore, 102, 274, 278
Mt. Desert Island, Maine, 133–139
Mt. Desert Festival, 127
Mt. Greylock, 144, 209
Mt. Greylock Reservation, 209
Mt. Holyoke College, 64
Mt. Hor, 190
Mt. Kearsarge, 150
Mt. Liberty, 201
Mt. Mansfield, 259, 261
Mt. Megunticook, 215, 217
Mt. Monadnock, 116–117
Mt. Monadnock State Park, 117, 121
Mt. Pisgah, 190
Mt. Snow, 174
Mt. Snow Craft Show, 174
Mt. Sunapee II, 149, 153
Mt. Sunapee gondola, 148
Mt. Sunapee State Park, 148–49
Mt. Washington, 100–101, 275
Mt. Washington Valley, 100–196, 273–279
Mt. Washington Auto Road, 101
Mt. Washington Cog Railway, 101
Mt. Washington Valley Ski Touring
    Foundation, 275, 278
Museum of Fine Arts (Boston), 77, 79, 83,
    235
Museum of Fine Arts (Springfield), 63
Museum of Newport History, 285, 290
Museum of Rhode Island History, 29, 32
Museum of Science, (Boston) 74, 235, 237
Museum of Yachting, 288
Mystic, Conn., 70, 241–244
Mystic Marinelife Aquarium, 70, 74,
    242–243, 244
Mystic Seaport Museum, 68, 70, 74,
    241–242, 244

Nantucket, Mass, 20–26, 159–161
Nantucket Historical Association, 21, 26
Naples, Maine, 184, 281
Nathan Hale Homestead, 15, 19
Nathan Hale Schoolhouse, 69, 73
Nathaniel Macy House, 21
National Park Outdoor Activity Center (Bar
    Harbor), 134
National Park Service Information Center

(Boston), 233
National Training Laboratories, 279
National Yiddish Book Center, 64, 68
Natural Bridge State Park, 208
Nature Center for Environmental Activities, (Westport) 94, 95
Naumkeag Museum and Gardens, 144, 146
Nauset Beach, 178, 183
New England Aquarium, 73, 232–233, 236
New England Bach Festival, 174, 177
New England Brewing Company, 92
New England Center for Contemporary Art, 17
New England Culinary Institute, 128
New England Maple Museum, 229, 231
New England Marionette Opera, 116, 120
New England Science Center, 266, 268
New England Ski Museum, 201, 203, 274–275, 278
Newfane, Vt., 301–302
Newfield, Maine, 186
New Hampshire State Parks, 117, 121
New Harbor, 112
New Hartford, Conn, 270
New London, Conn., 68–70, 72–74
New London, N.H., 148–50
New London Barn Players, 149
New Marlborough, Mass., 141, 144
Newport, R.I., 284–291
Newport Art Association Museum, 288, 290
Newport Casino, 287
Newport Historical Society Museum, 287
Newport Mansions, 285, 286, 290
Newport Winter Festival, 284
New Preston, Conn., 47
Niantic, Conn., 70
Nichols House, 76, 83
Nightingale-Brown House, 27
Noank, Conn., 70–71
Norfolk, Conn., 270
Norman Rockwell Exhibition (Arlington), 172, 177
Norman Rockwell Museum (Rutland), 229, 231
Norman Rockwell Museum (Stockbridge), 141, 142, 146, 256
North Adams, Mass., 208, 255
Northampton, Mass., 64–65
North Bridge, 9, 10
North Conway, N.H., 101–102, 103–106, 273, 274, 276–277
North End (Boston), 79, 233, 234
Northeastern College, 77
Northeast Harbor, Maine, 135, 126
Northeast Kingdom, Vt., 188–94
Northeast Kingdom Foliage Festival, 192, 194
North Ferry Islands, 217

North Light lighthouse, 113
North Shore Art Association, 35, 38
North Sutton, N.H., 150
Norwalk, Conn., 90–96
Norwich, Vt., 247
Nubanusit River, 117
Nubble Light, 107

Oak Bluffs, Mass., 123
Occum Pond, 248
Oceanarium Lobster Hatchery, 137
Ocean Beach Park, 70, 74
Ocean Drive (Acadia), 134
Ocean Drive (Newport), 284, 286
Ocean Point, 154
Ogunquit, Maine, 96–99
Ogunquit Museum of American Art, 97, 99
Ogunquit Playhouse, 97, 99
Old Bennington, Vt., 173
Old Brick House, 155
Old Burying Ground (Concord), 9
Old Burying Ground (York Village), 107
Old Cemetery Point, (Sandwich) 53
Old Constitution House, 151, 153
Old Corner Bookstore, (Boston) 78, 234
Old Customs House (Bath), 42
Old Customs House, (New London), 69
Old Deerfield Crafts Fairs, 206–207
Old Fort House, 156
Old Gaol (Nantucket), 21
Old Gaol (York Village), 107
Old Harbor, 111, 112,
Old Jail (Concord), 10–11
Old Lyme, Conn., 71–72
Old Lyme Art Association, 72, 74
Old Man of the Mountain, 199, 200, 276
Old Manse, The, 10, 11, 13
Old Mill, (Nantucket) 21, 26
Old North Church, 79, 234
Old Port Exchange, 57–58
Old Quaker Meeting House & Graveyard, 53
Old Saybrook, Conn., 72, 214
Old Schoolhouse, 107
Old South Meeting House, 78
Old Speck, 186
Old State House (Boston), 78, 83, 234
Old Stone House, 190, 193
Old Sturbridge Village, 263–265, 267–268
Old Whaling Church, 122
Olde Mystic Village, 243
Orchard House, 10, 11, 13
Orleans, Mass., 177, 178
Orleans County Historical Society, Vt., 190
Ottauquechee River, 4, 87
Otter Creek, 228
Otter Lake, 117

Pacific Club, 21
Paradise Falls, 202
Paradise Pond, 64
Patriot's Park, 15
Park Street Church, 233
Paul Revere House, 79, 83, 234
Peabody Essex Museum, 222–223, 225
Peabody Museum of Archaeology and
	Ethnology, 293
Peacham, Vt., 192
Peary-MacMillan Arctic Museum, 40, 44
Pejepscot Historical Museum, 41, 44
Pemaquid Point, 156
Penobscot Bay, 217
Percy and Small Shipyard, 42
Perkins Cove, 96, 97
Peterborough, N.H., 117–118
Peterborough Library, 118
Peterborough Players, 116, 120
Peter Foulger Museum, 23, 26
Philbrook Place, 186
Pickering Wharf, 223
Pico Mounain, 226, 227
Pico Alpine Slide, 228
Pigeon Hill, 35
Pilgrim Hall Museum, 196, 198
Pilgrim Monument (Plymouth), 195
Pilgrim Monument (Provincetown),
	179–180, 183
Pinkham Notch, 102, 276
Pioneer Valley, 62–68
Pittsfield, Mass., 141, 142, 144, 256
Pittsford, Vt., 229
Plainfield, Vt., 192
Pleasant Bay, 178
Pleasant Lake, 150
Pleasant Mountain, 184
Plimoth Plantation, 195, 197, 198
Plimoth Plantation Harvest Feasts, 197
Plummer's Sugar House, 299, 303
Plymouth, Mass., 194–199
Plymouth, Vt., 6, 8, 229
Plymouth Colony Winery, 197
Plymouth harbor, 196
Plymouth harbor cruises, 196, 199
Plymouth Notch Historic District, Vt., 6, 8,
	229, 231
Plymouth Rock, 194
Pomfret, Conn., 16
Pomfret Farms, 16
Pontoosue Lake, 134
Pool, The, 189
Pontoosuc Lake, 144
Popham Beach, 42
Porpoise Point, 165
Port Clyde, Maine, 217
Portland, Maine, 56–62
Portland Art Museum, 58, 61

Portland Head Lighthouse, 56, 59, 61
Portland Observatory, 59, 61
Portsmouth, N.H., 109, 250–253
Portuguese Princess Whale Watch, 183
Poultney, Vt., 229
Pratt House, 212, 214
Prescott Park, 250
Princeton, Mass., 266
Proctor, Vt., 228
Profile Lake, 200
Prouts Neck, 59
Providence, R.I., 26–32
Providence Arcade, 29, 32
Providence Art Club, 29, 32
Providence Athenaeum, 29, 32
Providence Festival of Historic Houses,
	27–28, 31
Providence Lands Visitor Center, 179, 182
Provincetown, Mass., 179–180
Provincetown Art Association and Museum,
	180, 182
Provincetown Heritage Museum, 180, 182
Provincetown Playhouse, 180
Provincetown Whale Watching, 180, 183
Prudential Center, 75, 77
Prudential Tower Skywalk, 77, 83, 234
Public Garden, (Boston) 76, 233
Putnam, Conn., 17
Putney, Vt., 299

Quaker Meeting House (Nantucket), 20
Quaker Meetinghouse and Graveyard
	(E. Sandwich), 53
Quechee, Vt., 5, 87–89, 247
Quechee Balloon Festival, 87, 89
Quechee Polo Club, 89
Quincy Market, 79, 234
Quinebaug River, 16

Race Point beach, 183
Rachel Carson Naional Wildlife Refuge,
	167
Radcliffe Yard, 294
Redwood Library, 288
Reid State Park, 42
Rhode Island School of Design Museum of
	Art, 28–29, 31
Rhode Island State House, 29, 32
Rhododendron State Park, 117, 121
Richard Sparrow House, 196, 199
Ridgefield, Conn., 93
Rindge, N.H., 118
Ripton, Vt., 127, 229
River Lily Farm, 97
Riverton, Conn., 270–271
Riverview Cemetery, 212
Robert Frost Cabin, 127
Robert Frost Memorial Drive, 229

Rock Harbor, 179
Rockland, Maine, 218
Rockport, Maine, 218
Rockport, Mass., 34–35
Rockport Art Association, 35, 37–38
Rockport Chamber Music Festival, 33, 37
Rocky Gorge (NH), 103, 202
Rocky Neck Art Colony, (Mass), 35
Rocky Neck State Park (Conn). 71. 74
Rodman's Hollow, 113
Roger Williams National Memorial, 29, 32
Roger Williams Park, 29, 32
Roost, The, 185
Roseland Cottage, 17, 19
Round Hill Scottish Games, 90–91, 95
Rundlet-May House, 251
Rutland, Vt., 228, 229

Sabbaday Falls, 103, 202
Sabbathday Lake Shaker Museum, 186, 188
Saco Bound, 102, 184
Saco River, 184
Saco River Valley, 102
Sailor's Memorial Museum, 218
St. Albans, Vt., 299
St. Ann's Episcopal Church, 166
Saint-Gaudens National Historic Site, 150, 153
St. James Church, 142
St. Johnsbury, Vt., 188–190
St. Johnsbury Athenaeum, 189, 193
St. Mary's Church, 288
St. Patrick's Church, 156
Salem, Mass., 221–226
Salem Halloween Happenings, 221, 225
Salem Maritime National Historic Site, 223, 225
Salem 1630: Pioneer Village, 223, 225
Salem Witch Museum, 221, 225
Salem Witch Village, 222, 225
Salisbury, Conn., 268–273
Salmon Falls, 207
Salt Pond Visitor Center, 179, 182
Sand Beach, 134
Sandwich, Mass., 51–56
Sandwich Glass Museum, 52–53, 55
Sandwich Town Hall, 52
Sandy Neck, 51
Sandy Point, 112–113
Satre Hill, 268
Saugatuck River, 93, 94
Sayward-Wheeler House, 108, 111
Scarborough Beach State Park, 59
Science Museum of Eastern Connecticut, 70, 73
Screw Auger Falls, 186
Seal Harbor, 134
Seal Ledge, 155

Seaman's Bethel, 123, 127
Seashore Trolley Museum, 167, 169
Sebago, Maine, 186
Sebago Lake, 184
Sebago Lake State Park, 184
Second Congregational Church, 288
Sentinel Pine Bridge, 201
Settler's Rock, 113
Seven Seas Whale Watch, 37
Sever Hall, 292
Shakespeare & Company, 142, 147
Sharon, Conn., 269
Sharon Arts Center, 118
Shaw Perkins Mansion, 69, 73
Shawme Pond, 52
Shawnee Peak Ski Area, 281, 283
Sheffield, Mass., 141, 257
Sheffield Island, 92, 96
Shelburne, Vt., 130–31
Shelburne Falls, Mass., 207
Shelburne Farms, 127–28, 129–130, 132
Shelburne Museum, 130, 132
Sheldon-Hawks House, 206
Sherburne Pass, 228
Sherwood Island State Park, 93
Siasconset, Mass., 22, 159–160
Sieur de Monts Spring, 134
Silvermine Guild Art Center, 91, 93
Simmons College, 77
Simon Pearce, 88, 150–51, 247–148
Ski Sundown, 270, 273
Skinner State Park, 65, 67
Skolfield-Whitter House, 41, 44
Sky Tower, 202
Sleepy Hollow Cemetery, 11
Sloane-Stanley Museum, 48, 50
Smith College, 64
Smith College Museum of Art, 64, 67
Somes Sound, 133, 135
Somesville, Maine, 135
Songo River Queen II, 184, 188
South Beach, 124
South Bridge Boat House, 11
Southbury, Ct., 46
South Carver, Mass., 194, 197
South Congregational Church, 166
Southeast Light, 113
South Egremont, Mass., 141
Southern Vermont Art Center, 171, 177
South Mountain Concerts, 142, 147
South Norwalk, Conn., 92
Southport Island, 154
Southwest Harbor, Maine, 135, 136
Southwest Harbor Oceanarium, 135, 139
Southwest Vermont, 169–177
South Williamstown, 256
Spirit of Ethan Allen cruises, 133
Spirit of the Sea, 42

Splashdown Amphibious Tours, 199
Spouting Rock, 166
Springfield, Mass., 62–64
Springfield Armory National Historic Site, 63–64, 67
Springfield Library and Museums, 63, 67
Springfield Science Museum, 63
Spruce Point, 154
Star Island, 109
State House (Boston), 76, 80, 233
Steamboat Dock, 211
Stellwagen Bank, 33
Stephen Douglas Homestead, 229
Stephen Phillips Memorial Trust House, 222
Stockbridge, Mass., 141, 142, 144, 256, 257
Stonington, Conn., 71
Stonington Lighthouse, 71
Storrs, Conn, 15, 16
Story Land, 103, 105
Stowe, Vt., 127, 259–63
Stowe Winter Carnival, 259–260. 263
Stowe winter sports, 261, 263
Stratton Mountain, 169, 170
Stratton Mountain Arts Festival, 169, 174, 176
Strawbery Banke, 109, 250–51, 253
Sturbridge, Mass., 263–268
Submarine Force Museum (and historic ship Nautilus), 70
Sugar Hill, N.H., 199–200, 276
Sugarmill Farm, 192
Summit Cave Walk, 202
Sunday River Cross Country Ski Center, 280, 283
Sunday River Ski Resort, 280–281, 283
Sundial Herb Gardens, 213
Sutton, Vt., 192
Swan Boats, 233, 237
Swan Island State Park Wildlife Area, 42
Swans Island, 136
Swanzey, N.H., 118
Swift River Valley, 202

Table Rock, 186
Tanglewood, 140, 141–42, 147
Tapping Reeve House and Law School, 48, 50, 271
Temple Street Post Office, 166
Texas Falls Recreation Area, 229
Thayercroft House, 216
Thomas Cooke House, 123
Thomas Macy Warehouse, 20, 26
Thomas Point Beach, 41
Thompson Arena, 248
Thorne-Sagendorph Art Gallery, 118
Thornton Burgess Briarpath, 53
Thornton Burgess Museum, 52, 55

Thunder Hole, 134
Thuya Gardens, 135, 139
Ticonderoga, 130
Tisbury Great Pond, 124
Tisbury, Mass., 123
Tony Carretta studio, 48, 51
Topsmead State Forest, 49, 50
Touro Synagogue, 287–288, 290
Town Hall (Vineyard Haven), 123
Town Hall-Opera House (Rockport), 218
Trapp Family Meadow, 127
Trinity Church (Boston), 7
Trinity Church (Newport), 288, 290
Truro, Mass., 178
Turtle, The, 211
Two Lights State Park, 59
Tyringham Art Galleries, 144, 146

UConn Dairy Bar, 16
University Hall, 292
University of Connecticut (UConn), 15, 16
University of Massachusetts, 60
University of Vermont, 128–129
U.S. Coast Guard Academy, 69, 73
U.S. Naval Submarine Base, 70, 74

Valley Railroad, 213
Vergennes, Vt., 119
Vermont Folklife Center, 131
Vermont Institute of Natural Science, 5, 8
Vermont Maple Festival, 299
Vermont Marble Exhibit, 228, 231
Vermont Mozart Festival, 127–128, 132
Vermont, southwest, 169–177
Vermont State Craft Center, 6, 129, 131, 151, 229
Vermont Wildflower Farm, 131, 133
Vesper Hill, 218
Virginia, 41
Victoria Mansion, 59, 61
Vietnam Veterans Memorial Skating Rink, 255
Village Middle Bridge, 4
Vinalhaven, Maine, 217–218
Vincent House, 123, 127
Vineyard Haven, Mass., 123–24
Vineyard Museum, 123, 127

Wachusett Mountain State Reservation, 266, 268
Wadsworth House, 293
Wadsworth-Longfellow House, 57, 61
Walden, Vt., 192
Walden Pond State Reservation, 10, 12, 13–14
Walker Art Building, 40
Walker Point, 166
Wang Center for the Performing Arts, 80

Wapack Trail, 117
Ware, Mass., 265
Warner House, 251
Washington, Conn., 44–46, 50
Waterbury, Vt., 261
Waterfront Park, 42
Waterford, Maine, 185, 282
Waterville Valley, 275
Wauwinet, Mass., 160–161
Wayside, 10, 13
Wellfleet, Mass., 178, 179
Wells, Maine, 167
Wells National Estuarine Research Reserve, 167
Wells-Thorn House, 206
Wendell Gilley Museum, 135, 139
Wentworth-Gardner House, 251
Wesleyan Grove, 123
West Arlington, Vt., 172–173
West Brookfield, Mass., 266
West Burke, Vt., 190
West Chop Lighthouse, 124
West County Winery, 207
West Dover, Vt., 174
Western Gateway Heritage State Park, 208
West India Goods Store, 223
Weston, Vt., 6
Weston Playhouse, 6
West Paris, Maine, 185
West Parish Congregational Church, 280
Westport, Conn., 93–96
Westport Country Playhouse, 94, 95–96
West Stockbridge, Mass., 141, 143, 257
West Tisbury, Mass., 124
West Townshend, Vt., 174
Whale Oil Row, 69
Whaling Museum, 21, 26, 161
Whitcomb Summit, 208
White Flower Farm, 49, 50
White Memorial Foundation and Conservation Center, 49, 50, 271
White Mountain National Forest, 103, 185
White Mountains, 100–106, 185, 273–279, 280
Widener Library, 292
Wildcat Mountain, 101, 274, 278

Wildcat Mountain Gondola, 101, 105
Wildcat Valley Trail, 275
Wilder, Vt., 246
Wild Gardens of Acadia, 134
Wild River, 185
Willard House and Clock Museum, 266, 268
William Benton Museum of Art, 16, 19
Williams College, 141, 254–55
Williams College Art Museum, 255, 258
Williamstown, Mass., 141, 142, 209, 253–258
Williamstown Theater Festival, 142, 147
Willowbrook, 186, 188
Wilmington, Vt., 173–174
Wilson Castle, 228, 231
Windjammer Cruises, 216, 220
Windjammer Days, 153
Windsor, Vt., 6, 150–151
Winooski, Vt., 129
Winslow Memorial Park, 39, 44
Winsted, Conn., 270
Witch Dungeon Museum, 222, 225
Witch House, 222, 225
Wolfe's Neck State Park, 39, 44
Woodbury, Conn., 45, 49–50
Woods-Gerry Gallery, 28, 32
Woodstock, Conn., 17
Woodstock, Vt., 3–8, 88, 226, 229, 247
Woodstock Historical Society, 4
Woody Jackson, 131
Worcester, Mass., 266
Worcester Art Museum, 266, 268
Words and Pictures Museum, 64, 67
Wright House, 206
Wyoming, 42

Yale-Harvard Regatta, 68, 73
Yale School of Music, 270
Yankee Fleet Whale Watch, 37
Yarmouth, Nova Scotia, 136
Yesteryears Doll Museum, 52, 55
York, Maine, 106–111
York Beach, Maine, 109
York Harbor, Maine, 109
York Lake, 144
York Village, Maine, 106–107

CATEGORY INDEX

Antiquing

Bennington, Vt., 173
Fitzwilliam, N.H., 118
Gaylordsville, Conn, 47
Kent, Conn, 47
Manchester, Vt, 170
Norwalk, Conn, 93
Ogunquit, Maine, 97
Pomfret, Conn, 16
Portsmouth, N.H., 251
Putnam, Conn, 17
Salisbury, Conn, 269
Woodbury, Conn, 45
Woodstock, Vt., 4–5

Arts and Crafts

American Craft Council Craftfair, 62, 67
Bennington Potters, 129, 173
Berkshire Center of Contemporary Glass, 143
Bonnema Pottery, 186
Connecticut River Artisans Cooperative, 213
Hildene Harvest and Craft Festival, 171
Jones Museum of Glass and Ceramics, 186, 188
Keene, New Hampshire, 118
Kent, Conn., 47
League of New Hampshire Craftsmen Fair, 148, 152
League of New Hampshire Craftsmen shops, 102, 247
Lunt Design Center and Marketplace, 207, 210
Mt. Snow Craft Show, 174
North Shore Art Association, 35, 38
Northampton, Mass, 65
Old Deerfield Crafts Fairs, 206–207
Sharon Arts Center, 118
Silvermine Guild Art Center, 91, 93
Stratton Mountain Arts Festival, 169, 174, 176
Vermont State Craft Centers, 6, 129, 131, 151, 229
Wellfleet, Mass., 178, 179

Beaches and parks

Acadia National Park, 33–34
Ballston beach, 183
Beartown State Forest, 144
Cahoon Hollow Beach, 183
Camden Hills State Park, 217–220
Cape Cod National Seashore, 177, 179, 182
Cape Cod National Seashore beaches, 183
Cape Neddick, 107–108
City Park, 42
Crawford Notch, 202, 276
Crescent Beach, 112
Crescent Neck Beach State Park, 59
East Beach, 124
Echo Lake State Park, 102
Ferry Beach, 59
Fish Beach, 155
Fort Allen Park, 59
Fort Griswold Battlefield State Park, 70, 74
Fort Williams Park, 59
Franconia Notch State Park, 200,203, 276
Fred Benson Beach, 112
Goose Rocks Beach, 166
Grafton Notch State Park, 186
Greenfield State Park, 117, 121
Halibut Point State Park, 36,38
Harkness Memorial Park, 69, 74
Head of the Meadow Beach, 183
Higgins Beach, 59
Katama Beach, 124
Kent Falls State Park, 47–48
Lake Waramaug State Park, 47
Marine Park, 218
Miller State Park, 117, 121
Mt. Monadnock State Park, 117, 121
St. Sunapee State Park, 148–149
Nauset Beach, 178, 183
New Hampshire State Parks, 117, 121
Ocean Beach Park, 70, 74
Pigeon Hill, 35
Popham Beach, 42

Rhododendron State Park, 117, 121
Roger Williams Park, 29, 32
Sand Beach, 234
Scarborough Beach State Park, 59
Sebago Lake State Park, 184
Sherwood Island State Park, 93
South Beach, 124
Swan Island State Park Wildlife Area,
42
Texas Falls Recreation Area, 229
Thomas Point Beach, 41
Two Lights State Park, 59
Wachusett Mountain State Reservation,
266, 268
Walden Pond State Reservation, 10, 12,
13–14
Western Gateway Heritage State Park,
208
White Mountain National Forest, 103,
185
York Beach, 109

Children's activities
Attitash Bear Peak Alpine Slide, 103, 105
Patriot's Park, 15
Bar Harbor Oceanarium, 136–137
Basketball Hall of Fame, 63, 67
Ben and Jerry's Ice Cream Factory, 261
Billings Farm and Museum, 5, 8
Boothbay Railway Village, 155,158
Boston for families, 233–237
Boston by Little Feet, 233, 237
Boston Tea Party Ship and Museum, 232,
235, 237
Brayton Grist Mill, 16, 19
Bunker Hill, 79, 234
Cabot Farmers' Cooperative Creamery,
192, 194
Candlelight Stroll, 250–251, 253
Cape Ann Whale Watch, 33, 37
Cape Cod Scenic Railroad, 53, 55–56
Capt. Bill & Son's Whale Watching, 37
Children's Museum of Boston, 234–235,
237
Children's Museum of Maine, 59, 61
Children's Museum of Southeastern
Connecticut, 70, 74
Computer Museum, 235, 237
Crowley Cheese Factory, 6
Dexter Grist Mill, 52
Dolphin Mini-Golf Course, 156
Drumlin Farm, 12, 14
Freedom Trail, 75, 78–79,233–234
Friendly Farm, 118, 121
Hancock Shaker Village, 140, 142–143,
257
Harlow's Sugar House, 299, 303
Heritage New Hampshire, 103, 105

Loon Mountain Gondola Skyride and
Cave Walk, 202, 204
Lost River Reservation, 202, 204
Maple Grove, 189–190, 193
Maple Sugaring, 299–300, 303
Maritime Aquarium at Norwalk, 92,
95–96
Montshire Museum of Science, 247, 249
Mt. Washington Cog Railway, 101
Mystic Marinelife Aquarium, 70, 74,
242–243, 244
Mystic Seaport Museum, 68, 70, 74,
241–142, 244
New England Aquarium, 73, 232–233,
236
Oceanarium Lobster Hatchery, 137
Old Sturbridge Village, 263–265,
267–268
Pico Alpine Slide, 228
Plimoth Plantation, 195, 197, 198
Plummer's Sugar House, 299, 303
Prudential Tower Skywalk, 77, 83, 234
Quechee Balloon Festival, 87–89
Salem Halloween Happenings, 221–225
Salem 1630: Pioneer Village, 223, 225
Salem Witch Museum, 221, 225
Southwest Harbor Oceanarium, 135, 139
Story Land, 103, 105
Swan boats, 233, 237
Valley Railroad, 213
Words and Pictures Museum, 64, 67

Cultural events
Acadia Repertory Theater, 136
Albany Berkshire Ballet, 142–147
American Repertory Theatre, 291
American Stage Festival, 116, 120
Apple Hill Chamber Players, 116
Arts Jubilee, 102
Aston Magna concerts, 142, 147
Bar Harbor Festival of Chamber Music,
136
Bar Harbor Music Festival, 136
Berkshire Choral Festival, 142, 147
Berkshire Opera Festival, 142, 147
Berkshire Theater Festival, 142, 147
Boston Pops Orchestra, 76
Boston Symphony, 140, 141–142
Brickyard Pond Arts Center, 116
Carousel Music Theater, 156
Connecticut Repertory Company, 16
Dartmouth Players Repertory Company,
150
Dorset Playhouse, 170
Eugene O'Neill Theater Center, 69–70
Gloucester Stage Company, 35
Goodspeed Opera House, 212, 213,
214–215

Harkness Memorial Park Summer Music, 69, 74
Hatch Memorial Shell, 76
Hopkins Center, 89, 150, 247, 249
Jacob's Pillow Dance Festival, 140, 142, 147
Levitt Pavilion, 94, 96
Loeb Drama Center, 294
MacDowell Colony, 117
Maine State Music Theater, 41
Maine Summer Music Festival, 41
Monadnock Music, 116, 120
New England Bach Festival, 174, 177
New England Marionette Opera, 116, 120
New London Barn Players, 149
Ogunquit Playhouse, 97, 99
Peterborough Players, 116, 120
Portland Ballet Company, 59
Portland Lyric Theater, 59
Portland Stage Company, 59
Portland Symphony, 59
Provincetown Playhouse, 180
Rockport Chamber Music Festival, 33, 37
Shakespeare & Company, 142, 147
South Mountain Concerts, 142, 147
Tanglewood, 140, 141–42, 147
Town Hall-Opera House, 218
Vermont Mozart Festival, 127–128, 132
Wang Center for the Performing Arts, 80
Weston Playhouse, 6
Westport Country Playhouse, 94, 95–96
Williamstown Theater Festival, 142, 147

Fairs and festivals
Chocolate Festival, 276
Cranberry Harvest Festival, 194, 197, 198
Daffodil Festival, 20, 22, 25–26
February Heritage Day, 280
Fryeburg Fair, 183, 184, 188
Maine Festival, 41
Newport Winter Festival, 282
Northeast Kingdom Foliage Festival, 192
Quechee Balloon Festival, 87, 89
Plimoth Plantation Harvest Feasts, 197
Salem Halloween Happenings, 221–225
Stowe Winter Carnival, 259–60, 263
Windjammer Days, 153

Historic sites
Aldrich House, 29
Ancient Burying Ground, 293
Arrowhead, 144, 146, 257, 258
Asa Stebbins House, 206
Ashley House, 205
Astors' Beechwood, 286, 290

Barrett's farm, 9
Bath Iron Works, 41, 154
Battle of Bennington monument, 173
Beacon Hill, 76, 235
Belcourt Castle, 286, 290
Blacksmith House, 294
Bullet Hole House, 9
Bunker Hill, 79, 234
Chateau-sur-Mer, 286
Chesterwood, 144, 146
Coles Hill, 195
College Hill Historic District, 27–28
Colonial Newport, 284, 285
Colonial Pemaquid State Historic Site, 156
Coolidge home, 6
Customs House (New London), 69
Customs House (Salem), 223
Dana House, 4, 7–8
Derby Wharf, 223
Deshon-Allyn House, 70
Dickinson Homestead, 65, 68
Drisco House, 109
Dwight House, 206
Eastern Cemetery, 59
Elizabeth Perkins House, 107
Elms, The, 286
Emerson House, 10, 13
Emerson-Wilcox House, 107
Faneuil Hall, 79, 234
Farnsworth Homestead, 218
First Baptist Meeting House, 29, 32
First Church of Christ (Sandwich), 52
First Parish Church (Portland), 57
First Parish Meetinghouse (Sandwich) 52
First Parish Unitarian Church (Kennebunk), 167
First Parish Unitarian Church (Cambridge), 293
Fisher House, 122–23
Florence Griswold Museum, 71–71, 74
Fort Griswold Battlefield State Park, 70, 74
Fort McClary State Memorial, 109
Fort William Henry, 156
Franklin Pierce Homestead, 119
Frary House, 206
Freedom Trail, 75, 78–79, 233–234
Frost Place, 201, 203–204
Gillettte Castle, 23, 215
Gingerbread House, 144, 146
Glebe House, 45, 50
Governor John Langdon House, 251
Governor Stephen Hopkins House, 29, 32
Granary Burying Ground, 233
Grandma Moses Schoolhouse, 173, 256
Grapevine Cottage, 11

Hadwen House, 22, 26
Hancock Shaker Village, 140, 142–143, 257
Harbor Walk, 235
Harlow Old Fort House, 196, 198
Hathaway-Cushing-Millay House, 216–217
Hayden Yard, 211
Hempsted House, 69, 73
Heritage New Hampshire, 103, 105
Hildene, 171, 177
Hinsdale and Anna Williams House, 206
Historic Deerfield, 205–206, 210
Historic Nantucket Properties, 64, 67
Hoosac Mountain Tunnels, 208
House of Seven Gables, 223, 225
Hoxie House, 52
Jefferd's Tavern, 107
Jethro Coffin House, 21, 26
John Bray House, 109
John Brown House, 20, 32
John Paul Jones House, 109, 251
Jonathan Trumbull House, 16, 19
Kings Chapel, 234
Kings Chapel Burying Ground, 234
Lady Pepperell House, 109
Litchfield Congregational Church, 271
Litchfield Historical Society, 48, 50
Lockwood-Mathews Mansion, 92–93, 95
Longfellow National Historic Site, 294, 298
Lyme Historical Society, 72
Major Gideon Hasting House, 280
Marblehead, Mass, 224
Marconi Wireless Station, 179
Mayflower II, 195, 198
Mayflower Society House, 196, 198
Meriam's Corner, 9
Minuteman National Historical Park, 9, 13
Moffatt-Ladd House, 251
Monte Cristo Cottage, 69, 73–74
Moses Mason House, 280
Mt. Washington Cog Railway, 101
Mount, The (Edith Wharton Restoration), 142, 146
Nantucket Historical Association, 21, 26
Nathan Hale Homestead, 15, 19
Nathan Hale Schoolhouse, 69, 73
Nathaniel Macy House, 21
Newport Mansions, 285, 286, 290
Nichols House, 76, 83
Nightingale-Brown House, 27
North Bridge, 9, 10
Nubble Light, 107
Old Bennington, Vt., 173
Old Burying Ground (Concord), 9
Old Burying Ground (York Village), 107

Old Cemetery Point, 53
Old Corner Bookstore, 78, 234
Old Customs House (Bath), 42
Old Customs House (New London), 69
Old Fort House, 156
Old Gaol (Nantucket), 21
Old Gaol (York Village), 107
Old Jail (Concord), 10–11
Old Manse, The, 10, 11, 13
Old Mill, 21, 26
Old North Church, 79, 234
Old Schoolhouse, 107
Old South Meeting House, 78
Old State House (Boston), 78, 83, 234
Old Stone House, 190, 193
Old Sturbridge Village, 263–265, 267–268
Old Whaling Church, 122
Orchard House, 10, 11, 13
Orleans County Historical Society, Vt., 190
Paul Revere House, 79, 83, 234
Percy and Small Shipyard, 42
Pilgrim Monument (Plymouth), 195
Pilgrim Monument (Provincetown), 179–80, 183
Plimoth Plantation, 195, 197, 109
Plymouth Notch Historic District, 6, 8, 229, 231
Plymouth Rock, 194
Portland Head Lighthouse, 56, 59, 61
Pratt House, 212, 214
Providence Athenaeum, 29, 32
Providence Festival of Historic Houses, 27–28, 31
Quaker Meeting House (Nantucket), 20
Quaker Meetinghouse and Graveyard (Sandwich), 52
Rhode Island State House, 29, 32
Richard Sparrow House, 196, 199
Robert Frost Cabin, 127
Roger Williams National Memorial, 29, 32
Roseland Cottage, 17, 19
Rundlet-May House, 251
St. Johnsbury Athenaeum, 189, 193
Salem Maritime National Historic Site, 223, 225
Salem 1630: Pioneer Village, 223, 225
Salmon Falls, 207
Sandwich Town Hall, 52
Seaman's Bethel, 123, 127
Second Congregational Church, 288
Sentinel Pine Bridge, 201
Settler's Rock, 113
Shaw Perkins Mansion, 69, 73
Sheldon-Hawks House, 206
Skolfield-Whittier House, 41, 44

Springfield Armory National Historic
Site, 63–64, 67
State House (Boston), 76, 80, 233
Stephen Douglas Homestead, 229
Strawbery Banke, 109, 250–251, 253
Tapping Reeve House and Law School,
48, 50, 271
Thayercroft House, 216
Thomas Cooke House, 123
Thomas Macy Warehouse, 20, 26
Touro Synagogue, 287–288, 290
Trinity Church (Boston), 7
Trinity Church (Newport), 288, 290
Victoria Mansion, 59, 61
Vincent House, 123, 127
Wadsworth House, 293
Wadsworth-Longfellow House, 57–61
Warner House, 251
Wayside, 10, 13
Wells-Thorn House, 206
Wentworth-Gardner House, 251
Whale Oil Row, 69
Wilson Castle, 228, 231
Witch House, 222
Woodstock Historical Society, 4
Wright House, 205

Museums and galleries
American Museum of Fly Fishing, 171,
177
American Precision Museum, 151, 153
Arthur M. Sackler Museum, 292, 298
Ballard Institute and Museum of
Puppetry, 15, 16
Bar Harbor Historical Society, 137, 139
Beauport Museum, 35, 38
Bennington Museum, 173, 256
Blue Heron gallery, 179
Boothbay Railway Village, 155, 158
Boothbay Region Art Foundation
Gallery, 155, 158
Botanical Museum (Harvard), 293
Bowdoin Museum of Art, 40, 44
Bread and Puppet Museum, 190
Brick Store Museum, 167, 169
Busch-Reisinger Museum, 292, 298
Cape Ann Historical Museum, 35, 37
Carpenter Center for the Visual Arts, 292
Chaffee Art Gallery, 229, 231
Clark Art Institute, 141, 253–254
College of the Atlantic Natural History
Museum, 137, 139
Concord Museum, 11, 13
Connecticut River Foundation Museum,
211
Connecticut Valley Historical Museum,
63
David Winton Bell Gallery, 28, 32

Fairbanks Museum and Planetarium, 189,
193
Fair Street Museum, 26
Farnesworth Art Museum, 218, 220
Florence Griswold Museum, 71–72, 74
Fogg Art Museum, 292, 298
George Walter Vincent Smith Art
Museum, 63
Gleason Fine Art Gallery, 155
Gunn Historical Museum, 46, 50
Hammond Castle Museum, 35, 38
Hart Nautical Galleries, 296, 298
Harvard Art Museums, 292–293, 298
Heritage Plantation, 51, 53–55
Higgins Armory Museum, 266, 268
Hitchcock Museum, 270
Hood Museum, 247, 249
Institute for American Indian Studies,
46–50
International Tennis Hall of Fame, 287,
290
Isabella Stewart Gardner Museum, 77, 83
James B. Owen Art Gallery, 280
John F. Kennedy Library Museum,
79–80, 83, 236, 296
Joshua L. Chamberlain Museum, 41, 44
Kendall Art Gallery, 179
Kent Art Association Gallery, 47
Kittery Naval Museum, 109
Larry LiVolsi studio, 48, 51
List Arts Center (Cambridge), 296, 298
Lyman Allen Museum, 70, 73
Maine Coast Artists Gallery, 218, 220
Maine Maritime Museum, 41–42, 44
Maria Mitchell Science Center, 21, 26
Maritime Aquarium at Norwalk, 92,
95–96
Martha's Vineyard Historical Society,
123
Mashantucket Pequot Museum and
Research Center, 71
Massachusetts Museum of Contemporary
Art, 208
Mead Art Gallery, 67
Montshire Museum of Science, 247,
249
Museum of Fine Arts (Boston), 77, 79,
83, 235
Museum of Fine Arts (Springfield), 63
Museum of Newport History, 285, 290
Museum of Rhode Island History, 29, 32
Museum of Science (Boston), 74, 235,
237
Museum of Yachting, 288
Mystic Seaport Museum, 68, 70, 74,
241–242, 244
Naumkeag Museum and Gardens, 144,
146

New England Center for Contemporary Art, 17
New England Maple Museum, 229, 231
New England Ski Museum, 201, 203, 274–275, 278
Newport Art Association Museum, 288, 290
Newport Historical Society Museum, 287
Norman Rockwell Exhibition (Arlington), 172, 177
Norman Rockwell Museum (Rutland), 299, 231
Norman Rockwell Museum (Stockbridge), 141, 142, 146, 256
North Shore Art Association, 35, 38
Ogunquit Museum of American Art, 97, 99
Old Lyme Art Association, 72, 74
Peary-MacMillan Arctic Museum, 40, 44
Peter Foulger Museum, 23, 26
Pilgrim Hall Museum, 196, 198
Portland Art Museum, 58, 61
Providence Art Club, 29, 32
Provincetown Art Association and Museum, 180, 182
Provincetown Heritage Museum, 180, 182
Rhode Island School of Design Museum of Art, 28–29, 31
Rockport Art Association (Mass), 35, 37–38
Rockport Photography Workshop Gallery (Maine), 218
Sabbathday Lake Shaker Museum, 186, 188
Sailor's Memorial Museum, 218
Saint-Gaudens National Historic Site, 150, 153
Salem Witch Museum, 221, 225
Sandwich Glass Museum, 52–52, 55
Seashore Trolley Museum, 167, 169
Shelburne Farms, 127–128, 129–130, 132
Shelburne Museum, 130, 132
Smith College Museum of Art, 64, 67
Southern Vermont Art Center, 171, 177
Springfield Science Museum, 63
Springfield Library and Museums, 63, 67
Thorne-Sagendorph Art Gallery, 118
Thornton Burgess Museum, 52, 55
Tony Carretta studio, 48, 51
Tyringham Art Galleries, 144, 146
U.S. Coast Guard Academy Museum, 69, 73
Vermont Folklife Center, 131
Vermont Institute of Natural Science, 5, 8
Vineyard Museum, 123, 127
Walker Art Building, 40

Wendell Gilley Museum, 135, 139
Whaling Museum, 21, 26, 161
Willard House and Clock Museum, 266, 268
William Benton Museum of Art, 16, 19
Williams College Art Museum, 255, 258
Witch Dungeon Museum, 222, 225
Woods-Gerry Gallery, 28, 32
Worcester Art Museum, 266, 268
Words and Pictures Museum, 64, 67
Yesteryears Doll Museum, 52, 55

Nature
Acadia National Park, 133–134
Agamenticus Wilderness Reserve, 108
Artist's Bluff, 201
Ashley Falls, 144
Asticou Gardens, 135
Atlantic White Cedar Swamp Trail, 179
Avalanche Falls, 201
Baby Flume, 201
Bartholomew's Cobble, 144, 147
Basin, The, 201
Berkshire Botanical Garden, 144, 147, 257
Black Top Path, 102
Block Island, 112, 113
Blowing Cave, 165, 166
Botany Trial, 171
Boulder Loop, 202
Brandon Gap, 229
Brewster Gardens, 196
Bridge of Flowers, 207
Cape Ann Whale Watch, 22, 27
Cape Cod National Seashore, 177, 179, 182
Cape Pogue Wildlife Refuge, 124
Caprilands Herb Farm, 14–15, 17, 18
Capt. Bill & Son's Whale Watching, 37
Cascade Falls, 186
Cascades, 188
Cathedral Ledge, 102
Cathedral of the Pines, 118, 121
Cathedral Woods, 155
Cedar Tree Neck, 124
Channing Blake Meadow Walk, 205
Cliff Walk, 284, 286
Connecticut College Arboretum, 70, 73
Darling Hill, 190
Deer Leap Trail, 228
Diana's Bath, 102
Eastern Point Sanctuary, 36
Echo Lake, 201
Evans Notch, 185, 186
Felix Neck, 124
Flanders Nature Center, 47, 50
Flume, The, 201, 302

Great Meadow National Wildlife Refuge, 12, 14
Headlands, 35
Heritage Plantation, 51, 52–55
Hopper, The, 209
Jeffreys Ledge, 33
Kancamagus Highway, 103, 202, 276
Lobster Cove, 155
Long Trail Hiking Path, 170, 228
Loon Mountain Gondola Skyride and Cave Walk, 202, 204
Loon Mountain, 201, 275, 278
Lost River Reservation, 202, 204
Lyman Plant House, 64
Marginal Way, 96
Maritime Aquarium at Norwalk, 92, 95–96
Massachusetts Audubon Society, 12, 179
Mohawk Trail, 204–210
Mohegan Bluffs, 113
Monhegan Island, 153, 154–55, 217
Moose Cave, 186
Mother Walker Falls, 186
Mt. Greylock Reservation, 209
Mystic Marinelife Aquarium, 70, 74, 242–243, 244
Nature Center for Environmental Activities (Westport), 94, 95
Naumkeag Museum and Gardens, 144, 146
New England Aquarium, 73, 232–233, 236
Oceanarium (Bar Harbor), 136–37
Oceanarium (Southwest Harbor), 135, 139
Oceanarium Lobster Hatchery, 137
Ocean Point, 154
Old Man of the Mountain, 199, 200, 276
Old Speck, 186
Paradise Falls, 202
Pemaquid Point, 156
Pleasant Mountain, 184
Pool, The, 189
Porpoise Point, 165
Portuguese Princess Whale Watch, 183
Provincetown Whale Watching, 180, 183
Public Garden (Boston), 76, 233
Rachel Carson National Wildlife Refuge, 167
Rocky Gorge, 103, 202
Roost, The, 185
Sabbaday Falls, 103, 202
Salt Pond Visitor Center, 179, 182
Sandy Neck, 51
Sandy Point, 112, 113
Screw Auger Falls, 186
Seal Ledge, 155
Shelburne Farms, 129–130, 132

Sieur de Monts Spring, 134
Sky Tower, 202
Somes Sound, 133, 135
Spouting Rock, 166
Stellwagen Bank, 33
Summit Cave Walk, 202
Sundial Herb Gardens, 213
Table Rock, 186
Thornton Burgess Briarpath, 53
Thunder Hole, 134
Topsmead State Forest, 49, 50
Vermont Institute of Natural Science, 5, 8
Vermont Wildflower Farm, 131, 133
Wachusett Mountain State Reservation, 266, 268
Wapack Trail, 117
Wells National Estuarine Research Reserve, 167
Whitcomb Summit, 208
White Flower Farm, 49, 50
White Memorial Foundation and Conservation Center, 49, 50, 271
Wild Gardens of Acadia, 134
Yankee Fleet Whale Watch, 37

Shopping
Bar Harbor, Maine, 136
Bennington, Vt., 173
Berkshires, 143,
Bethel, Maine, 186, 281
Block Island, 113
Boothbay Harbor, Maine, 155
Boston, Mass, 77, 78
Burlington, Vt, 129
Cambridge, Mass, 293–294
Camden, Maine, 217
Cape Cod, 178, 179
Concord, Mass., 11
East Arlington, Vt., 172
Freeport, Maine, 39
Grafton, Vt., 301
Hanover, N.H., 247
Kent, Conn., 47
Kittery, Maine, 109, 251
Manchester Center, Vt., 170
Nantucket, Mass, 22, 23
New London, N.H., 149
Newport, R.I., 286
Norfolk, Conn, 270
Northampton, Mass, 65
North Conway, NH, 102, 276–277
Ogunquit, Maine, 97
Plymouth, Mass, 196
Portland, Maine, 58
Portsmouth, N.H., 250–251
Quechee, Vt, 5, 88, 247–248
Riverton, Conn, 270
Salisbury, Conn, 269

Shelburne, Vt., 122
Stowe, Vt., 261
Sturbridge, Mass., 265
Washington, Conn., 46
Weston, Vt., 5
Williamstown, Mass., 255
Wilmington, Vt., 174
Woodbury, Conn., 45
Woodstock, Conn., 17
Woodstock, Vt. 4–5
York, Maine, 107

Sports and recreation
Appalachian Mountain Club, 102, 105, 144, 209, 276, 278
Appalachian Trail, 144, 209, 276, 278
Attitash Bear Peak Mountain, N.H., 101, 102, 103, 274, 276, 278
Attitash Bear Peak Alpine Slie, 101, 105
Attitash Bear Peak Chair Lift, 101, 105
Balmy Days, 158
Bascom Lodge, 144, 209
Basketball Hall of Fame, 63, 67
Bluenose Ferry, 136
Boothbay Harbor, Maine cruises, 158
Boston, Mass., harbor cruises, 83, 237
Bretton Woods, 102, 274, 275, 276, 278
Bromley Mountain, 170
Burke Mountain, 190, 191–192
Camden, Maine, cruises, 216
Camden Snow Bowl, 217
Connecticut River Cruises, 215
Cannon Mountain, 201, 274, 275, 278
Cannon Mountain Aerial Tramway, 201, 203, 274
Cape Arundel Cruises, Kennebunkport, 169
Cape Ann Whalewatching cruises, 33, 37
Cape Cod Cruises, 199
Cap'n Fish's Goodtimes Sightseeing Boat Trips, 158
Capt. John Boats, 199
Casco Bay Lines, 58, 61
Chapman Rink, 253
Connecticut Ice Yachting Club, 271
Craftsbury Center, 191
Dartmouth Outing Club, 248
Dartmouth Skiway, 248
Davis Rink, 248
Deep River Navigation Company, 215
Deer Leap trail, 228
Dorset Field Club, 170
Eastern Ski Jumping Championships, 268, 273
Fenway Park, 77, 80

Frenchman'Bay Company cruises, 136
Grafton Ponds Cross-Country Ski Center, 301
Great Glen Trails, 275, 278
Hopper, the, 209
Jackson Ski Touring Foundation,
Killington Gondola, 226, 228, 231
Killington Mountain, 226, 228,231
Killington Skyeship, 226, 228, 231
Lake Champlain ferry, 133
Lake Sunapee cruises, 149
Long Lake-Lake Sebago Maine, cruises, 184, 188
Long Trail Hiking Path, 170, 228
Loon Mountain, 201, 275, 278
Loon Mountain Gondola, Skyride and Cave Walk, 202, 204
Maine Highland Games, 41
Maine State Ferry Service, 217, 220
Merrell Hiking Center, 228
Mohawk Mountain Ski Area, 269, 273
Mt. Abram Ski Slopes, 281, 283
Mt. Mansfield (Stowe), 259, 261
Mt. Monadnock, 117, 121
Mt. Sunapee gondola, 158
Mt. Washington Auto Road, 101
Mt. Washington Cog Railway, 101
Mt. Washington Valley Ski Touring Foundation, 275, 278
Occum Pond, 248
Ogunquit, Maine, cruises, 99
Penobscot Bay, 217
Plymouth, Mass, cruises, 199
Portland, Maine, cruises, 61–62
Provincetown, Mass., cruises, 180, 183
Quechee Polo Club, 89
Round Hill Scottish Games, 90–91, 95
Saco Bound, 102, 184
Shawnee Peak Ski Area, 281, 183
Ski Sundown, 270, 273
Snowshoeing, 275–276
South Bridge Boat House, 11
Spirit of Ethan Allen Cruises, 133
Sunday River Cross Country Ski Center, 280, 283
Sunday River Ski Resort, 280–281, 283
Swan Boats, 233, 237
Thompson Arena, 248
Waterville Valley Ski Area, 275
Wildcat Mountain Ski Area, 101, 274, 278
Wildcat Mountain Gondola, 101, 105
Wildcat Valley Trail, 275
Windjammer Cruises, 216, 220
Yale-Harvard Regatta, 68, 73